BEING INDIGENOUS IN JIM CROW VIRGINIA

Being Indigenous in Jim Crow Virginia

Powhatan People and the Color Line

Laura J. Feller

UNIVERSITY OF OKLAHOMA PRESS: NORMAN

Library of Congress Cataloging-in-Publication Data

Names: Feller, Laura J. (Laura Janet), author.
Title: Being Indigenous in Jim Crow Virginia : Powhatan people and the color line / Laura J. Feller.
Description: Norman : University of Oklahoma Press, [2022] | Includes bibliographical references and index. | Summary: "Explores experiences and strategies of tidewater Virginia Indians, descendants of peoples of the seventeenth-century Algonquian Powhatan chiefdom, in maintaining, creating, and re-creating their identities as Native Americans from the 1850s through the Jim Crow era. Examines how tidewater Native individuals, families, and communities positioned themselves as red people, rather than Black or white, in an era when some white Virginians argued that Virginia's Indians were 'mulattoes' and 'colored people.'"—Provided by publisher.
Identifiers: LCCN 2021056426 | ISBN 978-0-8061-9065-5 (hardcover) 978-0-8061-9389-2 (paper)
Subjects: LCSH: Powhatan Indians—Race identity. | Powhatan Indians—History—19th century. | Powhatan Indians—History—20th century. | Tidewater (Va. : Region)—Race relations.
Classification: LCC E99.P85 F45 2022 | DDC 975.5004/97347—dc23/eng/20211129
LC record available at https://lccn.loc.gov/2021056426

The paper in this book meets the guidelines for permanence and durability of the Committee on Production Guidelines for Book Longevity of the Council on Library Resources, Inc. ∞

Copyright © 2022 by the University of Oklahoma Press, Norman, Publishing Division of the University. Paperback published 2024. Manufactured in the U.S.A.

All rights reserved. No part of this publication may be reproduced, stored in a retrieval system, or transmitted, in any form or by any means, electronic, mechanical, photocopying, recording, or otherwise—except as permitted under Section 107 or 108 of the United States Copyright Act—without the prior written permission of the University of Oklahoma Press. To request permission to reproduce selections from this book, write to Permissions, University of Oklahoma Press, 2800 Venture Drive, Norman OK 73069, or email rights.oupress@ou.edu.

S|H The Sustainable History Monograph Pilot
M|P Opening Up the Past, Publishing for the Future

This book is published as part of the Sustainable History Monograph Pilot. With the generous support of the Andrew W. Mellon Foundation, the Pilot uses cutting-edge publishing technology to produce open access digital editions of high-quality, peer-reviewed monographs from leading university presses. Free digital editions can be downloaded from: Books at JSTOR, EBSCO, Internet Archive, OAPEN, Project MUSE, ScienceOpen, and many other open repositories.

While the digital edition is free to download, read, and share, the book is under copyright and covered by the following Creative Commons License: CC BY-NC-ND 4.0. Please consult www.creativecommons.org if you have questions about your rights to reuse the material in this book.

When you cite the book, please include the following URL for its Digital Object Identifier (DOI): https://doi.org/10.38118/978080619607

We are eager to learn more about how you discovered this title and how you are using it. We hope you will spend a few minutes answering a couple of questions at this URL:
https://www.longleafservices.org/shmp-survey/

More information about the Sustainable History Monograph Pilot can be found at https://www.longleafservices.org.

To John, and to Lucy Pearman Scott

CONTENTS

Introduction 1

CHAPTER 1
"A Home in a Strange Land" 15

CHAPTER 2
Virginia's 1924 Racial Integrity Law 51

CHAPTER 3
Constructing Native Identities, 1865 to 1931 90

CHAPTER 4
White Ethnographers and Salvage Ethnography 126

CHAPTER 5
The Aftermath of the Racial Integrity Law, 1930s to 1950s 158

Epilogue 194

Acknowledgments 199

Notes 203

Bibliography 247

Index 265

Introduction

IN MARCH OF 2015, Kevin Brown, chief of the Pamunkey Indians, replied to opponents of the Pamunkey petition to join the list of federally recognized Native American tribes: "We met the English and John Smith. Pocahontas was Pamunkey. It's crazy that we're not recognized [by the federal government]. We should have been the first recognized tribe."[1] The Pamunkey effort succeeded and was confirmed in 2016. In the past, federal officials had argued that because the Pamunkey were party to colonial-era pacts rather than treaties with the United States, they were in the realm of the commonwealth of Virginia, not the federal government.[2] However, that does not explain why in 2015 the Pamunkey, who have continuously held their reservation lands in tidewater Virginia since the seventeenth century and whose political organization the state has recognized for generations, had some difficulty in the Bureau of Indian Affairs acknowledgment process.

In 2015, public opposition to the Pamunkey petition sprang from multiple bases and biases. Some opponents anticipated that the Pamunkey tribal government might at some point establish a casino. These included investors in a casino not far away in Maryland. A California group warned Virginians that the sovereignties of federally recognized tribes constituted "no taxation and unfair competition" with local non-Native businesses. Some convenience-store owners in Virginia expressed similar fears.[3]

Opponents also seized upon racialized arguments that the Pamunkey had faced for decades. For years, in the nineteenth and twentieth centuries, some white Virginians argued that because of the history of sex and marriages between Native Americans and African Americans, no one in Virginia should be considered a "full-blood" Indian. Some who opposed the 2015 Pamunkey bid for federal recognition raised again that old argument about Virginia Indians' "mixed" ancestry. One opposition group emphasized that at least one of the individuals cited by the Pamunkey as a tribal ancestor "was a free black man who didn't move onto Pamunkey land until he was in his late 20s."[4]

The argument that a person called a free Black in nineteenth-century government records must necessarily be non-Indian ignores a long history of inconsistent practices and methods that white officials used to ascribe racialized identities to indigenous Virginian individuals. It also ignores the realities of family-making and community-building among tidewater Native people who did not live on reservations. Over generations after 1607, Native American, European American, and African American individuals worked together, lived as neighbors, loved, married, and raised families across racial lines. But in spite of the plural nature of their society, white Virginians attempted to build "race" as a Black-white binary in which everyone was on one side or the other of a single, two-part color line. The existence of Virginian Native Americans, and their connections to African Americans and European Americans, challenged the notion of race as a Black-and-white matter, potentially and sometimes directly. As a result, official records did not always accurately or consistently reflect the cultural identities of indigenous Virginians.

Beneath that 2015 critique of a Pamunkey ancestor as a free Black also lurks the idea that "one drop" of African American "blood" must make a person Black or "colored." In antebellum years, government records such as census counts often lumped together Native Americans and free African Americans as free persons of color. Jim Crow-era census records might categorize a single individual as Black, "mulatto," or Indian in different census years. Clearly, one historic document that identifies a Pamunkey ancestor as a free person of color or Black is not necessarily a reliable indicator of the racialized identity ascribed by white officials to that individual over the course of his or her lifetime—and it likely tells us even less about how that individual defined her own identity. We can reject the idea that someone who had moved onto Pamunkey land as an adult was not, could not, and should not be regarded as Indian and part of the Pamunkey community simply because white officials had at some point categorized her or him as a Black person.[5]

Some opponents of the Pamunkey's application for federal recognition criticized them for past "civil rights violations" and discrimination against African Americans and women.[6] This critique ignores extreme pressures the Pamunkey faced, before the Civil War and as Virginia's Jim Crow regime developed, from those who insisted that there could be no "full-blood" Indians in Virginia because of a history of "race mixing." Those pressures stemmed from whites' desire to dismantle reservations—and otherwise to buttress the segregation and disfranchisement of all people of color—by denying that any Virginian not white could be other than Black (or "colored"). Claiming Indianness, these whites feared, could be a tool for escaping Jim Crow. Some Virginia Indians responded by denying historic family and community ties to African Americans and excluding them from Native organizations. In the era of segregation, for Native groups this probably looked like a matter of survival.

Thus, in their recent successful quest for federal recognition, the Pamunkey people heard both that they have too many Black ancestors to be Indians—and also that their historic efforts to assert their Indianness by denying ties to African Americans are a barrier to federal recognition. Both critiques echo painful episodes in the histories of the Virginia Indians descended from peoples of the seventeenth-century tidewater Powhatan chiefdoms, whether they live on or off one of the two present-day, state-recognized Pamunkey and Mattaponi Reservations.

My project focuses primarily on tidewater Indians historically and currently living between the James and Rappahannock Rivers—people historically descended from Algonquian-speaking groups related to that famed Powhatan chieftaincy—especially the Pamunkey, Mattaponi, and Chickahominy of New Kent, Charles City, and King William Counties, and their Indian neighbors in those counties who were not formally part of those organized communities. Other Virginia Native peoples, such as the Monacan nation, of Siouan heritage and living west of the tidewater, also suffered through Jim Crow; they largely conducted their affairs separately from Powhatan and Chickahominy indigenous people throughout the Jim Crow era. So did Nottoway peoples, historically Iroquoian-speaking, who live south of the James River in tidewater country.

The backstory of how tidewater indigenous peoples weathered decades of the ever-stranger career of Jim Crow is long. For centuries, in what is now the southeastern United States, African Americans, Native Americans, and European Americans lived, worked, had children together, and shared cultural riches (even as over those centuries racialized legal, economic, social, and political barriers could cruelly mar those unions and exchanges). Before the early national period, among many Southeastern Native American groups, adoption, marriage, community participation and observance of community norms (and sometimes a period of captivity) could cement group membership and relationships, in the absence of homogeneous "blood" and in the presence of "colored" ancestors, to make someone part of the community in ways not congruent with whites' ideas about race.[7] Parentage mattered and matters, but so did other forms of acceptance by the group. Clan kinship/membership, which among some Native communities derives from the status of the mother, could be a key factor; it could be conferred by adoption.[8] In short, European ideas about "blood" and race were foreign to structures of community and individual identity in many precontact Southeastern Native American cultures, whose practices differed from whites' genealogical and legal norms.

"Race" as Europeans conceived of it eventually gained influence among Southeastern Indians over decades in late colonial and early national times.[9] European Americans and the economic systems that they brought to the hemisphere exerted pressures that, in the long run, contributed to the erosion of matrilineal systems and infiltrated race into Native cultural and social life. Native peoples at some times and places came to accept, modify, or acquiesce to European American ideas about race and the status of African Americans.[10] That helped to shape post–Civil War efforts by tidewater Indians to separate themselves from their Black neighbors. Yet, as the anthropologist Melville Herskovits acknowledged years ago, significant numbers of African Americans claim some Native American ancestry.[11] Like Virginia's Moble Hopson, quoted in chapter 3, they "live black" but retain memories of ancestors who were Indian or lived among Native peoples.

Creating race fundamentally involved prohibiting "interracial" marriage. Virginia's first law forbidding such marriages, in 1691, explicitly included Native Americans among those forbidden to marry white individuals.[12] Another milestone in the centuries-long chain of Virginia's laws against interracial marriage was a 1924 Act to Preserve Racial Integrity, perhaps the most drastic in Virginia's litany of such legislation. The 1924 law also marked the moment when the notion that "one drop" of Black "blood" made a person legally Black (or colored) was enshrined in Virginia law. Remarkably, the 1924 act did that by defining what made an individual legally white. The law read: "For the purpose of this act, the term 'white person' shall apply only to the person who has no trace whatsoever of any blood other than Caucasian."[13] It excepted from that standard, making them legally white for purposes of this law, only individuals who had "one sixteenth" or less Indian "blood" and whose other, non-Indian ancestors were white, a standard now satirically nicknamed the Pocahontas exception. Before 1924, Virginia law had generally set the boundaries that put an individual on the not-white side of the color line by defining mixed-race identities in terms of fractions of ancestry—the blood quantum concept.

Behind this 1924 Virginia law was a long history of racialized ideas about personal and group identities, citizenship, sex, and marriage in the European American world: eighteenth-century efforts to explain differences among the world's peoples using natural history-based classificatory schemes; nineteenth-century "scientific" racism built on that earlier discourse; and late nineteenth-and twentieth-century eugenics. In Virginia's 1924 law, Jim Crow racism fed on the eugenics movement's argument that the genetic qualities of the human race could and should be improved by careful attention to the genes of potential parents. Eugenic rhetoric helped justify the 1924 law's ostensibly absolute "no trace whatsoever" standard for whiteness. But in its "one-sixteenth" measure of the number of Indian forebears allowable in a legally white person, the law referred also to legal traditions that defined race in terms of blood quantum. Thus, this law married that older notion of "blood" to the rhetoric of eugenics. This suggested that enforcement of the law could be grounded in verifiable, quantifiable biological and genealogical facts. Yet the word "blood" connoted not only ideas about genes and genealogy, but also blood as a semi-magical inheritance of racialized "gifts." Those gifts supposedly shaped essential, inherited racial identities that linked biology and culture. Whites have historically tried to justify and explain race in America as if it were a natural, self-evident concept with unquestionable explanatory and integrative powers. That is the unstable foundation of racialized stereotyping, and supposedly predictive, determinative descriptions and prescriptions about social and economic status, citizenship and mental capacities that still haunt this country today.

Peter Wallenstein has detailed that laws forbidding interracial marriage have colonial roots, and that after the Civil War, they became a cornerstone of Southern segregation, though not all states of the former Confederacy acted at the same time or in the same way to renew or reinforce legal prohibitions on "miscegenation." By 1924, such laws were widespread across the United States; most states, at one time or another, have had laws restricting interracial marriage. Massachusetts' version of such laws, for example, was in effect until 1843. California's stood until 1948, when it was struck down in state court. Across the country, these laws varied in their targets and their definitions of what constituted forbidden interracial unions. In some states they applied to racialized groups other than African Americans, using terms like "Mongolian" and "Malay" to describe Asian peoples.[14] For Mississippi Choctaw people, when the state legislature passed laws against interracial marriage from the 1880s on, those laws did not embrace Native Americans, likely because removal-era federal treaty language about the Choctaw who stayed in Mississippi and related state law of the 1830s ostensibly made them citizens on par with free whites in Mississippi, and also because of their small numbers, their social cohesion, and their relative obscurity in post–Civil War state politics.[15] In Louisiana, a state supreme court ruling in 1810 implied that since American Indians were "persons of color," they could not marry whites. The 1870 revision of the state's civil code did not include provisions forbidding interracial marriage. In 1894, interracial marriage again became illegal in Louisiana, and Indians remained persons of color within the legal lines that defined such marriages. In 1920, a Louisiana law declared "the union of an Indian and a person of the 'colored or black' race as miscegenetic." In 1932, Louisiana's attorney general opined that "marriage between white persons and Indians was not prohibited in Louisiana."[16] Louisiana's legalities of the 1920s and 1930s throw into relief the fact that in that era, indigenous Virginians were not forbidden by the state to marry Black partners, while legally they could marry a white person only if they met a spurious "Pocahontas exception." Shortly after statehood, Oklahoma established in effect that if an individual was not Black, he or she was white for purposes of marriage law—and situated Indians on the not-Black side of Oklahoma's color line.[17] As Sarah Deutsch put it, to do otherwise—that is, to identify the state's Indian peoples as not-white—would have raised the possibility that "whites could not only alienate large groups of Indian voters who knew quite well the status blacks held in white eyes, but whites could also shoot themselves in the foot in terms of access to [Indian] land through marriage."[18]

In early twentieth-century Virginia, indigenous Virginians had less influence and leverage, in numbers and control of land, than Indian people in Oklahoma, and so Virginia's 1924 legal standards for interracial marriage reinforced efforts to place Native Americans on the not-white side (whether Black, colored or "mulatto") of a color line. Legal enslavement of Indians in Virginia had ended in the distant past.[19] In eighteenth-and early nineteenth-century Virginia, some enslaved Virginians had even sought their freedom in court based on having Indian forebears.[20] Yet in antebellum years, Virginia's non-reservation Indians were generally officially labeled free people of color, with the legal disabilities that that status entailed. After passage of 1924's Act to Preserve Racial Integrity, opportunities for Native Virginians to establish their identities as Indian, not Black and not white, were as problematic as ever, as proponents of that 1924 law used eugenic rhetoric to justify their segregationist campaign.

By 1924, eugenics was embedded in American media and thought. Some eugenics advocates, in this era, had professional credentials and therefore some credibility in presenting eugenics as scientific. Writing about 1920s trends, Elazar Barkan noted that while some scholars like Franz Boas raised possible "alternatives to biological determinism," it took time for such alternatives to gain credibility not just in the general public but also within academic institutions. He argued, "Castigating these racist positions as pseudo-science is therefore anachronistic."[21] But we can acknowledge that race and class bigotries were fundamental to the worldview of eugenics advocates.

A rhetoric of eugenics was on full display, when in 1924 and 1930, the state of Virginia passed laws to re-articulate who would be considered legally white and Black and to define whiteness in more restrictive ways.[22] When the 1924 act allowed an exception for marriage between whites and individuals "with no other admixture of blood than white and American Indian," this blood-quantum language derived from legislators' desire to accommodate elite white families who proudly claimed descent from Pocahontas. But as chapter 2 demonstrates, that exception's "one-sixteenth" benchmark prompted the law's promoters to argue that all indigenous Virginians were really "colored," having African Americans in their family trees. They argued that potential marriages of Native Virginians to white partners were a serious eugenic threat to the "racial integrity" of the white citizenry, because if African American "blood" existed outside the recognizably Black population, it might easily spread unless marriages and official racialized identities were stringently policed. Given centuries of Black/indigenous/white relationships in Virginia, enforcement of the 1924 law was bound to collide with the realities of Indianness in Virginia and to expose complications and absurdities inherent in the Black-white dual racial divide that Virginia officials worked so hard to build and maintain. That 1924 law became a centerpiece in a campaign by Walter Plecker, head of Virgini's Bureau of Vital Statistics, to ensure that no one in Virginia could escape Jim Crow by claiming to be Indian rather than Black.

Narratives about tidewater Indian families and groups in the wake of this 1924 law may seem obscure tales from small places, but their stories illuminate American conceptions of race, racial and ethnic identities, community, family, and marriage. As a law against interracial marriage, the 1924 statute exemplifies how in the United States racialized identities have been integral to contests about class, sex, and reproduction. As Matthew Frye Jacobson observed, "The policing of sexual boundaries—the defense against hybridity—is precisely what keeps a racial group a racial group."[23] It is no coincidence that in 1924, Virginia also passed a law allowing for sterilization on eugenic grounds of Virginians living in state institutions who appeared "feeble minded" or "defective," a law that the U.S. Supreme Court notoriously upheld in its 1927 *Buck v. Bell* decision. (Virginia was far from the only state with a program for eugenic sterilization or institutional segregation of the eugenically "unfit.")

The 1924 Act to Preserve Racial Integrity arose in a world of racialized segregation, but also in the context of the rationalizing, modernizing ambitions of post-World War I state governments; of long-running contests about the meanings of citizenship in the wake of the Fourteenth and Fifteenth Amendments;

and of eugenic ideas applied to immigration. In 1924, the U.S. Congress authorized a round of yet more restrictive immigration quotas—restrictions based in racist, eugenic ideas and supported by advocates like New York lawyer Madison Grant. Grant helped popularize the eugenics-based argument that years of large-scale immigration by people who were not "Nordic" or "Anglo-Saxon" would damage the white racial "stock" of the United States. In Virginia, advocates of the 1924 racial integrity law sought Madison Grant's support, to put eugenic thinking in the service of Southern segregation. Many eugenicists in the United States at that moment were concerned about immigration from Southern and Eastern Europe, as sources of genetically "inferior," somehow not-quite-white-enough racial "stock." As Dan Kevles put it, in the United States between 1900 and 1930, "the biological distinctions that mainly obsessed eugenicists were not those between whites and blacks but those then believed to divide whites."[24] In contrast, white Virginians who promoted Virginia's "racial integrity" law of 1924 (and a follow-up law in 1930 that further defined Blackness and Indianness) were mainly fighting for a Black-white divide. Elazar Barkan has argued that the success of federal anti-immigration measures of 1924, along with America's relative isolation and prosperity in the mid-1920s, decreased some of the popular fear that fed eugenic thinking nationally in the United States.[25] In Virginia, though, proponents of the 1924 racial integrity law used eugenic-sounding appeals in their campaigns against Virginia's Indians precisely to stoke those fears, as outlined in chapter 2.

As the U.S. Congress in the 1920s mandated increasingly restrictive measures to limit the numbers of immigrants of certain ethnicities on eugenic grounds, in 1924 it also declared, as a blanket matter of law, that all individual American Indians born in the United States are citizens of the United States, which was welcomed by some indigenous people but also reflected the assimilationist goals of those who felt indigenous Americans must adapt to white society.[26]

Facing this national focus on race and assimilation, tidewater Indian people pursued varied strategies to maintain, retain, construct and reconstruct their identities as Native Americans. Their actions expose the instability of the construction of race as a Black-white divide. They were creative and persistent, while constrained and influenced by what Grace Elizabeth Hale called the "culture" of segregation.[27] At times, tidewater Virginia Indians in the Jim Crow era echoed some of the racialized ideas of the larger society in which they lived, as did other Southeastern Indian groups. For example, as Katherine M. B. Osburn observed, Mississippi Choctaw people labeled themselves "full-blooded" from the late nineteenth century in ways that they had not done earlier, and formally took up "blood quantum" language by at least 1934. However, their rhetoric suggesting a "lack of race mixing" in the community did not necessarily mean that the Mississippi Choctaw at that moment shared white Americans' ideas about race, phenotypes, Choctaw citizenship, or Choctaw identity.[28] A Black-white binary notion of race may not have fit Choctaw historic, lived experience of the "mixing" of indigenous, white, and Black people any more than it did the lives of Native Virginians.

Battles for Indian identities and communities in Virginia, as in the rest of the country, involved not only marriage law, but also dispossessing Native people of their lands. Over decades of effort by whites to classify Virginia Indians as free people of color, mulattoes, or Blacks, Virginia's reservations ultimately were disassembled as tribal lands, for practical purposes—except for those of the Mattaponi and Pamunkey that remain today. At times, whites justified their efforts to take Indian lands and dissolve reservations by arguing that intermarriages with Blacks made those Indian communities no longer Indian. And non-reservation tidewater Natives who did not join with reservation people or other organized tidewater indigenous groups (like the Chickahominy) also faced tricky choices about when and whether to identify themselves as Indians in legal situations and official documents.[29]

Michael Omi and Howard Winant have argued that since the early 1940s, many "Americans have come to view race as a variety of ethnicity;" that is, race may be seen as a social category in which culture and ancestry both contribute to personal and community identities. At the same time, "explicitly racial (and racist) perspectives on race, rooted in the formerly dominant paradigm of the prewar era, have lived on in the South (and to some degree in the Southwest)."[30] Even after World War II, tidewater Native people did indeed deal with that "formerly dominant paradigm." Virginia's 1924 Act to Preserve Racial Integrity remained in effect until the Supreme Court's 1967 *Loving v. Virginia* decision, which struck down laws against interracial marriage across the entire nation.

Since many white Virginians viewed Indianness as a racial and so largely biological category, would it have been possible for Virgina Natives to construct Indianness as an ethnicity in early twentieth century Virginia? If in that era some indigenous peoples in New England re-fashioned their identities by emphasizing ethnic over racial underpinnings, that strategy would seem more difficult for Southern Native groups in their Jim Crow setting.[31] Southern federally recognized tribes have had a long history with federally fostered, racialized methods of determining tribal membership based in blood-quantum concepts.[32] And for Southern indigenous peoples who are not federally recognized, the legal codification of race as a Black-white divide historically has had crushing power to place Natives on the Black side of that color line. Karen Blu suggested that the Lumbee people in North Carolina have a history of viewing themselves in terms "essentially 'ethnic' (rather than 'racial') at a time when only a few social scientists used the term," while asserting their indigenous status.[33] The Lumbee, a relatively large group, had remarkable success in gaining state recognition despite their Jim Crow circumstances. For smaller, non-reservation Native communities in tidewater Virginia, the road to state recognition was harder and longer.

Whether or not "ethnicity" was a viable option for Virginia Natives in Jim Crow times, that should not cloud the fact that First Nations (to borrow a Canadian term) have particular legal status and claims on the United States government. For Southeastern indigenous groups in general, there is and has been a looming question of how their sovereignty, if only as "semi-sovereign" or "domestic dependent" nations, intersects with their cultural and social distinctiveness. Did reservation Virginia Natives pursue nationalistic strategies to assert Indian identities, given their seventeenth-century treaties and their reservation lands? Some scholars critique nationalisms as tending to foster static, essentialist models that can contribute to rigid conceptions of racialized difference. On the other hand, "strategic essentialism," as Omi and Winant have labeled some kinds of responses by "subordinate racial groups" to a dominant society's power and prejudices, can provide unifying tools to resist racist moves by powerful outsiders.[34] For Native peoples, "strategic essentialisms" such as the use of pan-Indian imagery can be productive strategies. In chapters 3 and 5, we will look at tidewater Indians' uses of pan-Indianisms.

A question perhaps more salient for Jim-Crow era tidewater indigenous people is how group and individual cultural and social identities can draw on a sense of a shared historical experience. If some tidewater Natives at times accepted aspects of racialized ideologies to delineate themselves, they also drew on a common history that included the well-known narrative of their contact with the English colonists in early seventeenth-century Virginia to affirm their indigenous identities. As they contended with racialized concepts such as "blood," organized tidewater Virginia Indian groups announced their shared, local, and group-specific histories as descendants of famed seventeenth-century Algonquian Powhatan peoples. Such historical grounding can undermine static, monolithic notions about ethnic/racialized identities.

In looking at how tidewater Virginia Natives adapted to prevailing European American ideas about race, and retained, maintained, affirmed, invented and reinvented their Indianness after the Civil War, I draw on excellent historical literature on the development of ideas about race in the Southeast over centuries.[35] As that literature shows, some indigenous peoples in the Southeast eventually adapted or adopted European notions about race, and participated in the racialization and enslavement of African Americans. Also, many southeastern Indians eventually found themselves lumped with "free people of color," as white Southerners took legal steps, especially after 1830, to disfranchise and marginalize all non-whites.[36] As whites' conceptions of race accompanied increasing Anglo economic and political power, whites' ideas about "blood quantum" as an essential maker and marker of racial identity could be accepted by, adapted by, or imposed on, Native communities. This eroded other, more traditional, ways of defining who was, or was not, part of a Native community or polity.[37] For Native people who lived among and with African Americans, that could lead to cycles of denial of Black ties to Native families and groups. Toni Morrison's character Susan Byrd put it this way in *Song of Solomon:* "You know colored people and Indians mixed a lot, but sometimes, well, some Indians didn't like it—the marrying, I mean." Thus, in the Southeast, when ideas about blood quantum as applied to Indian peoples intersected with the "one-drop" notion of what makes someone Black, the results were especially pernicious to Native social life and tribal sovereignty. I argue, with other historians, that meaningful and realistic ways of defining Native identities reflect not blood quantum, but rather group participation and relationships of reciprocity among members of a community; shared language, history, and other cultural assets; and ideas about kinship—such as clan membership and adoption—that can transcend biological parentage.[38]

To ground this argument concretely in individuals' lived experiences, chapter 1 tells of the extended family and descendants of Lucy Pearman Scott and her second husband, William Scott. When Lucy and many members of her family left Virginia for Canada in the 1850s, at least two of her grown daughters stayed in Virginia. Probably only a handful of the descendants of those two daughters ever lived on Virginia reservations in King William County, though they had many links to indigenous families in New Kent and Charles City Counties. Census and other records treated their Indian identities in contradictory ways, exposing the vagaries of official racialized designations in Jim Crow Virginia. Yet in some of these non-reservation families descended from Lucy Pearman Scott, traditions of Native ancestry persisted over decades and generations despite official denials of their Indianness. Those of Lucy's descendants who stayed in Virginia showed that living near and marrying within other Native families were among key strategies for claiming and maintaining Indianness among non-reservation indigenous families after the Civil War and into the twentieth century.

To underscore what organized non-reservation groups like the Chickahominy, and families like the Pearmans, were up against, chapter 2 looks at contexts and motivations for the passage of Virginia's 1924 Act to Preserve Racial Integrity, and subsequent efforts to refine legal definitions of race in Virginia in 1928 and 1930. How was it that state officials came to focus on Virginia's Indians in their efforts to enforce that 1924 law? In doing so, those officials added to general pressures on non-reservation Indians to marry and live within clusters of other Native families, and they harassed Native individuals and families. Such harassment dramatizes the painful day-to-day, immediate, direct consequences of Jim Crow-era efforts to deny Indian identities to Native Virginians.

Chapters 3 and 5 look mostly at reservation and other organized Native groups, in contrast to chapter 1's emphasis on when and how non-reservation individuals asserted Indian identities in the Jim Crow era—and when they did not directly challenge a Black-white color line.

Chapter 3 examines trends before 1924, to explore how tidewater reservation-dwelling and other organized indigenous people had publicly been working to maintain, proclaim, reclaim and reimagine their identities as Indians after the Civil War. As whites entrenched a Jim Crow regime, Mattaponi and Pamunkey Reservation people maintained their tribal lands and organization. Some other non-reservation tidewater groups—the Chickahominy, Upper Mattaponi, and Rappahannock, for example—created new formal tribal organizations and built new community institutions, such as separate churches and schools. To some degree these tidewater Native groups did carve out a third category in the face of efforts to place them on the Black side of a binary color line, but they managed this at the cost of taking some measures that were exclusionary on racialized grounds. When organized tidewater Indian groups affirmed their separation from their Black neighbors, they implicitly accepted whites' notions about race. The reservation groups also demonstrated their Indianness in public performances that linked them to seventeenth-century Powhatan history. (As Kevin Brown's 2015 comment shows, the Pamunkey still emphasize their role in colonial encounters between Powhatan and English peoples more than four hundred years ago and point to the celebrity of Pocahontas.) Those performances embraced pan-Indian imagery. This, I argue, signified not a loss of cultural "authenticity," but rather the ability of reservation groups to connect their Southern experiences and history to a national history of Native persistence, colonialism, and whites' appropriations of Indian lands.

Chapter 4 shifts the focus to white ethnographers who ventured to affirm and describe Indian identities in tidewater Virginia. It explores fieldwork by ethnographers of the Smithsonian's Bureau of American Ethnology, and by the University of Pennsylvania's Frank Speck and his students, from the 1890s into the 1940s. These white ethnographers used their scholarly authority to assert that particular tidewater groups were *really* Indian. Their work reflected the era's assumptions about the importance of "blood"—and being "full-blood"—for Indian identities, but it did more than that. Frank Speck's lifelong interest in eastern and southern Native peoples whom some whites did not see as *real* Indians, and his willingness to comment on contemporary Virginia Indians' political battles, show that he took a broader view of cultural change and Native identities than some of his contemporaries. This chapter looks at professional ethnographers of the early twentieth century grappling with assumptions about the "vanishing" of Indian culture and what makes "authentic" Indianness, assumptions that continue to dog Virginia Native people today—as in the recent fight for federal recognition by the Pamunkey. While white ethnographers' interventions could be a mixed blessing, the work of these ethnographers also highlights Virginia Indians' skills in cultivating white allies for their own political and social purposes.

Chapter 5 explores consequences for Native Virginians of the 1924 Act to Preserve Racial Integrity, focusing on strategies that reservation and other organized tidewater Native peoples between the James and Rappahannock Rivers used to affirm their Indianness in the two decades following 1930. After 1930, these people faced sustained scrutiny and opposition from state officials who denied their indigeneity. In federal initiatives such as the census and the World War II selective service, they also encountered challenges to their identities as Indians. In response, tidewater Virginia Natives continued to build community organizations and to perform in public as Indians, strategies they had developed since the nineteenth century.

In this project, I intend to look with empathy at tidewater individuals and groups who challenged racialized ideas and practices by asserting their Indian identities in Jim Crow Virginia. It is impossible fully to imagine someone else's experience but attempting that leap of imagination is necessary. I do not intend to exploit anyone's historical pain, or to "speak for" a "subaltern." I hope that Virginia Native people will perceive that I do not pose as an authority on their cultures, histories, and social structures. I also hope that learning about the lives of some tidewater Native Virginians will give non-Native readers a vivid, concrete example of the fluidity, instability, and destructive power of the construction of race in America. Along the way, I hope readers will question assumptions behind the race-based arguments of opponents of federal recognition of the Pamunkey in 2015–2016, including the concept of being "full-blood." And I devoutly hope that Lucy Pearman Scott would find what I have written respectful, were she alive today.

Race, marriage, citizenship, and immigration remain arenas of conflict, but today Americans in general may be relatively more open to stories that erode the idea of race as a monolithic biological and therefore immutable phenomenon. Americans regularly hear about "mixed-race" celebrities (such as Tiger Woods and Meghan Markle) in popular media. In the 2000 census, for the first time Americans could check more than one box to indicate their racial identity(ies). Still, many Americans may assume that the fabled "one-drop" notion of what makes a person African American was historically ubiquitous, undisputed, indisputable and, as a matter of law, uniformly prevalent over time and across the country. If the idea of a color line as a rigid and natural Black-white divide is losing some of its grip in America today, stories of Native American people in tidewater Virginia constructing their Indian identities during Jim Crow contribute to our understanding of conflicts and resistance in the history of that invented binary conception of race.

We sometimes hear the suggestion that race is somehow not real if we no longer view it as a natural, biological phenomenon. To refute that, let us seek out stories about the history of race as a set of power relationships whose persistent strength we must acknowledge, if we are to move forward in public policy and as fellow citizens, friends, and neighbors of people who are not "like us." As Matthew Frye Jacobson remarked, "The challenge is not only to recognize the fluidity of race, but to find ways of narrating events, social movements, and the trajectory of individual lives in all their integrity along the convoluted path of an ever-shifting racial reality."[39]

CHAPTER 1

"A Home in a Strange Land"

On October 29, 1854, William C. Scott and Lucy Pearman Scott wrote to their "dear children" in rural tidewater Virginia, from Brantford in what is now Ontario, Canada:

> I am in good hopes that this may find you all well an making up you minds to leave old Virginia my morther home my hart morn with sorry to think that I had to seek a home in a strang land among strangers for the sack of my children it was hard for me to part with some of my good friends in Virginia, an so it will be with you all but for the sack of you children you all mus part from you good friends also and come to a land whar you children can be men an ... women.[1]

The Scotts had left Virginia to settle in Canada shortly before. Why did William and Lucy uproot themselves and then urge their children to migrate to Canada so their grandchildren could become true "men and women?" That question involves legal definitions of racialized identities and obstacles blocking free people of color in antebellum Virginia who sought educational and economic opportunity.

Some of Lucy and William's children did leave Virginia for Canada, but they left behind two of Lucy's married daughters, Ann Eliza Pearman Wynn and Susan Pearman Howell, Lucy's children from her first marriage to Michael Pearman of New Kent County, Virginia. They and their husbands were likely the intended recipients of Lucy and William's letter. In their letters to Ann Eliza, Susan, and their husbands, William and Lucy painted a picture of Canada as rich in possibility for farming and educating children. Perhaps as further enticement, they added, "also thar is a good many indians in this province an some of them ar very rich they one a good deal of land and some of them has very rich farmes I am told an doing very well thar is very few blacks in this city indeed to look hear an in some other citys that I have bin in since left old Virginia thar is such a few that some times I think I left them all behind in old Virginia."[2]

The Scotts' interest in Six Nations people in the Brantford area, and in African Americans and African Canadians, was not casual. In the 1850 census for Henrico County, Virginia (p. 473), William Scott, Lucy Pearman Scott and others in their household appeared as "mulatto." Their letters suggest that that designation did not precisely reflect William and Lucy's ideas about their racial position, though these texts do not explicitly claim Indianness. However, succeeding generations of their extended family included multiple individuals who claimed indigenous identity, despite inconsistent official labeling of their racial status. Lucy's son Macfarland Pearman, for example, figured in different censuses over the years as "mulatto," Black, and Indian. Thus, the letters of Lucy Pearman Scott and William Scott to their Virginia children are a window on the experiences of a cluster of related families maintaining their Native identities over generations despite formidable, racialized barriers. Only a few individuals in those families lived within tidewater Virginia's formally organized Powhatan Indian groups. But some of Lucy and William's descendants who remained in Virginia pursued strategies for guarding and presenting their Indianness that included marrying within other Indian families, living in proximity to related families, and helping one another economically. Their persistence in asserting their Indianness through the Jim Crow era demonstrated the tenacity of Native communities in the commonwealth.

Individual white Virginians occasionally recognized Virginia Indians' indigenous identities (as when Lucy Pearman Scott's son Macfarland Pearman was enumerated as an Indian in 1900). Generally, though, from antebellum years to the 1920s and beyond, powerful white Virginians argued that after centuries of unions between African Americans and Native Americans, all Virginia Natives should be considered Black or of "mixed race." State officials committed to the concept of race as a Black-white binary lumped together and marginalized all mixed-race and non-white people. "Free person of color" and "mulatto" functioned as catch-all labels that whites applied to some individual Virginians who saw themselves as Indian. All over the South, Native people faced white officials haunted by the facts of "interracial" sex and marriages. The experiences of Lucy Pearman Scott's descendants in Virginia show that whites' efforts to construct race as a Black-and-white dichotomy clashed with the reality that for centuries indigenous, white, and Black people lived, worked, and loved together in Virginia, long before Lucy Pearman Scott left the state in 1854. The stories of non-reservation Virginia Indians situated like the descendants of Lucy Pearman Scott show the rickety underpinnings of the unrelenting fight that white Virginians waged for white "supremacy." That fight exposed incongruities and inconsistencies in whites' official, legal definitions of race, but those definitions were not arbitrary or capricious. Through them, white people protected and reinforced the legacies of slavery, and rationalized racial segregation and disfranchisement. To that end, some white officials tried to deny the history, and to minimize future possibilities, of intermarriages that could blur the legal color line drawn around African Americans. That pressure fostered in-group marriage and residence among Native Virginians asserting Indianness after the Civil War.[3]

Why did Lucy Pearman Scott and William Scott abandon Virginia in the 1850s, when they were each around fifty years old? Did they consider themselves Indians and resent being assigned the status and legal disabilities of "free people of color?" Their surviving letters invoke race matters, but they are especially explicit in addressing two related and intertwined factors that probably became increasingly urgent as Virginia tightened legal restrictions on free people of color in the antebellum era. One was the family's goals for profitable work and economic opportunity. A second was Lucy and William's emphasis on schooling for their grandchildren. Constraining their opportunities for work and education were a range of legal restrictions aimed at all antebellum Virginia's free non-whites. For example, laws required free people of color to register and obtain certificates attesting to their free status, and there were checks on their freedom to move out of their county of residence.[4] To cite just one example of legal impediments to economic opportunity, the profession of river pilot was closed to free people of color. After 1831, the state made it illegal to hold public gatherings to educate African Americans. Such tightening legal pressures on free people of color caused some to leave the state, like Lucy Pearman Scott and William Scott.[5]

Complicating the grim situation of free people of color who remained in antebellum Virginia were Virginia's murky legal definitions of race. Some such definitions were couched in "blood quantum" terms that seemed to call for precise classification of generations of ancestors, ancestors who might be hard or impossible to trace. In practice, legal proceedings also could reflect assumptions that racialized identities clearly manifested themselves in bodily characteristics readily available to (whites') visual inspection. However, physical appearance, like ancestry, was not a straightforward matter in a place like Virginia where whites, Blacks, and Indians had lived and loved together for generations. Local reputation and associations also influenced official, legal ascription of racialized labels to Virginians in the antebellum era.[6]

The experiences of William Scott and Lucy Pearman Scott's descendants reflect this instability in the concept of "free persons of color" in Virginia and shed light on how non-reservation Virginia Indians built communities and families that sustained their Indian identities. As noted, two of Lucy's daughters from her first marriage to Michael Pearman stayed in New Kent County when William and Lucy and other relatives went to Canada in the 1850s. Ann Eliza Pearman had married John Carman Wynn, and Susan Pearman wedded John Howell. Pearman, Wynn, and Howell are surnames that the anthropologist Helen Rountree notes among "New Kent fringe people."[7] Instead of positing a simplistic, in-or-out dividing line, she used "fringe" to describe people with varying connections to "core" Powhatan Native American groups (Pamunkey and Chickahominy) who might not always share the full range of the core's cultural markers, and might have less frequent or less intimate associations with individuals in the core. She acknowledged that "these fringe people without reservations or tribal councils should not be considered as anything other than 'Indian Virginians.'"[8]

In the case of tidewater Virginia Indians, though, the concept of a fringe and core, if read outside Rountree's sophisticated and realistic anthropological framework, could perpetuate stereotypes about who is a real Indian. The idea that one drop of African American blood makes someone Black coexists and contrasts with blood-quantum notions about how much Indian blood makes a real Indian. Historically, Virginia whites have used both notions to deny the Indian identities of Native Virginians. Those two contrasting ideas about blood, given centuries of race mixing, made Virginia's non-reservation Indians vulnerable to those devoted to white supremacy. Today, the one-drop idea that one Black ancestor makes a person Black, as well as the assumption that Indians must prove multiple Native ancestors, remain potent. In that context, calling non-reservation Indians a "fringe" could fuel the idea that their status as Indians is not as real as that of a core group. So, to explore the identities of William Scott and Lucy Pearman Scott, her children, grandchildren, and their extended families, let us attend not only to their ties (or lack thereof) to core Powhatan people, but also to the richness of interactions, close contacts over generations, marriages, and community-building efforts among these New Kent County non-reservation Indian families, including some of Lucy's descendants.

What kinds of cultural identities could an Indian family assert in the face of official efforts to deny that there were any real indigenous Virginians? How did they respond to pressures from the larger society? What constrained their responses? The Pearman-Scott letters witness the harsh climate for free people of color in antebellum Virginia, as sectional tensions and Southern whites' fears of slave rebellion grew, especially after Gabriel's plan for insurrection in 1800 and Nat Turner's uprising in 1831. By the middle of the nineteenth century, for people like the Pearman-Scott family, Virginia's legalized racial dichotomies could be crushing. This was true even though, in face-to-face, daily interactions, perhaps especially in rural counties, white neighbors and local officials sometimes recognized the Indian identities of families known to them over generations, giving the lie to the theoretical rigidity of racialized categories expressed in statewide laws, policies, and politics.

Before we return to the Pearman-Scott letters, here is a selective overview of the tangled historical processes that shaped legal definitions of race and slavery over centuries in British North America, and so molded William and Lucy's world. In late seventeenth-century Virginia, "what began with legal initiatives to defend the boundaries of slavery expanded to incorporate protection for legal concepts of race."[9] Those boundaries and concepts entangled Native peoples as well as African Americans. Unlike earlier British trading ventures in Africa, seventeenth-century English colonization in North America created a context in which "Englishmen distinguished between the heathenisms of Indians and of Negroes."[10] Yet while English attitudes toward those two groups differed, at least one minister cautioned prospective early English colonists about the evils of intermarriage with "heathen" Indians.[11] From early days in their Virginia colony, English officials sought to control contacts, including trade, between colonists and the Algonquian-speaking groups in the tidewater paramount chieftaincy led by Powhatan.[12] As the English expanded their grip on lands within Virginia during the seventeenth century, pushing aside Powhatan peoples, the demographic facts for Virginia Natives were grim. By the late 1630s, it is possible that there were more English than Powhatan people in tidewater Virginia.[13]

After about 1660, African and Afro-Virginian populations in the colony increased, and chattel slavery took on the broad outlines of its ultimate legal shape. This set the stage for whites' further marginalization of Powhatan groups as well as free Black people. Virginia's Indians continued to lose ground and numbers. The English applied to them a variety of legal restrictions designed to shore up the racialized order embedded in the institution of slavery. For example, a 1691 Virginia law forbade marriages of any "English or other white man or woman" to Blacks, mulattoes *or* Indians, to minimize "the abominable mixture and spurious issue" that would result from any such marriages.[14] Kathleen Brown called this an early use of the term "white," rather than "English" or "Christian," to denote racialized distinctions in Virginia law.[15] Over time, legal processes in Virginia tended to make a fundamental legal distinction between whites and all others. For example, Virginia law of 1705 included Indian and "mulatto" slaves along with Black enslaved people in affirming that enslaved individuals could be inherited in accord with practices for real estate.[16] Statute defined "mulatto" to embrace a person whose parentage included Native American, as well as African, ancestors. These laws restricted "negroes, mulattoes, and Indian servants, and others, not being christians" from office-holding and from acting as witnesses in general courts.[17]

These exclusionary processes were not monolithic, and in daily informal interactions their workings were probably uneven. By the beginning of the eighteenth century, tidewater Virginia's Indian population was relatively inconspicuous, and legally recognized Indian slaves were not a major factor in the colony's workforce.[18] For non-reservation Indians, Helen Rountree has argued that despite the repressive nature of that 1705 legislation, among those who stayed out of court, "There was no day-to-day disability involved in being identified with other non-Whites, so long as people possessed nothing that avaricious Whites might want."[19] She suggested that before 1830 such people were likely "content merely to be known by others as Indian-descended non-Whites and to continue to live quietly with their neighbors."[20] This may describe Lucy Pearman Scott's situation. But despite the possibility of that kind of uneasy quiet, legal discrimination was a threatening backdrop for the daily lives of non-reservation Indians. For example, a 1723 law (reflecting earlier Virginia taxation practices) provided that free Black women, Indian women, and "wives of negroes, mulattoes, or indians" would be tithable, but, generally, not white wives of white husbands.[21] This put all free non-white families at a disadvantage in building a secure family economy.

In some cases heard in colonial-era courts "free Indians may have enjoyed some slight advantage over their free African counterparts." Kathleen Brown wrote that "although individuals of Indian descent suffered from many of the same disabilities as Afro-Virginians, they could and occasionally did use claims to Indianness to achieve some relief." Local officials might see "Indians and Africans as different peoples, while discouraging their mixture out of the fear that such unions would make racial categories more precarious and racial identification more complicated." Brown contended that by the end of the eighteenth century, despite laws designed to homogenize Virginia's non-white people, whites understood free Black and Indian populations as having "historically distinct relationships with white Virginians."[22] That may have been truer for people on reservations, and for those who claimed Anglo-Indian rather than African

Indian ancestry. In the long run, non-reservation Indians, especially the children of their unions with African Americans, faced legal disabilities based on ideas about race. Inconsistent or infrequent enforcement of legal restrictions can be an effective tool of social control. If getting involved in politics or the courts, or possession of economic resources coveted by whites, was risky for Virginia Indians, that cast a shadow over daily life.

Despite the long history of Virginia law against racial intermarriage, in the eighteenth century some white Virginians engaged in theoretical introspection and speculation about white-Indian "amalgamation." A few whites conceived of intermarriage as a means of inculcating white cultural norms and, in effect, making indigenous people into white ones. Robert Beverley, William Byrd, and Thomas Jefferson conjectured about the desirability of Indian-white marriages as a means by which peace—and the movement of Indian lands out of tribal hands—might have been secured long ago. For them, this dream of dispossession-without-violence was probably an abstract, romantic, and nostalgic possibility shrouded in the past or—perhaps—some gauzy, distant future.[23]

While descendants of Pocahontas's son Thomas Rolfe included elite white Virginians, whites could and did marginalize the children of ordinary Indian-white or Indian-Black unions. Romantic literary images of the noble savage or Indian "princess" that whites attached to the figure of Pocahontas were not useful for non-reservation people like the descendants of Lucy Pearman Scott—even as Pocahontas' biological, elite descendants basked in a sentimental glow around the marriage of their long-ago, safely-distant Native American ancestor to a white man.

As the antebellum nineteenth century brought further hardening of legal restrictions on all free non-whites, erosion of Indian land bases made the pain and risk worse, even though several Native groups held land patents that dated from the seventeenth century. For example, at the Gingaskin Reservation in Northampton County on Virginia's Eastern Shore, in 1812–1813 the Gingaskin's county-appointed trustees instigated the legal break-up of the reservation and allotment of its lands to reservation residents. Whites justified this by claiming that, because some Gingaskins had married Blacks, many residents of the reservation were not "real" Indians. They also claimed that the reservation harbored disreputable free Blacks and mulattoes. (Whites in Virginia had long been fearful that the presence of free Blacks would contribute to unrest among enslaved people.) After the allotments, the Gingaskin legally no longer existed as a corporate body—and after that, official records could erase their Indian identities, labeling them variously "other free persons," free people of color, Black or mulatto.

Still, many Gingaskin individuals retained their parcels of the allotted land for years. Then, in the wake of Nat Turner's 1831 uprising, Northampton County officials pressured free Blacks to leave the county, in a campaign that included efforts to disperse remaining residents of Gingaskin allotments.[24] By 1854, when Lucy Pearman Scott and William Scott departed Virginia, the only reservation parcels remaining in the state were those of the Pamunkey and Mattaponi, and the Nottoway south of the James River.[25]

Even the Pamunkey and Mattaponi people, despite their retention of reservation lands, faced threats to their identities as Native Americans and as organized Indian communities. In 1843, for example, whites in King William County petitioned the state legislature either to sell the Pamunkey lands and give the proceeds to those "as can show their descent from Indian stock," or to divide all the land among individuals who demonstrated Indian ancestry. These petitioners anticipated that, in the latter case, individual Pamunkeys' right to sell their allotted land would "in the progress of time, lessen or remove the present grievance." The petitioners' stated grievance was multifaceted. They wrote that Pamunkey group claims to the land should be voided because unions with Blacks made them legally "free mulattoes" rather than Indians. The petitioners also claimed that the reservation represented grave danger to local slaveholders, as a body of free people of color "in the midst of a large slave holding community," and as a refuge for fugitive slaves and disreputable whites.[26] For the Pamunkey, by this time, keeping some distance from people of African ancestry probably appeared a matter of group survival.

In many parts of the Southeast, antebellum whites used their vision of racialized differences to explain and justify such legal, political, and economic pressures on all free people of color, with drastic consequences for Southeastern Native peoples. For example, when in 1835 North Carolina law disfranchised free persons of color, who lost the ability to vote and other legal rights such sitting on juries, North Carolina's Lumbee Native people were included in the category of free persons of color. Karen Blu has suggested that this new rigidity also shaped social realms in North Carolina. Before that, whites and Indians in the state might attend the same churches and the same schools.[27] (This echoes Moble Hopson's comments about his early life in Virginia, quoted in chapter 3.) As among the Lumbee, in Virginia the antebellum tightening of restrictions on free people of color in Virginia, and then post-bellum Jim Crow strictures, demonstrated the risks to indigenous Virginians of accepting as community participants people whom whites regarded as Black or "colored."

Like the communities now known as Lumbee and Tuscarora in North Carolina, other Southeastern Native people found niches in relatively isolated places, participating, if sometimes marginally, in the larger economy surrounding them, often through farming. Some people, undoubtedly, lost the desire to continue to claim Native identities as families, as individuals, or as communities, and lived as Blacks or whites. But all along the eastern coastal plain and piedmont from New Jersey to northern Florida, Gerald Sider argued, were groups who looked "settled" and spoke English, but their strategy was "*not* simply acculturation but the framework for *social* isolation—for being left alone, for being seen as neither Black nor Indian nor, in some profoundly ambiguous ways, White—an isolation revealed by the long-lasting continuing separateness of many of these peoples, who have endured as distinct groups until the present."[28]

That kind of semi-isolation and "social and cultural quietness" could be hard to maintain, especially given major social, political, and economic changes in the aftermath of the Civil War. For example, it seems that in North Carolina, as Jim Crow took hold, "after the Civil War, previously open and friendly relationships between Lumbees and their African American neighbors became much more tense."[29] Gerald Sider argued that alliances of Lumbee people and Blacks peaked between 1864 and 1884, but deteriorated after that, following 1885 legislation by which North Carolina formally recognized as Indians the group now called Lumbee. That law provided a basis for a system of schools for Lumbee students separate from those for Black and white children.[30] Karen Blu wrote that "for many years, [Lumbee] Indians have refused to marry Blacks (those who do are ostracized from the Indian community) or to attend Black schools" because they saw how such associations encouraged whites bent on treating Lumbees as African Americans.[31]

As in North Carolina, as restrictions on all free non-whites tightened, Virginia Native people sought distinctions within the Black-white binary that framed so much Virginia law. Perhaps urged by Nansemond Indians, whose homelands are south of the James River, an 1833 state law provided that individuals of "English" and Indian descent might be considered "persons of mixed blood, not being free Negroes or mulattoes," if at least one white person would support this claim in county court. Nansemond individuals used this law, but there may be no evidence that Indians other than the Nansemond, and one Nottoway person, took advantage of it.[32]

What did it mean in Virginia to be labeled a free person of color, a person of mixed blood, or a mulatto? Jack Forbes, in writing about "red-black peoples," argued for close analysis of the contexts and meanings of terms used in historic documents to describe people as "mixed" or "colored," since such words were often not used historically as we understand them today. He noted fluidity and changes over time in the definitions of an array of words—like mulatto, mestizo, mustee—used to describe people of mixed ancestry in the Americas. He contended that in the United States, it was in the aftermath of the Civil War that many whites commonly used "colored" as synonymous with "negro," rather than as a catch-all category for an array of non-white people. We should not assume that in antebellum use, "colored" was synonymous with terms like "free negro" that connote African or African American ancestry or identity, given the "ethnically diverse and culturally pluralistic" nature of nineteenth-century non-white peoples on the Atlantic seaboard.[33]

Forbes's idea that there was a post–Civil War collapse of a distinction between "colored" and "negro" seems relevant to pressures that Virginia Indians faced after the war. Lucy and William Scott's antebellum letters refer both to Black and mixed-blood people. If in antebellum years whites had been less insistent that all colored people were Black, that could be part of the context for Helen Rountree's suggestion that before the 1860s, Powhatan groups might accept into their communities, "at least as fringe members," Black individuals who had married into the group, on the basis of social ties.[34] Even before the Civil War, some white Virginians argued that marriages of Indians with African Americans meant a loss of Indianness. And even when the laws of Virginia defined "mulatto" or "colored" as a distinct category, the legal status of free Blacks and free people of mixed blood was similar for some official purposes.[35]

In postbellum testimony, New Kent County people remembered this threatening climate. In 1877, William H. Brisby, a forty-year-old African American farmer, fisher, blacksmith, onetime member of the state legislature and county supervisor, in speaking about his Pamunkey neighbor William Cooper Langston, reflected that before the war the Pamunkey "were generally treated about the same as the colored people, they had no vote and were but a step from the slave and were most of them union [that is, loyal to the U.S. during the Civil War] people."[36] Langston had been the only person listed as Indian in the 1860 censuses of New Kent and Charles City Counties (New Kent County census, p. 873). In 1874, William Langston's son, John H. Langston, testified: "We are Pamunkey Indians. . . . He [William C. Langston] has been a Union man always," adding that "we all thought if the rebellion [the Civil War] succeeded they would have turned us all into slaves."[37]

The establishing of Indian identities in nineteenth-and twentieth-century Virginia was complicated not only by ideas about blood and race, but also by whites' stereotypes about Native American cultures. Over centuries after 1607, among Virginia Indians many economic and cultural practices evolved in ways that did not fit whites' notions about real Indians. By the 1830s, to most Virginia whites (and African Americans) the material and religious culture of Virginia's Indians probably looked mostly similar to that of Virginia whites. Virginia Natives attended Christian churches and usually dressed like their non-Indian neighbors. Non-reservation and reservation tidewater Natives spoke English. As Helen Rountree put it, "By 1830, the core people among the Powhatans had Anglicized so much that they were no longer easily recognizable to outsiders as 'real'—that is, pre-Contact—aborigines."[38] This made it easier for white people to categorize them as mulattoes or "mixed bloods," and to deny that any real Indians lived in Virginia.[39]

This is what William Scott and Lucy Pearman Scott fled in 1854 when they departed Virginia for Canada. Legal restrictions on free people of color and meager educational opportunities for their children led them to abandon a home where their identities as people of Native American ancestry were probably understood by some of their neighbors, even when not officially recognized.

Lucy Jarvis of York County had married Michael Pearman in 1819; in 1842 she was living, as Lucy Pearman, in New Kent County. By 1848, she had married William Scott and by 1849 she was living with him in Richmond with some of her younger children. A letter from William and Lucy dated August 26, 1849, shows that they maintained affectionate contact with Lucy's adult offspring, their "dear children," who remained in nearby New Kent County.[40]

When they and the rest of their household were called "mulatto" in the 1850 Henrico County census (p. 473), Lucy Pearman Scott and William Scott were, respectively, forty-six and forty-nine years old.[41] Living with them were seventeen-year-old Caroline V. Pearman; Macfarland Pearman (fourteen years old); and Nancy Pearman, aged twelve, three of Lucy's children from her previous marriage to Michael Pearman. Living nearby and listed as "mulatto" were George E. Pearman and two men who may have been William C. Scott's sons from his previous marriage: William P. Scott and Richard Scott, with their families. It is possible that William P. Scott's wife, Louisa, was Lucy's daughter, and that Lucy was also the mother of Richard's wife Frances (called Fanny).[42] If so, this may be a manifestation of what the anthropologist Theodore Stern (more on this below) called "paired sibling marriage" in his 1952 study of the Chickahominy.

In Richmond, William Scott was a deacon of the First African Baptist Church, where Lucy Pearman Scott was also a member.[43] Some antebellum

Virginia Baptist churches embraced whites, free and enslaved Blacks, and Indians. First African Baptist was founded by and for a Black congregation.[44] As a deacon, William Scott had an important role, one that he perhaps would not have played in a congregation dominated by whites. Virginia law at that time required that a church's minister be white, but deacons had significant responsibilities in the Baptist tradition.[45] Thus, this Black Baptist church was a community where Scott could be, and was, a leader. His and Lucy's membership may reflect that opportunity, and the fact that whites ascribed to them a "mulatto" status, rather than indicating that the Scotts identified themselves as African Americans.

William Scott was dismissed from the church on July 16, 1854, in keeping with Baptist practice of taking formal leave of a congregation in circumstances such as a move like the one the Pearman-Scott family was undertaking. The family's move was part of a wave of departures from First African Baptist over decades after Nat Turner's 1831 uprising, a wave that crested between 1853 and 1855. Gregg Kimball found that between 1841 and 1859, a significant proportion of those who left First African Baptist were free congregants. Some of them, like William and Lucy, severed their ties with the church because they were leaving the area.[46]

As family letters show, William and Lucy were questing for economic and educational opportunities lacking in Virginia. Reports about the potential rewards and problems of making a new life in the north came to Richmond through networks fostered by mail, rail, and shipping. Surely, William and Lucy knew of African Americans who took refuge in Canada in the wake of the federal Fugitive Slave Act of 1850. Probably they were also aware of the American Colonization Society's efforts, since the first minister at First African Baptist, Robert Ryland, had connections to that society.[47] But given some of their descendants' later public assertions of Indian identity and the tenor of William and Lucy's surviving letters, it seems unlikely that Lucy and William saw themselves as part of an African American diaspora to Canada.

William and Lucy's letters seem to echo currents in antislavery rhetoric of the time, in their emphasis on piety, literacy and education, and industriousness. This rhetoric, of course, was shared by many middle-class strivers of whatever race. Abolitionists, though, made special use of it, to argue that by leading exemplary lives, free people of color countered proslavery rhetoric about the failings of African Americans as workers, entrepreneurs, and citizens.[48] Perhaps their position as strivers who were persons of color weighed on William and Lucy, even if they did not regard themselves as Black. This is not to suggest that Lucy was a "race" woman as that term later came to describe Black individuals committed to uplifting all African Americans. Rather, she shared aspirations for respectability widely held in her day and devoted herself to lifting up her own family.

William and Lucy uprooted themselves and their family in a quest for profitable work and schooling for their descendants, but their economic situation was likely not desperate when they lived in Virginia. According to the 1850 federal census, William owned real estate worth three thousand dollars. Lucy had been born into a family of means. When her father William Jarvis died, by 1827, he "left a considerable estate real and personal," including fourteen enslaved individuals, to his children, grandchildren and his widow, Mary Maund (or Mound) Jarvis.[49] (In the antebellum era, Lucy Jarvis's siblings and their families living in York County were categorized in the federal census as "free colored persons" or "mulatto." Generally, their households included enslaved as well as free non-white people.[50]) In the 1810 York County census, the household of William Jarvis included no white people; in it, nine individuals were listed as free non-white persons, and seven were enumerated as slaves (p. 4/302). In the 1820 York County census (p. 315/157A/152) William Jarvis's household consisted of eight "free colored persons" and eleven enslaved people.[51] In Virginia, sometimes free people of color technically, legally owned enslaved members of their family because, after a free relative bought a family member away from his or her enslaver, they then faced the grim reality that after 1806 Virginia law required manumitted slaves to leave the state after gaining their freedom. There were official avenues for an emancipated person to seek legal permission to stay in Virginia, but that was a cumbersome and risky process. As a result, sometimes a relative remained legally enslaved to a family member to avoid being forced to leave home and family.[52] However, it seems unlikely that William Jarvis's slaves were in that situation, given the tenor of chancery court records about the division of enslaved people among his children in the settlement of his estate.

Lucy's first husband, Michael Pearman, like her father William Jarvis, owned slaves and was labeled a free person of color in the federal census. Lucy, thus, was born and married into propertied non-white families who were invested in the slavery system and had some financial wherewithal. Michael Pearman, in fact, explored a range of economic opportunities. In the 1820 New Kent County census (p. 211), his household consisted of three "free colored persons" and five enslaved individuals; two people in the household engaged in agriculture, one in commerce, and two in "manufactures." This pattern repeated over generations when members of Lucy's extended family pursued multiple lines of work as farmers and artisans. In the 1830 (p. 33) and 1840 New Kent County censuses (p.100), everyone in Michael's household was again classified as a "free colored person" or as enslaved.

The 1850 Henrico County census did not indicate that William and Lucy Pearman Scott held slaves. It did note that Lucy's second husband William Scott was a "laborer" and quantified his real estate holdings. The census taker listed real estate ownership for no one else enumerated near William and Lucy. Neighbors who were likely extended family—William P. Scott and George E. Pearman—worked as a carpenter and wheelwright, respectively. If the wealth of Lucy's father William Jarvis and of her first husband Michael Pearman, some of it in the form of enslaved people, had dissipated by 1854, the family still had skills and enough capital to manage the move to Canada.

When William and Lucy left Virginia in 1854, they journeyed through Ohio with the help of Lucy's son William F. Pearman, before settling in Brantford, Canada. William F. Pearman had moved to Ohio by 1852. In August 1854, William F. Pearman wrote to his "brother" (probably his brother-in-law John Carman Wynn) that he had gone to meet the "old people" in Columbus, Ohio, during their trip.[53] Likely his example and assistance helped to inspire William Scott and Lucy Pearman Scott to go north.

Shortly after, Lucy wrote back to the family in Virginia from Columbus that she and William Scott had decided to go on to Canada West (now Ontario), because in Columbus "bisness is not good for wheelwright as it is in Canada," perhaps a prime consideration because of George Pearman's skills. She urged the recipients of her letter to join them and promised to write as soon as she was settled in Canada. Finding work and land in Canada were on her mind, but her letter is also filled with concern about schooling for her grandchildren. Sadly, Richard Scott, husband of Lucy's daughter Fanny had died, leaving bereft his widow and young children. Lucy found some consolation in the prospect that:

> his children will be school free thank god for that and I fine kind gentelmen an ladyes in Ohio as well as in Virginia so the lord will porvid for us all.... so my dear children I will not be saddysfied till you children is whar thay can be school for men is [put?] out hear to go on look out for the poor mixed blood children as well as they look out for the poor white in Virginia for to look at littel boys an girls how well thay read an right and speack proper I can but look then think and morn but the good peopel in Virginia was sorry for us I no, thar was not a gentelman an lady in Richmond an New Kent County but was sorry for us.[54]

Does Lucy's reference to "mixed blood children" show that she accepted a mixed-race label for her family? Did she use "mixed blood" here to encompass both Anglo-Indian and African Indian ancestry? Was Lucy suggesting that her own family was a particular, singular object of elite whites' sympathy? If so, did she feel that not all white Virginians saw her and her family as part of an undifferentiated mass of mixed blood, mulatto people? If so, was this because of their Indian identities? Lucy's use of "poor" and "good" here, and her references to "ladies" and "gentlemen" show her understanding of class distinctions in Virginia. Her reference here to "good" Virginians who felt "sorry for us" may also reflect Lucy's experiences over years as the legal status of free people of color deteriorated in antebellum Virginia. Perhaps she felt that some white neighbors were sympathetic as she and her family endured tightening legal racialized restrictions.[55]

What if, in Lucy's mention of "good" people, "ladies and gentlemen," in Virginia who felt "sorry" for the Scott-Pearman families, she was referring to someone who had helped members of the family learn to read and write? In 1831, Virginia's legislature prohibited public gatherings of "free negroes and mulatoes" or enslaved individuals for purposes of learning to read.[56] Does Lucy's language here hint at the utility of some kinds of white patronage? William and Lucy themselves were literate and highly valued literacy; it is a recurring theme in the surviving Pearman-Scott family letters, and not only those written by William and Lucy. For example, in 1852, William F. Pearman wrote from Sandusky, Ohio, to William Scott (his "Dear Father") in Richmond, to ask Scott to welcome and help a friend who was about to visit Richmond. Pearman recommended his friend to Scott as a man engaged in "geating up schools for the Cholord Children."[57] While it is not entirely clear that members of Lucy's extended family called themselves "colored," perhaps they did accept this loosely defined term, either because others imposed it on them, or because they understood it to encompass Indian as well as African ancestry at that time.

Lucy and William's first surviving letter to family back in Virginia after they reached Ontario was full of urgency about schooling and future opportunities for younger members of the family. Pressing the recipients to join them in Canada, William and Lucy wrote about how hard it had been to leave home and friends in Virginia (quoted above), but expressed their conviction that this was necessary so that the children could grow up to be "men an women." Lucy and William understood the significance of gendered roles and literacy for social respectability. For them, literacy was also a key to the pursuit of economic security. The letter promised, "butiful schools hear you can school you child for 25 cent per mont and mak him man up to bisness I lick this place better than I do Ohio tho you do not pay anything thar for schooling but you can mack a better living in this place than in Ohio tho land is very high hear but very good an easily cultivated." Lucy and William extolled crops in Canada West, reflecting the family history of farming along with other kinds of labor. As further evidence of opportunities in Canada, they reported their intention "to keep a grosery and bording house." They carried out their plan; the 1861 Canadian census described William as a grocer (p. 109, Town of Brantford, Brant County). They wrote that brother George (probably George Anderson Pearman) worked as a wheelwright, and "Mackfalland and thomas king" were working together as carpenters. (King was one of Lucy's sons-in-law.) Opportunity was inseparable from education, and both were stymied in Virginia:

> you sisters elizabeth can right as pretty[?] a hand as any of our ladys in old Virginia her little boy is very small but he can spell well. . . o my Dear childarn yo all are always in my mind you littel childarn groing so fast an if you don't brin tham from thar all you working will be northing I think if [I?] had brot my childarn from thar when thay was small what a good thing it wod have ben for tham but so it is you all mus try an do all you can and come in the spring. . . an you all no there is no chance in Virginia all the gentelmen an ladys in Virginia will [say?] so too an thay no [you have?] a [pretty?] parsel of childarn that if they was cultivated thay wood be men an women.⁵⁸

By the fall of 1854, multiple family members had joined William and Lucy in Canada, apparently sharing their vision of the potential rewards of a move north, and sometimes living near one another. Surviving family letters mention numerous relatives present in Canada, including Thomas King and William King (Lucy's sons-in-law); Lucy's daughter Caroline Virginia; William P. and Louisa Scott; Lucy's son Macfarland; and the family of Lucy's widowed daughter Fanny. Fanny and her children, including her son Gideon Scott, appeared in the 1861 Canadian census listed next to William and Lucy in the town of Brantford (p. 109). William P. Scott and his wife Louisa (who was perhaps Lucy's daughter), were also enumerated on that same page, just as Fanny's and Louisa's families had appeared on the page with William and Lucy in the 1850 Henrico County census. The letters also refer to "brother George" in Canada; this George Pearman appeared in the 1871 Canadian census for Burford, Ontario (p. 41) listed as Indian, with his family that included a daughter named Pocahontas.⁵⁹

In a later letter, William C. Scott again emphasized education for the children in these families, reporting that, "Sister Fanny and her three little Boys are well the oldest one Gideon Scott is going to School every Day and I hope it will be in my power this September to send the other two William P. Scott and his Family are well and their two Childern are going to School every day."⁶⁰ Lucy's hopes for the education of Fanny's children were being realized. In Brantford, the Black community had established a school in 1837. At the time, schools in some parts of Canada were racially segregated, a segregation that was legally reinforced in 1850. In Brantford, though, some whites enrolled in the Black community's school, which eventually was merged with a "common" school.[61] Perhaps grandchildren of Lucy and William attended it.

That first surviving letter from Lucy and William in Canada West (Ontario), quoted at the beginning of this chapter, makes ambiguous references to race. In it, Lucy and William noted the presence of Indians in the province, while coaxing their Virginia relatives to come to Canada. Did they seek to reassure those relatives that Indian identities were recognized and respected in Brantford? Did they mean to suggest that the families of Lucy's daughters, Susan Howell and Ann Eliza Wynn, who were still in Virginia, might find acceptance as Indians if they came to Canada? William and Lucy wrote that, "thar is very few blacks in this city indeed to look hear and in some other citys that I have bin in since left old Virginia thar is such a few that some times I think I left them all behind in old Virginia altho I sopose as we stoped at the hotells all the way that I never saw but very few so when you all stop the hotells is the best place to stop at in traveling."[62] Her "so" suggests that maybe Lucy was not merely mentioning hotels as convenient places to rest. Did Lucy feel it would be best for family members to avoid being seen in the context of groups of Black people while on the journey north? If so, was she especially concerned because that journey would take them to places where their racialized reputation was unknown? She was probably well aware of kidnappings of free Blacks in the North in the wake of the Fugitive Slave Act of 1850. She evidently did want family members in Virginia to understand that, once in Brantford, they would not be surrounded by large groups of "blacks." Was this because she felt that if her family were not seen in the company of Black people, they might more readily avoid racialized categorization— there being relatively few Blacks in Brantford to frame them, visually or socially, as not-white? Perhaps Lucy thought that absent evidence that her family associated with Black people, questions about their race might lie dormant among Canadians they encountered, and/or that in an area with a significant Six Nations populations they might more easily be recognized as Indians. Maybe she was concerned about living among Blacks as opposed to colored or mixed people? Given her earlier letter's reference to "poor mixed blood children," is it revealing that Lucy referred to Black people as "them?" Did she conceive of Black and colored as significantly different categories, sometimes accepting the colored label for her family but seeing danger in being perceived as Black? If so, this recalls Jack Forbes's argument that before the Civil War-era whites had not always conflated the term "colored" with African ancestry. In any case, the 1861 Canadian census called her, William, and others in their extended family "mulatto."

If Lucy was suggesting that her relatives could or should avoid "blacks" by staying at hotels, that may seem inconsistent with William and Lucy's participation in the First African Baptist Church back in Richmond. In an undated and ambiguous letter from Brantford to her children in Virginia, as Lucy cajoled them to come to Canada, she reminded them to bring their "church letter tell the minister to say the baptis church and no more be carful."[63] "Church letter" here probably refers to correspondence that in Baptist practice formally introduced a departing congregant to a new congregation. Was Lucy concerned that if such a letter came from a church whose name identified it as an African American congregation, that would perpetuate a Black (or colored) identity for her family in their new home in Canada? If so, it may be that Lucy's caution stemmed from experiences in Virginia, where she and her family faced an increasingly rigid racialized regime that made it hard for Indian people to create spaces for themselves other than as mulatto, mixed race, colored, or Black.

Emphasizing the importance of religion and education, William C. Scott wrote back to Virginia in April 1859, that

> money has been very scarce and property very low but we have every reason to bless and praise the Lord and we do bless him and praise his Holy name for his mercies to us all 'poor unworthy Creatures' for we have suffered for nothing since we have been in Canada . . . and we do bless the God of all mercy for his mercies and goodness towards us, that our lot was cast in a Land where we can sit under our own vine and fig tree and none dare to make us afraid and oh my dear Children what a great blessing it is to have the freedom of Speech and to be where we can send our little Children to School together all taught together and that for love instead of hating each other and calling each other names too hard to be borne by one that knows that God has created all things created them to his own Glory and what is man that he should find fault of his Creator.[64]

William's critique of the fear, silencing and "hard" names visited upon him and his family in Virginia clearly had deep roots in Christian texts, as well as a solid political grounding. His gratitude for "freedom of speech" in Canada seems a direct comment on the failure of the state and country of his birth to live up to their rhetoric of liberty. He also indicts his native land for a lack of Christian love. If he understood Indianness as part of his extended family's identity, perhaps that helped fuel a sense that his family was particularly victimized by Virginia's legal structures that denied full citizenship to all free people of color.

William and Lucy, focused as they were on freedom, work, and literacy, expressed their religious faith with just as much fervor. William's service at Richmond's First African Baptist Church, and his letter of April 1859, evidence his religious devotion. In his conception of the family's blessings quoted above, William expressed gratitude that "all of our family belong either to the Methodist or Baptist Church them that had fallen from Grace are restored." He urged his family to "let us hold on to do good to them that hate us and dispitefully use us so that when our Heavenly Father shall call us we may have a conscience void of offense both to God and Man."[65] His faith, then, was integral to his conception of his familial responsibilities. In 1869, when he was nearly seventy years old and in poor health, William wrote to his "dear children" in Virginia (probably to Susan and John Howell, Lucy's daughter and son-in-law) that he intended to travel to see his daughter Ellen Scott Charity and hoped also to see the recipients of his letter. He explained that

> one of my great [objects?] Is to see you and all the children So that I mit in Parat [impart] to tham Sum spiritual instruksion and not to tham only but to all Wharaver I may go for the lord have ben very good to me And I feel it my Duety to talk of his grat goodness to me in taken my feet out of the myery clay and Puting tham upon the Rock crist Jesus And have put a new song in my mouth to Prase him and I have Ben trying to Du so for 49 yers and in tend to Du so by his grace untell he silence this tung of mine in dath.[66]

Clearly, Pearman-Scott family members shared the aspirations of many Virginians for literacy, liberty, economic opportunity, a life of Christian piety, and seeing their children grow up to be proper "men" and "women." They left the United States to seek those things.

Surviving family letters vividly depict William and Lucy's economic, educational, and religious ambitions, and show that those ambitions were thwarted because of their precarious racialized status. These letters do not definitively tell us how they identified themselves within the racialized vocabulary of their era but indicate that they were regarded by others as "mixed." The letters suggest that they saw their racialized position in Virginia as unfair, and that with the move to Canada, they may have been reluctant to be associated with Blacks. In talking within the family, did they acknowledge African American ancestors, or Native American forbears? Did William and Lucy have any objections to the slavery regime in Virginia? These letters do not directly address slavery or the enslaved people among whom Lucy had lived in New Kent and York Counties before she moved to Richmond. The letters do, though, tell us about how they themselves experienced racialized prejudice in Virginia's slavery times.

In 1850s Virginia, William and Lucy felt themselves hemmed in and maligned; going to Canada was their answer. Though many of their children were willing to join them in Canada, Brantford was less than the promised land for some among the Scott-Pearman extended family. In a poignant 1862 letter, Lucy wrote to her children that "tomas" (probably her son-in-law Thomas King) had left Brantford in the depth of winter, taking his "poor littel children" with him: "it melted my poor hart in sorry to see them in the snow.... I ask him to let me no how he was getting along but I have not heard one word from him since."[67] Lucy's son Macfarland Pearman departed Brantford at least temporarily in 1858 or 1859, though he was probably back in Canada in 1869.[68] But by 1900, he had left Canada and resettled in New Kent County.

Staying in Virginia

Some descendants of Lucy Pearman Scott remained in Virginia, dealt with its racist structures, tried to prosper, and sometimes publicly asserted their Indianness as Virginia's Jim Crow systems developed after the Civil War. Despite William and Lucy's entreaties and encouragement, Lucy's daughters Ann Eliza Pearman Wynn, who married John Carman Wynn, and Susan Pearman Howell, wife of John Howell, did not move to Canada.[69] However, they and their families were far from isolated as they remained in Virginia. Both couples, and their children and grandchildren, maintained ties to other Virginia Natives over generations, marrying and living within clusters of other tidewater Indian families.

The Wynn Connection

For example, John Carman Wynn, Ann Eliza Pearman Wynn's husband, was likely from an extended group of families named Wynn at times acknowledged by white people to be Indian in New Kent and Charles City Counties. In marrying a Wynn, Ann Eliza connected herself to some of the most prominent individuals recognized as Indians in those counties. The Indian roots of these

Wynns are documented from the early nineteenth century when, as Helen Rountree noted, at least one child of the white couple Gloucester and Sarah Wynn of King William County married a Pamunkey person. Gloucester and Sarah Wynn's son, William Wynn, had a son named Ferdinand Wynn (some of his descendants shared the name Ferdinand). This Ferdinand Wynn, the elder, "moved to New Kent County and joined the intertribal fringe there. Some of his descendants are Chickahominies today."[70] Though I have not yet found documentation to substantiate this, it seems quite possible that John Carman Wynn, Ann Eliza Pearman's spouse, was a brother of this elder Ferdinand Wynn.

Like other non-reservation Indian families in tidewater Virginia, Ferdinand Wynn and his descendants received varied and inconsistent racialized labels in government records. For anyone who imagines race as a well-defined, unambiguous fact of every individual's personhood, consistent through the course of life, the variations in census descriptions of these families may be startling. Federal census data for generations of tidewater Indian families connected to Lucy Pearman Scott and William Scott demonstrate in concrete, personal ways that they maintained family traditions of Indian identity even though recognition of their Nativeness could be snatched away from one census to the next.[71]

Ferdinand Wynn, the elder, his son Ferdinand, and other members of their households were called "mulatto" in censuses from 1850 to 1880. Yet Ferdinand the elder identified his father William as Indian in his federal Southern Claims Commission file of 1873. In that file, Ferdinand testified that he "didn't like the way the Southern people treated the colored folks. I had travelled up North considerable and knew what liberty was."[72] This may or may not suggest that Wynn saw himself within a catch-all category of "colored folks," but here he was quite clear about his Native ancestry. Up in the air is the question of his attitude toward slavery, since Ferdinand the elder, according to the 1850 federal census slave schedule for New Kent County, held one enslaved person that year, as did his likely brother, John Carman Wynn, husband of Lucy's daughter Ann Eliza.[73]

Ferdinand's son, Ferdinand (call him "the younger"), with his wife Rebecca Stewart Wynn, their children, and a cousin living in their household, were all enumerated as Black in the 1900 federal census for New Kent County (p. 261B). Like her husband, Rebecca Stewart Wynn came from a family with Indian roots, though her father was white.[74] Ten years later, in 1910, Ferdinand the younger (then sixty-six years old), Rebecca, and the four children living with them were classified as Indian in the census (p. 225A, New Kent County). Separately, in that 1910 New Kent County census, three other young men named Wynne, one a twenty-six-year-old named Ferdinand, were categorized for "color or race" as "other," with a marginal notation suggesting they had Indian ancestors (pp. 199A and 199B, New Kent County 1910 census).⁷⁵ Was this the enumerator's expression of his knowledge of their family history? Did these young men press the enumerator not to list them as mulatto? The twenty-six-year-old "other" Ferdinand was likely the son or the nephew of Ferdinand the younger.⁷⁶ Previously, in the 1900 census, both the son and the nephew named Ferdinand had been listed as Black.

In 1920, Ferdinand the younger and his wife Rebecca Stewart Wynn were again enumerated in New Kent County as Indians (p. 107A). In the 1930 census for Richmond city, though, Ferdinand was classified as white (p. 191A). In the 1940 Richmond census, Rebecca, then living in the household of her son Ray, was called white, as were Ray and others in the household (p. 3A, Jefferson Ward).

The Family of John Howell and Susan Pearman Howell

Children and grandchildren of Susan and John Howell linked themselves to multiple Indian families in addition to the Wynns. Some Howell descendants married into other tidewater Native families, and those who stayed in tidewater Virginia often appeared in census data evidently living near one another.

Other non-reservation tidewater Virginia Indians also manifested these patterns of residence and marriage within clusters of Indian families. The anthropologist Theodore Stern, writing in the post-World War II-era about the Chickahominy, noted that "by far the greatest proportion of unions have been made within the community. Genealogies exhibit the intricately involved web of relationship characteristic of small endogamous communities." Non-reservation Virginia Natives may have been no more or less likely to live and marry within geographic clusters based on kinship and racialized identities than Black or white families in these rural counties. However, Stern noted one aspect of Chickahominy endogamy that seemed not as common among their white or Black neighbors: "'paired-sibling marriage.' This practice involves the union of two or more siblings, of the same or opposite sex, with similarly related individuals in another family." Stern described this pattern as most striking "in the generation living about the time of the Civil War," and becoming less common in later generations.⁷⁷ As noted, two of Lucy Pearman Scott's children may have participated in such unions with William Scott's children from his first marriage.

Endogamy was especially salient for non-reservation, tidewater Indians because they were small groups compared to their white and Black neighbors, and because they were targeted by those who denied their Indianness on the basis of participation with African Americans in Native communities. Tidewater

Natives who remained in Virginia readily saw that close association with African Americans could erode their ability to assert indigeneity, adding incentive for non-reservation families to live and marry within clusters of their own extended families and other Native families.[78]

Sometimes, white individuals in the rural counties of New Kent, Charles City, and King William acknowledged that certain families had been recognized locally as Indians for generations (see chapter 2 for an example of this, in testimony by white people about Ray Wynn's Indian ancestors, including his mother Rebecca Stewart Wynn). Staying in a place where that family history was known and accepted by non-Indians likely provided the occasional respite from officials who denied that Virginia was home to any real Indians. Of course, when whites' perceptions of, and testimony about, racialized identities had more influence than Indians' identification of themselves, that buttressed the prevailing racialized order. Nonetheless, whenever whites supported individual Virginia Indians who asserted Native identities, those Indian individuals could strategically use that support.

A complete social and cultural history of the descendants of Susan Pearman Howell and Ann Eliza Pearman Wynn in Virginia is beyond the scope of this project. Here, the focus is on what their situations tell us about the construction of race in Jim Crow Virginia and about their strategies for asserting their Indianness in a world that was supposedly Black-and-white. But part of the context for their stories is that, despite their economic disadvantages as people of color, families descended from William and Lucy included farmers, skilled mechanics, slaveholders, and landowners. For example, the 1850 New Kent County census (p. 310) listed Ann Eliza Pearman Wynn's husband, John Carman Wynn, as a blacksmith. He held one ten-year-old enslaved person (1850 New Kent County census slave schedule). That same census (also p. 310) enumerated the family of Susan Pearman Howell and her husband, John Howell, right next to John Carman and Ann Eliza (Pearman) Wynn's household, noting that Howell, a wheelwright, held two enslaved teenagers (1850 New Kent County census slave schedule) and owned real estate worth some two hundred dollars. The slave schedule for 1860 New Kent County does not indicate that Wynn and Howell still held slaves, but they remained people of some means. In 1860, the New Kent County census (p. 882) valued John Carman Wynn's personal property at five hundred dollars; his brother-in-law John Howell (p. 870) possessed real estate worth three hundred dollars.

While John Howell and his wife Susan had financial resources, they and their descendants occupied ambiguous racialized positions, marked by variations in their census racial classifications from decade to decade. The federal census of

1850 New Kent County (p. 310) classified the Howells (and the neighboring family of Susan's sister Ann Eliza Pearman Wynn) as "mulatto."

Ten years later (1860 New Kent County census p. 10/870), the family of John and Susan Pearman Howell, again classified as "mulatto," appeared on the same page with two households headed by Pearmans. One was the family of Thomas Pearman, a seventy-seven-year-old farmer, with his son Jones, Jones's wife Lizzie, and the young couple's daughter, Victoria, who were also called "mulatto." (Lizzie—Rebecca Elizabeth Langston, called Rebecca E. and Elizabeth R. in other censuses, was a daughter of William Cooper Langston, a Pamunkey man mentioned above.) This elder Thomas Pearman was possibly a brother of Michael Pearman, Lucy Pearman Scott's first husband. If so, Thomas was Susan Howell's uncle. Another of John and Susan Howell's neighbors was John Pearman, a thirty-five-year-old mulatto blacksmith, another son of Thomas Pearman.

On that same 1860 census page was the household of Major P. Bailey, including his wife, Martha, and her sister Marie (or Mary Ann) Pearman. Martha Bailey (also known as Patsey) was a daughter of the elder Thomas Pearman. (Her siblings, then, included John; Thomas the younger; Mary Ann/Marie; and Jones Pearman.)[79] That year, all in the Bailey household were labeled "mulatto" except one eight-year-old identified as Black. Mary Ann Pearman lived with her sister Martha's family, the Baileys, for years, exemplifying the shelter these extended families gave one another. (See New Kent County censuses, p. 10/870 for 1860, p. 522A for 1870, p. 358D for 1880.) Over those decades, the Baileys consistently appeared in the census close to the family of Jones Pearman, brother of Mary Ann and Martha. These families provided support to their relatives within their households and also as neighbors.

The census' racialized descriptors of members of these intertwined households varied from one census to the next. In 1870, for example, within the household of Major Park Bailey (listed next to Jones Pearman's family), his wife Martha (Patsey) and her sister Mary Ann Pearman were listed as "mulatto," while Park and the children were classified as Black. Perhaps this was an enumerator's comment on the sisters' appearance, or maybe the enumerator understood the sisters to have a mixed-race identity that included Indian ancestry. Members of Jones Pearman's household were similarly called "mulatto" in 1870, except for Armistead Pearman, who was classified as Black.[80]

From 1850 to 1880, in fact, each New Kent County census categorized Jones Pearman as "mulatto" (p. 337 for 1850, p. 10/870 for 1860, p. 522A for 1870, p. 358D for 1880). Despite that mulatto label, Jones was also known and accepted locally as a person of Indian descent. In 1889, in response to a circular that the Smithsonian ethnographer James Mooney sent to selected people in the mid-Atlantic region inquiring about the names of local living individuals "of Indian descent," a Dr. Archer of Henrico County replied, "There are a few persons of mixed blood in my neighborhood, said to be of the Pamunkey tribe. The best known of them is J. T. Pearman."[81] Very likely this was Jones Pearman.[82] To cite one example of his descendants' being recognized as Indian, William Walter Pearman, son of Jones and Lizzie Rebecca Pearman, was labeled "mixed Indian" on his death certificate.[83]

Though Jones Pearman was consistently called "mulatto" in federal censuses, for other non-reservation tidewater Indian individuals, racialized categorizations could vary from one census to the next. In 1870, for example, the census taker again assigned the family of John and Susan Howell the "color" mulatto (1870 New Kent County census, pp. 512–13). Then in 1880, the census described John Howell as "mulatto," but listed his wife Susan and their children in the household as Indian. That year, the Howells were living near a cluster of Pearman kin: Jones Pearman's family; Jones's brother the younger Thomas Pearman; the household of Park M. and Martha Bailey and Mary Ann Pearman; and Edward (James E.) and Victoria Holmes, Jones Pearman's daughter. Those families were enumerated as "mulatto" (1880 New Kent County census, pp. 358D, 359A). Why that year were the Howells thus distinguished, racially, from neighboring kin?

Unlike the 1870 and 1880 censuses, the records of an 1870s U.S. Southern Claims Commission (SCC) case had acknowledged John Howell as Pamunkey. In that case, Howell testified skeptically about William Cooper Langston's claim for compensation for food and fodder that U.S. Army troops had taken from Langston during the Civil War. Unlike Howell, Langston had been enumerated as an Indian in the 1860 New Kent County census. (A SCC special agent reported that two others who gave depositions casting doubt on Langston's claim, John Pearman and Thomas Bailey, were "very respectable colored men.") That agent noted that Langston's claim was "prepared by a colored man by the name of Brisby, who is a prominent politician and has represented the County in the legislature." The agent implied that this man, William H. Brisby, was perhaps not quite "honest," maybe because the agent resented the way Brisby's prominence signified African American empowerment in the Reconstruction era.[84]

William Cooper Langston's Southern Claims Commission file sheds light on the racialized identities of people in the New Kent County Indian community, on when they did or did not assert their Indianness publicly, and on the intricate network of kinship relationships among them. John Pearman was a brother of Jones Pearman; Jones's wife, Rebecca Elizabeth Langston, was William Cooper

Langston's daughter. Perhaps Thomas Bailey was related to Major P. Bailey (see p. 334B, 1850 New Kent County census), who had married one of John and Jones Pearman's sisters. The SCC file also hints at webs of economic relationships among Indian, Black, and white neighbors. Men who testified in this case farmed and engaged in carpentry, fishing, smithing, and milling.

The file details how tensions could erupt among kin in this racialized environment. To rebut the skepticism of John Howell, John Pearman, and Thomas Bailey, William Cooper Langston in 1877 submitted a deposition in which he denied that Howell and Pearman were able to know of his affairs during the war years and explained that each was hostile to him and so unlikely to support his claim. Langston claimed John Pearman was antagonistic because he thought Langston had had something to do with John's having been "cut off" in his father's will in favor of John's brother Jones "who married my daughter." A family quarrel also caused the animosity of Thomas Bailey: "Bailie who styles himself a preacher is a brother-in-law of mine." Langston opined that John Howell's hostility arose because soon after Virginia was re-admitted to the Union, Langston had asked a man in Richmond for aid to establish a school in the neighborhood. Howell helped Langston build the schoolhouse. Then, the Richmond man "sent us a splendid teacher who was a colord man well educated. Howell objected to him on account of his being black and refused to do anything toward supporting the school and was angry with me because I would not have him sent back and get a white man and because I stood by him and the school and kept it up and boarded him at my house during the entire session."[85] John Howell's work on the schoolhouse shows that, like his mother-in-law Lucy Pearman Scott, he yearned and worked for educational opportunities for his children. However, he opposed associating his family with African Americans, even in the service of schooling those children. This echoes both Lucy's pleas for educating the family's children and her possible caution to the families of John Carman Wynn and John Howell in her letter of October 29, 1854, about being seen with Black people if they made the trip north.

Langston's SCC file named John Howell as Pamunkey. Another example of official recognition of the Howell family's Indianness appeared in 1910, when Susan and John Howell's grandson (Lucy Pearman Scott's great-grandson) John Clayton Howell married Grace L. Stewart in New Kent County. Their marriage license described both as Indians.[86] The pair divorced, and when John Clayton Howell remarried in 1913, he wed another woman from an Indian family, Elizabeth Wynn, a daughter of Winslow Wynn and Joanna Holmes Wynn. Winslow was a son of Ferdinand Wynn the elder. The New Kent County marriage register noted that John Clayton Howell and Elizabeth Wynn were Indian.[87]

Subsequently, though, when John Clayton Howell appeared in the Richmond city censuses of 1920 (p. 244B), 1930 (p. 223B), and 1940 (p. 1B for Jefferson Ward) with Elizabeth and their children, all of them were listed as white.[88]

John Clayton Howell was not affluent. In his suit for divorce from Grace Stewart, while he was living in New Kent County, he described himself as a "laborer."[89] After he moved to Richmond, the federal censuses for 1920, 1930, and 1940 listed him variously as fireman at a packing house and cold storage facility and engineer for a railroad company. Poignantly, although his grandfather John Howell and great-grandmother Lucy Pearman Scott so valued education, in surviving court records John Clayton Howell said that "he could 'scratch' some and sign his name to papers but does not write well."[90]

Other descendants of John and Susan Howell, not just John Clayton Howell, married into families with surnames common in tidewater Indian communities, such as Stewart, Bradby, Miles, and Collins.[91] For example, Pinkey Howell, daughter of John and Susan Howell, married Simeon Collins in 1882.[92] The infant Simeon Collins had shown up in the 1860 King William County census (p. 605) as "mulatto" (like many others in his community that year). But the 1900 King William census (p. 140A-B) enumerated him, Pinkey and their six children among the county's "Indian Population" on the special form used that year for Indians. Pinkey thus had married into the Indian community in King William County across the river from New Kent County—site of Virginia's Mattaponi and Pamunkey Reservations—though it does not appear that she and her family lived on reservation land in 1900. That year, the census listed Pinkey and her family as being of the Powhatan tribe, and as having parents who were also Powhatan. The family were recorded to have "½" percent of white "blood." Was this "quantum" of white blood a figure that the family volunteered? Was it instead based on the enumerator's perception of their community associations, their reputed ancestry, or their physical appearance? Simeon was a fisherman at the time; their sons living in the household did farm work and their daughters were in school. (Pinkey's grandmother Lucy Pearman Scott would have applauded their efforts at education.) In 1910, when Simeon and Pinkey's daughters Ella and Carrie lived in Richmond, working as cooks in private households, they were both enumerated in the Richmond census as Indian (pp. 54A, 192A). Some of Pinkey Collins's children also married within the Indian community. For example, Simeon and Pinkey's son George Raymond Collins married Virgie Lillian Wynn, a daughter of Ferdinand and Rebecca Stewart Wynn, in 1909.[93]

When, also in 1909, the widowed Simeon Collins himself remarried, to Gertrude Miles, bride and groom were called Indian in the King William County marriage register.[94] He and Gertrude appeared, enumerated as Indians, in the 1930 census for King William County (p. 245B) on a page with others listed as Indians. In 1940, though, Simeon lived in Richmond and was listed as white; he lived on the street where John Clayton Howell (Lucy Pearman Scott's great-grandson and Pinkey's nephew), resided (p. 1B, Jefferson Ward). Moving to Richmond, then, might mean being officially called white, but did not necessarily erode extended-family ties. And in the case of Ella and Carrie Collins in 1910, moving to Richmond did not preclude being enumerated as Indian.

The 1900 census of New Kent County provides another vivid demonstration that children of John and Susan Howell maintained proximity to extended-family kin. Six households with connections to Pearman and Wynn families appeared in a row on a single page that year (p. 262B/14B for Cumberland Magisterial District). These included three households formed by John and Susan Howell's married daughters. The 1900 census classified all six of those related families as Black, but records on other years and other generations indicate Indianness. Such inconsistencies demonstrate how malleable these racialized terms were, in theory and in application to individual human beings.

James P. Miles, who had married John and Susan Pearman Howell's daughter Henrietta (Honey), had been widowed by 1900 and was listed on that census page with three children, Alice, James M., and Journey.[95] Twenty years earlier, in 1880, James and Honey V. Miles and two sons, Harold and Journey, had been called white (New Kent County census, p. 391B), but in 1900 James and the three children living with him were listed as Black, as noted. However, the 1910, 1920, and 1930 King William County censuses enumerated Journey Miles and his family as Indians. In the 1910 census, Journey and his family showed up living on the Pamunkey Reservation, and the 1920 census also indicated he lived in "Indian Town Reservation" on the Pamunkey River (King William County censuses, p.76/3A for 1910, p. 50A for 1920, p. 245B for 1930). In chapter 3, Journey Miles will appear again as a member of a reservation group participating in the 1907 Jamestown Exposition.

Edmonia Howell Stewart, Dick Stewart, and their children were also listed as Black on page 262B of the 1900 New Kent County census. Edmonia was one of John and Susan Howell's daughters. Dick (called Robert A. and Richard in other censuses), was a son of Margaret Stewart, and a brother of Rebecca Stewart Wynn, the wife of Ferdinand Wynn the younger.[96] The 1910 census (p. 225A, New Kent County) enumerated the family of Dick and Edmonia Howell Stewart as Indian, next to Ferdinand and Rebecca Stewart Wynn, also then counted as Indian.[97] When their son Llewellyn Wilton Stewart in 1910 married Maude

C. Wynn, a daughter of Ferdinand and Rebecca Wynn, the New Kent County marriage register called the couple Indian.[98]

Yet another of John and Susan Howell's daughters, Fanny, who had married Jim (James A.) Stewart, was enumerated with three of her children on that same page in 1900 New Kent County. Like Dick Stewart, Jim was a son of Margaret Stewart and brother of Rebecca Stewart Wynn.[99] Thus, the marriages of Fanny Howell and Edmonia Howell to Stewart brothers represent the "paired sibling" marriage practices noted by Theodore Stern. Fanny and her children were enumerated as Black in 1900, but her daughter Hattie, Hattie's husband Walter Miles, and their children were listed as Indians in the 1920 King William County census (p. 50B), living on the "Indian Town Reservation."[100] This is among the relatively few instances of Lucy Pearman Scott's descendants living within the reservation community—that being perhaps the most potent sign of Indian identity available to them. Managing to assert their Indianness though not living on reservation land, Fanny Howell Stewart's son Oliver and his family were enumerated as Indian in Charles City County in the censuses of 1930 (p. 246A) and 1940 (Harrison Magisterial District, p. 26A). This likely reflects the fact that Charles City County was home to many families organized as Chickahominy people by that time.

A tight network of family relations did not guarantee harmony, as evidenced in the Southern Claims Commission file of William Cooper Langston. In a chancery court cause settled in 1921, John Clayton Howell (Lucy Pearman Scott's great-grandson) sued his stepfather, Charles H. Langston, about ownership of some land in New Kent County that his father John Beverly Howell had held at the time of his death in the 1880s. The property in question, known as "Wigwam," was about 110 acres adjacent to lands at one time held by John Beverly Howell's father John Howell (husband of Lucy Pearman Scott's daughter Susan).[101] Apparently the Wigwam land had once belonged to Ferdinand Wynn, the elder, and his wife Leticia (or Luticia).[102] (As noted, Ferdinand the elder was possibly a brother of John Carman Wynn.) Perhaps the elder Ferdinand Wynn gave the land that name in token of his Indian identity, even though, unlike some of his descendants, the federal census never recognized him as Indian.

Family of John Carman Wynn and Ann Eliza Wynn

As with the Howells and their descendants, federal census enumerators inconsistently categorized the race of the family of Ann Eliza Pearman Wynn and John Carman Wynn. The 1850 New Kent County census (p. 310) called John Carman, Ann Eliza, and their three young children, like their neighbors and kin the Howells, "mulatto." A record of John Carman Wynn's taxes for 1853, though, carries the notation "Indian."[103] Someone could have added that notation in later years, but this might be a rare early official recognition of an individual Indian in nineteenth-century New Kent County records, and it shows that some local officials could be open to tidewater Natives' assertions of their Indianness. The census again applied the "mulatto" label to the family in 1860 (New Kent County, pp. 882–83)—including seven children. Then, in 1870, the New Kent County census categorized Ann Eliza Pearman Wynn, John Carman Wynn, and their children as Indian (p. 488). John Carman Wynn was a blacksmith, farmer, and sometime landowner, but his property and skills did not ensure economic security for his family; he had had some financial trouble by the time of his death in the mid-1870s.[104] By 1880, Ann Eliza Pearman Wynn and some of her children were living together in nearby Hanover County, where they were enumerated as Indians (1880 Hanover County census, p. 148). In 1900, some of those children remained in Hanover County, living in households of their own. That year, John Carman and Ann Eliza's son John Solomon Wynn and his family were classified as Indians in the Hanover County census (p. 340A). John Solomon's wife at that time, Lena L.—they later divorced—was his cousin, one of John and Susan Pearman Howell's daughters.[105]

Ann Eliza Pearman Wynn and John Carman Wynn's daughter Susan Virginia married a Hanover County man, Christopher Hawes White. In 1900, she and he and their six children were apparently living near her brother John Solomon Wynn (p. 340A, Hanover County census). Susan Virginia Wynn White and her children were classified Indian that year, but her husband Christopher White was listed as white. Then, in the 1910 census for Hanover County, the entire White family was classified as white. Did that reflect a desire by the enumerator, or by Christopher and Susan Virginia Wynn White, not to create a record of a mixed-race family, especially not one that involved a white man? Perhaps, by 1910, the fact that Ann Eliza's family departed New Kent County years earlier made it harder for her children to assert an Indian identity. Maybe as the family's time in New Kent County faded into the past, their ties to other Indian families also dimmed. That year, the census categorized Susan Virginia's brother John Solomon Wynn, still living nearby, as "mulatto" (p. 193B/9B Henry District), even though he and Susan had the same parents. In the 1920 Hanover County census (p. 273A) and in 1930 (p. 229A), the Whites and the rest of their household were again classified as white. John Solomon Wynn appeared again in the Hanover County census in 1940, aged eighty-three and also enumerated as white (p. 252A).

This long-term proximity of some of John Carman Wynn and Ann Eliza Pearman Wynn's children was not without tensions. After Ann Eliza's death, some of those adult children were in chancery court to settle the distribution of family farmland in Hanover County, in what may have been a contentious case. John and Ann Eliza's son Hiram, and their daughter Susan Virginia Wynn White, asked that their allotted shares of the farm be contiguous, and expressed their desire to avoid "wholly breaking up the family."[106] Judging from the surviving records of this case, John Solomon Wynn and his siblings Hiram and Virginia were closely linked over the course of their adult lives, working on their mother's business affairs and the family farm, and sometimes living near one another when they were no longer under their mother's roof. For them, the family was a focus of economic support and perhaps economic rivalry. Still, their close connections did not ensure that these siblings' Indian identities were consistently recognized in the census when they no longer lived in the same household. Did their proximity help them sustain family traditions of Indian identities in private, despite the times when official records denied those identities?

Macfarland Pearman

Surviving records about Lucy Pearman Scott's son Macfarland also evidence the importance of living near extended family and how tenuous and fleeting governmental recognition of Indianness could be. Macfarland moved back to New Kent County sometime before 1900. There, he "purchased the original Pearman homestead as well as other real estate in said county," according to records of the chancery court settlement of his estate. He died possessing several tracts of land, one of about 114 acres and another estimated at 440 or 450 acres.[107]

As family letters show, Macfarland was in Canada with William Scott and Lucy Pearman Scott in the 1850s and probably into the 1860s, but apparently, he was restless. In 1858–1859, MacFarland departed Brantford, perhaps only temporarily at that moment. We know this because his stepfather William Scott wrote to family members that he (William) had received an inquiry on behalf of the purchaser of the family's "Glebe land" in Virginia about the deed for that land. William had responded that he would "attend" to this when Macfarland returned to Brantford.[108] Evidently, Macfarland retained some stake in that land transaction. In 1870, Macfarland was working as a cook and living in a hotel or boarding house operation in Mansfield, Ohio (1870 census, Mansfield, Richland County, Ohio, p. 157). That year in Ohio, as in the 1850 Henrico County census, he was enumerated as "mulatto."

Macfarland's subsequent return to Virginia may reflect a deep attachment to that former family land in Virginia, and a strong desire to live near members of his extended family in New Kent County. Given his work as a carpenter and cook over the years, it seems remarkable that Macfarland had enough capital, on his return to Virginia, to buy considerable acreage in New Kent County. Other chancery court records, not just those about settling his estate, confirm that he owned hundreds of acres in New Kent County by 1905. He was not always free of debt, and at one point sold timber off his land to repay a "small sum of money" he owed. In another example of the continuing connections of these non-reservation Indian families, Albert Williams, one of the younger Thomas Pearman's heirs, was involved in that transaction.[109]

Macfarland was enumerated in the 1900 New Kent County census (p. 279A) as a sixty-four-year-old single farmer, and as an Indian; he was the only person in the county acknowledged to be indigenous in the federal count for the county that year. Because the enumerator listed him on the census form for "Indian Population," which had "special queries" for Indian people, the record elaborated on his ancestry and status. The census data identify him and his parents as belonging to the "Pocahontas" tribe, noting that he had one-third "white blood." If this was what Pearman told the enumerator, perhaps he identified as "Pocahontas" because he felt little connection to organized Pamunkey, Mattaponi, and Chickahominy groups. Maybe, instead, Macfarland—or the enumerator— simply used "Pocahontas" as a handy label generically recognizable as Indian. In contrast, in 1900 King William County, among those on the "Indian Population" census form, "tribe" names were listed as Powhatan, Mattaponi, Chickahominy or Pamunkey— except for Powhatan, these were all names attached to specific individual organized tidewater communities of that day. (There is just one possible reference to a "Pocahontas" ancestor.) On the "Indian Population" forms for 1910 King William County, though, some references to "Pocahontas" appear in the form's blocks for "tribe" names—a generic label, unattached to any specific organized tidewater Native community. The challenges and ambiguities involved in asserting tidewater Indian identities are evident here.

Macfarland's entry in the 1900 census reflects another ambiguity. In the column for citizenship status, the form recorded that Macfarland acquired citizenship in Ohio in 1876. This is puzzling, given that Macfarland was born in the United States to free parents who seem never to have been part of any federally recognized tribe or other reservation group. Legally, some Indian individuals in federally recognized tribes, such as those who had participated in federal efforts to allot tribal lands to individual tribal members, were considered citizens, even before Congress passed a blanket law in 1924 conferring United States citizenship generally on all Native Americans born within the United States. That does not seem relevant to Macfarland's case, though. He was not part of a reservation group, so it seems unlikely that he saw himself as lacking U.S. citizenship from his birth. If at some point Macfarland had taken Canadian citizenship, perhaps that was why the census referred to his time later in Ohio as the occasion of his U.S. citizenship.

Probably, part of the context for this puzzle is that as the nineteenth century wore on, the complexities of census labeling and counting individual Native Americans grew increasingly obvious to the Bureau of the Census. Instructions to census enumerators about Indians not living on reservations or in tribal contexts suggest this. In 1880, those instructions reminded enumerators that the constitutional provision on excluding "Indians not taxed" applied to "Indians living on reservations under the care of Government agents, or roaming individually, or in bands, over unsettled tracts of country." At the same time, the 1880 instructions told enumerators that: "Indians not in tribal relations, whether full-bloods or half-breeds, who are found mingled with the white population, residing in white families, engaged as servants or laborers, or living in huts or wigwams on the outskirts of towns or settlements are to be regarded as part of the ordinary population of the country for the constitutional purpose of the apportionment of Representatives among the States, and are to be embraced in the enumeration."[110] Similarly, instructions to enumerators for the 1900 "Indian Population" form specified that "detached Indians living either in white or negro families outside of reservations should be enumerated on the general population schedule . . . as members of the families in which they are found."[111] Given that direction, Macfarland was probably living alone that year. In any case, Macfarland's 1900 census designation testifies to the persistence of the Pearman family's Indian identity and his enduring connection to New Kent County. In order to be listed as the lone Indian in the county in 1900, Macfarland may have expressed his Native identity to the enumerator with energy and determination.

In 1910, though, the New Kent County census (p. 238B) listed seventy-seven-year-old Macfarland "Mack" Pearman as a Black man, living in the household of Ballard R. Bailey and his wife, Alice. Alice was a daughter of Henrietta (Honey) Miles and James P. Miles.[112] Henrietta Miles was a daughter of Susan Pearman Howell (Macfarland's sister); Alice, then, was Macfarland's great-niece. This is another example of the shelter and support Lucy's descendants might provide to members of their extended family.[113] Despite the fact that the 1910 census listed Alice Bailey, her husband Ballard, and their two children as "mulatto," the register of her marriage to Ballard Bailey in 1908 had indicated that she and her spouse were "white & Indian."[114] Later censuses listed her and her family as white (p. 124A in the 1920 New Kent County census, p. 234B in the 1930 Henrico County census, and page 4A in the Varina Magisterial District in the 1940 Henrico County census).

Alice Bailey's name appeared in the list of Macfarland's survivors in chancery court records of the 1918 settlement of his estate. A bill of complaint in those records recounts that Pearman ancestors came from Corsica in the eighteenth century.[115] It seems unlikely that many Corsicans transplanted to Virginia in the eighteenth century, though census records for nineteenth-century Richmond do include some immigrants from that island. This mention of Corsica may suggest that in 1918, in this particular legal matter, a claim of Indian identity by non-reservation Indian families like descendants of William Scott and Lucy Pearman Scott seemed potentially disadvantageous, dangerous, or likely to be dismissed. Perhaps at that moment the family felt it best not to assert their Indianness in this court setting, since such an assertion could have provoked white officials and lawyers to imagine that the family was African American or colored. Maybe the family or their legal advisors thought that claiming a southern European connection could help them avoid curiosity or questions about their race and color in these court proceedings. The records of this case are silent about the family's Indianness. Choices about when and whether to publicly affirm Indian identities likely depended on a specific strategy and context. Perhaps local clerks who recorded marriages were more likely to be sympathetic than chancery court officials.

The lives of Lucy Pearman Scott's children and grandchildren reflect the impact of race as, in Kathleen Brown's words, "a historically produced technology of power."[116] In their Southern context, Virginia Indians faced a system designed—legally, politically, economically, and socially—to maintain white supremacy and to build race as a binary Black-white system in which labels such as "mixed race," "mulatto," or "free person of color" were ambiguous or conflated with Black. In the South, this led to sharp contrasts in the ways whites historically tried to ascribe and impose indigenous and Black racialized identities. Some whites argued that one drop of Black blood made a person Black. In contrast, white officials have long tried to measure Indian identities using a very different yardstick, in which a considerable number of Native ancestors was a criterion for recognizing Indian individuals.

In response to the resulting pressures on all free people of color, many in the Scott-Pearman extended family left Virginia in the 1850s, seeking refuge in the north where they hoped to prosper and educate their children to be "men and women." Departing "my mother home" was a wrenching experience for William Scott and Lucy Pearman Scott, but apparently to them the alternatives within Virginia's institutionalized racism looked even worse. Though William and Lucy's letters do not say they were Indian, it seems possible that their sense of an Indian or mixed identity added to their resentment of racialized economic and educational constraints, "names too hard to be borne" and other injustices they suffered in Virginia, contributing to their decision to leave a place their families had called home for generations.

The experiences of these Pearman, Howell, and Wynn families show that Virginia's legalized racism had formidable power to disrupt community and family relationships among non-reservation Native Virginians. Some simply left their rural homes for other states, including Ohio, sometimes settling in cities. Given the forceful racism that denied their identities as Indians, perhaps for them Jim Crow Virginia came to feel like a "strange land" even though it was their mothers' home, for it was a place where their persistence and existence as Native people required strategic courage and patience.

The stories of Lucy Pearman Scott's descendants also demonstrate that Indian identities and family ties endured despite these formidable obstacles. Macfarland Pearman's return to Virginia is one poignant reminder of the lasting strength of family bonds and family traditions of Native identity. Like Macfarland, others among Lucy's descendants who stayed in Virginia sometimes publicly asserted their Indian identities. They married within other Indian families and lived near one another in rural tidewater counties and in Richmond. Given whites' assertions that marriages with African Americans made them not-Indian and Virginia's laws against interracial marriage, strategies like in-group marriage could buttress Virginia Natives' denials in the postbellum era that African Americans had historically lived and married within Virginia Indian communities. For non-reservation families like the Pearmans, Wynns, and Howells, living close to, and marrying within, other Indian families look like especially crucial strategies for maintaining and asserting their Indianness in Jim Crow times.

As chapter 2 shows, Virginia's 1924 Act to Preserve Racial Integrity on interracial marriage, and follow-up legislation in 1930, were steeped in a "one-drop" notion of what made an individual Black—even as the 1930 law retained "blood-quantum" notions about what made someone Indian. In objecting to such legal efforts to put them in the "colored" category, some Virginia Indians publicly echoed rhetoric about so-called racial purity to argue for their own racial integrity and to deny connections with African Americans—just as John

Howell objected to having a Black teacher for his children after the Civil War. Thus, while Virginia Indians conceptually posed a challenge to the notion of race as a Black-white binary, their resistance might sometimes entail acceptance of unrealistic one-drop notions about Blackness.

Still, despite the pervasive power of whites' ideas about one drop of Black blood, and about the level of blood quantum that made someone Indian, the lives of the descendants of William Scott and Lucy Pearman Scott remind us that such racist systems are not and were not eternal or impregnable. They arise within, reflect, and shape specific historic contexts and power struggles. They do not represent immutable, universal, "natural" or inevitable practices. Listen to the Pacific Studies scholar Teresia Teaiwa: "In the culture of my father's people, te I-Banaba, from the central Pacific Islands of Kiribati, there is no such thing as being part Banaban. You either are or you aren't Banaban. Mixed blood does not lessen one's claim to being Banaban or one's authority as a Banaban. As a result, intermarriage is not threatening to Banaban people. But Banabans have never been satisfied with intermarriage as a way of strengthening their gene pool. A key feature of our social organization is adoption."[117]

Similarly, Barbara Krauthamer and Theda Perdue have argued that, even when chattel slavery was developing among the Southeastern so-called Five Civilized Tribes, there was a moment when, for marriages of Indian women and white men, there existed "social conventions that cast their children as 'Indian,' rather than 'mixed blood' or 'half breed'."[118]

In the late twentieth-and twenty-first centuries, multiple non-reservation groups in Virginia have successfully, publicly, proclaimed and reclaimed their identities as Indian people, not mixed people on the Black side of a racial color line, getting recognition by the Commonwealth of Virginia and the federal government. Their continued organizational and political work emerged out of the experiences and persistence of people like Macfarland Pearman, Jones Pearman, and Ferdinand Wynn. Mixed blood and intermarriage were and remain potent exclusionary concepts in the United States, but such concepts conflict with the historical realities of other ways of building communities and constructing cultural and social identities, in Virginia just as on the islands of Kiribati.

In the next chapter, we will see the power and inherent contradictions of ideas about "blood" and interracial marriage erupting in Virginia in the mid-1920s. That story illuminates the strength of the racism that built segregation and the formidable obstacles that confronted Lucy Pearman Scott's descendants in Virginia in asserting their indigeneity—but it also demonstrates Native Virginians' resilience and persistence in the face of those obstacles.

CHAPTER 2

Virginia's 1924 Racial Integrity Law

THE CENTERPIECE OF VIRGINIA'S 1924 Act to Preserve Racial Integrity was this language: "It shall hereafter be unlawful for any white person in this State to marry any save a white person, or a person with no other admixture of blood than white and American Indian. For the purpose of this act, the term 'white person' shall apply only to the person who has no trace whatsoever of any blood other than Caucasian; but persons who have one-sixteenth or less of the blood of the American Indian and have no other non-Caucasic blood shall be deemed to be white persons."[1] Following that law's enactment, Virginia's Native peoples faced a renewed onslaught of official efforts to buttress Virginia's segregation regime. For example, in January 1925, William Archer Thaddeus Jones sat in the offices of Virginia's Bureau of Vital Statistics answering questions about his parents, grandparents, and siblings and their race, questions designed to sort out his racialized identity, and that of his children. Jones replied matter-of-factly; his responses included the fact that one of his grandmothers was "a white woman," and he called himself "mixed." He noted his extended family's Pamunkey and Chickahominy connections. Of one woman from a separate family, he explained that she "was what was called at that time a colored lady, (you know they just had colored and white at that time)," but added that "she was said to have Indian blood." Jones expresses here his clear understanding of whites' efforts to construct race as a Black-white binary, while reporting on the actualities of mixed-race people in his family and community. He noted that his sister's children attended the Roxbury school established by the Chickahominy in Charles City County, one of a handful of schools in Virginia for Indians. And he acknowledged that he himself "didn't go in" to join the Chickahominy people after they initially legally organized, decades before this interview. Jones noted that the children of his brother Newton, then living in Newport News, were not allowed to attend white schools in that city. Finally, the interviewer queried Jones to clarify the power relationships at stake:

B. [Albert O. Boschen]: Now Jones, you want to establish your racial standing so that your children can attend the "Indian" school, the same as your sister's?

J. Yes sir.

B. You understand, Jones, this is simply to get your children into the "Indian" school, and not to allow you the privilege of riding on the white cars and intermarrying with white people.

J. Yes sir, for nothing else.[2]

As this interview shows, for Virginia's Native people, as enforcement of the 1924 racial integrity law played out, sex, marriage, and segregation were entwined. That 1924 act on its face focused on restricting interracial marriages, but as white officials targeted Virginia Indians in implementing the law, they also fretted about other challenges to segregation, as in schools and public transportation. They subjected individual citizens to detailed, intrusive scrutiny.[3] In response, Mr. Jones acknowledged, and subtly contested, efforts by white officials to impose on him and his children a Jim Crow binary of a Black-white racialized scheme.

This chapter examines how Walter Ashby Plecker, John Powell, and Earnest Sevier Cox, among the most vocal and energetic proponents of Virginia's 1924 Act to Preserve Racial Integrity, perceived the challenges posed by Indian Virginians to their conception of the color line. (Peter Wallenstein, Paul Lombardo, Brian William Thomson, Richard Sherman and J. Douglas Smith have explored other aspects of the passage of this 1924 law.) Powell, Plecker, and Cox dramatized the threat they perceived from Native Virginians whom they considered mixed and therefore especially eugenically dangerous to white racial integrity. As small but distinctive groups, Native Virginians became targets for Plecker in his efforts as head of Virginia's Bureau of Vital Statistics to enforce the 1924 law. Indians on and off reservations, as small communities claiming an identity neither Black nor white, were relatively recognizable and identifiable, but not affluent or possessed of great statewide political influence.[4] In Virginia's plural yet segregated society, this made them obvious quarry whom Plecker could pursue to bolster segregation and white supremacy, through legalization of a "one-drop rule" for Blackness in Virginia.

The Campaign to Pass the Act to Preserve Racial Integrity

In their advocacy, Powell, Plecker, and Cox sounded an alarm about the racial realities and ambiguities that William Archer Thaddeus Jones's ties to the Indian community presented. In pressing for the 1924 law, building on centuries of Virginia legislation forbidding interracial marriage, Powell, Plecker, and Cox pushed for a definition of whiteness that was new to Virginia law; under the 1924 act it would belong only to those with "no other admixture of blood than white and American Indian." Before and after the law passed, they singled out Native Virginians in their efforts at advocacy and enforcement.

In this fight, Plecker, Cox, and Powell sometimes touted their identities as Southern whites, to show the roots of their commitment to white supremacy. Plecker (1861–1947), born in Staunton, Virginia, was a physician who became head of Virginia's Bureau of Vital Statistics. Powell (1882–1963) was a concert pianist and composer from Richmond who trained and performed in Europe and maintained an interest in American music. Cox (1880–1966), from Tennessee, studied at the University of Chicago, traveled in Africa and other parts of the world early in his life, and then settled in Richmond by 1922. Plecker and Powell promoted Cox as someone who had made a deep study of the "race problem" internationally and advised correspondents to read Cox's book *White America*.[5] Perhaps Cox also subscribed to a lost-cause version of Southern history, for at the 1907 Jamestown Exposition, he lectured on Civil War battles. Maybe while there he witnessed, or was aware of, performances by Virginia Natives at that exposition in which they asserted the Indian identities that so alarmed Cox and his white-supremacist allies (see chapter 3).

Plecker, Powell, and Cox were aware of the nationwide popularity of eugenic thinking in the 1920s, so they linked their ideas about segregation and white supremacy to eugenic rhetoric. Echoing the anti-immigration campaigns of Northern eugenicists like Madison Grant, they reached out to potential supporters who shared their interests in racial purity all over the country. Cloaking racism in eugenic arguments, Cox posited that if two "races" lived in close association, "amalgamation" would inevitably result, and that if the "mixing" involved white people the resulting population would just as inevitably be racially "inferior" to the "true" white race.[6]

Plecker, Powell, and Cox dabbled in Mendelian-sounding language and eugenic rhetoric, but their strongest devotion was to segregation and to the concept of race as a color line separating African Americans from white people. In that project they were necessarily drawn into conflicts with Virginians with Native American identities and ancestry. Some Native Virginians were vocal in their opposition. Though their actions are not as well documented as those of Plecker, Powell, and Cox, they acted, reacted, and resisted. Plecker and Powell acknowledged that some people in Virginia were of mixed race, but they were adamant that having any African American ancestors placed individuals on the Black side of the color line. They asserted that there were no real Indians in Virginia (that is, Native people with no Black ancestors), and joined eugenic rhetoric to the popular one-drop rule that any "black blood" at all made a person Black.

Until 1924, Virginia's legal definitions of race were not precisely in line with the one-drop notion. Rather, Virginia law had generally attempted to create racial identities by outlining how many Black or Native forebears might make a person colored or Indian, expressed as a fractional number of such ancestors. Inevitably, official efforts to define racial identities in terms of "blood quantum" were and are fraught with practical and moral difficulties. The genealogical certainty that blood quantum fractions imply was not and is not available to many of us. Such legal blood quantum definitions pretended to an unrealistic precision, given centuries of kinship and cohabitation across racial lines in Virginia. In practice, Virginia courts sometimes recognized that factors such as physical appearance, community association and participation, and social reputation provided clues for defining an individual's race in court—but using such factors belies the precision implied in blood-quantum fractions.[7]

The notion of blood quantum was entrenched in statute, but in Virginia law the precise fractions that defined "black" or "colored" shifted over time. In 1866, the Virginia legislature described what made an individual legally "colored" this way: the individual in question had one-fourth or more "Negro blood." (So a person with less than one-fourth Black ancestry could be legally white.) That 1866 law also sought to define Indianness in Virginia, using that same one-fourth fraction to specify the minimum blood quantum that made one Indian, but it added that no one was legally Indian who could be defined by law as colored. Thus, Black ancestors trumped indigenous ancestors in this legal arena. In 1910, the Virginia legislature redefined the standard for "colored" status; the new legal benchmark was "one sixteenth or more of Negro blood." The criterion for being legally Indian did not change in 1910.[8] That these legislated fractions could and did change is yet another sign that such legal definitions were far from self-evident, immutable, or natural.[9] Perhaps the most innovative feature of the 1924 racial integrity law was the attempt to set an absolute legal standard for whiteness: "no trace whatsoever of any blood other than Caucasian" (except for Virginians with "one sixteenth or less of the blood of the American Indian ... and no other non-Caucasic blood").

While the 1924 law was remarkable for this new definition of whiteness, it was not remarkable in the sense that it dealt with interracial sex and marriage. As early as 1662, Virginia law provided that "if any Christian shall commit fornication with a Negro man or woman, he or she so offending shall pay double the fines imposed by the former act."[10] In 1691, Virginia, like Maryland before it, enacted a law against interracial marriage. That law defined interracial marriage as a union between an "English or other white man or woman" on one side and, on the other, "a Negro, mulatto, or Indian man or woman."[11] From the colonial era, then, Virginia's laws against interracial marriage made the biggest distinction that between whites and all other racialized groups, including Indians, as Virginia attempted regulation, discipline, and punishment of citizens' choices of marriage partners.

Such colonial-era laws on interracial marriage may be read as an aspect of a modernizing state apparatus in the British North American colonies. In the twentieth century, state power was still an important tool, in the eyes of progressive-era eugenicists who questioned whether many people would voluntarily adhere to eugenic principles.[12] In the 1920s, Plecker, Powell, and Cox pointed to modern centralization and ramification of governmental powers to buttress their notion that government could and should act vigorously to police citizen's racialized identities and maintain record-keeping systems about those identities in the service of segregation and the eugenic integrity of the white race. In this sense, Plecker, Powell, and Cox fit the profile of eugenics supporters who considered themselves "middle-class professionals applying scientific expertise to solve pressing social problems through governmental intervention."[13]

These progressive-era attitudes also shaped the activities of the governor who signed the racial integrity law of 1924, Elbert Lee Trinkle. For example, Trinkle favored Virginia's participation, along with other state governments, in the "good roads" movement.[14] Perhaps he thought better roads were desirable not only for commerce and tourism, but also for policing and enforcement of a range of government policies and laws related to public health and social order. Yet the mobility that individuals found in a modernizing road system raised the stakes for state action to control the consequences of that mobility in matters of sex, marriage, and segregation.

To Powell, Cox, and Plecker, local, community mechanisms for policing racialized identities and preventing interracial marriage were not adequate. As some Virginians moved from rural to urban environments, these three men saw in that mobility potential threats to the proper racialized classification of Virginia's citizens. (As chapter 1 shows, some of Lucy Pearman Scott's descendants who moved to the Richmond area were called white in federal censuses.) Powell, Plecker, and Cox felt that, to combat such threats, the capacities of a modernizing state government should be put in the service of their eugenic, racist program.

Given the power of the state to prescribe and enforce racial identities, Virginia's Native people were especially vulnerable to rhetoric that joined Jim Crow and one-drop ideas to eugenic thinking. Plecker and Powell claimed that "near whites" were most dangerous to the purity of the white race, because they would be more able to evade Jim Crow restrictions and gain acceptance in white communities. They argued that Native Virginians, because their appearance cloaked their Black blood, might more easily blend into the white population. They feared that individual white Virginians would not always perceive and isolate Virginia Indians as Black, mixed, or near-white people. Thus, Plecker, Powell, and Cox cast Virginia Natives as a potential leading edge in a eugenic threat to whiteness.

Stoking such fears, by 1924 tidewater Virginia Indians for decades had demonstrated that they were willing and able, publicly and politically, to assert their positions as indigenous, not "near white" or "colored" people. Plecker, Cox, and Powell were provoked by Virginia Native people's actions, from the waning years of the nineteenth century, to organize and to get attention from white anthropologists who saw them as real Indians, and to establish access to railroad cars reserved for whites. Betsy Nies pointed out that nationally, "Eugenicists seemed particularly unaware of Indians as a living population in the country. The Indian Citizenship Act passed one week after the Immigration Act of 1924 without a murmur from them."[15] In that 1924 immigration law, Congress authorized new restrictions designed to limit immigration from "non-Nordic" countries. Robert Berkhofer noted that among U.S. congressmen that year, "The influx of millions of southern and eastern Europeans appeared more dangerous in their eyes than a few hundred thousand pacified Indians."[16] Proponents of Virginia's 1924 law, though, were vocal and active in voicing the eugenic threat they imagined Virginia's Indians posed.

Plecker, Powell, and Cox counted not only on the popularity of eugenic thinking, but also on Virginia's developing state bureaucracy. Because Virginia's 1924 law defined whiteness in a spectacularly absolute way, it would be easy to overlook a mundane aspect of government operations in the modernizing commonwealth: renewed emphasis on keeping track of births, deaths, and marriages at the state level. In 1912, Virginia had passed legislation authorizing a Bureau of Vital Statistics that would focus on centralized, consistent statewide collection of birth and death records, based on a model endorsed by the American Medical Association, the American Public Health Association, and the Bureau of the Census.[17] This renewed attention to statewide vital statistics came not so long after the commonwealth had strengthened aspects of its Jim Crow regime, including disfranchisement of African Americans, under a new state constitution of 1902.

In 1912, Walter Plecker became a state official, charged to implement this new vital statistics regime, and he served as state registrar of the Bureau of Vital Statistics until 1946.[18] In 1918, a new state law reinforced Plecker's reach, making the Bureau of Vital Statistics responsible for certain existing records of past births, deaths, and marriages and for future maintenance of up-to-date records of marriages and divorces.[19] Plecker was thus in a key position to consolidate state record-keeping on Virginians' racialized identities, to monitor and challenge individuals' racialized identities when records of births and marriages came to his office, and to respond to queries from local and state officials and others about individuals' official racial categorizations. To reinforce his role, Plecker collected older Virginia tax, marriage, birth, and death records. As a physician with experience in the field of public health, Plecker's access to a range of state records likely bolstered his credibility as a proponent of eugenics and segregation.

Aware of gaps in state collection of records for births and deaths between 1896 and 1912, advocates of what became the 1924 racial integrity law initially proposed a registration program requiring that every resident of Virginia have a certificate attesting to his or her racial identity. In the final version of the law, the registration program was voluntary. Later, Plecker took some credit for saving the bill when the proposal for mandatory registration encountered opposition, by offering that optional registration could be substituted for a compulsory system.[20]

As the campaign for the 1924 law got underway, Plecker's medical background complemented Earnest Sevier Cox's claims to ethnological expertise. In a draft letter of 1907, Cox had expressed interest in the "social and political sciences," and in doing a "thesis on the condition of the Negro under other governments." He wrote that he wanted to investigate "the development of the race problems in the European colonies and also [be?] acquainted with the general conditions of the native."[21] Attempting to sound scholarly, Cox showed awareness of nineteenth-century "scientific" racialism's debates about whether the races all derived from a single, common human ancestry—an argument that arose in spite of Christian orthodoxy that humans descend from one shared genealogy (an idea known as *monogenesis*). Though Cox distanced himself from nineteenth-century polygenists who proposed that the "races" came from separate ancestries, he held that "from many evidences we may assume that the differentiations, at least with regard to the primary stocks of man, had their beginnings in the very remote past."[22] Cox's separatist ideas were not new to him in 1924. In 1906, he had vitriolically suggested that African Americans face deportation in the wake of a race riot in Atlanta.[23] Cox later was in contact with a man connected with the American Colonization Society about his belief in "repatriation" and what he called the "Abraham Lincoln plan for colonization."[24]

In the World War I era, Cox had worked on a manuscript he called "Decay of Culture," which may have been an early version of his *White America*.[25] Hoping to gain public attention for his ideas about repatriation, he attempted to interest publishers in his text by asserting that the public should be receptive to those ideas because "recent violent symptoms of race discord" showed "that race friction will grow more intense with the increase of the races." To argue for the feasibility of the project, if backed by a government organization, he cited his experience with World War I army embarkation camps as evidence of "the adaptability of the principles of military movements to the rapid and orderly movement of civilian populations."[26] He viewed wartime mobilizations as evidence of the potential technical abilities of government to deal with racialized "problems" in peacetime.

Cox was aware of the movement that eventually led to the eugenically inspired federal law of 1924 mandating more restrictive immigration quotas. By 1920, Cox was corresponding with a supporter of such restrictions, the New York lawyer and eugenics advocate Madison Grant, author of *The Passing of the Great Race*.[27] Grant primarily focused on opposition to immigration into the United States by people from southern and eastern Europe whom he considered eugenically unfit as not "Nordic" or "Anglo-Saxon." In private, Grant encouraged Cox, Plecker, and Powell as they sought to strengthen measures to cordon off Blacks and Indians in Virginia. In 1920, Cox wrote to Grant about "exclusion and removal" of Blacks from the United States, noting that his book attempted to show the "negro problem to be but a phase of a world-wide and age-old color problem," seemingly to link his ideas with Grant's notions about immigration. Here, addressing a white elite Northerner, Cox acknowledged that his proposals for "removal," as the production of a white Southerner, could be seen as "harsh and adversely critical of the negro." Cox perhaps hoped that Grant's support would make his book seem less extreme.[28]

Cox in that same letter to Grant mentioned a recent public gathering of the Ku Klux Klan, writing, "Personally I am opposed to any secret organization of this nature," and that "there is much opposition among conservative Southerners to the attempt to revive the Ku Klux Klan." Still, Cox suggested that Klan activities might "force the negro problem to the immediate attention of many people in the South" and that his proposal's "peaceful methods" might "get a better hearing" when contrasted with Klan violence.[29] Grant responded: "I am interested in seeing the revival of the Ku Klux Klan all over the country. I think they should be approached with a view to spreading the proper kind of information on the relations of the races throughout the country. Do you happen to know how they could be reached for this purpose?"[30]

Precisely how Cox, Plecker, and Powell's links to the Klan operated is not entirely clear, but John Powell's papers show that at least one former Klan member remembered Powell's connection to past activities of Virginia Klansmen.[31] In 1922, the Richmond chapter of the Klan voted to leave the national Klan organization and join the local arm of Anglo-Saxon Clubs being formed by Powell.[32] Maybe Cox's self-image as a "conservative Southerner" of a certain class, and as a "scientific" observer somehow above the secretiveness and violence of the Klan, would have been at risk had he linked himself too openly and publicly to the KKK.[33]

In any case, in Cox's search for allies, he reached out to people who might share his ideas about racial separatism—including some African Americans with nationalistic aspirations. In 1923, Cox wrote to a friend that due to mechanization, competition for some jobs was so serious that only "selfish" whites would argue against a plan to restore "the Negro to the homeland of his ancestors and establish him in independence and plenty." He referred to comments by Marcus Garvey, the famed Black nationalist leader of the Universal Negro Improvement Association (UNIA), on the likelihood of growing "competition of the races," to suggest that someday "both races" would seek Blacks' "repatriation."[34] Madison Grant advised Cox to get in touch with Garvey "as it might be worthwhile to back his proposition."[35] By June 1925, Cox was in correspondence with Garvey.[36] Rhetoric within Garvey's UNIA about separation of the races suggested to Cox that Garvey would be sympathetic to some of Cox's ideas about racial purity. Perhaps Cox also thought Garvey's support would make his proposals for repatriation seem less draconian.

While Cox at times emphasized international aspects of the race problem, Plecker and Powell often brought their focus down to race in Virginia. As early as 1923, the three men mounted a public relations campaign advocating legislation for Virginia along the lines of what became Virginia's 1924 Act to Preserve Racial Integrity. Their offensive included articles in major Richmond newspapers, and the formation, largely credited to Powell, of "Anglo-Saxon Clubs."[37] While adopting some of the rhetoric of eugenicists like Madison Grant who sounded a public alarm about the threat to whites' racial purity from immigrants from southern and eastern Europe and Asia, they joined that anti-immigrant language with Southern racists' rhetoric about African Americans—and included Native Americans in that mix.

As the campaign for the 1924 law got underway, Powell and Plecker used arguments beyond their Virginia-specific cause. In 1923, Powell's Anglo-Saxon Clubs of America adopted a constitution that said the clubs stood for "the wise limitation of immigration and the complete exclusion of unassimilable immigration," for "the preservation of racial integrity; [and] for the supremacy of the white race in the United States of America, without racial prejudice or hatred."[38] Perhaps out of concern that their program would evoke visions of lynchings and the Ku Klux Klan, the writers of the clubs' constitution thus publicly avowed their devotion to white supremacy as if the clubs' program was founded not on personal animosities or ancient Southern bigotries, but rather on a modern need to protect white "civilization." They aimed to make institutional racism sound reasonable and reasoned, and to sell Jim Crow as a national, not just regional, need.

If Powell, Plecker, and Cox desired to distance themselves from the most overtly brutal aspects of Southern racism, the clubs' disavowal of "prejudice or hatred" may reflect their conceptions of, and anxieties about, their class identities. In any case, their attitudes about class as a dimension of the problem likely resembled those expressed by Madison Grant to Powell: "It is the insidious increase of mixed breeds in the lower strata of society which has heretofore undermined and ruined many white civilizations. The process goes on subtly, scarcely noticed, but ultimately pushes its way into the upper classes." Grant linked this "process" to Native American as well as Black people and added a layer of gender anxieties: "When the crossing of races is condemned by the law of the land, such mixture as takes place is between low-grade whites and Negro or Indian women."[39]

Against this backdrop, a piece published in the Richmond *News Leader* on June 5, 1923, announced the development of a petition by the newly formed Anglo-Saxon Clubs to the Virginia legislature, urging legal action for:

- a system of "registration and birth certificates showing the racial composition (white, black, brown, yellow, red) of every resident of the state;"
- restriction of marriage certificates to those possessing and presenting such a registration/birth certificate;
- renewed commitment to the idea that "white persons may marry only whites" based on the proposition that whiteness meant "no trace whatsoever of any blood other than Caucasian."

Clearly, Native people as well as African Americans were on the minds of the petitioners. Here, the clubs promoted their program as a reflection of a "wave of patriotism that swept over the country during the world war," when the stresses of war "displayed in a relentless glare certain deficiencies and weaknesses" involving immigration, the "intensification of racial frictions and animosities," and "the rapid breakdown of the traditional American virtues and principles." This article advocated both "intelligent selection and exclusion of immigrants," and "fundamental and final solutions of our racial problems in general, most especially of the negro problem." The "Asiatic problem" on the West Coast rated a mention; the piece cited Pacific coast state laws against "admixture with Asiatics" as responses to the need for an absolute color line.[40] This focus on immigration and interracial marriage reflects the desire of Powell, Plecker, and Cox to garner support nationally from northern eugenicists like Madison Grant and from white westerners with racialized fears of immigration.

That June 5 article also claimed, since there were already laws on the books in Virginia against interracial marriages, that the new legislative proposals were "not revolutionary nor even novel." (Plecker in another context wrote that this "one-drop" definition of whiteness was indeed a significant change.) "The proposed definition of the term 'white persons' constitutes merely the legal recognition of the general consensus of opinion" and simply extended a historic trend in Virginia law to tighten legal definitions of "colored" status through increasingly stringent blood-quantum fractions. If not novel, though, this new program needed urgent, immediate action because, "Even under the present law, racial admixture is rapidly spreading... if the color line is to be maintained, even temporarily, it must be made absolute."[41] The supposed absolute nature of the threat was that "no race has ever maintained its civilization when tainted even slightly with African blood." Thus, the article suggested that "the impossibility of an immediate final solution of the negro problem necessitates legislation that will ensure us a breathing space pending the final solution."[42] Perhaps this refers to some voluntary form of repatriation or colonization of African Americans; for a post-Nazi-era reader, the term "final solution" is frightening.

John Powell's public advocacy of the ideas behind the 1924 racial integrity law and his uses of eugenically tinged language were on full display in a piece published under his name in the Richmond *Times-Dispatch* on July 22, 1923. In it, he appealed to "history, ethnology, and biology" as bases and contexts for his arguments.[43] Powell used some Mendelian-sounding language; insisting that "'one drop of Negro blood makes the Negro,'" he wrote, "In this conviction there is nothing defamatory or derogatory to the Negro, but merely the recognition that under the laws of heredity, he is a predominant strain." Therefore, Powell argued, the continued danger of past or future racial "crossing" was both long-term and dire. "It is true that there are fewer hybrids of the first crossing than formerly. But we have no assurance that this decrease will remain constant." Besides, in Powell's eyes, a great danger lay not only in the "first crossing" but also in subsequent generations "from individuals of dubious racial purity."[44] Likely he was thinking of Virginia Indians among people who represented centuries of intermarriage and interracial sex.

In that July 22 *Times-Dispatch* piece Powell explicated more fully the reference to newer immigrant groups in the June 5 *News Leader* piece, and his thoughts about the intersections of biology and culture. In his view, such immigrants might marry outside their race because they were possibly "more deficient in the pride of racial integrity than our native stock. Moreover, it is undeniable that the Negro as a whole is becoming whiter." He attempted to pull back from the most bald, virulent assertions of the "inferiority" of non-white peoples and claimed that the Anglo Saxon Clubs "do not propose any categorical or dogmatic solution of the Negro problem," yet he pointed to African Americans as a grave threat to "Anglo Saxon civilization in America." Powell wrote that here, "The term 'Anglo-Saxon' is used in no narrow racial sense, but rather in a cultural sense. Ethnologically, the term has no right to existence."[45] Perhaps Powell was attempting to address arguments of his day about a "modern split between biology and culture" by embracing both.[46]

Like Powell, Earnest Sevier Cox also wrote about immigration for newspapers in the early stages of the campaign for the 1924 law. In a July 22, 1923, article, billed as a "Word-Famous Ethnologist," he called the Anglo-Saxon Clubs' petition and program "the expression of an ideal, for it would prove to be literally impossible to perfectly segregate the whites" given increasing numbers of "Brazilians, Cubans, Porto Ricans, San Domingans and other Latin-Americans, many of whom possess colored blood." Cox included American Indians in his screed: "our grave danger lies in the absorption of the blood of the negro rather than in the absorption of the blood of the yellow and red races. There is no doubt that the blood of the negro is prepotent when mixed with the blood of any other race." But while Cox wrote in support of the Anglo-Saxon Clubs' proposed definition of whiteness, he also suggested that "practical politics will probably differentiate between the various colored races. It may prove to be advisable to classify an individual of one-eighth or less of the red or yellow race as 'white.' Especially is this true of the Indians of the Cherokee type, who according to capable ethnologists, are probably either a part of or closely related to the white race . . . our chief danger is not from that source." However, Cox's nod to "practical politics" did not mean that those campaigning for a racial integrity law in Virginia saw Virginia's Indians as "of the Cherokee type." Cox closed this article on an absolutist note: "amalgamation or separation," he wrote, were the "two solutions to a race problem."[47]

Walter Plecker also had his say, as the head of the state's Bureau of Vital Statistics, in the pages of the Richmond *Times-Dispatch* on August 4, 1923. Virginia Indians were much on his mind. In this piece, he wrote about some "communities in Virginia which have perplexed us greatly." He mentioned a community in Halifax County that extended across the state border into North Carolina, another group in Amherst and Bedford Counties, and some people in Greene County. (Amherst and Bedford Counties are within the homelands of the Monacan people.) The Halifax group he described as "a tribe of people of mixed descent which gave us trouble at first to classify." According to Plecker, those Halifax people were not accepted by whites and did not associate with Blacks. Even in rural Virginia, at that time, probably it would have been difficult for such a community to maintain a high degree of social or economic insularity, so it seems likely that this situation was, racially and socially, far more fluid than Plecker represented it. For the Halifax group, he wrote, "We have compromised upon the term 'Indian' and admit them thus to the record." For Plecker, "the record" was a tool to define, standardize, and regulate not only individual identities, but also an entire community's view of itself. Plecker here only grudgingly applied the word "Indian;" perhaps he felt that to foster public faith in the authority and finality of the vital records system he was building, he might sometimes find minor compromises strategically valuable.[48]

Evidently, Plecker sometimes found individual and community identities more ambiguous and complex than he wished to admit. He wrote of the Halifax people, "They are swarthy in appearance, resembling closely neither the white nor the colored race."[49] Plecker thus in effect acknowledged the difficulties of officially classifying the Halifax community on racial lines through genealogy and blood quantum, and fell back on other indicators: physical characteristics as stereotypical indicators of race and community associations.

Plecker was concerned about inconsistencies in official racialized classifications, citing a family in which some children had been labeled white and some colored. He wrote, "A puzzling situation arises when births are reported, the parents being married (probably in other states) though of different colors. As it is a violation of Virginia law for white and black to live in marriage relations, I always report such cases to the commonwealth's attorney of the county. None of these officers, however, has brought the cases to court." Plecker responded to this "puzzling situation" with confidence in his power as a state official, in his eugenic, segregationist mission, and in a proposed new absolute definition of whiteness. He had written to officials in Amherst and Bedford Counties, home to Monacans, "asking them to unite and decide the status of these people," and not to classify them as white "if they have even a trace of negro blood on either side."[50] This seems a bold request, given that the legal definition of whiteness had not yet changed, as it would when the 1924 racial integrity act introduced a one-drop standard into Virginia law.

For Plecker, nineteenth-century state vital and tax records, physical appearance, and community reputation and associations were all evidence he could muster in his fight to impose his vision of their race on Virginian Indians. Sometimes, that evidence did not immediately motivate local officials on whom he had to rely for information and enforcement.[51] As implementation of the law unfolded, there were tensions surrounding the certainty sometimes expressed by Plecker, as he attempted to create an aura of rationality and objectivity, asserting that historical records admitted of only one interpretation: that a given Indian individual was Black.

The campaign by Powell, Plecker, and Cox bore fruit in the spring of 1924, when the Virginia General Assembly passed and Governor Elbert Lee Trinkle signed the Act to Preserve Racial Integrity. Powell was particularly visible in his public support of the proposed law; he even addressed the General Assembly.[52]

That same year, another law passed by the Virginia legislature permitted sterilization of individuals who were in state institutions and were considered eugenically "feebleminded" or "unfit." Though Powell, Plecker, and Cox at times espoused eugenic thinking about the dangers of reproduction by the "feeble-minded" within a single "race," they focused more on interracial sex. Paul Lombardo has remarked on Plecker's interest in sterilizing white women with mulatto children; and Brian William Thomson noted that Plecker recommended sterilization of at least one white woman "who seems to have given birth to one or two mulatto children."[53] It seems that Plecker was more concerned about enforcing a one-drop racial rule than he was about non-racial aspects of eugenic belief systems about what made someone "unfit."[54]

The final version of the 1924 racial integrity law differed somewhat from the agenda first laid out by the Anglo-Saxon Clubs. For example, an early version of the bill had proposed that the standard for being legally white, in cases of people who had both Indian and white blood, be set at one-sixty-fourth of Indian blood. In the law as passed, that bar was one-sixteenth Indian blood.

Implementation of the 1924 Act to Preserve Racial Integrity

Having achieved their objective to make Virginia law define whiteness in an absolute way, Powell, Plecker, and Cox pursued their segregationist mission after passage of the 1924 act. Cox went on arguing his case for repatriation of African Americans, pamphleteering and writing letters. Plecker as a state official and Powell as a public figure used similar avenues. They sought legislative refinement of the 1924 law to amend what they considered its flaws; urged enforcement of segregation in individual cases through contacts with local officials and individual citizens, such as William Archer Thaddeus Jones; took an interest when legal challenges arose in state courts; continued publishing articles to encourage public support for enforcement of the racial integrity law; and advocated that similar laws be passed in other states and the District of Columbia.[55] Their campaign went on for years, but in this chapter, the focus will be on their activities in the immediate wake of the passage of the 1924 law.

Revising Legal Definitions of Race after 1924

Virginia's legislature took up bills to refine provisions of Virginia's legal code defining "race" at its sessions in 1926, 1928, and 1930. Though seemingly not directly engaged in the legislative debates of 1924, Virginia Indians expressed concern about these later bills and involved white allies in publicly commenting on them. In 1926, proposed legislation that would have defined as "colored" anyone with "any known, demonstrable, or ascertainable admixture of Indian or Negro blood," failed to pass. Some of the opposition came from whites concerned that the bills could reclassify as "colored" some prominent whites who claimed Indian ancestors, even though the bill included language intended to exempt those descended from Pocahontas.[56]

A Virginia Baptist weekly, the *Religious Herald*, reported other objections to the 1926 bill, arguing, "The whole truth is that the bill originated with a few men who have had a sort of obsession on this business. The races in Virginia were never more distinct than they are at the present time, and there is no reason to suppose that we are in any kind of peril in this direction." One state senator, apparently like the *Herald* a firm believer in racial purity and in white Virginians' success in maintaining it, " 'resented the advertising which had been given Virginia as a State that was fast becoming mongrelized.' " Another lawmaker, perhaps less swept up in rhetoric about "mongrelization," noted that under the 1926 bill, a person could be charged with a felony for seeking to marry "if their ancestors were registered as of mixed blood." One senator said that "the effect of the bill on Foreign Mission activities would be highly injurious;" likely he had in mind Baptist missionary activities involving groups such as the Chinese.[57] By 1928, such legislative debates had raised concerns among white Baptists about the racialized status of their Indian Baptist brothers and sisters (more on this in chapter 3).

In 1928, in response to new legislative proposals to further the goals of the 1924 law, the Pamunkey chief George Cook told the Senate Court and Justice Committee, "I will tie a stone around my neck and jump in the James River rather than be classed as a Negro. It would be far finer to perish in the waters of this stream, upon whose banks my ancestors fought to help the 'pale faces' achieve independence from England than to suffer such an indignity after being chief of mine ancient and honored tribe for nearly a quarter of a century."[58] Thus, these 1926 and 1928 legislative discussions gave Virginia's reservation groups additional reasons and opportunity publicly to reject the idea that their communities historically had included African Americans. In so doing they accepted, or acquiesced in, certain notions about racial purity. Perhaps Chief Cook was opposed to an effort to impose on his group *any* identity other than Indian, but in Jim Crow Virginia, to say that ascribing any African American ancestry to Virginia Indians was an "indignity" worse than death probably resonated as an affirmation of the racism aimed at Black Virginians.

Louise Burleigh, a playwright who married John Powell in April 1928, reported to him about legislators' discussions surrounding bills introduced in early 1928 that had so stirred Chief Cook. She wrote to Powell that at one Senate debate, a speaker said that "this bill is aiming at one thing and one thing only: to humiliate and oppress the remnants of the Indian tribes who have dwelt peacefully among us for so long." In Burleigh's view, "Indian sympathy" among lawmakers was a significant factor in the legislature's deliberations. She noted that the Dover Baptist Association, home to several Indian churches, was among those opposed to the proposed legislation. She witnessed an exchange in which one legislator asserted that the bill under consideration would not affect any Indian in the state, and another lawmaker responded, "Oh! They seem to think it would."[59] Clearly, Virginia's Native people were making their case directly to legislators and others, including Baptist allies.

Virginia Native groups publicly spoke out about bills to revise definitions of race in Virginia's legal code in the aftermath of the 1924 law, using multiple strategies and cultivating sympathetic whites. They drew Louise Burleigh's scorn: "In the hearing before the Senate Committee, these people dressed in department store regalia, were much in evidence with their lawyers and sympathizing sentimentalists." She was outraged that Virginia Native people lobbying the General Assembly in 1928 publicly asserted their Native identities, using pan-Indian dress. "They may loudly proclaim that they have for one hundred years rejected the negro from their embrace, and that it is their desire to intermarry only amongst themselves," even "expelling from the reservations those of marked negro characteristics," but in her view nothing could diminish the facts of long-ago "negro mixture" in Virginia Indian communities. Burleigh was angered not only that Indian Virginians "began to make a show of excluding the negro," but also that they demonstrated strategic political skills. They raised money for legal fees and tried to influence individual legislators; they "readily recognize and reward their white friends by gifts of fish and game for words spoken on their behalf;" and they "are eager to serve white sportsmen who in words at least accept them on their own claims."[60]

Pressures behind the 1926 and 1928 bills had been building since at least 1925. As a state official closely connected with implementation of the 1924 law, Walter Plecker remarked that carrying out that law appeared to him an overwhelming task and opined that the law's provision for a program of voluntary, optional registration had somewhat backfired in actual practice. In his view, those most likely to try to register under the law were individuals whose racial identity was ambiguous, some of whom sought registration simply to try to cross the color line into whiteness.[61]

Native people in Virginia figured prominently in his complaint. Plecker lamented to the editor of the Richmond *Times-Dispatch* after the 1924 law passed that the rise of individual families as well as "some half dozen groups of people claiming most vociferously that they were 'Indians'" forced his office "to take up the rather difficult task of classifying, as to race, this population, totaling nearly two thousand." He noted that "historical and ethnological facts available," and vital statistics records dating back as far as 1853, had been supplemented by the testimony of "many responsible citizens of the localities where these people, claiming to be Indians, live." Thus, Plecker cited documentary "facts" including genealogical data, but he also sought local opinion about community reputation. He granted that, because of their history of recognition as Indians and their reservation status, the legal status of the Pamunkey as Indians had some protection. Nonetheless, he suggested that if Vital Statistics Bureau records were more complete, the Pamunkey, too, could be exposed as "a composite race of black, white, and in most cases of a small amount of Indian admixture." He pushed a one-drop notion of colored identity, and he wrote as if past investigations by the U.S. Bureau of American Ethnology supported his position.

Leaning on old state vital statistics records, on centralizing state records systems, on his selective interpretation of work by white researchers, and on equally selective uses of local informants, Plecker denied "that there are any native born Virginian Indians of unquestionably unmixed blood, and none under our new law entitled to the privilege of intermarrying with white persons."[62] It seems likely that Plecker's thinking in 1925 about tightening racial integrity legislation was a reaction not only to the existence and resistance of organized Indian groups, but also to a Richmond controversy that involved interracial marriage and school segregation.[63] The fall of 1925 found him "preparing for a suit against the Richmond School Board by several families of mixed people from Charles City and New Kent Counties" who "have been sending their children to the white schools of Richmond and have been intermarrying with white people."[64] This was likely the case of Ray Wynn—son of Ferdinand Wynn the younger—and some of his neighbors, including John Clayton Howell (Lucy Pearman Scott's great-grandson), described below.

In December 1925, the Chickahominy leader E. P. Bradby wrote to Governor Trinkle because he was aware that Plecker wanted to push new legislation. In his initial reply Trinkle assured Bradby of his willingness to help ensure that Bradby got a hearing before the appropriate legislative committee and expressed confidence that "no one would want to do the Indians of this State an injustice." Trinkle coaxed "The Indians have certainly given me no trouble since I have become Governor, and I hope they will continue to follow this course."[65] He wrote to Plecker about this exchange: "I do not know what you have in mind along this line, but I am sure you are going to be conservative and reasonable and not create any ill feeling if it can be avoided between the Indians of Virginia and the State government. From reports that come to me I am afraid sentiment is moulding itself along the line that you are too hard on these people and pushing matters too fast."[66] Trinkle declared that "no one could be personally more in favor of the racial integrity law than I," but he also urged on Plecker political prudence, "extreme caution and careful advancement."[67] Despite such political cautions, and despite the failure to pass the 1926 and 1928 bills, in 1930 the legislature adjusted the definition of "colored" in Virginia law so that it better meshed with the standard for whiteness in the 1924 law. Although the 1924 law had defined whiteness stringently, it had not explicitly altered the 1910 legal "one-sixteenth or more of negro blood" definition for determining who in Virginia was a colored person. The 1930 law provided: "Every person in whom there is ascertainable any Negro blood shall be deemed and taken to be a colored person, and every person not a colored person having one-fourth or more of American Indian blood shall be deemed an American Indian; except that the members of Indian tribes living on reservations allotted them by the Commonwealth having one-fourth or more of Indian blood and less than one-sixteenth of Negro blood shall be deemed tribal Indians so long as they are domiciled on such reservations."[68] Apparently, in 1930, the legislators thought that a one-drop rule defining what made a Virginian colored should be relaxed only for Virginia Indians on reservations. Under this law, reservation people seemingly risked losing their tribal Indian status, not because they had chosen a new identity, or because they had somehow magically gotten new and different forebears, but simply because they had moved away from one of the two state-recognized reservations.[69]

Virginius Dabney of the Richmond *Times-Dispatch,* reporting on the 1930 bill to the *New York Times,* wrote that it was prompted by a "discovery" that some "negroid" children were attending white schools (and might therefore ultimately gain entrance to white colleges and universities in the state), a situation that could not be prevented until the state changed the 1910 "one-sixteenth" legal standard for being "colored" to match the 1924 law's definition of whiteness. Dabney explained that, "the Indian question has given the advocates of racial integrity in Virginia more trouble than any other." Plecker claimed there were no real Indians in Virginia, but as Dabney wrote, "The Indians have thousands of white friends in the State who feel that the redskins have suffered enough and that they should be left alone. When attempts were made in 1926 and 1928 to strengthen Virginia's racial integrity law it was found that in one way or another the Indians would be adversely affected, and there was a great uproar. Similarly, the movement at the present [legislative] session to change the definition of a "colored person" roused friends of the Indians who felt that the Chickahominys and Rappahannocks, as well as various groups in Halifax, Amherst, and Rockbridge Counties calling themselves Indians, should be excluded from the terms of the act, as well as the [reservation] Pamunkeys and Mattaponis." Dabney noted that Powell and Plecker countered with their standing argument that so-called white civilization would be destroyed in the United States "unless the mingling of the white and negro races in this country is stopped at once."[70]

Thus, as proponents of the 1924 and 1930 laws voiced their segregationist and eugenic-sounding concerns about enforcement of those statutes, they particularly targeted indigenous Virginians. They continued to argue that Indians were dangerous because, although many had Black ancestors, that aspect of their parentage might not be immediately or visually obvious. Thus, an Indian with a Black person in the family tree might be able to cross the color line to marry a white person. Louise Burleigh wrote that even if their Indian status were legally recognized, that "will not prevent ambitious young men from leaving for other localities and ensnaring thoughtless females into believing that they are something great."[71] Thus, she wrapped notions of female weakness around acknowledgment of the glamour of noble savage imagery that existed alongside and within whites' presumptions about Native American racial inferiority.

In practice, enforcing the law was a continuing struggle, exacerbated by the fact that, as Plecker admitted, some Indian Virginians appeared to him neither Black nor white; a mixed-race status had to be squared somehow with the legal maintenance of a color line as a simple Black-white binary divide. The 1930 law's contorted language about reservation Indians seems counter to the rhetorical stance of Powell, Plecker, and Cox about "ascertainable" Black blood, since that 1930 act retained a blood-quantum measure for legally defining Indians (but not for Black Virginians), and made legal racialized categories among reservation Indian people contingent on place of residence. The law's exception for reservation lands shows that absolutist segregation rhetoric was not always made legally absolute. The 1930 law, like the 1924 law's "Pocahontas exception," made it obvious again that the construction of race in Virginia's marriage laws stemmed from the politics of white supremacy, barely cloaked in eugenic "science."

Surveillance and Enforcement

Even before passage of the 1924 law, Plecker had involved himself in policing racial classifications of individual Virginians. For example, in early 1924 he corresponded with a lawyer who apparently had requested, on behalf of their mother, birth certificates for children who "had been suspended from the white schools, pending an investigation as to whether they were white or colored." The family's surname does not appear in the copy of this letter in John Powell's papers, but whether or not this correspondence involved an Indian family, Plecker's response foreshadowed his activities against Native people. He replied, "There is a very serious condition existing in many parts of Virginia caused by the mixture of the races as in this case. Our office is taking a firm stand against the admission of any individual as into the white race if they bear the slightest trace of negro blood."[72] Apparently Plecker was intent on enforcing a restrictive definition of whiteness even before the 1924 legislation was signed into law in March of that year.[73] Opposition by individuals and communities to enforcement of the 1924 law forced Plecker to explain his stance. Sometimes he emphasized absolutist aspects of his one-drop argument, and at other times he pleaded practicalities in making his case against interracial marriage. He portrayed his positions as the fruit of a scientific, coherent, logically integrated argument, even in the face of practical challenges that arose in his interactions as state registrar with mixed-race individuals and communities. Anyone in Virginia claiming a Native identity faced in Plecker an opponent who was doctrinaire, yet tried to sound pragmatic.

Immediately after passage of the 1924 law, Plecker issued a *Virginia Health Bulletin* "extra" edition providing direction for local registrars and other officials with responsibilities for enforcement of the new law. Apparently, he suspected that not all local registrars would be enthusiastic about implementing the voluntary registration program authorized by the law or about risking confrontations with neighbors and acquaintances in enforcing new strictures on interracial marriages. He wrote: "It is preferable that local registrars confine their efforts at first to their own territory, but if neighboring registrars do not push this registration, permission is given to other registrars after three months after the law goes into effect, to solicit and accept this form of registration outside of their own bounds. Special registrars or agents of the Bureau [of Vital Statistics] may be appointed for this special work if needed." This sounds like a threat and warning to any registrars who did not exert themselves in these matters. Plecker was willing to assume ultimate responsibility for carrying out the law if local officials were uncooperative, and he intended to go far to take bureaucratic control, writing that, "the Bureau of Vital Statistics should be notified of all doubtful or suspicious cases."[74]

Yet Plecker was placing in the hands of local officials a responsibility for determining racial identities that in other contexts he had admitted was difficult to carry out. He instructed: "As color is the most important feature of this form of registration, the local registrar must be sure that there is no trace of colored blood in anyone offering to register as a white person.... Equal care must henceforth be used also in stating the color of the parents of children registered at birth under the 1912 law."[75] Plecker urged local officials to "warn any persons of mixed or doubtful color as to the risk of making a claim as to his color, if it is afterwards found to be false." He recommended that registrars delay for "further investigation" if they had doubts about the racial identity of a registrant. In this pamphlet, Plecker endorsed making "further explanation" on the back of a birth certificate about a child's racialized identity in cases of doubt or dispute.[76] Over decades, that practice aroused anger and resentment among Virginia Indians.

Plecker already had reason to think that some local officials could be intimidated by, or perhaps sympathetic to, local residents. In 1923, a registrar and businessman had written about his dealings with Monacan people of Amherst, Rockbridge, and Bedford Counties: "These people have their own churches, schools, etc., and do not associate with either class, yet they are registered as white on the voting list, and the only thing I could see to do without being very injurious to my business, was to let the birth registers go on as handed in to me by the midwives as white."[77]

On the eve of passage of the 1924 law, Plecker had complained to a state senator about the wariness of at least one registrar (possibly the man quoted above), and about physicians who might report "mixed-breed" births as white "because of the lack of recorded evidence to the contrary and for business reasons." He added that his office had, in some of these cases, changed some certificates "from white to colored after securing additional information."[78] While it is more than likely that local white officials generally supported racial segregation, Plecker's "Instructions" bulletin and some of his letters show that he anticipated local complications.

To make matters more complex, Plecker in his "Instructions," stressed the importance of using "color terms accurately," and offered definitions of "mulatto," "quadroon," and "octoroon." He added, "The terms 'Mixed,' 'Issue,' and perhaps one or two others, will be understood to mean a mixture of white and black races, with the white predominating." ("Issue" as a term for "mixed-race" Virginians echoes language in Virginia's 1691 law against interracial sex and marriages.) He noted of such "mixed" people: "That is the class that should be reported with the greatest care, as many of these are on the borderline, and constitute the real danger of race intermixture." He admonished, about "mixed" people: "The term 'Indian' will no longer be accepted for that class, but must be applied only to those of known pure Indian blood, or those mixed with white. If there is a mixture of negro they must not be classed as Indians but as 'Negro' or 'Mixed Indian.'" Here, Plecker encouraged the use of a broad range of words to describe "colored" and "mixed" people. Perhaps Plecker raised words like "mulatto" or "octoroon" because of the 1924 law's language authorizing voluntary registration forms as vehicles to describe in some detail the "the racial composition of any individual, as Caucasian, negro, Mongolian, American Indian, Asiatic Indian, Malay, or any mixture thereof, or any other non-Caucasic strains."[79] Plecker seemingly aimed to foster an archaic vocabulary that was in tune with his one-drop notions about African American and mixed identities.

As years passed, in his surviving correspondence with state officials and ordinary citizens, Plecker sounded increasingly dogmatic, rigid, and strident in his contention that no one in Virginia was really Indian.[80] He expressed ambivalence about the "compromise" (mentioned in his 1923 newspaper statement noted above) with Native people in Halifax. As early as December 1924, he wrote:

It is very likely that there was some Indian admixture in the Halifax tribe, but I believe there is very little doubt as to their composition being chiefly negro and white.... At the time of our inquiry they resented being classed as negro; as descendants of 'free negroes' always do. We compromised on the term 'Indian' in order that we might know that they are not white. Now that term is being used as a stepping-stone to being classed as white.... Under the new Racial Integrity law we are not accepting that term as conclusive.[81]

Legal challenges to enforcement of Virginia's new restrictions on interracial marriage were not long in coming and developed early in Monacan territory—Amherst, Bedford, and Rockbridge Counties—among people whom Plecker had already found "perplexing." In the spring of 1924, Plecker wrote to a range of school officials, local registrars, and county clerks in that part of Blue Ridge and Piedmont country: "Our office is trying to investigate the families of mixed blood under the new racial integrity Act." Noting that Amherst and nearby counties have "a large number of these people," Plecker wrote, "I desire to warn you especially to use every precaution not to issue marriage license for one of these people to intermarry with a person of known pure white blood."[82]

Plecker cited, among the "proofs" underlying his enforcement efforts, genealogical information drawn from records dating as far back as the mid-nineteenth century. But he also recognized the need for local knowledge in statewide enforcement of the 1924 law. In the case of mixed-blood families in Amherst and Rockbridge Counties (presumably Monacan individuals), he also leaned on the work of two eugenically inspired writers, Ivan E. McDougle and Arthur Estabrook. They were working on a book they would publish in 1926 as *Mongrel Virginians: The WIN Tribe*. By July 1924, Plecker was aware of their assertion that those mixed families of Amherst and Rockbridge Counties descended from "Indians who mixed with white and negro people" and who should therefore not be considered "pure white."[83]

That summer, Plecker complained that the 1924 law's provision for optional registration was having unintended consequences, since "our near white friends" in "the Amherst crowd are all trying to register as white and we have written to the local registrars that they must give their money back rather than accept them as such."[84] Plecker reported that resistance in that part of the state had reached a high pitch. "Our Amherst County colony is up in arms and are on the verge of a race riot, threatening the life of one of our local registrars for giving out information concerning them. About 47 from Irish Creek, Rockbridge County, who belong to the Amherst tribe sent in registration cards all white, though we know positively that most, if not all of them are mixed."[85]

Shortly after, Plecker boasted that he had a network of midwives, physicians, local registrars, undertakers, and county clerks who had been "very carefully instructed as to the law and warned as to enforcement." He said this network showed "zeal in getting this matter straight and in furnishing us with information. Even the midwives are writing us letters giving us lists of the mixed people for whom they practice and asking advice."[86]

In the fall of 1924, "the Amherst crowd" brought legal challenges to a head, calling into question Plecker's claims to definitive knowledge about them. The Rockbridge County clerk declined to issue a marriage license to a couple, based upon his understanding that one of applicants, Dorothy Johns, had some Black as well as white and Indian ancestry. Johns sued, and Judge Henry Holt ruled against her. Shortly after that, another couple, one of whom was reputedly racially mixed like Dorothy Johns, came before the same judge, who ruled that the prospective bride, Atha Sorrells, should be considered legally white for purposes of Virginia's marriage law.[87] Plecker monitored the Johns and Sorrells cases, and testified in both. He maintained that nineteenth-century records listing Atha Sorrells's family as "colored" were proof that she had some African ancestry.[88] Sorrells contended that in her case, those records meant that there were Indians among her ancestors. The judge, while apparently sympathetic to the fundamental premises of the new racial integrity law, noted the practical difficulties of proving, over countless generations, that an individual had no ancestors who were not white.[89] This counters Plecker's contention that, from nineteenth-century vital records and other sources, he had adequate genealogical evidence for enforcement of the 1924 law.[90] In individual cases, the ostensible precision of blood-quantum fractions and of legal language like "no trace whatsoever of any blood other than Caucasian" and "ascertainable" could dissolve into fuzziness.

Plecker and Powell perceived the Sorrells ruling as a threat to implementing the racial integrity act. They considered further legal action. In the wake of the Sorrells decision, Leon M. Bazile, then an assistant attorney general for Virginia, told Powell and Plecker that Judge Holt had threatened, should the state appeal his ruling, to "amend his opinion, and declare the racial integrity act unconstitutional." Faced with this, Bazile advised against an appeal. Since "the law seems to be working all right outside of Judge Holt's circuit, we would run the risk of losing a great deal on the chance of reversing him in one case." Nonetheless,

Bazile wrote to Powell that, "if you and Dr. Plecker wish the case to go to the Court of Appeals, this office will take it there," and he solicited Powell's further views.[91] Decades later, as a judge, Bazile convicted Richard and Mildred Loving of violating Virginia laws against interracial marriage, a case that ultimately led to the invalidation of all such laws in the United States, when the U.S. Supreme Court reached its 1967 *Loving v. Virginia* decision.

Plecker professed to be undaunted by the practical difficulties and cruelty of enforcement of the new law. In the wake of the Dorothy Johns case, he wrote to editors of the *County News* of Lexington and the Lexington *Gazette*, "We cannot afford to let pity for these miserable people influence us in what is safe and right."[92] In this, Plecker echoed arguments developed as white people entrenched racialized categories and ideologies as somehow "natural" and objective, to the effect that this scientific racism required that questions of human sympathies be set aside, since harsh measures that might ruin individual lives served a racialized greater purpose.[93]

Plecker's belief in the righteousness of his crusade emboldened him to try repeatedly to constrain individual Virginians' daily lives and their future life chances, especially in marriage and in schooling. Take, for example, his message to a mother in Lynchburg. A midwife had signed a birth report for a child born to Mrs. Robert Cheatham in 1923 that categorized both mother and father as white, but Lynchburg city officials had submitted a "correction" to the effect that the child's father was "a negro." Plecker threatened Mrs. Cheatham: "This is to give you warning that this is a mulatto child and you cannot pass it off as white. A new law passed by the last Legislature says that if a child has one drop of negro blood in it, it cannot be counted as white. You will have to do something about this matter and see that this child is not allowed to mix with white children. It cannot go to white schools and can never marry a white person in Virginia. It is an awful thing." Whether Plecker meant that the child, or the circumstances of the child's birth, or both, were "awful," his language is chilling, and not just because he referred to a child as "it." Plecker also threatened the midwife involved: "This is to notify you that it is a penitentiary offense to willfully state that a child is white when it is colored. You have made yourself liable to very serious trouble for doing this thing. What have you got to say about it?"[94] The Cheatham family likely did not claim an Indian identity, but this correspondence captures Plecker's belligerence, which he also aimed at Virginia's Native people.

Plecker continued such activities for years, boasting that his office would unilaterally alter records submitted to his office to ensure that mixed people were not identified as white. He involved local officials by writing to functionaries such as the "Clerk and School Superintendent giving them they [sic] information which we have."[95] By 1928, he had developed a standard "warning which we are now attaching to the backs of birth certificates where we are now in possession of facts which a hundred years from now might not be available."[96] Generations of Virginia Indians have resented such alterations of their official records.

Within months of passage of the 1924 law, Plecker turned serious attention to Native peoples of the tidewater. Prior to a meeting with Chickahominy people of Charles City County, he wrote:

> In the eastern part of the State there are three or four tribes of Indians who are sufficiently pure to be classed as Indians, though in one of these tribes now under investigation, the Chickahominy tribe, their Chief is engaged in separating the Indian—colored—white from those he claims are free from negro blood. The latter class I believe will be much in the minority. I have an arrangement to meet with him at their Church on December 21st, and arrange definitely as to accepting them in the records of our office as Indian, the others to be classed as mixed-colored, though they probably have some Indian blood. Another tribe, the Rappahannock, is in just the same situation and I expect to make a similar investigation of them. The Pamunkey Indians are probably the purest of all. We have not, however, seriously considered the Halifax, Amherst, and Rockbridge tribes as being of sufficient Indian blood to be classed as such.[97]

Plecker's "investigation" was likely a divisive episode for the Chickahominy and a clear warning that their status as an Indian community was under siege. He evidently intended that Chickahominy leaders participate in sorting their membership along blood lines. Here, Plecker made a broad distinction between Native groups in the eastern and western parts of the state, but he was also eager to split up eastern communities, in line with his rationale for denying the Indian identities of Amherst (Monacan) and Halifax groups en masse. Perhaps this episode helped spur opposition by tidewater Indians in 1926 and 1928 when revisions to the 1924 law were considered in Virginia's General Assembly.

Possibly Governor Trinkle, in his desire to avoid public controversy, influenced Plecker's decision to have that face-to-face meeting with the Chickahominy in their own community. After that meeting, Plecker noted that Governor Trinkle had been among the whites who "paid them [the Chickahominy] a little attention." One of Plecker's white informants reported that the governor had joined those who attended Chickahominy "fish frys" intended to cultivate white supporters. Plecker informed him that the governor "knows now" that the Chickahominy were not Indians but were "mixed with negro."[98]

In preparing for his meeting with the Chickahominy, Plecker continued his practice of asking help from local officials. A local registrar told Plecker of "two negroes, J. F. Bowman and Peter Tyler of Ruthville, who claim to know a good deal about the race origin of the Charles City Indians." Plecker wanted to see those two men as part of his trip to meet with the Chickahominy.[99] Probably he anticipated that Bowman and Tyler would tell him things that would undermine Chickahominy claims to be pure Indians, individually or as families.

After the meeting at the Chickahominy church, Plecker noted that the occasion gave him, "the opportunity to tell them plainly that they were mixed with negro and would not be allowed to marry with white people. I told them that they would be allowed to write 'mixed Indian' on their birth certificates, which means in our office that they are a mixture of negro-white and Indian." For their part, the Chickahominy asked Frank Speck, a well-known University of Pennsylvania anthropologist and folklorist, to send a representative to the meeting who addressed the gathering at the church after Plecker spoke. Following the meeting, Chickahominy leaders made visits to Plecker and to Governor Trinkle.[100]

William Archer Thaddeus Jones's interview (quoted above) held on January 31, 1925, in Richmond also revealed methods and consequences of Plecker's attention to tidewater Indians. At that meeting, Jones expressed his wish to place his children in the Chickahominy school near Roxbury, in Charles City County. The superintendent of schools for James City, Charles City, and New Kent Counties had taken the position that for the children to be placed in that school, "It will be necessary for him [Jones] to be recognized by the Bureau of Vital Statistics as a 'mixed Indian.'. . . This stand was taken due to the fact that neither the School Board nor I care to pass on the race of a man where there is a Bureau established, you might say, for this purpose." This superintendent linked his stance to Plecker's presentation to him of "a list of people living in Charles City County whom he [Plecker] has listed as 'mixed Indian'. . . " and whose children were attending the Roxbury school.[101] The superintendent cited state record-keeping and segregation practices; perhaps he was also hesitant to take the lead in asking a question that might cause confrontations with or among his neighbors.

William Archer Thaddeus Jones's testimony focused on both his genealogy and his community associations. In his interview he affirmed that his mother, Emma Langston, was "a full-blooded Pamunkey Indian" and that his sister, Mattie B. O. Jones, wife of Curtis J. Wynn, sent her children to the Roxbury school. The web of connections among these non-reservation Indian families was dense. Curtis J. Wynn's father was Ferdinand Wynn the younger, whom we met in chapter 1. Mattie B. O. Jones was Curtis's first wife; his second wife was Delia Canaday, a granddaughter of Jones Pearman.[102] The questions posed to Jones were designed to sound objective, but racialized categories underpinning Jim Crow segregation were shifty and contingent. What did Jones think about having to submit to such an examination about his racial standing in order to get his children into a school their cousins already attended?

Plecker's "investigation" of the Chickahominy also included a meeting with Ferdinand Wynn the younger (Curtis Wynn's father) whose father, Ferdinand Wynn the elder, Plecker accepted as a person whose Indian blood was traceable. Plecker said the Chickahominy community brought Wynn "into my office as their Indian exhibit, and he does bear some marks of Indian blood." He emphasized, though, his conversations with local non-Indians about the reputation of the Chickahominy: "Some five or six leading men of Charles City County have visited my office and furnished me with the pedigree of these people, and all emphatically claim that they are of negro-white descent, except those descended from this man Wynn, who would still have a faint trace of Indian. Their statements fully agree with our records and the historical quotations referred to."[103]

In the letter quoted above, Plecker went on to talk about the "Rappahanocs," a group who, in his view, had only recently adopted that name. Though he had not yet "traced out" the families of this group, he already believed that they, too, "contain a trace at least of negro blood." Plecker sometimes touted his genealogical precision, but here he showed that lack of documentation did not necessarily shake his confidence in his opinion about the racialized identities of Chickahominy and Rappahannock people. He gave great weight to the word of local white "leading men," against the testimony of a Native community and the analysis of contemporary scholars like Frank Speck.[104]

Plecker wanted to suppress research that endorsed tidewater Natives' Indian identities. To John Powell he wrote: "I hope that we have stopped the issuing of Speck's report on the Essex and King and Queen group. Suppose you call upon the Indian Museum people and tell them a few things."[105] Plecker here referred to the ethnographer Frank Speck's monograph on the Rappahannocks, published by the Heye Foundation in 1925.

Speck had already written to Plecker at least once, in response to Plecker's request for access to Speck's writings on Virginia Indians. Speck took that opportunity to lament that Virginia's State Historical Society had earlier dismissed a chance to see his manuscripts, so that he lost an opportunity to help inform "a decision on the racial status of the Indians in Virginia in view of the 1924 racial integrity law." Speck then critiqued the 1924 law, arguing, "that assimilation is biologicaly [sic] practically inevitable; that the act may possibly result in moral injustice to many whites and the near-whites; that it may also have an effect toward the increase of illegitimacy where it might be avoided without harm; that the heredity theories upon which the Statute is based are not scientifically valid, especially that which assumes the 'purity' of any existing type as a 'white' race."[106]

Plecker also attempted to influence U.S. Census Bureau officials who would conduct future census counts of Virginia Indians. In early 1925, Plecker informed federal census officials that his investigations were confirming that "we have no Indians in Virginia that are not heavily mixed with negro as well as white blood." He wrote that at his recent meeting with the Chickahominy people, "there was only one woman who could be classed as Indian in comparison with those that we see in the west. The others were all clearly and distinctly negroid." Here, Plecker cited physical appearance, not just the genealogical documentation of which he sometimes boasted. Since the Rappahannock group, like the Chickahominy, were pressing for recognition of their Indianness, Plecker countered, "They probably contain a strain of Indian blood but possibly to a less degree than the other three tribes mentioned" (that is, Chickahominy, Pamunkey, and Mattaponi people). Here, he cited the marriage record of a Rappahannock leader's grandparents who had been called by a county clerk "free negroes," in his effort to refute Rappahannock claims. Plecker also noted that the census for Amherst County showed increasing numbers of Indians after 1900. "That colony has such a slight strain of Indian blood that it is entirely erroneous to class them as Indians. We have the direct history of them as descendants from free-negroes." In citing these cases Plecker requested that for the 1930 census count "our bureau ... be permitted to co-operate with you if we are able in establishing the racial status of the so-called Indians of Virginia."[107]

Public Advocacy after Passage of the Racial Integrity Act

Following passage of the 1924 law, Plecker, Powell, and Cox continued to speak publicly and to write newspaper and magazine articles, letters, and pamphlets making the case for their segregationist program inside and outside the state. Linking their activities to the national eugenics movement, they sought to reach general and professional audiences across the country. Their attitudes toward Virginia Indians were integral, not incidental, to their racist campaign, which they aimed to make national in scope.

In November 1924, Plecker presented to the Southern Medical Association a paper titled "Shall America Remain White?" In it, Plecker referred to eugenic rhetoric about the "unfit," and "reversion under Mendel's law," but he devoted some text to his theory of history. In his view, from ancient Egypt and India to South Africa and the United States, nowhere "have white and colored races lived together without ultimate amalgamation, and without the final deterioration or complete destruction of the white or higher civilization." In the wake of the Johns case, he emphasized the "dangers" of "a mongrel race of white-black-red mixture, the most undesirable racial intermixture known, as I can testify from my own observation of similar colonies in Virginia."[108]

Plecker also read a paper before the American Public Health Association in October 1924 that appeared in *The American Journal of Public Health*. In abbreviated form, it reappeared in the national magazine *The Literary Digest*, on March 7, 1925. In this piece, for public health peers and a countrywide popular audience, Plecker rehashed his historical theories, and insisted that biological "indubitable scientific fact" backed up his notions about the "ruin" that results from race "hybrid mixture." Plecker added, "Our chief trouble is with some of the near-white who are desirous of changing from the colored to the white class." Among the "near-white," Plecker likely had in mind Native parents who sent their children to white schools, like Ray Wynn and John Clayton Howell, and people like Atha Sorrells.[109]

Plecker had the full text of his Public Health Association paper reprinted by the commonwealth of Virginia, in a booklet titled "Eugenics in Relation to the New Family and the Law on Racial Integrity." In it, he prefaced his essay "Virginia's Attempt to Adjust the Color Problem" with comments that placed it firmly within eugenic rhetoric of the day about "fit" families in America and the importance of teaching young people to make eugenically sound choices in choosing marriage partners. In those prefatory remarks, he contended, "The worst forms of undesirables born amongst us are those when parents are of different races." He sounded again his fear of "negro-Indian-white intermixture."[110]

Cox, Plecker, and Powell coordinated correspondence and opportunities for public speaking and promoted one another's work. Plecker recommended to correspondents, and helped distribute, Cox's pamphlets and Cox's *White America*.[111] In the course of this outreach, they had contacts with African Americans, for example in correspondence with the Alliance of Colored American Citizens in Philadelphia. Plecker asked Cox to respond to one of their letters.[112] An alliance broadside accompanies this correspondence in Cox's papers; it emphasized the long history of African Americans in America, reminding readers, "We are one hundred per cent Americans by birth with undivided allegiance." As a point for their Americanness, this broadside in effect claimed Pocahontas as an ancestor, describing her as "a young colored woman" and "a beautiful brown maiden" and celebrating her marriage to John Rolfe: "This union of the Colored and White groups was consummated in the midst of general rejoicing."[113] As this alliance affirmed the Americanness of African Americans, they here staked out commonalities among non-white people, perhaps in response to Marcus Garvey's separatism and nationalism.

As noted, Cox's outreach efforts included Marcus Garvey and others in his Universal Negro Improvement Association. In May 1925, not long after Plecker presented his papers for the Public Health Association and Southern Medical Association, Cox published a pamphlet, "Let My People Go," which he dedicated to Marcus Garvey.[114] Garvey wrote Cox praising the pamphlet, noting that he, too, saw the dangers of a "mongrel America."[115] After Garvey was convicted on politically motivated federal charges of mail fraud, Plecker and Cox wrote letters in 1927, advocating that Garvey's application for pardon be granted.[116] Cox's efforts to gather Garveyites' support did not always work, though; letters to him from the president of the Richmond division of the UNIA informed Cox that Garvey's contact with Cox, Powell, and Plecker was controversial among some of Garvey's supporters.[117]

Powell, for his part, wrote a series of articles that appeared in the Richmond *Times-Dispatch* between February 16, 1926 and March 2, 1926 using the evocative title "The Last Stand: The Necessity for Racial Integrity Legislation in Virginia as Shown by an Ethnological Survey of the State by Congressional Districts."[118] Powell's allusion to George Armstrong Custer's defeat links his argument to broader narratives about "manifest destiny" and the dispossession of Native Americans across the continent. However, these articles mostly rehashed arguments that he, Plecker, and Cox had been making about the urgent need for further action to combat racial "mongrelization," situated in their vision of the history of slavery and race in Virginia. In addition, Powell presented "ethnological" information, citing cases in which, "Certain mix-breed groups, claiming descent from the aboriginal Indians, are pressing against the color line and in many instances are succeeding in passing over." Powell's anecdotes encompassed "interracial" marriages and instances in which the children of such "mix-breed" families attended white schools. As an example of dangers of the situation, he pointed to Nansemond people in Norfolk County, "claiming, and to some extent possessing, a strain of Indian blood," who had succeeded in getting some federal attention and a school of their own, and who in Powell's view were "negroid."

Powell noted that some of the Nansemond, having moved to the nearby cities of Norfolk and Portsmouth, "intermarried with white people—usually Poles or other foreigners—and have tried to enter white schools." Thus, while he focused on Blackness, Powell made Indians and recent immigrants integral parts of the "problem."[119] Virginia Natives were much on their minds as Powell, Plecker, and Cox advocated for enforcement of the racial integrity law.

Advocacy for Similar Laws in Other States

Shortly after passage of the 1924 racial integrity law, Governor Elbert Lee Trinkle sent letters to governors of other states about the law, recommending its provisions for their consideration. John Powell likely encouraged the governor in this action.[120] Plecker assisted and followed up in his own correspondence to suggest that people in other states advocate for similar legislation.[121] Plecker mailed about 1,200 copies of the text of the 1924 law to the Louisiana Club for Segregation and offered also to provide that club copies of the state-published pamphlet that reprinted his essay on "Virginia's Attempt to Adjust the Color Problem."[122]

Plecker lamented, to out-of-state audiences and authorities, that under the 1924 law's optional registration system "it is chiefly the near-white undesirables who are trying to register as white," surely a reference to Virginia Indians.[123] His concern about Virginia Indians shaped his advocacy for similar or "better" legislation in other states, as in a letter he wrote to a man in Cleveland, Ohio. He emphasized the 1924 Virginia law's stringent definition of a white person as its "most important feature," while acknowledging that Native people had created pressure for some legislative compromise:

> We had considerable trouble in establishing the position of the American Indian and admitted those with one-sixteenth or less of Indian blood to accommodate our Pocahontas descendants and one or two other cases known to us in the State. That clause, however, has given us much trouble, as a number of groups who have but a trace of Indian blood, the rest being negro and white, are claiming exemption under that clause. In at least one county some who are descendants of ante bellum "free negroes" with a considerable admixturer [sic] of illegitimate white blood are claiming themselves Indians and seem to have been meeting with success.[124]

This comment likely refers to events in Amherst and Rockbridge Counties in 1924, including the Johns and Sorrells cases. Plecker wrote to a California man that for Native people, Indian status was a stepping-stone ultimately to get "sufficient white illegitimate admixture" to be classified as white.[125] Likely Plecker's perception of a threat to enforcement of the law, as in the Johns and Sorrells cases, contributed to his sense of urgency in advocating that other states follow Virginia's lead.[126]

Plecker corresponded with fellow public health officials in several states about the racial integrity law.[127] He wrote to the Arkansas state health officer offering counsel about how Arkansas could avoid some of the pitfalls he saw in Virginia's 1924 act, advising, "The serious objection to the registration law is that the 'near-white' people, especially those with a trace of Indian blood, have been the first to register as white."[128]

In response to a request from Senator Morris Sheppard of Texas, and with help from Virginia's Legislative Reference Bureau, Plecker even provided a draft text for a law that would have banned "intermarriage between negroids and whites" in Washington, DC. This draft included a provision that would have also prohibited "extra-marital intercourse between the races" in the District. Plecker wrote to Sheppard that on this point in Virginia, "we have found that it will be necessary to have our law amended at the next legislature . . . as that is now becoming in Virginia almost the only form of racial intermixture, but it has always been the chief one."[129] Thus, Plecker expressed confidence about the success of his efforts to enforce the 1924 racial integrity law to prevent interracial marriage if not interracial sex, about the prospect of expanding that legislation, and about the significance of that law as a national model, barely a year after the 1924 law had passed. Native people were much on his mind as he pushed his campaign outside Virginia.

Conclusion

Richard B. Sherman has pointed out that in 1924, "The campaign for racial integrity in Virginia was not the product of a great popular ground swell. Rather it was primarily the work of this dedicated coterie of extremists who played effectively on the fears and prejudices of many whites."[130] Certainly, Plecker, Powell, and Cox seem extreme in their dedication to legalizing a one-drop rule, and they effectively exploited whites' racist fears. In many ways, though, they were in the mainstream of their day. They married older, well-established justifications of Southern segregation with eugenics, the latest, popular, and pervasive, brand of so-called scientific racism. When they described a threat posed by African Americans and mixed-race people, they clothed long-standing belief systems underpinning Jim Crow regimes in nationally accepted popular eugenic thinking. In this sense, Plecker, Powell, and Cox did not need a "great popular ground swell;" they rode powerful currents that already existed.

In their publicity-seeking, they cast themselves as sounding an alarm, to wake whites out of a complacent acceptance of impending eugenic danger. They dramatized that threat, to engage support from old-school Southern segregationists and northern eugenicists, but even without such melodrama their efforts would seem certain to bear legislative fruit among Virginia's lawmakers. In the 1920s, Southern whites' commitment to the Jim Crow regime was at least as strong as it had ever been. Racism's national reach was demonstrated in the resurgence of the "second" Ku Klux Klan, the narrowed immigration quotas mandated by Congress in 1924, and the fact that so many states had laws against interracial marriage. If some scholars like Frank Speck were voicing reservations about eugenics, others who presented themselves as having scientific credentials were effective eugenics advocates.

About this era, there is an argument that nationally the idea of race was shifting from the notion that racialized identities existed as a complex set of numerous categories (with Nordic, Alpine, and Mediterranean races dividing Europe, for example), toward the use of race primarily as shorthand for a Black-white divide. Plecker, Powell, and Cox can be seen as reflecting that trend, since their primary fear was African Americans marrying whites. Add to this Plecker's place in the state bureaucracy, which positioned him to manipulate administrative levers of government at the state and local levels. Given those contexts, the racial integrity campaign of Plecker, Powell, and Cox would seem unlikely to generate much controversy or require much persuasion among whites in 1924 Virginia, even if those actively campaigning for the 1924 law were a small, loud group.

For Virginia's Native people (both those in organized groups and other individuals outside those groups, like Ray Wynn and John Clayton Howell), the 1924 racial integrity law represented one more rolling crisis in a long history of threats to their identities and communities. After passage of 1924 and 1930 racial integrity legislation, Virginia's Indian people were especially vulnerable to the arguments of Plecker, Powell, and Cox, who contended that it was precisely people of mixed genetic inheritance who constituted the most insidious danger, not just to whites' political power but also to white culture. Plecker, Powell, and Cox connected their campaign with eugenic language about the "new family" and the genetically "defective." But they used that rhetoric chiefly to argue that segregation had to be even more stringent to protect the white race from the consequences of racialized mixing, a phenomenon that they saw conspicuously represented by Virginia's Native Americans. From the start of their racial integrity campaign, Virginia's Native people were a particular concern and target for Plecker and Powell. In part, Plecker, Powell, and Cox had been inflamed by the public organizing of non-reservation groups like the Chickahominy and Rappahannock to assert their Native identities before 1924. In response, some indigenous Virginians, like Chief Cook, denied community connections with African Americans, in effect accepting aspects of the racialized arguments that their white foes were making against Virginia Indians. It is easy to see how that strategy seemed necessary, given the circumstances at that moment, to Virginia Indians.

One example of the immense yet daily pressures involved came in the summer of 1925, when Richmond officials refused to re-enroll sixteen Richmond schoolchildren for the upcoming school year at the Robert Fulton Elementary School (a school for white students). Their parents, Ray Wynn, John Howell, John T. Jones, Eva Dennis, and I. C. Stewart wrote to the Richmond City School Board to request a hearing, so they could respond to "certain charges" that their children were not "entitled" to attend white public schools. (The children involved were Thomas Dennis, Richard Dennis, Thelma Dennis, Herman Dennis, Lucille May Wynn, Lloyd Wynn, Russel Wynn, Herman Wynn, Ethel Wynn, Herbert Howell, Walter Howell, Evelyn May Jones, Alva Jones, Daisy Stewart, Louis Stewart, and Stanley Stewart.)[131] In requesting this hearing, these parents did not use the word Indian, or describe the charges, or specify who raised those charges.

The *Richmond Times-Dispatch*, *The Richmond News Leader*, and *The Richmond Planet* (edited by the prominent African American entrepreneur and civic leader John Mitchell Jr.), however, reported that Richmond school officials had turned to Walter Plecker when some parents at the Fulton school raised doubts about the race of the sixteen children in question, and that records supplied by Virginia's Bureau of Vital Statistics purported to show that the children had "a colored woman in their family tree," though their "parents claim that they are Indians with no drop of negroid blood."[132]

In fact, Ray Wynn (son of Ferdinand and Rebecca Wynn), John Clayton Howell (Lucy Pearman Scott's great-grandson), John T. Jones, and Irvin Clyde Stewart were sporadically recognized as Indians in official records. At the hearing requested by the parents, lawyers representing the parents pointed out inconsistencies in official documents and questioned Plecker's reliance on racial labels in nineteenth-century records. Several individuals spoke about the racialized identities of the families involved. During the proceedings, Plecker testified that Wynn was a "near white." Ray's father, Ferdinand Wynn the younger, then in his eighties, affirmed the families' reputations as Indians. White and Black witnesses also testified. A judge and the clerk of court in Charles City County both wrote letters about the families' claims of indigeneity, showing again the utility of whites' testimony to vouch for Virginia Natives' Indianness.[133]

Probably in response to this very public argument, the city established an Indian school for the 1927–1928 school year on Nicholson Street, in the Fulton neighborhood where the families involved in the 1925 hearing lived. In its initial year, the school served nine students and its only teacher was white. In one of the paradoxes of Jim Crow, at this moment, while Richmond officials segregated these Indian children, other students in the school system "played" Indian in their classrooms. In 1928, the superintendent of Richmond public schools wrote, "The study of Indian life is always an endless source of information and pleasure to the children. They have dressed up as real Indians and have made wigwams on the floor, and for the time being they have been Indians." [134] How would the Wynn, Howell, Jones, Dennis, and Stewart families have viewed the idea that such play made Indians out of non-Indians "for the time being," while their own children were separated and segregated?

There were ten students in the Indian School in the Fulton neighborhood in 1928–1929, and eight in 1929–1930, but it seems that the school no longer operated in the school year 1930–1931.[135] Perhaps school administrators found this school unsustainable because the student body was small, or because they found it ideologically difficult to support a separate school for students who were neither Black nor white, or because the children of the Native families in the Fulton neighborhood were growing out of elementary school age.

This episode reflected long-standing strategies among generations of the descendants of Lucy Pearman Scott: their emphasis on education; dense networks of kinship connections among non-reservation Virginia Indians from New Kent and Charles City Counties; and their reluctance to be associated with African Americans. In this 1925 case, John Clayton Howell's desire that his children attend a school for white students echoes his grandfather John Howell's objection to hiring a Black schoolteacher for a newly established local school after the Civil War, recounted in chapter 1.

For generations, people in the extended Wynn, Stewart, and Howell families had been living near one another and marrying into one another's families. For example, Ray Wynn's first wife, Isola Myrtle Langston, was a half-sister of John Clayton Howell.[136] In 1911, the New Kent County register of marriages coded

Ray and Isola Myrtle's race as "I," presumably for "Indian."[137] Ray and Isola Myrtle moved to Richmond by 1918, and in 1920 they lived on State Street, near other parents who requested the school board hearing in 1925.[138]

Like Ray Wynn's family, the families of three other petitioners for that hearing—John Clayton Howell, Irvin Stewart, and Eva Dennis—were enumerated as white people in 1920 Richmond (Richmond City census, pp. 244B, 208B–209A, and 209B). But other records testify to their Indianness—and their extended-family connections stretched back generations, persisting after they moved to Richmond. John Clayton Howell's great-uncle John Carman Wynn was likely a brother to Ferdinand Wynn the elder, Ray Wynn's grandfather. Petitioner Irvin C. Stewart was part of the extended Bullifant-Stewart clan of Charles City County that included Rebecca Stewart Wynn, wife of Ferdinand Wynn the younger, as well as Olivia Stewart Howell Langston (John Clayton Howell's mother). In the Richmond Register of Marriages for 1914, Irvin Stewart and his bride Hattie Collins were called Indian, demonstrating that living in Richmond had not precluded all official recognition of their Indianness. By 1940 they were living on the Pamunkey Reservation and the census classified them as Indians (p. 16B, West Point Magisterial District, King William County census). (Perhaps this 1940 listing of Irvin and Hattie's race reflects the 1930 Virginia law that differentiated between Indians living on or off Virginia's two reservations.) In 1940, Irvin, Hattie, and their children were enumerated on the same page as Journey Miles, who was, like John Clayton Howell, a descendant of Lucy Pearman Scott. Like Irvin Stewart, petitioner Eva Stewart Dennis was connected to the Bullifant-Stewart families; she may have been Irvin's sister.[139] Her husband Thomas Dennis was likely a son of Keziah Langston Dennis and Thomas Dennis, born into a family enumerated over decades as Indians in Virginia censuses.[140] Petitioner John T. Jones had married Virginia Lee Wynn Jones, Ray Wynn's sister. In the 1920 Charles City County census (p. 32A), their family was enumerated as Indian, and John's World War I draft registration card calls him a "citizen" Indian.[141]

By 1925, when this school board episode was underway, Isola Myrtle Wynn had died, and Ray Wynn had married again, to a white woman named May Wilson.[142] On November 5, 1925, during the school board hearings, lawyers for Wynn wrote to the Richmond school board superintendent, "We have, however, today learned that an indictment has been procured against Wray Wynn, the father of the above-mentioned Lucille May Wynn, wherein he is charged with being a negro and having violated the laws of the State of Virginia by intermarrying with a white woman, one May Wilson." Ray Wynn's attorneys requested that the school board postpone further hearings until this charge against him and his wife was settled.[143]

Among the witnesses who testified in the subsequent trial of Ray and May Wynn were Sarah J. Bradby, a Native person more than eighty years old, General Henry T. Douglas, and James J. Cardine, the latter two elderly white men of New Kent County. A report of Bradby's testimony informed the court that for forty years, she had known Ray Wynn's grandmother, Margaret Stewart, the mother of Rebecca Stewart Wynn. She testified that Margaret Stewart "was indian and white and that she had no negro blood in her ... also that the Father of Rebecca Stewart was a white man with whom the said Margaret Stewart cohabited and lived with as his wife, viz; One Jordan Bullifant and that of this union there were born a number of children including the said Rebecca Wynn the Mother of Ray Wynn.... That Margaret Stewart had a red skin and long straight black hair and had no appearance of negro blood." The court record described Bradby as "the only Indian woman of her age who could testify to the above facts."[144]

The eighty-seven-year-old H. T. Douglas presented himself as a former Confederate officer and a railroad engineer who had served in the Spanish-American War. Speaking of Ferdinand Wynn the elder and his son Ferdinand the younger (Ray's grandfather and father, respectively), he said:

> I always knew them and heard them spoken of as Indians, and never heard it stated that they had any negro blood in them, but always heard them spoken of as a mixture of indian and white, with the indian blood predominating. I never heard Rebecca Stewart classed as a negro and always understood that she was Indian and White. These persons always were known as Indians in Charles City and New Kent Counties to the best of my knowledge and belief, and they always lived separately and to themselves and never to my knowledge associated with negroes.[145]

This testimony about the local reputation of the family of Ferdinand Wynn is at odds with the variable census designations the family received over the years, as mulatto, Black, Indian, and white. Also striking is General Douglas's report that the family did not associate with African Americans, echoing arguments by other tidewater indigenous people in the Jim Crow era that they were not intimately connected to their Black neighbors.

J. J. Cardine, at ninety-two years old, testified similarly about the reputation of Rebecca Stewart Wynn's family as Indians who did not "associate with negroes." Like Sarah Bradby, but unlike Douglas, he mentioned Margaret Stewart's connection to the white man Jordan Bullifant, adding that Bullifant recognized her children as his. He said of Margaret, "I know that the negroes did not like her because she did not associate with them and would not allow them to visit her."[146]

The stakes for Ray and May Wynn in this case were high, for violating Virginia's laws against interracial marriage could be punished by imprisonment. Despite the fact that the 1924 racial integrity law had considerably tightened and heightened the legal definition of interracial marriage, a jury acquitted Ray Wynn in December, 1925.[147] Perhaps by emphasizing Ray's white and Native ancestry, Wynn's lawyers had raised sufficient doubt about Ray's racial identity, given the 1924 law's "Pocahontas exception" and the six specific elements the court identified as major aspects of the crime charged against him and his wife.[148] The court had instructed the jury that, in order to find Wynn guilty, they had to find that the state had proved all six of those elements beyond a reasonable doubt. Apparently, the jury found no such clarity.[149]

Today, given the *Loving v. Virginia* and *Obergefell v. Hodges* cases, it may take some effort to grasp the cruelty and absurdity of the situation of Ray and May Wynn, hauled into court and told that their marriage was illegal. In the aftermath of the trial, Ray and May Wynn stayed in the Richmond area for years. In 1930, living in Henrico County just outside Richmond city, the couple were enumerated as white, though three children from Ray's first marriage who lived with them—Ethel, Herman, and Horace—were listed as Indians (Henrico County census, p.157A). (Ethel and Herman were among the children denied enrollment in the Fulton school in 1925.) Perhaps that listing of Ray and May as white in 1930 reflects caution on their part after their experience in the court case of 1925. In 1940, Ray and May were back in their old Richmond neighborhood, living with his mother Rebecca Stewart Wynn and his daughter Ethel; all were listed as white that year (Richmond City census, Jefferson Ward p. 3A).[150] John and Virginia Jones's son (Ray's nephew) Carlisle C. Jones was living with them, in another demonstration of the close intergenerational ties among these Indian families and the support that flowed from those connections.

Walter Plecker's activities in the wake of the 1924 Act to Preserve Racial Integrity directly afflicted the Wynns, Howells, and other Indian families as he fought his segregationist campaign not just against interracial marriage but for all forms of segregation, especially in schools. In 1854, Lucy Pearman Scott lamented, "I had to seek a home in a strang land among strangers for the sack of my children," and their education. And in 1925 Richmond, Lucy Pearman Scott's great-grandson John Clayton Howell struggled to provide educational opportunities for his children. Lucy's descendants who stayed in Virginia could be refused official recognition of their Indianness at any moment.

CHAPTER 3

Constructing Native Identities, 1865 to 1931

AFTER 1924, WALTER PLECKER engaged in a spasm of official activity against Virginia Native people—but long before Plecker's campaign, Virginia Indians knew well how vulnerable their claim to indigeneity could be. After the Civil War, they pursued varied strategies publicly to claim, proclaim, and reclaim their Indianness, developing new tribal political organizations, as well as their own churches and schools. They also engaged in public performances of their Indianness that linked them not only to Virginia's storied seventeenth-century history, but also to modern pan-Indian imagery.

At least one scholar has written that nationally, racial prejudice against Native Americans was less monolithic than that aimed at African Americans; "Prejudice against Indians tended to be local, directed against local Indians on local reservations."[1] In tidewater Virginia, reservation and non-reservation Indians grappled with racialized strictures that were inextricably tied to the pervasive racism directed at African Americans. As chapter 2 shows, white Virginia officials invested heavily in defining race as a Black-white color line and connected Native positions and Indian identities to white supremacy issues that were national as well as local.

As a result, in dealing with Jim Crow-era restrictions, organized tidewater Native peoples worked to establish and maintain identities distinct from those of African American Virginians. After centuries in which whites, Indians, and African Virginians in tidewater Virginia lived together and shared work, love, and marriages across racialized lines, disclaiming connections to Black Americans ran counter to realities of personal, family, and community life. Nonetheless, in asserting their indigeneity, organized groups of Virginia tidewater Indians sometimes created structures that excluded other Virginians whose families remembered Indian ancestors but who chose, or felt they had no choice but, to "live Black." On or off reservations, Virginia Natives had limited options and tools for asserting their Indianness.

Moble Hopson, an elderly blind man in Poquoson, Virginia, born in 1852 or 1853, testified about just how limited those options were. In November 1936, in an interview in the Federal Writers Project program for recording the memories of ex-slaves, Hopson recounted that his mother was Indian, and his father was white; "least-ways he warn't no slave even effen he was sorta dark-skinned." Hopson explained:

> Yuh wanta know why I'm put with the colored people? Sure, ah got white skin, leastwise, was white las time ah seed et. Well, ah ain't white and ah ain't black, leastwise not so fur as ah know. 'Twas the war done that. Fo de war dere warn't no question come up 'bout et. Ain't been no schools 'round here tuh bothuh 'bout. Blacks work in de fields, an' de whites own de fields. Dis land here been owned by de Hopson's since de fust Hopson cum here.... Ustuh go tuh de church school wid ole Shep Brown's chillun, sat on de same bench, ah did. But de war changed all dat. Arter de soljers come back home, it was diff'runt. First dey say dat all whut ain't white is black. An den dey tell de Injuns yuh kain't marry no more de whites. An' den dey tell usen dat we kain't cum no more tuh church school. An dey won't let us do no bisness wid de whites, so we is th'own in wid de blacks. Some uh our people move away, but dey warn't no use uh movin' cause ah hear tell et be de same ev'y wheer. So perty soon et come time tuh marry, an' dey ain't no white woman fo' me tuh marry so ah marries uh black woman. An' dat make me black, ah 'spose 'cause ah ben livin' black ev'y sence.[2]

Hopson here shows us how, in the South, the conception and construction of race as a Black-white duality required unremitting work by white people to construct, maintain, and enforce. He pointed out that racialized identities shifted in response to specific events, pressures, and circumstances—including war and marriage. Before the Civil War, Hopson suggested, the Black-white divide was different, at least for him and his family. Then, he said land ownership operated as a marker of racialized status, separating Black from white in a setting where Black mostly meant enslaved, and white implied not just free but propertied. Racial segregation, he told us, was human-made, not god-given. After the Civil War, the development of institutional and economic segregations altered how whites drew the color line, for Hopson and others. Hopson described himself as neither Black nor white, but "living black," yet he did not explicitly call himself Indian, either. In effect, he asserted that Virginia's legal definitions of Blackness and whiteness were historically constructed, not immutable and natural. As he remarked, the people with whom one lived and associated—and especially whom one could marry—shaped racialized lines, and he pointed out that churches and schools were key institutions in these processes.

Long before Hopson's interview and Walter Plecker's racial integrity campaign, reservation and non-reservation people faced challenges in seeking legal, governmental recognition of any racial status other than a free person of color, Black, mixed blood, or mulatto.[3] In responding, Native peoples' successes in building Indian organizations, identities, and spaces brought attention from people like Walter Plecker and his supporters, as well as some kinds of support from white allies. At a hypothetical level, white Virginians sometimes recognized social differences between Native Americans and African Americans. In everyday social and economic exchanges, local officials and white neighbors could acknowledge people of mixed blood as Indians.

Still, after the Civil War, Virginia developed a regime in which the most important single racial distinction was a Black-white color line. If before the 1860s, Powhatan groups accepted "at least as fringe members" people who participated in the group, an acceptance based not solely on Indian ancestry but also upon marriage and other forms of kinship and social connections, that apparently shifted over decades after 1865.[4] Part of the context for that shift was pressure from white people who feared that Native peoples' Indianness complicated the Black-white categories designed to clarify who was subject to Jim Crow.

Thus, Virginia's reservation groups took some explicit steps to emphasize social separation from African Americans. A published version of Pamunkey tribal laws, adopted in 1886–1887, prohibited marriages with non-Indians or non-whites. That was the first on a short list of tribal rules.[5] Tidewater Virginia Indians also worked to distinguish themselves from African Americans in other systems of segregation. As mentioned in chapter 2, the reservation Pamunkey got a ruling that gave them an exception within Virginia law on racial segregation in railroad cars. In an article published in 1907, the Smithsonian ethnographer James Mooney reported: "To prevent annoyance when traveling, under recent Virginia legislation the Pamunkey now carry official certificates of tribal membership; and for similar reasons the unorganized Chickahominy and Nansemond are recently making strong effort for state recognition as Indian tribes, such as is accorded the Pamunkey and Mattapony and the so-called 'Croatan Indians' [now known as Lumbee and Tuscarora] of North Carolina."[6]

A new state constitution in 1902 accelerated racialized disfranchisement in Virginia, and around this time non-reservation Virginia Natives began to create new tribal organizations. These formal organizations had legal charters, rules, and sometimes tribal rolls. The people on what is now known as the Mattaponi Reservation (who had been generally regarded as part of the Pamunkey community) created a separate tribal organization of their own in 1894.[7] The Chickahominy, who were without a reservation, formed a modern legal organization as a tribe in 1901. By 1904, the Chickahominy were issuing certificates attesting to tribal membership. A surviving example shows the depth of organization the Chickahominy had created. It was signed by a chief, second chief, clerk, and trustees for the tribe, to "hereby certify that the bearer, John J. Jefferson, is a member of the Chickahominy Tribe of Indians, and is entitled to all rights and privileges accorded the said Tribe of Indians."[8] (This John J. Jefferson may have been the same man who married Sarah Canaday, a granddaughter of Jones Pearman.)

If Virginia tidewater Indians posed an implicit challenge to construction of a Black-white color line, for the most part they did not directly question the existence of racialized segregation. Their separate institutions, including tribal organizations, churches, and schools, both asserted their Indianness and distanced them from their Black neighbors.

Baptist Churches

Beginning in response to the changed climate at the end of the Civil War, people of the Pamunkey and Mattaponi communities hived off from existing congregations to form their own Baptist churches.[9] To this day, churches remain important institutions among tidewater Natives. When the Dover Baptist Association, a regional grouping under the umbrella of the statewide Baptist organization in Virginia, held its annual meeting in 2006, it convened at the Samaria Baptist Church, which formed as a Chickahominy congregation in 1901. The association's minutes for that 2006 gathering reported that "Ken Custalow of the Mattaponi Indian Church, opened the meeting with a prayer in the native Algonquian language." The meeting also featured "craft demonstrations, a traditional Native American meal, and an intertribal drum prelude," and "an historical overview of the roles played by the Native American tribes in Virginia history." Chief Stephen Adkins of the Chickahominy, and Wayne Adkins, Chickahominy assistant chief, spoke; both were Samaria congregants. There was testimony by people representing each of "the six tribes and the six related Dover churches." A concluding benediction was "interpreted...in Indian Sign Language."[10] This meeting represented long-standing traditions of public performances of Indianness and reminded whites of the long history of Powhatan peoples.

By 2006, Virginia's state-recognized tribes had firmly established themselves as public bodies, so Native leadership at that meeting is not surprising. What may surprise is that by 2006 tidewater Native Baptist people had been active for more than a century within individual Indian congregations and in the Dover Baptist Association. The establishment of Indian churches within the association, from 1865 on, was a major facet of concerted efforts by tidewater Virginia Native peoples to build their own separate (and not-Black) community institutions.

White and Black Baptists in the South, of course, have long histories together and apart. In antebellum times, whites and African Americans might worship under the same roof or in separate churches. At the Lower College Baptist Church (later called Colosse Baptist) in King William County, as a Works Progress Administration history noted, "Early membership included Pamunkey Indians and Negroes."[11] The thirteen Indians documented in 1791 as members of the Lower College Baptist Church may be the earliest records of Native membership in a Virginia Baptist church.[12] Ambiguities and disabilities of Baptist membership for enslaved people were manifest in the history of the Lower College Church. The church's minute book includes a November 1827, resolution that "this church receive no more slaves as members of this church except they bring notes from their masters, mistresses, or overseers."[13] Still, the mix of people—Black, indigenous, and white—within the church allowed for some influence and action by African American and Native congregants. In June 1828, at a church meeting held "at the Pamunkey Indian town" and attended by a majority of the church's male members, "A committee of coloured members was appointed to deal with coloured members in New Kent belonging to this church" and to "report their proceedings to the church." Some of the "brethren" on the committee seem to be identified only by first name, which might be a sign of enslaved status, while others received an honorific "Mr."[14]

Baptist worship services were held on the Pamunkey Reservation at least as early as 1859, before there was a separate organized Pamunkey church or church building.[15] As a form of acknowledgment by whites, such services were probably among the reasons an antebellum tidewater Indian might choose to be Baptist. By 1854, there were forty-two Native American members of Colosse, and "while they attended Colosse's services once a month, they also held religious meetings of their own on the reservation every Sunday. John Langston, a member of the tribe, was the leader of the religious meetings."[16] Undoubtedly, meeting locally was more attractive because travel on bad roads was difficult, but part of the attraction for the Pamunkey also was the opportunity for leadership and community-building work right at home.

After the Civil War, distances between southern Black and white Baptist congregations widened. Virginia's Dover Baptist Association bears witness to that trend. In 1865, six or seven Black Baptist churches moved to the Shiloh Baptist Association from the Dover association.[17] This move by African American congregations to a Black regional grouping in the wake of emancipation indicates African Americans' imperative to exercise autonomy and authority in their lives as churchgoers. It also suggests that white Baptists resisted that quest; perhaps whites actively opposed the presence of Black congregants after emancipation.

In 1865, just as multiple African American congregations were leaving the Dover association, a new church—the Pamunkey Indian Baptist Church—organized. Native congregants left Colosse and formed a church for a specifically Indian congregation.[18] Virginia Baptists today recognize this church as the first of the state's organized Indian Baptist churches. Perhaps Colosse's white congregants pushed at that moment for non-whites to depart the church. Still, for tidewater Indians, the benefits were clear. Indian churches marked Native communities as places separate and distinctive and provided spaces for building intragroup community and identity. Black Baptists in Virginia had already achieved some churches and congregations of their own before the Civil War, but tidewater Natives established separate Indian churches only in the postbellum period. When African Americans departed the Dover Baptist Association, making it a grouping of white congregations, Indian tidewater Baptists sought membership for their new Indian churches in that association of whites, rather than forming their own association or joining the Shiloh organization.

Participants in the initial organization of the Pamunkey Baptist Church included white clergy, a white deacon from Colosse, two white laymen, and "twenty-five Indian members of the Colosse Church," who met in April 1865.[19] (Some of those twenty-five had been identified as mulatto in the 1860 census of King William County.) Subsequently, the Pamunkey church became part of the Dover Baptist Association, but the church's members did face whites' concerns about their racialized identities. At first, the Pamunkey church's delegates to Dover association meetings were not its Indian congregants. The Pamunkey church petitioned the association that "it should be represented by its own members." A "Committee on Application of Pamunkey Church," appointed in 1868 apparently to review this request, reported back: "The committee, to whom was referred the question of altering the first article of our Constitution, so as to omit the clause, 'all of whom shall be white persons,' respectfully recommend that the change be not made."[20] By the 1880s, though, Pamunkey individuals were representing their church at Dover annual meetings.[21]

From its beginnings, this Pamunkey church was a focal point for expression of Pamunkey identity and community. At the dedication of the Pamunkey Baptist Church building in 1866, a white pastor delivered a sermon that included standard exhortations to the congregation "to live Christ-like lives and to train their children to glorify God in their homes." What was not standard was that this minister also spoke of Powhatan Indians as people who shared a distinctive cultural past and history, referring to their first contacts with English colonists.[22]

By 1873, a Pamunkey man served as pastor of the church. The pattern of Native leadership in managing this church's affairs continued, though sometimes white men were its pastors over the years. In 1901, the Pamunkey leader George M. Cook seems to have been the first Indian member-delegate to the statewide Baptist General Association. By 1891, the Dover association articulated in principle that, "when a member of Pamunkey church shall give good evidence of being called of God to the ministry" he might receive help "in securing educational qualifications for preaching the Gospel."[23] Perhaps this recommendation indicates uneasiness among the Dover association's white Baptists about levels of formal education among the Pamunkey. Perhaps, instead or also, it was part of a general discussion about professionalism and the ministry; Baptists debated about education among ministerial qualifications in nonracialized contexts, too. In either case, by 1891 this Indian church could seek association help in developing ministerial skills among its congregants.[24]

While representing the community to a white Baptist world, the Pamunkey church served intracommunity functions, such as hosting an annual "Home Coming."[25] As more tidewater Indian congregations formed over the years, they also marked congregations' Indianness for non-Indians, and reinforced group ties within individual Indian communities. Sometimes these churches also fostered connections between Native communities when Indian individuals attended churches of neighboring groups. Except among the Nansemond people, who have had a Methodist church, tidewater Indian churches were all Baptist congregations and became part of the otherwise-white Dover Baptist Association, facilitating intercommunity personal contacts and formally connecting these churches.

Among non-reservation groups, the formal establishment of a separate church sometimes linked to the establishment of a legal tribal organization, even where it did not follow immediately on the heels of a group's incorporation. Schools, too, were connected, for they sometimes housed religious functions before construction of a church building. Chickahominy people, for example, organized their own congregation, the Samaria Church in 1901, around the time of their formal organization as the Chickahominy tribe, and for a while "they worshiped in a schoolhouse."²⁶

Such churches demonstrated Indianness and also separation from African Americans. Helen Rountree reported "oral tradition" that the formal development of a Chickahominy church followed a period when another local church, which had been multiracial before the Civil War, became a largely Black congregation, and at that point some Chickahominy people moved to another local church attended by whites. She found that some Chickahominy families who remained in the Black church were among those who did not later join the Chickahominy tribal organization.²⁷

Years later, a pastor of the Samaria Church testified to white Baptists' questions about Indian identities. In 1920, the Reverend Mr. Philip Throckmorton, a white man, wrote a notarized statement that when he was considering becoming minister at Samaria Indian Baptist Church in 1901, he made inquiry of a local judge who assured the pastor "that these people were reconized [sic] by his court as Indians and that he held them in high esteem and advised me to eccept [sic] the call. After receiving his letter I accepted the call." Likely, Throckmorton in 1901 was seeking assurance that the congregation was not regarded as Black. Throckmorton added, "Since I have had this charge I have married about forty couples from that tribe and this court always issues the license as Indians."²⁸ (Throckmorton officiated in 1910 when, as noted in chapter 1, Lucy Pearman Scott's great-grandson John Clayton Howell married Grace Stewart.)

Tsena Commocko Church formed in 1922, in the context of a division of Chickahominy people into eastern and western groups, a split that involved questions about who should be pastor at Samaria, and whether the Chickahominy should seek to establish a reservation.²⁹ This new church did not spring from nowhere, though; in 1920, "a group of ladies from the First Baptist Church of Richmond" and from the Dover Baptist Association had organized a Sunday school in the community.³⁰

The reservation Mattaponi, who were closely connected to the Pamunkey and formally separated from the reservation Pamunkey in 1894, organized a separate congregation in 1932, "bringing letters from Pamunkey church" in accord with Baptist practice.³¹ Like the Pamunkey church before it, this congregation sought ties to the Dover Baptist Association. The organization of this church crowned a process in which various Baptist pastors had held missionary services in the

Mattaponi school building from about 1914.³² A Baptist periodical reported that "representatives of the Pamunkey, Chickahominy and Rappahannock Indian Tribes, and many prominent citizens of the county, of Richmond, and other places" attended the Mattaponi church building dedication in 1935.³³ Thus, while the church served intracommunity functions, it also fostered recognition and support by other tidewater Native groups and whites.

The Upper Mattaponi—who incorporated in the 1920s and are separate from the reservation Mattaponi—built their own church, Indian View, in 1941 or 1942. It became part of the Dover association in 1946. Church history holds that the Upper Mattaponi had been attending churches established by the reservation groups, but in 1920, Sunday school and other services were held in their Sharon school building, around the time when the Upper Mattaponi "were organized into a body."³⁴ Thus, as at Mattaponi and among the Chickahominy, the Indian View church had connections to another important community- and identity-building institution: a school for Indian children. By at least 1950, like the Pamunkey church, the Indian View church was holding a "Home Coming," fostering ties within the community.³⁵

Minutes of the annual meetings of the Dover Baptist Association in the 1920s show involvement by tidewater Indians in the association's affairs as they managed their own congregations. Tidewater Natives acted as delegates from their churches to the association's annual sessions and participated in discussions and reporting at those meetings. For example, Chief G. M. Cook was one of a group of three who submitted the "Report on Temperance to the Dover Baptist Association for the Year 1921." In 1921, Cook also served on the association's standing committee on Home Missions. At its 1921 meeting, the association heard a report about "home missions" that included Baptist work "among the foreigners, Indians and negroes."³⁶ (Typically that committee's report recounted the years' activities by the national Home Mission Board of the Southern Baptist Convention.) Did Chief Cook want to be on the Home Missions committee to underscore his congregation's status as established Baptists on par with other association congregations, who could help guide missionary activities rather than needing missionizing?³⁷ Perhaps Cook wanted to secure some influence in the tone and content of reporting within his home association on Baptist work among other Native groups nationwide?

Ties to the Dover Baptist Association proved helpful to the organized tribes in the wake of the campaign Plecker and his colleagues unleashed against Virginia Natives after passage of Virginia's 1924 Act to Preserve Racial Integrity. Minutes of the Dover Baptist Association annual meetings do not evidence that the association took a position on legislative debates preceding passage of that

1924 legislation. By 1928, though, tidewater Indians had publicly established their resistance to a new bill then before the state legislature. When supporters of the 1924 act advocated new legislation to address what they regarded as weaknesses in the 1924 law (see chapter 2), the Indian Dover congregations involved the association. At the 1928 Dover Baptist Association annual meeting, Tsena Commocko Church was well represented. Perhaps that congregation was particularly active because Plecker had targeted Chickahominy people, as shown in chapter 2. In the association's minutes for the first day of its 1928 annual meeting, a "Report of the Executive Committee of the Dover Association" noted, among other items of business: "At the recent session of the General Assembly of Virginia, a bill was introduced by certain individuals which would have altered the traditional civic and social standing of our Indian brethren and produced serious complications in the long established relations of their churches to this body. A number of the members of your Committee took an active part in informing the Senators of the facts in this matter, and with the able leadership of Senators Wickham and Haddon, the bill was overwhelmingly defeated."[38]

R. A. Bradby, a member of the Tsena Commocko Church, gave an address about Virginia Indians on the day after this Executive Committee report, and it seems likely that the committee's action reflected a concerted effort by members of Indian churches that began before the annual association meeting.[39] Mr. Bradby may also have seen this as an opportune time to continue educating association delegates about his community's Native identity and their "traditional civic and social standing."[40]

The willingness of the Dover Baptist Association to engage in direct advocacy about proposed legislation of any kind seems remarkable in the context of contemporary Baptist discussions about separation of church and state. The candidacy of Al Smith had raised concerns about temperance and so about Southern Baptist allegiance to the Democratic Party. On July 18, 1928, the Dover Baptist Association resolved: "We recognize fully that Baptist churches and our other denominational bodies exist for spiritual ends, and that they can properly take no action in purely political affairs or exercise authority over the individual conscience in any matter."[41] Despite this Baptist reticence about political activity, tidewater Indians made white Dover Baptists their allies in the 1928 fight.

Schools

In Virginia's tidewater Indian schools, as at Indian churches, Virginia Natives built and nurtured Indian identities and communities, and like the churches these schools were also sites of segregation. By 1890, a Richmond newspaper noted approvingly and reassuringly that the Pamunkey Reservation people, "support their own schools, and provide their own teachers. They have their own places of worship, which are under the control and direction of the Baptist denomination of Christians. They are amiable and unoffending in their intercourse with their white neighbors." Perhaps this writer also meant readers to understand that by 1890 these separate institutions distanced the reservation community from African Americans, despite acknowledging that Pamunkey "progenitors for several generations having intermarried with whites, mulattoes, and blacks."[42]

The history of the bare handful of separate schools established for Virginia's reservation people and non-reservation Powhatan groups in some ways echoes local-school segregation all over the Jim Crow South. But separate Indian schools in Virginia met perceived needs of Virginia Indian communities in asserting their identities as indigenous, rather than colored, Black or white. The existence of the few Virginia Indian schools fostered Native community and identity, served some Virginia Natives' desire for social distance from African Americans, and linked tidewater Native groups in some ways. However, Virginia's Indian schools were small, discrete institutions compared to the system of Indian schools among the Lumbee people of Robeson County, North Carolina. In Jim Crow-era Mississippi, between 1882 and 1900, state legislators authorized separate schools for the Mississippi Choctaw, administered by county governments, since public schools for white students generally did not accept Choctaws, and some Choctaw parents, like Virginia's tidewater Indians, would not send their children to Black schools. (Before the Removal era, there had been government-and missionary-supported schools and churches in the Choctaw nation.) As in Virginia and North Carolina, segregated "third race" schools served important functions for Mississippi Choctaw identity and community cohesion, as well as skills for dealing with a white-dominated society and economy that engulfed them.[43]

Such state-sponsored schools contrast the Jim Crow experiences of Southeastern indigenous people with those of reservation-based western Native groups in that era, when federal reservation day schools and boarding schools for federally recognized tribes developed into a national system. An obvious fundamental contrast was that segregated schools for Indians in Virginia did not involve federally recognized tribes. Also, Virginia's tidewater Indians, as small groups surrounded by Black and white communities, did not live in the kinds of remote places that justified the establishment of day schools on western reservations or federal Indian boarding schools. Indian schools in tidewater Virginia addressed and augmented social distances essential to Jim Crow segregation, not geographic distances.

Hazel Hertzberg has argued that the federal program of Indian boarding schools, by the 1890s, fostered communication and cooperation across tribal lines. Presumably this was an effect unintended by the Bureau of Indian Affairs, which designed its schools to make American Indians more like European Americans, sometimes in extremely oppressive ways. At federal boarding schools, students could make connections with people from other federally recognized groups. For students and graduates, English could then function as a common language they could use in forging relationships and alliances with members of other tribes.[44]

Some of these factors operated, but in very different ways, among tidewater Virginia Indians. Virginia Indians spoke English. As "amiable and unoffending" Indians who lived much as their white and Black neighbors did, white Virginians probably did not view the Powhatan groups by this time as in need of the kinds of harsh assimilative pressures prevalent at BIA schools. Still, like the federal boarding schools, the few small Indian schools in rural tidewater Virginia provided opportunities for communication and cooperation across tribal lines in Virginia, in some cases connecting reservation people with organized non-reservation Powhatan groups. Whereas federal Indian schools aimed until the 1930s to weaken tribal identities, Virginia's few tidewater Indian schools, as day schools, were Native places and focal points for community activities and construction of Powhatan identities until state support vanished in the aftermath of the 1954 *Brown v. Board* decision.

Part of the impetus for these schools was organized Powhatan groups' assessment that to send their children to colored schools would erode their ability to assert Indian identity, providing whites additional reason to claim that tidewater Natives were Black, colored, or mixed, and not indigenous. When and if their own efforts proved insufficient to support adequate community schools, some Virginia Indian parents saw "only two choices for their children, if they could not teach them themselves: illiteracy or 'colored' schools."[45] When Indian parents could not or would not send their children to local schools for whites or Blacks, children might not attend school—or their parents might seek schooling far from their homes and families.[46] Some tidewater Virginia Indians sent their children to Indian schools in places as far-flung as Bacone College in Oklahoma or the federal school at the Cherokee Reservation in North Carolina, for a secondary-level education that was hard to finance within small, rural tidewater Native communities.

As that 1890 Richmond *Daily Times* article noted, Virginia Natives for many years were largely responsible for support of their separate, local Indian schools.

Tidewater Native peoples' continuing efforts to secure and increase state funding for Virginia Indian schools yielded some results, but state aid was always inadequate. Like southern African American parents of this era, Virginia Natives did not receive an equitable share of state or local government school funding. Virginia Indians sometimes responded as did many African American communities and parents; they organized schools and built school buildings themselves. Tidewater Indians' connections with Virginia Baptist organizations could augment support for these schools, but Native parents were the prime movers.

State support was more forthcoming after 1917, when Virginia's assistant attorney general "gave an opinion that the Pamunkey and Mattaponi were wards of the State." This generated some funding for elementary schooling for schoolchildren on the two reservations.[47] The tenuous nature of state government support for Indian schools even on the reservations did not diminish their importance or the commitment of Indian communities. The Pamunkey reportedly had had a school on their reservation soon after the Civil War, just as they formed a separate church in that turbulent time. In 1890, the Smithsonian ethnographer Albert Gatschet reported of the Pamunkey, "In every house there are children and a school is established for them in the reservation."[48] Though "is established for them" suggests outside support for the school, "it is uncertain whether the state supplied a teacher for the children" in the 1870s.[49] The Mattaponi seem to have had access to the Pamunkey school, but around 1917 they sought and got a school of their own.[50] After the Mattaponi formally organized their own Baptist church in 1932, its pastor "led them in an effort to get a modern and adequate school building on the reservation, which was accomplished. It is a credit to any small community. During these years, the school and church had been using a small building, altogether inadequate."[51]

The Tsena Commocko and Samaria schools, both Chickahominy-based and built by Chickahominy people, also had links to Baptist churches. As noted, among the Chickahominy, the idea of a separate school gained traction around the time when they were also working to establish a Chickahominy tribal organization and separate Baptist congregation.[52] In 1922, pressure by the Chickahominy, who had been soliciting testimony from whites about their reputation as real Indians (recall the notarized statement by the Reverend Mr. Throckmorton cited above), persuaded Charles City County and the state government to help pay teachers' salaries at a school the Chickahominy community had built, but this support seems to have been meagre over the following decades.[53]

According to Baptist reports about the Sharon school built to serve the Upper Mattaponi people in 1919, "the King William County School Board erected a small one-room building, unfurnished. The parents had to purchase desks and other equipment."⁵⁴ However, the National Register of Historic Places documentation for the Sharon school says that the 1919 Sharon school building initially was "built, furnished and staffed by tribal members at their own expense." (Upper Mattaponi tribal history mentions an earlier, short-lived school in the late nineteenth century.) The community's initiative for the Sharon school apparently involved assistance from the two reservation groups, indicating how these schools could link Native communities. The Upper Mattaponi themselves ran the Sharon school at first, and then in 1925 the King William County Board of Education took responsibility for its management, after which the county staffed and equipped it.⁵⁵

A surviving state audit book summarizing some state-related school expenditures in the years 1922–1928 shows sums in the hundreds of dollars distributed to a few local-government treasurers for Indian school purposes, generally once or twice a year, between 1923 and 1927. Additional, more frequent, and typically smaller sums appear in a separate category. This account book has Indian-school related entries only for Charles City County, New Kent County, and Halifax County. It has no Indian school entries for King William County, where the reservation schools and the Sharon school were located. That could mean simply that the types of funds recorded in this account book were specific to a particular legal mandate, and so this audit book does not include other forms of state or county aid.⁵⁶ Still, the general impression from these auditors' records seems consistent with Virginia's underfunding of Indian education.

That underfunding persisted, despite the dilemma created if Native parents objected to sending their children to Black schools and were denied access to white schools. As expectations of universal secondary-school attendance became more institutionalized nationally, in Virginia the contrast between educational opportunities for whites and those for Indians looked ever more obvious. For years, Indian schools in Virginia offered little (or no) class work at the secondary level.⁵⁷

As early as 1900, as the Chickahominy formally organized, at least one of their white allies saw this need and encouraged them to get access to the nearby normal school at Hampton Institute (now Hampton University), just miles from tidewater Indian communities.⁵⁸ That famed historically Black university, for decades, admitted Indians from tribes across the country, but it is not clear that any of Virginia's tidewater Indians attended Hampton Institute in that era. Perhaps their struggle to distinguish themselves in institutional settings from African Americans made Native Virginian parents reluctant to send their children there, despite Hampton's inclusion of other Indians and its proximity—even though Hampton was attended by Eastern Cherokee students, and even when the school's recruitment patterns increasingly embraced other eastern Indians. Donal Lindsey wrote that the institute "was generally regarded as offering opportunities that helped an Indian with black ancestry find a place in American society."[59] If that was a common perception, perhaps that reputation helped persuade Virginia Natives against sending children to Hampton Institute, for fear of emphasizing "black ancestry." Instead, as noted, some tidewater Native parents sought to send older children for secondary and postsecondary work to Indian schools such as Haskell in Kansas, Bacone in Oklahoma, and the reservation school in Cherokee, North Carolina. They may have hoped that attending those places, far from home and family, could bolster students' claims to an indigenous rather than mixed identity.

Local schools for tidewater Virginian Indians could be sites of recorded incidents of acquiescence and participation in racialized segregation. (It is hard to imagine an effective strategy for challenging school segregation in pre–World War II Virginia.) A newspaper story in 1894 noted as an example of Pamunkey "race pride" their "recent indignant refusal to accept a colored teacher, who was sent to them to conduct the free school which the state of Virginia provides for them. They are very anxious to keep their blood free from further mingling with that of other races." This chimes with John Howell's resistance to having an African American teach his children after the Civil War, described in chapter 1. To help make the case for that Indian "blood," the article also mentioned that "the laws of the tribe now strictly forbid marriage with persons of African descent" and said the Pamunkey were seeking "immigration from the Cherokees of North Carolina."[60] This may foreshadow the interest of Virginia Indians in the federal Indian school at Cherokee, North Carolina. The tidewater Indian schools could also be a focus of whites' segregationist disdain; a long-time teacher at the Sharon school in later years reported, "The other teachers were very cool to me."[61]

Public Performances

In addition to tribal organizations, separate churches and schools, Virginia tidewater Native people in the late nineteenth and early twentieth centuries used public dramatic performances to present their distinctively Indian histories and identities. As early as the 1880s, and over more than thirty years, Virginia's reservation groups presented public theatricals in which they placed themselves at the center of Virginia's colonial past and embraced images of John Smith, Pocahontas, and Powhatan. As they tapped this Powhatan-specific, yet national, narrative about seventeenth-century Jamestown, they also made use of pan-Indian images, particularly through costuming, at staged performances and other public ceremonies such as regular presentations of a "tribute" of game to Virginia's governor.[62]

The use of such pan-Indianisms is especially striking because by 1830 Powhatan people in their daily lives displayed few of the obvious material markers that outsiders quickly and stereotypically perceived as Indian. By the late seventeenth and early eighteenth centuries, when Powhatan individuals wore clothing in traditional shapes, they might make those garments out of English cloth, and they might also wear garments cut in European forms. The anglicization of aspects of Pamunkey material culture likely accelerated after the early eighteenth century, as Pamunkey people adapted European American goods. By the middle of the eighteenth century, one white visitor to the Pamunkey Reservation noted that their housing was not European-style, but they wore Anglo-style clothing.[63] More than a century later, the anthropologist James Mooney recorded Pamunkey memories of one visible distinctive aspect of personal grooming. Mooney's informant, Terrill Bradby, remembered that men before the Civil War wore their hair long, and that some older men did so even after the war; this practice may be seen in later photographs of tidewater Native people.[64] In Jim Crow Virginia, such a display could perhaps help differentiate Indians from Blacks in whites' eyes, given whites' stereotypes about African American hair—and it also evoked pan-Indian styles.

When Powhatan peoples' descendants re-enacted Pocahontas's "rescue" of John Smith in Jim Crow times, they evoked seventeenth-century history when Powhatan peoples began their long journeys of conflict and accommodation with European Americans and African Americans. In harking back to that earliest colonial era, Virginia Natives were citing a moment when English colonists had to reckon with Native political and economic power. By the late nineteenth century, such dramas also look like a strategic appeal to whites' nationalistic myth-making about the Jamestown story. As in the early nineteenth century, Pocahontas could still be useful to Southern white Americans as part of a story of national origins and sectional pride. For whites, she represented a "good" Indian—the Indian "princess" who, in helping to ensure the survival of white colonists, lost her life or her status within her tribe. Against a backdrop of racialized segregation, late in the nineteenth century, Powhatan people made strategic, public use of their connections to Pocahontas to stake their claim to a specifically Native heritage that whites could easily recognize and applaud, since whites used Pocahontas as a symbol in a tale of their national beginnings and Native accommodations.

A printed flyer of 1898 advertised a dramatic offering that embraced not only a reenactment of the "Capture of John Smith and the saving of his life by Pocahontas," but also a war dance, snake dance, and green corn dance, suggestive of precontact histories and cultures. Featured characters included a powerful, famed non-Powhatan hero, Tecumseh—someone not easily construed, unlike Pocahontas, as an accommodating figure.[65] That flyer was designed to advertise multiple events in varied locations; it has blank lines for filling in places and dates of performances and noted separate admission fees for adults and children. The polished look of the flyer affirms a crisp, business-like approach to this production.

The importance of these dramatic representations could manifest itself in other areas of life. The 1898 flyer noted that Howard Lee Allmond (a girl probably about eleven years old at the time) would perform as Pocahontas, and E. R. Allmond, the assistant manager of the troupe, would portray Big Diver. In the 1900 census for King William County, when the census used two-part special forms for Indian populations, Allmond appeared first by that name, and then as Big Diver in the second half of the form, in a column labeled "Other Name, if Any." His daughter Howard Lee was enumerated first as "Howard L." and also as Pocahontas.

In such dances and dramas, tidewater Natives used pan-Indian emblems of Native Americans' cultural persistence. Christian Feest described "heavily fringed and partly beaded regalia, which grew ever more elaborate with each passing year." An 1881 photograph of the performers in costume for such a production shows many of them in multifeathered headdresses, with tunics and pants that seem inspired by images of Plains Indian clothing and stereotypes of pioneer garb.[66] In this, the costumes seem to reflect the popularity of Wild West shows and other mass-produced images of hunters and soldiers on the western plains. Feathered headdresses were not exclusively a Plains tradition; John Smith's map of Virginia in his 1624 *General Historie of Virginia* includes a figure wearing a feathered crown. Still, details of these Powhatan peoples' late nineteenth-century costumes have a pan-Indian flavor, rather than referring to clothing styles specific to any individual eastern Native group. Tidewater Native peoples seemingly understood well the power and popularity of the imagery crystallized and magnified in Wild West shows, nineteenth-century dime novels, and twentieth-century movie and television westerns. White people have long used such images to try to exoticize, homogenize, and romanticize Native Americans' histories and cultures. Commercialized Wild West images were ubiquitous; when Otis Mason of the Smithsonian's National Museum attended the 1889 Paris Congress of Prehistoric Archaeology and Anthropology, he reported that "the bill of fare" included Buffalo Bill's famous show.[67]

Some consider such homogenized pan-Indian cultural markers a concession to, or embrace of, stereotypes of Native cultures.[68] But their use has been a productive strategy for tidewater indigenous peoples. Christian Feest wrote that in their Jim Crow-era performances, tidewater Indians "began to play to the often naive and simplistic expectations of their white neighbors about 'savage' life and behavior."[69] George Pierre Castile, though, acknowledged that incorporation and fusion of elements from a dominant non-Indian society as well as from other Native groups has "necessarily" been a feature of pan-Indian movements. Castile argued that to dismiss such practices is to accuse Native participants of naiveté.[70] In tidewater Native peoples' uses of pan-Indian regalia, the innovation, borrowing, and adaptation involved in adopting such out-group markers looks strategic, even if it reflects stereotypes widely held by white people. This is not to downplay the value and significance of tightly held in-group cultural systems— traditions that are the fruit of intensive training, community participation, and life experience passed along over generations in cohesive cultural community frameworks. It is a suggestion that other kinds of cultural borrowing and expression may also be constructive.

Some progressive-era reformers were troubled by these Wild West images and their ubiquity. For example, some members of the Society of American Indians considered that Wild West show images of Native Americans were a distraction from the need to work within the larger society and deal with whites' cultural and political power. When Arthur C. Parker was a leader within the Society of American Indians (SAI), the association "eschewed anything which savored of the medicine show Indian, though Indian costume might be worn in certain circumstances, provided these were dignified and controlled." Apparently, Parker, with training in anthropology and a career in museum work, had limited tolerance for showier forms of pan-Indian dress. On seeing a photograph of a Six Nations gathering in Brantford, Canada, that depicted some in Plains-style costume, he lamented, "Indians to be recognized as such must 'play' Indian!"[71] (Did any of Lucy Pearman Scott's descendants in Brantford witness the photographed event?) When the SAI met in Chicago in 1923, there was an encampment with ceremonials and dancing in full regalia. One Chippewa observer "expressed his regrets that it is only when he exhibits Indian war dances and ancient ceremonies that the public evinces any interest in the Indian."[72]

Some SAI members emphasized distinctively Indian contributions to the larger society and the importance of traditional ways. Some progressive-era pan-Indian political activity, on the other hand, bent toward pragmatic accommodations.[73] But in the aftermath of World War I, SAI members struggled with ideas about self-determination and separatism. Some Native people nationally understood whites' nativist backlash against immigration in the 1920s as part of the larger problem of racialized prejudice (and this backlash played out among advocates for Virginia's 1924 racial integrity law). By 1922, Arthur C. Parker withdrew from the SAI, apparently discouraged about prospects for productive assimilation, and he focused more on Native Americans as individuals and their rights to self-determination.[74]

While the phrase "pan-Indian" can apply to political movements such as the SAI, it also embraces other forms of cooperation and social and cultural exchange across tribal lines. Some pan-Indian activity was social, religious, expressive, and creative. For example, today pan-Indian styling appears at intertribal powwow gatherings across the country where dancing, drumming, and costuming express shared Indianness across Native American linguistic, social, and cultural groupings. Such powwows reflect a history of alliances and trade patterns that have bridged traditional cultural and language differences.

Thus, tidewater Natives were not unusual in their strategic use of pan-Indianisms in public performances. Given their position in the Jim Crow South, as they worked to distinguish themselves from their African American neighbors, perhaps the use of such symbols, going back at least to the 1880s and 1890s, felt especially crucial and urgent as signifiers widely recognized by whites. Continued use of pan-Indian material culture since the 1970s, in the context of "red power" and other national civil rights movements, suggests its long-term utility for tidewater Virginia Natives, as a tool for asserting cultural identity as Powhatan people and as a visual link to other indigenous peoples across the country.

To complicate matters, there was the popular phenomenon of whites' "playing Indian": adopting Native cultural markers, romanticizing Native American cultures, and linking their nationalistic ideas with nostalgic primitivism.[75] This cultural play and work are relevant to Powhatan dramatic performances in Virginia, and they also lie at the roots of ethnography in the United States, as seen in the career of Lewis Henry Morgan, a founding figure in American anthropology. Frank Hamilton Cushing more famously adopted Pueblo dress on occasion, but Morgan also dressed up "Indian" early in his career, inspired by romantic literary and nationalistic concerns. Philip Deloria has described how figures like Morgan were part of a cultural process whereby, for white Americans who "played Indian" in the late nineteenth and early twentieth centuries, Indians became the focus of a sometimes touristic search for some kind of authentic, "primitive" cultural vigor.[76] In this cultural mix, the famous Dakota physician Charles Eastman, who was active early on in the SAI, advocated teaching white children about Indian ways as an antidote to the artifices of modern life, in writings for the Boy Scouts. Arthur C. Parker, too, could espouse primitivist ideas about the virtues of Indian cultures.[77]

Tidewater Virginia Native people's costumed performances tapped into that strain of whites' romantic notions about the primitive. Locally, while Powhatan people themselves performed their Indianness, white students at the nearby College of William and Mary were also known to costume themselves as Indians.[78] If whites could dress as Indians, and if a Wild West show could be presented to an international audience of anthropologists in 1889 Paris, why should not Powhatan people use pan-Indian, Plains-influenced dress to promote public recognition and acceptance of their Indian identities and history?

Historical dramas performed by Powhatan people in the late nineteenth century and the early twentieth century represent more than a display of symbols that non-Indian audiences would instantly recognize as generically Indian. Such staged events, including appearances at the 1907 Jamestown Tercentennial Exposition and reservation leaders' periodic visits to Richmond to place a tribute of game before the governor of Virginia, also represented Virginia Indians as key actors in a historical narrative about Jamestown that was integral to whites' notions about the colonial roots of the American republic. While taking advantage of whites' nostalgia and primitivism, tidewater Natives also evoked with specificity their historical roles and identities to underscore their communities' heritage and continued existence.

Certainly, the ceremony of Powhatan tribute to Virginia's governor engendered sentimentality among white Virginians as a relic practice by Indian people whom many whites considered almost relics. It was a cozy sentimentality that could bolster Virginia whites' acceptance of Virginia Indian identities. In 1890, for example, the *Daily Times* of Richmond ran a two-part article on Pamunkey history that concluded with a section titled, "Still a Remnant." This piece noted that the contemporary Pamunkey were not "of pure Indian blood, their progenitors for several generations having intermarried with whites, mulattoes, and blacks. Notwithstanding this, the distinctive physiognomy of their race strongly asserts itself." The writer affirmed them "to be the real descendants of the tawny warriors of 1607," despite their current status as "peaceful peasants and fishermen." As evidence of their current deference, but also their peculiar nationhood, the article noted the history of tribute to Virginia governors based in a colonial-era treaty:

> The habit thus acquired has ever preserved in their minds a sentiment of fealty to the State. Although long ago delivered from this exaction, to this day it is the pleasing custom of their Chief and his head men to make a complimentary visit to each newly inaugurated Governor, and testify their respect for his office and person by a present of fish and game from the waters and forests of their ancient habitat. Thus, have lived in security for more than two centuries, among the descendants of their ancient enemies a remnant of the race to whom the land we love originally belonged. During all this time their little State [the reservation lands] has remained as distinct an autonomy among greater powers as Andorra among the Pyrenees, or San Marino by the sea. They now represent probably the only organized community of aboriginal Americans left on the Atlantic slope; and with their disappearance will have passed away forever the last of their race to be found east of the Mississippi.[79]

This article's narrator thus folded present-day Virginia reservations into whites' long-running narrative about Native peoples as a "vanishing race." The *Times* reassured its readers, in a year that ended with the death of Sitting Bull and the Wounded Knee massacre, that the Indians of the Virginian reservations were harmless, tamed, peaceful "remnants" of a once powerful group.

This newspaper piece can also be read as evidence of the effectiveness of Pamunkey strategies. The *Times* article positioned Pamunkey people as disappearing remnants, but also as heirs of a grand tradition within a national, colonial, narrative dear to Southern whites. The writer affirmed Pamunkey status as a separate people, indigenous rather than Black or white, despite a history of marriages across racial lines. Thus, the photo op tribute of game to the Virginia governor created a ceremonial space for the reservation people outside Jim Crow's Black-white color line—while it positioned them as historic actors and present-day citizens.

Tidewater Natives involved in the ceremony of bringing a wild game tribute to Virginia's governors likely saw it as a distinctive, persuasive public performance. It may be that the ceremony shifted over decades toward increased uses of Indian regalia. One photograph of Chickahominy people making a gesture of tribute around 1919—possibly to assert a status similar to that of the reservation groups—shows no one in pan-Indian garb.[80] Similarly, a photograph of Pamunkey tribute-givers dated 1921 captures no obvious pan-Indian dress. Another photograph of perhaps the same occasion (or around the same time) reveals that the chief's hat has a distinctive decorative band; his clothing otherwise seems conventionally Anglo.[81] Also in that photograph collection, other mostly undated photographs that seem more recent, including an image from 1940, show that on other occasions of tribute to the governor, such pan-Indian garb was more prominent, including fringe, beads, and at least one full Plains-style feathered headdress.[82] When the Mattaponi make their tribute to the governor in more recent times, Helen Rountree wrote, "their representatives wear at least one item of 'Indian' regalia for the occasion, in accordance with the tribe's bylaws."[83]

Twelve of about fifty-seven photographs in a collection of Cook-Bradby family photographs show this tribute tradition; Cooks and Bradbys have long been prominent Pamunkey leaders. In these images, some Pamunkey representatives wore conventional clothing—that is, business suits and neckties for the men. If these photographs are representative of entire groups of the Pamunkey people in attendance, women may have been more likely than men to display pan-Indian elements of dress on these occasions. Five of the photographs seem to date from before 1942, the year when Tecumseh Deerfoot Cook became the Pamunkey chief. Three of these photographs show at least one man in full Plains-inspired feathered headdress and an elaborately decorated and fringed tunic and pants, including rounded fringed collars like those in an 1881 photograph of pageant players. The remaining photographs in this grouping perhaps were taken between 1942 and 1974. Except for one photo that features Pocahontas Cook, they show Chief Tecumseh Cook consistently clothed in feathered headdress and fringed, elaborately decorated garments. In what may be the latest photograph of this sequence, he wore somewhat less elaborately ornamented fringed clothing and a pair of moccasins that may have been mass produced. In another photograph, he held a drum. Women in these later photographs wore headbands, fringed garments, beads, and sometimes braids and a single feather in their hair.[84] Usually in these photos, among the men present, a leader and sometimes one other man were outfitted most elaborately, while other men wore standard business suits.

The clothing in these tribute photographs was part of an occasion that signaled Indianness broadly and unmistakably to white audiences. How a specifically Pamunkey or Powhatan identity and history fit into these uses of pan-Indian dress is a question the photographs do not answer. The Native participants probably did intend such regalia at these tribute ceremonies to evoke generalized pan-Indian symbols. The Native participants in conventional business dress were also, simultaneously, signifying that the communities paying tribute claimed their place as present-day citizens of a modern state on par with other citizens.

In these tribute photos, Virginia Indians not only portrayed themselves as real Indians to white state officials, they also joined themselves and their history to national issues of Indian identity. Pan-Indian garb connected them to a continental sweep of centuries of the dispossession of Native peoples. This move seems particularly productive for Southeastern Native groups trying to emerge from a long history of being assigned to catchall categories such as "free person of color" or "mulatto." Wearing such clothing was more than a way to mark oneself as an Indian for an uninformed Southern white public. It evoked a major American historical narrative that Powhatan people used to link themselves to Indianness nationwide in powerful, if generic, ways.

Those links could resonate within their own communities and in personal identity-building, not just in contacts with non-Indians. In addition to images showing the public ceremony of tribute to Virginia's governor, some of the older pictures among the Cook-Bradby family collection suggest more intimate, personal uses of pan-Indian-style dress. These nontribute shots are mainly portraits of individuals or small groups, mostly undated. Especially in such a small community, this use of pan-Indian clothing in group and private settings may reflect community consensus about the varied options for denoting Pamunkey, Powhatan, or generically indigenous identities. (The Cook and Bradby families have officially represented their reservation community often over the years, and so perhaps they owned more such garb than some of their neighbors.) Some of these photographs look like studio portraits. Among those are images shot against the kinds of backdrops sometimes used by commercial photographers. Subjects in these more formal studio pictures may wear pan-Indian and/or Anglo-style clothing. One such portrait shows an unidentified woman in a dress and hat of conventional 1890s European American styling. Luzelia Bradby Dennis, on the other hand, appears in a photograph wearing clothing that looks very much like what she wore for a picture of the Pamunkey group that performed at the 1907 Jamestown Exposition. Capitola Cook, in long braids, headband, fringe, and beads, poses against a studio backdrop; those overt signifiers of Indianness may not indicate that this picture was intended for a white audience. In another photo, taken when Capitola was somewhat older, she wore a polka-dotted dress and her hair styled in a conventional matronly way. John Bradby sported a neat cravat, moustache, short hair, and vested suit in a portrait made when he was a young man. He also appeared, somewhat older, in a 1921 tribute photograph, still looking dapper in a suit, hat, tie, and dark overcoat. In that image he carried on his shoulder one end of the pole carrying dead game for the governor. There are portraits of Chief Tecumseh Cook's grandparents, dressed conventionally and projecting solid middle-class propriety. Would they have approved of their grandson's later engagement with pan-Indian symbols? Tecumseh Cook's mother, Theodora Dennis Cook, appeared in several photographs looking dignified and matriarchal, in a fringed and decorated costume, her hair caught under a feathered headband. Thus, for formal individual and family portraits, sitters in these families used images of overt (if generic) Indianness by at least 1907. Perhaps the pictures capture some sitters prepared for a public occasion when they wore pan-Indian dress for the benefit of non-Pamunkeys. Nonetheless, if the subject was not someone who served as a chief, it seems unlikely that all portraits in which the subject is wearing pan-Indian articles of clothing were intended mainly for viewers outside the family. If some capture a public face, they seem also to document personal images treasured within the family.[85]

Less formal group photographs in this Cook-Bradby collection also document uses of both pan-Indian and conventional Anglo-style clothing and grooming. These snapshots of small groups often show that all the subjects in the photo have made similar choices about whether to wear Indian-or Anglo-style garments. There are two exceptions in which some people are conventionally dressed and others are in pan-Indian garb. The circumstances and settings for these two informal photographs are not obvious, but it may be that these two images document family gatherings rather than public events.

Other group photographs may show family members together in more formal occasions, when pan-Indian clothing might have been worn primarily with non-Indian viewers in mind. At least four group photographs have a posed quality that seems to indicate that they were shot in the context of public festivities or other promotional occasions that involved non-Pamunkey audiences. One shows three women, probably at the reservation trading post or museum, working on pottery with designs that seem intended to evoke generic ideas about Native American art. The women are wearing headbands and fringed, beaded garments. Two other photographs show two men working on a fishing net in full feathered Plains-style headdresses.[86]

Another cluster of these Cook-Bradby collection photographs is informal snapshots of individuals. Like other photographs, they document pan-Indian as well as conventional clothing choices made by Pamunkey people. Their context is not always clear, whether public occasions or more intimate family gatherings. Many of these snapshot portraits show a subject clothed either in entirely conventional Anglo-style dress or overall pan-Indian styling. Perhaps most of these informal images that show full pan-Indian outfitting related to a ceremonial or public gathering. In one photograph, the subject is wearing Anglo-style clothing, but his headgear tells an Indian story; Chief Tecumseh Cook, standing in shallow water in boots and a conventional pair of pants and jacket, wears a feathered crown headdress. One of these snapshots is another view of Tecumseh Cook's mother, Theodora Dennis Cook, still looking very much the matriarch, but without her headband. In this portrait, she wore conventional clothing with her hair pulled back as any white or African American woman of her age at that time might have done. She has, though, also chosen multiple strands of round beads, which look ordinary except that she is wearing several necklaces in different lengths. Perhaps her choice in this jewelry reflects her interest in presenting a pan-Indian aesthetic.[87]

Thus, pan-Indian clothing, as adopted by the Pamunkey and Mattaponi, seems integral to their strategies for proclaiming and reminding their neighbors of their identity as Indians. Such garments and grooming were important aspects of public presentations, from historical pageants to the trip to Richmond to give the governor tribute. Pan-Indian garb was not limited to chiefs. If pan-Indian costume was most commonly reserved for formal occasions and portraits, it was also used on occasions when non-Indians were not the primary audience. For example, in the cemetery on the Mattaponi Reservation, accessible to the general public but clearly a community space, several headstones have plaques reproducing photographic portraits, and a number of these images include pan-Indian items. Maybe, over time, such garments grew in importance as part of the communities' assertion of their identities as Native Americans.

These pan-Indian signals and indicators, used in public pageants, ceremonies, and dances, likely helped to engage the interest not only of a curious white public but also of white scholars. As we will see in chapter 4, the Bureau of American Ethnology took notice of, and began to gather information about, Indians in tidewater Virginia around 1889. Possibly among the sparks that ignited the bureau's efforts were Pamunkey public performances of the so-called "rescue" of John Smith by Pocahontas.[88] The existence of the 1898 flyer, mentioned earlier, in the bureau's files evidences the BAE's interest in these performances.

With or without the bureau's encouragement, the Pamunkey developed an interest in national and international expositions.[89] For example, Alfred Gatschet, in a notebook he kept after 1893, remarked that a carpenter and newspaper correspondent had collected Pamunkey "stone relics" for a "New Orleans exhibition," possibly the New Orleans Exposition of 1884.[90]

In recent decades, scholarship on the presence and presentations of Native peoples at major nineteenth-century expositions in Europe and the United States has explored the colonialist, primitivist, paternalistic, and racialized cast of such ethnographic displays. Despite all that, Virginia Indians saw and seized opportunities to pursue their own ends at Chicago's World's Columbian Exposition of 1893. William Terrill Bradby, one of James Mooney's informants, traveled to the 1893 exposition in Chicago, to represent his tribe. On the way he stopped in Washington to donate Pamunkey materials at the Smithsonian's United States National Museum, including "specimens of Pamunkey pottery," a tomahawk, ax, and spear heads. Besides depositing these items, which seem calculated to emphasize Pamunkey precontact traditions, Bradby also visited the office of the commissioner of Indian Affairs.[91] Mooney's notes about correspondence in Bradby's possession refer to a trail of endorsements and introductions that Bradby garnered for the 1893 exposition. If these were customary within exposition protocols, they also show how carefully Bradby prepared to secure multiple layers of whites' endorsements of his Indianness. The clerk of King William County and the office of Virginia's governor attested in writing to his status as a "member of the Pamunkey Tribe," and to the fact that the tribe held a reservation sanctioned by the state of Virginia. On Bradby's behalf, Otis Mason of the Smithsonian's U.S. National Museum wrote to the commissioner of Indian Affairs vouching for Bradby's status as a Powhatan descendant and as someone well known and "serviceable" to Mason in Smithsonian efforts to look at Pamunkey history. This in turn led to a letter from the assistant commissioner of Indian Affairs to Frederic Putnam of the Peabody Museum, co-organizer of ethnographic displays at the 1893 exposition, recommending Bradby as "one of the very few remaining" descendants of the historic Pamunkey group. Putnam responded by acknowledging Bradby's interest in Putnam's exhibitions and naming him an "honorary assistant" in the fair's Department of Ethnology.[92] Bradby thus sought multiple forms of official white recognition, probably convinced that a presence in the Smithsonian collections and at the Chicago exposition would bolster recognition of Pamunkey Indianness back home among Virginia whites.

He had another mission as well: to discuss possibilities of intertribal marriages with representatives of other tribes. At least one newspaper reported at the time that the Pamunkey representative to the 1893 fair planned "to invite other civilized Indians to come and settle on their reservation and amalgamate with their tribe. The Pamunkey's have rich lands and are in prosperous circumstances, but they have entermarried [sic] so long that the tribe is in danger of extinction. The delegates took the precaution of obtaining from the governor of Virginia a certificate to the effect that they were genuine Indians and have a secure tenure of their lands."[93] The theme of potential extinction from intermarriage recurs here, but this article also testifies to tenacious Pamunkey work to counter that narrative, to persuade white state officials to vouch for their Indianness and reservation status, to make new connections with Native groups outside Virginia to buttress their own reputations as Indians, and to get publicity for those efforts.

The Pamunkey were persistent in their quest for participation at expositions. In 1898, William Terrill Bradby's group used their connection to Otis Mason at the Smithsonian to request that the Indian Office sanction a Pamunkey delegate to the Omaha Trans-Mississippi and International Exposition and received a reply that that exposition had closed.[94] The Pamunkey also tried for representation at a turn-of-the-century Paris exposition (presumably the Exposition Universelle of 1900). A Washington, DC., newspaper reported in 1899 that their chief and others from the Pamunkey council had met with Virginia's governor "to tell of their grievances" and request state support for sending a Pamunkey delegation to Paris, specifically "a creditable company to produce a play representing the saving of Captain John Smith's life by Pocahontas" that would include tribal officials among the actors.[95] The governor replied that the state had no authorizing power in the matter.[96] There may be no record of what they told the governor about their grievances.

A Powhatan group performed at the 1907 Jamestown Tercentennial Exposition, held in Norfolk, Virginia. In a photograph of that group, men and women wear costumes similar to those in other surviving photographs of Powhatan performing groups, including ornamented, fringed Plains-flavored clothing and feathered headbands. Since Virginia's reservation Powhatan groups were and are relatively small communities, this photo of about fifteen people may signify that a sizeable slice of adult reservation residents participated in this dramatic public performance.[97] This photograph showed performers costumed for a play or pageant, but among them were two men not dressed in Indian costume. One, in a suit and tie, was identified in a key to the photograph as the "white man who organized Indian participation." The other, who was likely playing John Smith, wore a vaguely cavalierish costume including a wide-brimmed hat; he was identified as Journey Miles. Journey Miles, who figured in chapter 1, was the son of James and Henrietta (Honey) Miles and a great-grandson of Lucy Pearman Scott.[98]

Powhatan participation in the 1893 and 1907 expositions took place at a fraught time in federal policies toward Native people. Frederick Hoxie has analyzed how, at major expositions such as the ones in Philadelphia in 1876, 1893 in Chicago, and in 1904 Saint Louis, public representations of Native Americans at the fairs reflected white policymakers' and scholars' shifting visions of the possible futures of Indian peoples. Hoxie argued that in the context of industrialization and immigration patterns of the 1880s and 1890s, whites' earlier notion of a one-size-fits-all march to assimilation of Native peoples was tempered by Indian resistance and a general inability of whites to arrive at "complete acceptance" of Native peoples. As a result, by 1920, Hoxie argued, many white policymakers still envisioned that Native peoples would be incorporated into "majority society," but on a basis that "bore a greater resemblance to the position of the United States' other nonwhite peoples than it did to the 'full membership' envisioned by nineteenth century reformers." As Hoxie pointed out, Indians in the United States faced the same trends that brought ever-more stringent segregation of African Americans, exclusion of Japanese immigrants, and ultimately reductions in immigration from parts of Europe.[99] Virginia's Indian peoples faced a campaign by proponents of Virginia's 1924 racial integrity law that fanned fears about immigration, as described in chapter 2.

As noted, William Terrill Bradby used connections with Otis Mason of the Smithsonian to approach Frederic Putnam and the office of the commissioner of Indian Affairs in preparation for his visit to the 1893 Chicago Exposition. As Hoxie pointed out for the 1893 Chicago show, Putnam of Harvard's Peabody Museum conceived and organized a display that emphasized antiquities but also the continuing, yet somehow essentially premodern, cultural distinctiveness of contemporary North American Indians. The commissioner of Indian Affairs, in contrast, presented a vision of federal assimilationist programs designed to make Indians culturally indistinguishable from white citizens, with model schoolhouse classrooms as a focus.[100]

At the 1904 Louisiana Purchase Exposition in Saint Louis, there was again an Indian schoolhouse on the exposition grounds, but Hoxie argued that by then, "these divergent themes had been resolved. Interest in the Indians' 'primitive' character was paramount." At the Saint Louis fair, "No longer portrayed as both a 'people in transition' and a breed of primitive exotics, Native Americans had become members of one of the world's many 'backward races.'" They were part of a grand display of "primitive peoples of the globe" that included Ainu, Patagonian, and Philippine individuals.[101]

Just a few years after the Louisiana Purchase Exposition, the Jamestown Tercentennial Exposition of 1907 had some similar features, but on a smaller scale. However, at this exposition, contemporary tidewater Natives seem to have been relegated to the fair's popular entertainment section.

The 1907 exposition was intended to underscore the technological prowess and military might of the United States on a global and national stage. Attended by celebrities such as Theodore Roosevelt and Mark Twain, the exposition was staged on the Hampton Roads harbor in Norfolk to provide for display of naval strength by the United States and other countries. It was billed as a fair whose architecture, dominated by colonial revival styles, was more modest (and perhaps more tasteful) than that of some other recent expositions. This seems like a nod to mythologies of Southern whites' "gentility" in a romanticized colonial past, a past represented as less contentious and painful than the eras of Civil War and Reconstruction. (It was likely also a nod to the difficulties of fundraising.) Confederate references and organizations, though, were on display at this exposition.[102] Given these circumstances, it seems almost inevitable that Virginia's Native citizens would be marginalized at the exposition.

The Jamestown exposition celebrated the English colonization of Virginia as a story of American national origins. Various fair publications featured images of John Smith and Pocahontas and romantic portrayals of the first encounters of English colonials with Powhatan peoples in Virginia. But the romance of history took a back seat to other concerns; promoters noted, "Industrial and scientific progress will be demonstrated in various ways, but the distinctive feature of the Exposition will be the great military and naval drills, parades and manoeuvers."[103]

Special features touted in promotional literature included not only international displays of military might, but also congresses and conventions of business and civic organizations and federal government-sponsored displays representing U.S. progress and global reach. The federal presence included "Special Alaska and Philippine exhibits," "Special Indian exhibits," and "Special Negro buildings and exhibits."[104] Seemingly, federal work in this area was relatively restrained compared to the extravaganza of "primitives" presented at Saint Louis. As at earlier fairs, the Smithsonian was involved in representations of Native cultures at the 1907 exposition. In Norfolk, the Smithsonian had a building with historical displays representing a broad sweep of American history and technological progress, including a "life-sized lay figure group depicting Captain John Smith trading for corn with the Powhatan Indians."[105] The Smithsonian's efforts embraced the history of early contact between English colonists and Eastern Indians, placing Virginia Indians within a major national-origins narrative. The Smithsonian display did not overlook a premodern, primitivized past; it included "examples of aboriginal handiwork" from across the country, from Maine to Texas and from "Porto Rico and Santo Domingo," and an archeological display on "stone-implement makers of the District of Columbia."[106]

In contrast, the Bureau of Indian Affairs (BIA) exhibits, consistent with Hoxie's observations about other fairs, emphasized its schools as vehicles for "civilizing" Native groups. Displays of the work of Indian students at federal Indian schools affirmed the bureau's success in teaching business courses, dressmaking and sewing, embroidery, blacksmithing, shoemaking, and carpentry. The BIA exhibits did include some more "traditional" images of Native American "specimens of native arts and industries." Maps acknowledged the existence of Virginia communities of Native people, showing "locations of Indian reservations and the areas occupied by the remnants of Indian tribes in Virginia."[107]

That is one of the very few mentions of contemporary Virginia Native people in extant publications on the exposition, despite multiple graphic and textual references in those publications to Powhatan peoples in Virginia's distant colonial past. Jamestown's Tercentennial fair literature gestured toward Powhatan, Pocahontas, and Powhatan peoples' early contact with white colonials in seventeenth-century Virginia. Graphics of generic Indian figures graced promotional literature for the exposition. The grounds of the exposition were mapped with "Powhatan's Oak," the site of an old "Indian burying ground," an "Indian spring," and streets named Algonquin, Pocahontas, and Powhatan.[108]

There was also "playing Indian" at the 1907 fair. Among the many "state and special days" events, exposition publications advertised May 15 as "Virginia Red Men Day." On that day, as members of a white men's fraternal organization known as the Improved Order of Red Men, "The Great Council of *Red Men* paraded in Norfolk and then captured the Exposition. One hundred painted and fearless braves swarmed over the grounds and through the buildings of the Exposition."[109] These white men impersonated the "savage" Indian fighter, reflecting the popularity of such "redface" dating from at least the days of the Boston Tea Party.

The midway section of the fair, reserved for popular entertainments, was similarly freewheeling and stereotyping. On it were a 101 Ranch Wild West show, "A typical Oklahoma ranch showing a great array of Cowboys, Cowgirls, Mexicans, and Indians illustrating actual life in the far-west. Bucking broncos, lassoing wild steers, Indian dances, and other startling attractions may be seen." Capitalizing on the popularity of the Philippines display in 1904 Saint Louis, the

Jamestown exposition also offered a Philippine exhibit with "Igorrots in native costume. These people are capable of high development but are now next to lowest type of human beings on the Islands."[110] In the context of these displays and those of the BIA, the Jamestown exposition seems to reflect tensions between the notion of assimilating Indians and the vision of Native Americans as exoticized primitivized peoples, as Hoxie has described.

Despite the presence, mere miles from the exposition site, of Pamunkey, Mattaponi, and Chickahominy groups who proudly asserted their status as the people of Powhatan and Pocahontas, many promotional publications and official reports on the Norfolk exposition did not mention the presence of Powhatan Indians performing at this fair. Perhaps the photograph of those 1907 performers now in the National Anthropological Archives, and a stereocard photo (see fig. 3), depict a performance that happened only for a short time during the fair. In any case, it seems that those Powhatan performances happened at the midway section of the fair, the entertainment district—which was oddly called the "War Path."[111]

While the BIA offered a vision of contemporary Indians' movement toward what whites viewed as progress and the 101 Ranch celebrated mythic images of Native people in a "wild west," Powhatan people at the 1907 exposition apparently had little opportunity to position themselves as the present-day inheritors and representatives of a major historical narrative about the colonial origins of the nation. Native Virginians' relative obscurity at the 1907 exposition seems even more glaring given that a plan was hatched for an exhibit by New York State Tuscarora people, described in exposition promotional literature as having historically "ruled" parts of Virginia and the Carolinas. The New York Tuscaroras were billed as possibly having some Welsh origins and therefore being "of a much lighter complexion than any of the other tribes of the North American Indian."[112] Like Walter Plecker, apparently, some people involved in the 1907 exposition felt that tidewater Virginia Indians were too colored to be really Indian.

Thus, at the 1907 fair, white men played Indian, a wild west show titillated visitors with images of dangerous Plains warriors, seventeenth-century Powhatan people were celebrated for rescuing John Smith and his fellow English colonists from starvation, and the Bureau of Indian Affairs and Smithsonian Institution presented images of assimilating western Indians as well as examples of archeological and modern Native handiwork. But in the midst of all this mythmaking, the Powhatan people living in 1907 Virginia were barely visible in official publications at an exposition in their own back yard.

Similarly in 1931, to mark the 150th anniversary of the Revolutionary War battle at Yorktown and a formal dedication of the new Colonial National Monument, Virginia Indians, while not exactly invisible, occupied a contained, constrained position. As part of the official ceremonies, white organizers envisioned a series of pageants on the colonial period and the Revolutionary War. Those pageants barely depicted African Americans. Black attendees were segregated in grandstand seating and elsewhere on the grounds. Native people's histories fared no better. In one of the pageants, white people in redface acted the parts of Native Americans. Two prominent white organizers expressed and acted upon attitudes, like those of Walter Plecker, that Virginia Natives were not real Indians but were, rather, "Mulattoes masquerading as Indians." White planners did invite a Pamunkey, Mattaponi, and Chickahominy presence in a separate area they called a village, echoing their limited participation in the Jamestown 1907 exposition. "Relegated to the farthest corner of the premises, the display included, at the insistence of the coordinators, tepees 'of the types they used in those days' and 'entertain[ment] by means of ceremonial and war dances,' providing 'a most interesting' insight into colonial times."[113]

However small and compromised the space they occupied at the 1907 exposition and the Yorktown sesquicentennial, public performances of Powhatan people retained urgency and utility for organized tidewater Virginia Indians in publicly asserting their indigeneity at a time when white officials treated them as non-whites within Virginia's segregation regime. In those performances, sometimes tidewater Indians used pan-Indian costuming that connected to larger narratives of Indian survival in North America—and they asserted themselves not only as Virginians with a special role in Virginia's founding, but also as distinctively and distinct Native people and citizens of the present day.

From the Civil War and into the 1930s, through public performances and institutions such as churches, schools, and tribal organizations, Powhatan people maintained, formed, displayed, invented, and reinvented their Powhatan identities to create and preserve Native spaces in tidewater Virginia. Given the racialized pressures Native Virginians faced over decades of official opposition, their achievement is remarkable. Their separate institutions, though, entailed a level of acceptance of racial segregation. By the time of the Jamestown exposition, for example, the Chickahominy people—non-reservation "citizen" Indians—had formed an organization that affirmed their Indian identities as a group. That organizational effort entailed assembling a list of members, a tribal roll, backed by the advice of William Terrill Bradby and the Smithsonian ethnographer James

Mooney.[114] It seems likely that the impetus for this roll was not only to include Chickahominy individuals, but also to exclude some people with Black as well as Native ancestors. Tidewater Native Virginians worked in the arena of the color line even as they carved out for themselves spaces that were neither Black nor white. They did not exit the playing field of race, nor is it likely that that would have been possible for them in Jim Crow Virginia.

Ethnographers like James Mooney participated in these processes. Chapter 4 will look at involvement by late nineteenth and early twentieth-century anthropologists, such as Mooney and Frank Speck in varied activist—and separatist—moves of Virginia's tidewater Indian groups.[115]

FIGURE 1. Pamunkey School Children, ca.1920, photo by Walter Washington Foster. Credit: The Virginia Museum of History and Culture, photographic print 2002.645.27. The museum notes, "In a letter dated 5/9/1994 from Warren Cook, the women are identified as [standing left to right] Irma Page; Unidentified Girl; Teacher, Mrs. Kyle; Douglas Miles; (?) Miles and [seated] Martha Bradley; Thelma Dennis."

FIGURE 2. Pamunkey Indian Group, photo by Walter Washington Foster. Credit: The Virginia Museum of History and Culture, photographic print 2007.5.40. The museum notes that this photograph was most likely taken on the same day as 2002.645.27.

FIGURE 3. Stereocard image of the Pamunkeys' performance of "Pocahontas Pleading for the Life of John Smith" at the Jamestown exposition, 1907. Published by the Keystone View Company. Credit: The Virginia Museum of History and Culture, stereocard photograph 2008.37.42.

CHAPTER 4

White Ethnographers and Salvage Ethnography

IN 1928, FRANK G. Speck reflected on his fieldwork as an anthropologist among Indian peoples in tidewater Virginia: "The task of trying to reconstruct Powhatan ethnology has indeed been like conjuring. There seems to be little on the surface, yet shadows of remote customs and modified survivals of old economic life persist.... Many pleasant weeks have been passed consorting with the much-diluted Indian remnants of the tidewater country, yet each season creates a deeper feeling of respect for their loyal tenacity to their Indian traditions. This is responsible for the survival of many desirable facts hidden away in memory's closets."[1] Speck described his work as the retrieval from "memory's closets" of "hidden" cultural and economic survivals among "much-diluted Indian remnants," engaging significant arguments about the nature of authenticity and tradition. While Speck's Powhatan contacts likely appreciated his "respect for their loyal tenacity to their Indian traditions," they probably did not think of themselves as "much-diluted" or manifesting only "shadows" of their cultural inheritance.

Along with Speck, several late nineteenth-century and early twentieth-century white ethnographers affirmed the Indianness of some tidewater Native people; they thus gave valuable political aid to indigenous Virginians, but at the cost of injecting into the debate ideas at odds with more fluid and realistic ideas about cultural change. These scholars grappled with ideas of their time about the "aboriginal" and "traditional" as markers of authentic indigeneity. They appraised, and sometimes tried to influence, processes of community identity formation among tidewater Natives. They examined not only survivals from the past, but also cultural revivals, "salvage," and creativity—processes entangled, in Virginia, with Jim Crow segregation.[2]

Before Speck's arrival among them, tidewater Native people had already learned about anthropology and ethnographers. James Mooney and Albert Gatschet of the Smithsonian's Bureau of American Ethnology (BAE) had taken an interest in Eastern Seaboard Indian groups in the late nineteenth century.[3]

Speck's involvement in Virginia, spanning the 1920s and 1940s, was later and longer term than that of the BAE, and he brought to his work among tidewater Algonquian groups long-term experience among other eastern and northern Algonquian-speaking peoples.

Mooney and Speck worked in times when some ethnographers looking at non-Europeans emphasized supposedly timeless, unchanging, "primitive" aspects of their social and cultural systems, thereby framing non-white cultures as exotic and somehow outside of modernity. Rooted in nineteenth-century American thinking about race and cultural difference was an assumption that Europeans and European Americans existed in passing time as the subjects of history, and that "other" peoples whom whites considered primitive lived somehow outside history, in a static, timeless space. Some early United States anthropologists believed that each human society could be located on a continuum from savagery to barbarism to "civilization," and was to be judged by its progress (or lack thereof) on that scale. In the minds of many white Americans, real Indians represented a stage of human development antecedent to civilization and so disconnected from the flow of modern history.

Despite all that, the Native Virginian subjects of Mooney and Speck's research strategically managed their relationships with those ethnographers to advance their own cultural, social, and political goals. Segregationist white officials' opposition to their assertions of Indian identities was fueled by racist "scientific" rhetoric. So when Speck and Mooney wrote and published on Native groups in tidewater Virginia, their position as social scientists and authoritative voices on what was "authentically" Indian was useful for tidewater Natives. White ethnographers could affirm Virginia Powhatan peoples' Indian identities by showing that indigenous tidewater peoples fit some of whites' stereotypes of what made a real Indian—and/or by arguing that even where and when Virginia's Indians did not exactly fit those stereotypes, authentic Indian traits could still be uncovered or recovered to testify to a distinctive Indianness.

Looking back, the work of these ethnographers seems like a double-edged tool. Virginia's organized Indians gained significant support from Mooney and Speck during a virulently segregationist era of Virginia history. That support, however, came from outsiders who had their own visions of race and what made someone authentically Indian. Ethnographers' work sometimes leaned heavily on explicit or implicit searches for cultural remnants from a pre-1492 world. Such searches fed from and into whites' misconceptions about the static nature of Native cultures. Thus, in this period when Virginia's tidewater Native people traveled on anthropologists' terrain, they operated on a landscape with multiple barriers against more realistic, historically grounded ways of looking at cultural change and contingency among Native peoples over the centuries since 1492 or 1607. James Mooney and Frank Speck did far more than perpetuate primitivist stereotypes and visions of a hierarchy of cultures. At the same time, early ethnographers' analyses of Powhatan peoples sometimes led into what today look like dead ends—because they did not always stress the fluidity and historically conditioned nature of culture, community, identity-building, and kinship. When ethnographers among Virginia tidewater Indians used terms like "full blood," or assumed that out-marriage caused dilution of Indianness, they were in effect trying to distance Virginia Indians from their long histories of interactions—love, work, kinship, and neighborliness, as well as conflicts—with European Americans and African Americans.

The involvement of the BAE and Frank Speck with tidewater Natives unfolded at a time of transition in the practice of ethnography. Between the 1890s and the 1940s, anthropological study of Native Americans in the United States was shifting somewhat from its roots in museums—where some of its early practitioners, trained in the natural sciences, were inclined toward systematic, encyclopedic schemes of classification of cultures and collections. In the late nineteenth century, John Wesley Powell, as head of the BAE, and Frederic Ward Putnam (who welcomed William Terrill Bradby to the 1893 Columbian Exposition) emphasized comprehensive descriptive typologies, patterned on natural history traditions of collection and display of specimens using overarching taxonomic schemes of classification.[4] By the 1940s, though, American anthropology's major figures were more often found in college and university faculties than in museums, and many ethnographers had embraced Franz Boas's 1887 dictum that "classification is not explanation." Boas cautioned against overly rigid, universalized theoretical frameworks, arguing that "ethnological phenomena are, in the same way as geological or biological phenomena, the result of definite historical happenings."[5]

In the era of Boas's greatest influence, professional ethnographers often did studies focused on a single point in time, a trend reinforced by Boas's emphasis on a particular kind of in-the-moment fieldwork. What James Clifford described as the "notion of the 'ethnographic present,' the idea that that moment of fieldwork could stand in for any moment in the life of the people being studied" was influential in ethnographic discourse and analysis when Frank Speck was involved with tidewater Indians.[6] As a student of Franz Boas, Speck participated in a profession that sometimes prized that "moment of fieldwork" over analysis of change over time.

Speck, however, had a high level of confidence in his ability to look back from the present moment to try to accomplish "the task of trying to reconstruct Powhatan ethnography," based on his extensive fieldwork among other Algonquian cultures. As a result, when Speck described work among Powhatan people as "conjuring," he seemed to place himself, rather than his informants from those "much-diluted Indian remnants," in the position of the conjuror. When he looked at Powhatan peoples in the Jim Crow era, his work—like that of BAE ethnographers before him—to some extent affirmed notions about Native cultures as compromised and riddled with losses and gaps because of long-term contact with Europeans and European Americans, but he also envisioned Native communities rebuilding their Indianness with help from his work.[7]

The Bureau of American Ethnology and Tidewater Indians

The Bureau of American Ethnology's involvement with southeastern Native Americans is not as well known as some of its projects among Native peoples west of the Mississippi, such as James Mooney's famed work on the Ghost Dance. But in keeping with John Wesley Powell's aspirations for systematic, taxonomic, continentwide studies of Native peoples, the bureau did not restrict its work to western groups. James Mooney began his research on Cherokee people early in his BAE career in 1887 and did some of his earliest field work among the eastern Cherokee in North Carolina.[8]

A few years later, Mooney (1861–1921) began making inquiries about Native people in the southcentral Eastern Seaboard. A BAE colleague, Albert Gatschet (1832–1907), whose primary interests were linguistic, joined Mooney in looking at this region.[9] Their work reflected John Wesley Powell's intention that the BAE establish the study of Indian languages as a primary field of American ethnology. For Powell, linguistics could help to place groups within classificatory schemes for ranking human societies' stages of "progress."[10] Powell also saw in linguistics a tool for examining historical processes such as geographic movements of peoples and intergroup contacts.[11] In 1893, Gatschet wrote that he and Powell had settled on Algonquian languages as "the most important and most accessible" for "advantages to science."[12] Thus, Powell's ambition for a research program that was strategic, scientific, and systematic was part of the motivation for BAE efforts to look at relatively small and obscure Virginia Powhatan groups who had historically spoken Algonquian. (Algonquian tongues are widespread in North American; Powhatan peoples were among the southernmost Algonquian speakers.)

It also seems likely that the pageantry that some Pamunkey people had been staging in the 1880s attracted BAE attention.[13] The fact that the Pamunkey and Mattaponi held state-recognized reservation lands likely also helped spur Smithsonian inquiries. As early as 1877, Otis Mason of the Smithsonian's National Museum had noted the interest of a local minister named Dalrymple in the Pamunkey and Mattaponi, including "preservation of their ancient modes of making pottery." In 1878, at least one piece of Pamunkey pottery collected by Dalrymple was accessioned into the National Museum collections. Smithsonian accession records noted that it was, "Made by the last survivors of the Pamunkey and Mattaponi Indians in the year 1801."[14] The notion of the vanishing Indian was pervasive on the eve of Mooney's work among those Powhatan groups; "last survivors" those pottery makers were not.

Despite the conceit that Indians were vanishing, Mooney looked at whether and where there might be Indians in Virginia in addition to those on the two remaining reservations. In the spring of 1889, Mooney sent a questionnaire to about one thousand addressees in Maryland, Delaware, Virginia, and northeastern Carolina, over John Wesley Powell's name, posing a short list of queries about evidence and "remains" of former Indian presence on the land, and also about living persons of "pure or mixed Indian blood in your vicinity." In the bureau's tenth annual report to the Smithsonian's secretary, Powell noted that Mooney's circular was intended as a preliminary step toward "a monograph on the aborigines of the Middle Atlantic slope, with special reference to the Powhatan tribes of Virginia."[15]

Mooney had sent that questionnaire to prominent whites and to at least one Pamunkey leader. His questions showed his interest in archeological relics, ethnographic data, and finding additional informants. First, he asked, "What local place names in your county or immediate vicinity seem to be of Indian origin?" He seems to have hoped that such place names, presumably reflecting the memory of Indian groups who no longer occupied their former homelands, might help him trace present-day Native-descended peoples. As he later put it, he guessed that "the largest bodies of Indian admixture would still be found where the largest tribes had originally resided."[16] Second, Mooney asked respondents for "names and addresses of any individuals of pure or mixed Indian blood in your vicinity, and state to what tribes they belong." This question reflected common preoccupations with the notion of pure blood among Indian communities and individuals. Mooney's third query was about "Indian remains ... including mounds, graves, town-sites and shell heaps and Indian pictures and carvings."[17] Mooney's fourth question requested "names and addresses of any persons who may be able to give additional information."[18] With this questionnaire, Mooney intended to lay the groundwork for further efforts to find indigenous and mixed people in a region where few Native groups, other than the Lumbee in North Carolina, had received much official government recognition. Later, in summarizing his research, he noted that red-Black racial "admixture" had been at work; "it is in place to state that there is undoubtedly a considerable infusion of Indian blood among the negroes of the whole south Atlantic tidewater region."[19]

Mooney's methods and questions here reflected the state of the field of ethnography, including prevalent vocabularies of "blood." In his initial outreach, he would use local whites to try to locate Native contacts and informants. The first secretary of the Smithsonian, Joseph Henry, had a vision of the institution as a focal point for coordinating a network of scientifically minded correspondents who could report back to the Smithsonian their careful observations of a range of scientific issues to extend the Smithsonian's reach across the continent. Mooney's modest, nontechnical questionnaire about mid-Atlantic Indians echoed Joseph Henry's vision, presuming no special ethnographic expertise in respondents.[20] Probably most white recipients of Mooney's questionnaire were prominent enough to be considered elite. Judging by the number of medical doctors who responded, it may be that Mooney sought out physicians for his survey. But if Mooney relied on the testimony of local whites in preliminary planning of his work, he did not end his inquiries there.

Mooney's white respondents were generally cautious about recognizing Indian identities among non-reservation people. As noted in chapter 1, a Henrico County physician noted, "There are a few persons of mixed blood in my neighborhood, said to be of the Pamunkey Tribe. The best known of them is J. T. Pearman." This man, likely Jones Pearman, was the sole individual that doctor named as a potential source; "I do not know of any person likely to give any additional information."[21] One respondent (likely Dr. B. C. Harrison) named Ferdinand Wynne and A. Q. Franklin of New Kent County as people "of the Pamunkey tribe. very slight infusion of Indian blood."[22] E. C. Wynne, living near Williamsburg, responded to Mooney's question about present-day Indians this way: "only one near here Joseph P. Wynne Part negro and industrious black smith and accumulating but given to drink. One of the Pamaunkee tribe." At the other end of the social-class spectrum, E. C. Wynne mentioned as a possible source the wife of Dr. Charles Coleman of Williamsburg. Though Mrs. Coleman was "a niece of John Randolph who was a descendant of Pocahontas," Wynne did not name her among "individuals of pure or mixed Indian blood."[23] Cynthia B. T. Coleman of Williamsburg, in her reply to Mooney, referred only to "A tribe of Pamunkies" in response to Mooney's second question.[24] If she was Mrs. Charles Coleman, this may exemplify how elite Virginians proud to claim Pocahontas as an ancestor emphatically saw themselves as white, not mixed. A response from Buckingham County (west of Richmond) mentioned no present-day Indians except that "we have Bollings, Hubbards, and Eldridges all lineal descendants of Pocahontas in Buckingham."[25] A Norfolk respondent said, "There are, I understand many persons claiming Indian progenitors—such as the relatives of President Harrison."[26] For this respondent apparently it seemed safe to relegate "Indian" to the category of vanished "progenitors," to highlight elite whites with Powhatan ancestry. Impulses that later shaped the 1924 racial integrity law's "Pocahontas exception" seem at work here. A respondent from Amelia County, in south central Virginia, mentioned an elite family of "Indian descent," and then also noted, "There are some colored people formerly slaves who claim Indian kinship, and many of them rightly; but nothing definite in their history can be obtained."[27] Compared to the reticence of some respondents, this man was relatively more open to the idea of Native identities, or at least Indian ancestors, in both Black and white families.

Some responded to Mooney's question about "individuals of pure or mixed Indian blood" with simple "no" answers. A woman who lived across the James River from Charles City County reported, "There are no individuals of Indian blood in this vicinity," though "Many Indian Arrow points have been found around us, and we have in our Hall an Indian axe and hatchet picked up near our residence, of rude stones."[28] At that moment, the Chickahominy, across the James River from her in Charles City and New Kent Counties, had yet to create their modern formal organization. This woman's vision of Indians as long-gone people who made "rude" things signals how hard it might be for contemporary Virginia Natives to achieve such recognition.

Other responses were more nuanced. One respondent from near Lynchburg reported that in his vicinity there were "none [no Indians] worth the mention."[29] Given his conditioned, condescending denial, perhaps this person was aware of Monacan people in nearby Amherst and Bedford Counties who later caused Walter Plecker such anxiety. Like some other respondents, this individual mentioned stone and pottery artifacts as markers of the past presence and current absence of Indians; for him, recognition of archeological evidence of long-gone Natives was easier than acknowledging present-day Indian people. From Fairfax Court House, Mooney's queries elicited a response that "we have no pure Indians, some negroes claim to have Indian blood."[30] At least these Plecker-like denials, though dismissive, mentioned claims of Indianness among people of color.

Similarly, William B. Shands of Southampton County cited the breaking-up of Nottoway tribal lands in his southeastern part of Virginia "a few years since." He explained, "There are no pure blooded indians" at least in part because historically some Indian women "formed connections with negroes and others." Thus, he acknowledged mixed Nottoway people in the area, while suggesting that the Nottoway as a social or ethnic body no longer existed. Shands subscribed to the narrative that "these prehistoric races are passing away ... is not this the history of all the continents the higher races coming to drive out the lower and bring a higher civilization."[31] (Virginia formally recognized two Nottoway groups as Indian people in 2010.)

Even white respondents who acknowledged the social and political position of Mattaponi and Pamunkey people living on reservation lands hedged about their reservation neighbors' Indianness. A King William County respondent said, "Indian Town on the Pamunkey is quite a settlement of mixed blood.... There is also a settlement on the Mattapony, but very few are left."[32] A man from neighboring King and Queen County described those reservation communities this way: "The Indians are not pure & some shew but little traces of Indian blood. They elect their chiefs." Rather than referring Mooney to those chiefs, he mentioned some elite white Virginians as possible sources of "correct" information.[33] S. F. Harwood, another King and Queen County respondent, similarly said about the "remnant" of the Mattaponi people, "They have dwindled to a small number now, mostly by removals, and those that remain are right much mixed with negro and white." Harwood reported that the minister Dalrymple (mentioned earlier) "had a number of pieces of pottery made by the Mattapony Indians," in order to "ascertain whether the component parts were the same as that in the pottery found in the Western Mounds & He told me afterwards that it was."[34] Harwood showed somewhat more openness about the question of Indian identity than some other white respondents to Mooney's questionnaire, but he cited links to a misty pan-Indian continent-wide pre-Columbian past in doing so.

W. A. Bradby replied to Mooney's questions as chief of the Pamunkey. Bradby's response seems calculated not only to answer Mooney's questions, but also to introduce Mooney to the Pamunkey as a people with a distinctive Native economic and political base. He remarked that the "Indian Town" people relied largely on "hunting and fishing for a living," that they had their own chief, council, and trustees, and that they made and enforced their own laws. Bradby's response sometimes referred to his group in the third person, and at other times he used first-person "we," "us" or "I." This may reflect his experience of the difficulties of representing the Pamunkey to someone from a larger society that questioned his community's legitimacy. Perhaps Bradby was also positioning himself as someone competent to look at the community simultaneously from the outside and the inside. If so, perhaps there is here some kind of "two-ness" of vision, a variation on what W. E. B. Du Bois described as one response to a racialized position from which you face the question "How does it feel to be a problem?" In contrast to white respondents who mentioned arrowheads and other archeological evidence of ancient Indian occupation, Bradby's reply to Mooney's question about "Indian remains" such as mounds, graves, and town sites was simply, "All of those have disappeared from us."[35]

Mooney and his BAE colleague Albert Gatschet followed the survey effort by visiting tidewater Native people to do fieldwork. Some responses to Mooney's questionnaire had implied that being of racially mixed ancestry diluted claims to Indian identity. Mooney seems to have begun his fieldwork assuming admixture. Once in Virginia, though, he heard Native informants' perspectives.[36]

Mooney made visits to the tidewater in 1899 and 1901.[37] Right after his 1899 trip, Mooney wrote back to the bureau about the Pamunkey: "I was surprised to find them so Indian, the Indian blood being probably nearly ¾, the rest white, with a strain of negro. Some would pass unquestioned in any western tribe." For Mooney, a real Indian appearance involved images from west of the Mississippi and the notion of blood quantum. Yet Mooney also mentioned other markers of Indian identity. The Pamunkey, he noted, "have their own chiefs & tribal organization, and also an Indian dance society.... They are entirely Indian in feeling, altho native arts (except a little pottery), dress & language have entirely disappeared." While on his 1899 trip, Mooney mentioned "three bands of Powhatan Indians living in that neighborhood," the Pamunkey, Mattaponi, and Chickahominy. The Pamunkey told him of Nansemonds and Accomacs (on the southside of the James River and the Eastern Shore, respectively), affirming the Indianness of those groups. Mooney likely did not visit the nearby Chickahominy on the outbound leg of this trip, but Pamunkey informants told him the Chickahominy group was probably almost as large as the Pamunkey community.[38]

Mooney thus looked beyond the reservation groups as he sought to identify Native people in the tidewater and to describe what made them Indian. He corresponded with a man prominent among the Nansemond of Norfolk County, south of the James River, in 1899. Here again, Mooney used prominent whites in his search for contacts; the Norfolk County clerk was his source for the address of Augustus Bass. After Bass replied to him, Mooney visited the Nansemond.[39] He did this despite the fact that Bass painted a picture of a community who paid taxes like other citizens, supported themselves chiefly by farming, did not remember the "old language," and did not make "Indian pottery." Bass described the Nansemond as "our Tribe," though at that moment, they had "no organization with chief." They had a church, but its preacher was white. Bass told Mooney that Nansemond children received schooling supported by the county financially "as other white schools," that the school was "Indian school, No 9 of Norfolk Co" and had an "Indian teacher." Bass was eager for Mooney to provide information about, or facilitate contacts with, any of "my Kins People." He asked the names of tribes that Mooney had visited.[40] Bass's hunger to connect with other Virginia Natives shows that Frank Speck's later efforts to facilitate intergroup connections addressed a need already felt among tidewater Indians.

Later, in writing about his field visits, Mooney noted that responses to his questionnaire pointed to the existence of "unorganized" groups in addition to the reservation people, and that his visits in 1899 and 1901 confirmed this: "resulting in the discovery that not only the Pamunkey and Mattapony, but also the ancient Chickahominy and Nansemond, were still represented by several hundred mixed-bloods. Smaller groups of the same mixed pedigree were also heard of, but not visited. In all of these bands the blood of three races is commingled, with the Indian blood sufficiently preponderating to give stamp to the physiognomy and hair characteristic. It is probable that from intermarriage nearly the same mixture is in all alike." Echoing his 1899 letter, Mooney wrote that some of these people looked like "ordinary negroes," some looked white and "a few families and individuals might pass as full-blood Indians in any western tribe." He noted: "Notwithstanding the large percentage of negro blood, the Indian race feeling is strong. [crossed out here in Mooney's notes on his manuscript is "and the color line strictly drawn"] This is largely due, according to their own statement, to the fact that intermixture was frequently forced upon them in the old days, with the deliberate purpose of claiming their children for slavery. Their one great dread is that their wasted numbers may lose their identity by absorption in the black race, and against this they have struggled for a full century." Mooney added that "intermarriage with the negro race is now forbidden by Pamunkey law and frowned upon in the other bands."[41]

Mooney also heard about the people who later organized as the Upper Mattaponi and Rappahannock, describing them as "small groups or detached families of mixed-blood stock of the same Powhatan origins."[42] Though Mooney used this language of "blood," historical "admixture" for him did not necessarily completely invalidate the claims of these not-yet organized people to Powhatan ancestry and "Indian race feeling."

Albert Gatschet also looked at non-reservation groups as well as reservation people. He got wind of a group related to the Pamunkey who were identified to him as "Cumberland" Indians. These may have been people Helen Rountree has called the "New Kent County fringe," which included families and individuals related to Ferdinand Wynn and Lucy Pearman Scott, focal points of chapter 1.[43] In 1890, Gatschet visited what he called "three of their remnants" in New Kent County with William Terrill Bradby.[44] Perhaps he met some of Lucy Pearman Scott's descendants on that occasion.

Like Mooney, Gatschet placed some emphasis on physical appearance and his assumptions about how real Indians looked, in assessing racialized identities. Gatschet's visits to Virginia produced his assessment that the Chickahominy "stick hard together; show Indian blood better than Pamunkeys." To Gatschet's eye, the reservation "Women look more like Indians than men and are lean; they have a yellow complexion going into the olive color. Men have thick heads, receding foreheads and some look mulatto-like or negroish."[45]

Gatschet's papers include an 1890 newspaper piece annotated "written by 'Dora,' from correspondence sent by Albert S. Gatschet in November, 1890." That piece echoed Gatschet's description of the appearance of the reservation people, and it reflected whites' notions about the superiority of whites' domestic arrangements. Of the Pamunkey, the article reported: "They have so long been civilized that they have utterly forgotten their own language . . . and in religion they are Baptists. They have comfortable homes, dress neatly and have acquired most of the habits and customs of the whites." Readers of this piece learned that despite their adoption of whites' "habits and customs," the Pamunkey remained a distinctive people in appearance and in their ways of making a living: "These Indians are industrious but more in their own than the white man's ways. They like to fish with the seine, trap and hunt, and prefer the uncertain income from these sports, and the manifold exposures to life and health, to the steady occupation of husbandry."[46] Thus, this article echoed whites' centuries-long preoccupation with assimilation of Indian peoples to whites' agricultural and economic habits and systems.

Gatschet and Mooney both looked for linguistic material. Mooney's informants reported of the Chickahominy that "one old man who died among them last year had a good (?) knowledge of the old language, & his son is believed to know some words."[47] Note Mooney's question mark here. Later, Mooney wrote, "According to the statements of several persons of middle age, their parents some fifty years ago had conversational knowledge of the old language." Mooney expressed some skepticism about that, for he found only one older man, "Wm.

W. Weaver, a Nansemond," who had any Native-language vocabulary.[48] In the end, Mooney's conclusions about Powhatan language survivals were pessimistic. In earlier stages of his work, he had been more excited about the potential for linguistic survivals, as in a letter he wrote to Gatschet in 1887: "I thought you would be surprised, as I was, to learn that there were Pamunkies among the Catawbas. They are all descendants of a single man.... Most of these Pamunkies or 'Pamunks' followed some Mormon missionaries to Utah this spring—possibly partly owing to the unfriendliness of the Catawbas.... It is possible that a few words of Powhatan's language are still remembered at Salt Lake."[49]

As they lamented the loss of Algonquian language skills among Virginia Indians, they searched diligently for surviving scraps of words. Albert Gatschet's notebooks include listings of Native vocabulary drawn from published seventeenth-century English accounts of Virginia, as well as a handful of "Pamunkey dialect" words collected by the Reverend Mr. Dalrymple in 1844.[50] In 1892, Gatschet reported on the progress of his "office work" that "the remnants [penciled in, above "remains"] of the Virginian or Powhatan language ["that are known" is penciled in here] were also made accessible by carding the terms."[51] Gatschet perhaps thought that if sufficient pieces of Algonquian vocabulary "remnants"could be collected and indexed, larger patterns might emerge, but he also saw limits to linguistic research among the tidewater Virginian Indians.

In 1940 came a coda to the story of Gatschet's and Dalrymple's linguistic efforts. That year, John R. Swanton at the Smithsonian Institution received a letter from Raphael Semmes of the Maryland Historical Society. The society had acquired a manuscript that "once belonged to Edwin A. Dalrymple" of Virginia, in which the minister "has the meaning of a number of Indian words which were in 1844 'collected from the Indians on the Pamunkey River, King William county, communicated by Molly Holt and Roda Arnold.'" Swanton passed this inquiry along to Frank Speck, a student of Algonquian dialects, who wrote back that except for one word, "The others are a counting-out rhyme used in a game. How funny to find this worked into an actual glossary."[52]

After the flurry of interest manifested by Mooney and Gatschet in the 1880s and 1890s, Smithsonian involvement with Powhatan groups was limited for several decades. Still, into the 1970s, the organized tidewater Virginia Native groups apparently considered the Smithsonian an important repository where placing objects and papers would help affirm their Indianness. For example, in 1943 the Chickahominy chief donated to the BAE material that included copies of papers such as birth certificates documenting instances in which white officials had accepted Chickahominy assertions of Indian identity, including testimony about the Indianness of the Chickahominy from the white minister P. E. Throckmorton noted in chapter 3. In sending these copies, O. Oliver Adkins wrote, "These may be helpful in establishing proof as to our identity as American Indians, and also prove to you our social separateness from the colored race."[53] For Adkins at that moment, those two things were conjoined.

The work of Mooney and Gatschet likely encouraged the Pamunkey as they sought more recognition of their Native American identities.[54] Nonetheless, Mooney and Gatschet's approach seems a mixed blessing. From whites' perspectives, Native people who had not retained tribal lands, languages, tribal organization and other traditional ways frequently "were reduced to the status of 'descendants of Indians'—granted the racial attribution but denied the culture."[55] Mooney and Gatschet affirmed the Indianness of the Powhatan groups they studied, but they also positioned tidewater Indians as racially mixed people who had lost important aspects of traditional Indian cultures. Rather than seeing these tidewater Virginian Indians as communities evolving historically just as white communities do, Mooney and Gatschet saw them as compromised biologically, racially, and culturally.

Frank Speck and Powhatan Peoples

Frank Gouldsmith Speck (1881–1950) was the next major white ethnographer active among tidewater Powhatan groups on reservation lands and among non-reservation people. Speck did his research and collecting at a time of ferment in pan-Indian and intertribal cultural and political connections. Despite that ferment, primitivist notions about Indianness and ideas about vanishing Indian cultures were common among whites. In that setting, what could an early twentieth-century anthropologist accomplish by working with marginalized not-white and not-Black Southern communities facing Jim Crow discrimination? Frank Speck's fieldwork in Virginia aided Powhatan groups representing their claims to a past and a social and cultural identity that was not Black, white, or somehow mixed. Speck encouraged varied Powhatan groups to organize and work together. Sometimes Speck spoke of his fieldwork as reconstruction and/or unearthing lost bits of traditional cultures. Practitioners of such "salvage" ethnography are vulnerable to criticism that they help fabricate invented new traditions for indigenous groups. Here, I argue for appreciating Speck's work in light of his commitment to studying and engaging the political situations of eastern Native Americans rather than the western tribes who attracted many white ethnographers.[56]

On his death in 1950, a colleague praised Speck for his choice "to concentrate on languages and cultures which were nearing extinction."[57] Viewed in that context, Speck's ideas about salvage ethnography and building bridges between Native groups look constructive. Speck sometimes bogged down in the search for what he could label as pure survivals of precontact cultural traits and material culture. (He saw some cultures as more "complex" than others.[58]) Still, he took seriously the history of cultural borrowings and advocated for new intertribal connections among Algonquian groups. Speck could see cultures and communities as ongoing works-in-progress. Influenced by Franz Boas, his interests in borrowing and diffusion of cultural traits kept him from focusing exclusively on precontact aspects of the communities he encountered.

Like Mooney and Gatschet, Speck felt as a serious gap and loss the lack of Algonquian language skills among Virginian tidewater Indians. Speck's personal ethnological interests and his training embraced linguistics. Over time, he worked with a wide range of Algonquian-speaking groups. It seems likely that Speck's long-term work and experience with Algonquian languages were a major source of the sense of authority that he brought to his Virginia fieldwork and his relations with Powhatan people.[59]

Three areas seem especially fruitful to examine here: Speck's views of cultural change, racialized identities, and folkloric tradition among tidewater Virginia Indians; his approaches to collecting and his interest in material culture; and his advocacy as he lent support his Virginia informants' assertions of their indigeneity.

Speck had already displayed his interest in cultural change, Native identities, and folklore in the Jim Crow South back in 1911 when he began working among the Nanticoke people in Delaware, shortly before he ventured into tidewater Virginia. He was aware that some white officials contested the recognition of such mid-Atlantic groups as Indian rather than mixed-blood, colored, mulatto or Black.[60] He did not spend long periods of time in Virginia, and his scholarly work took him to many other places. Still, into the 1940s, he continued to bring and send students to tidewater Virginia communities, and to write letters in support of Virginia Native groups and to advocate acceptance of their identities as Native Americans.

In his approach to cultural change, continuity, and loss, Speck felt urgency about gathering information about what he considered aboriginal culture that could be remembered and perhaps resurrected. But his fieldwork also embraced a broad range of data related to the present-day lives of his informants, including material culture and folklore. Speck's Boasian training in ideas about cultural change—especially how cultural traits spread and get shared—gave him a platform for seeing Algonquian Powhatan culture as involved in broad pre-1492 patterns of exchange between Algonquian groups and other Native Americans of the Southeast and the Gulf area. He acknowledged the complexities of regional cultural and trade relationships. He wrote, for example, that in attempting to describe culture-area boundaries, scholars could find groups who shared material, cultural, and social traits, even though they did not share a language.[61]

In his fieldwork among contemporary Powhatan groups, Speck also acknowledged processes of postcontact cultural change. His intent was "to deepen the existing knowledge of ethnic properties of a people early transformed from their original native estate by ruinous association with Europeans; also to place their culture group on the map of ethnological comparisons in the East—nothing more. In days to come, when living sources open for investigation are absolutely closed, the real intensive study of this area, once rich in development, will be made."[62] This may be read as a modest Boasian statement about the primacy of fieldwork to gather ethnographic data first; theorizing could be done later. He apparently felt that once a specific generation of bearers of older traditions died, the remaining members of the community would lose a vital link to their past, and anthropologists would lose opportunities to collect data about a time when communities still practiced out of connections to that "original native estate." The popular notion of Indians as vanishing peoples lurks behind the idea that opportunities to speak with crucial "living sources" would someday be "absolutely closed." The concept that Indian cultures were "transformed . . . by ruinous association with Europeans," if not dying, added to Speck's sense of urgency about fieldwork. This meant that in tidewater Virginia, he saw himself doing salvage ethnography, collecting and protecting remnants and fragments wherever he could, in service to "much-diluted" tidewater Indian communities headed for irreparable cultural losses.

Still, Speck also saw that Native American cultures were not static, timeless monoliths but rather sites of ongoing, complex processes of cultural exchange. In other southern fieldwork, Speck showed some flexibility in this area. His 1934 *Catawba Texts* gathered and translated stories from a few Catawba informants in the Carolinas. He presented these stories without emphasizing whether their origins predated European contact. Perhaps this was partly because in that project he was most interested in Catawba language traditions.[63] His published monographs on Virginia's Powhatan groups devote much space to uncovering "survivals" traceable to pre-European-contact life. But as a student of Boas, Speck sought to record lots of data, and that included information that he did not analyze solely in terms of whether it reflected pre-contact culture. If Speck was not entirely free of prevalent ideas about Indian cultures as bound for extinction, he did explore Native communities as places that remained Indian spaces through centuries of cultural change.[64]

In the southern setting of his Chesapeake-area fieldwork, Speck saw that indigenous peoples, by their existence, challenged the idea of race as a Black-white color line. He wrote of Virginia's Powhatan groups:

> Very little attention has been paid to them by writers, whether ethnologists, historians, or folklorists. Some indeed have even assumed to deny their existence under the implication of there being no longer pure-blood Indians among them. Elimination, however, on this ground would involve a maze of controversy, for it would mean that many existing Indian groups all over North, Central, and South America, maintaining active tribal tradition, even government, would be consigned to the anomaly of classification as "whites" or "colored people." Nevertheless, the Powhatan descendants persist within the confines of their ancient territory despite the efforts to crush them that began in 1608, and which, after reaching a climax during Bacon's Rebellion in 1676, have continued to menace them, though with declining force, until the present time.[65]

Speck here acknowledged that many established indigenous groups throughout the hemisphere were mixed if judged by a standard of blood purity. He was suggesting other standards: "active tribal tradition," political organization, and persistent presence on ancient homelands. He thereby raised questions about what constitutes an ethnic group and about the history of cultural sharing and race mixing in the Americas. Of Powhatan groups, he believed that "for the whole region there is need of actual exploration of their industrial, social, and folkloristic properties. It will reveal much that will elucidate the principles of race-and culture-blending among American folk-communities." He used the word "survivals," suggesting some longing for a story in which some remnants remained unchanged as pure reflections of some distant past.[66] But Speck also embraced "active tribal tradition" and the study of cultural and social blending. He mentioned race in the same breath with "folkloristic properties" and "culture blending among American folk-communities," suggesting his understanding that ethnic/racial boundaries could be fluid, despite Virginia's Jim Crow regime. Speck saw the need to analyze race and ethnicity as complex ongoing processes embedded in specific historical contexts.[67]

Like his teacher Franz Boas, Speck did not entirely discount the possibilities of studying biological traits in attempting to understand human activities and personalities. But also like Boas, he saw that culture matters greatly, and racial labeling of individuals based upon visual, physical, characteristics could be dubious.[68] His 1915 monograph on the Nanticoke, in southern Delaware, devoted some attention to physical appearance. "Physically the community exhibits a great lack of racial homogeneity, the types of physiognomy, color, and hair ranging from the European, the mulatto, and the Indian through all the usual gradations." Speck recorded Nanticoke traditions of "Moorish" ancestors, and he also reported that the Nanticoke community of his day "refuses particularly to recognize marriage with negroes."[69] If a search for racial homogeneity could seem fruitless to Speck, he could not ignore the politics of that concept. About the Rappahannock, in 1925 Speck wrote that they had "neither indulged in nor permitted intermarriage with representatives of the other peoples surrounding them for almost a century—drastic homogamy to compensate for earlier laxity." He framed that discussion by pointing out the futility of attempting to prove "pure Indian blood" over the "potential two thousand ancestors that each would have had in the eleven generations elapsed since their first contact with the races of the Old World." Still, Speck's use of the word "laxity" invites critique: historic traditions of openness among Indian communities to new members may be viewed as socially and culturally productive, not "lax." Speck noted "variability" in physical appearance among the Rappahannock but stressed that the overall impression is of "the predominance of Indian blood." In this, Speck affirmed the importance of physical appearance—but he also reassured readers about his authoritative judgment that, despite variations in indigenous bodies, the community was *really* Indian. Speck's monographs on Rappahannocks, other Powhatan groups, and Nanticokes are larded with portrait photographs perhaps intended to demonstrate visually a "predominance of Indian blood." Yet Speck also downplayed physical appearance when he wrote, "These racial considerations are entirely aside from the determination of their social tradition."[70]

In writing about his fieldwork in Virginia, Speck did not engage in in-depth examination of, or extended speculation about, cultural influences flowing between African and Native American groups. He acknowledged the significance of diffusion of cultural traits from one Native group to another, but he devoted less attention to cultural sharing between African Americans and indigenous Americans. In one article about the "Southeastern Algonkian" he did judge that in general, "Even though a fairly large body of folk-lore and superstition remains among the Indian descendants, there is nothing ethnically distinctive about it.

Animal tales and some personal narratives of European and negro extraction, locally adapted to the condition of recent Indian life in the region, are all that we now have to represent the oral tradition of this area."[71] Speck here was perhaps disappointed in a lack of distinctively Indian material in "folk-lore and superstition," rather than fascinated by cultural borrowings across racialized lines.

Maybe Speck's relative reticence in this area had two sources, one political and the other more personal and professional. He knew that talking of their connections with African Americans was politically risky for tidewater Indians threatened by whites who saw them as mulattoes, colored or mixed people.[72] Perhaps he was reluctant fully to explore African American cultural influences so as not to cloud ongoing efforts of Indian communities fighting to assert their Native identities in the face of official repression. Speck's relatively small interest in cultural exchanges involving African Americans possibly also stemmed from a feeling that his personal, proper realm of expertise was the study of Indians.

Since the 1960s, Frank Speck has been criticized on grounds that his "romantic enthusiasm for discovering traditional continuities ... ran afoul of the dictates of 'holism' and Boasian contextualism."[73] I argue that Speck embraced Boasian perspectives on processes of cultural change and did so in creative tension with ethnographic approaches that emphasized the study of single moments in time. Speck understood that Algonquian and other southeastern Native American groups had lengthy histories of cultural exchanges up and down the Eastern Seaboard. Even given his interest in "traditional continuities," Speck saw that cultural change can involve borrowing and usually does not stem from monolithic processes in which the new wipes out all that historically preceded it.

Perhaps this explains why he saw a legitimate role for himself in sharing with Powhatan people of Virginia cultural information from other Algonquian groups. Take for example Speck's activities among the Rappahannock, as described by his student Robert Sollenberger in 1940. Sollenberger's field notes recorded that Speck's Rappahannock informants retained the memory of a dance "acquired from contact with Nanticoke band (Ind. River, Del.) during Thanksgiving reunions of Powhatan Confed. groups annually through 1925–1935.... Dance introduced about 1922 to Nant. by Gabe Paul (Penob.) [presumably Penobscot] and FGS."[74]

Another scholar noted that "Speck, greatly impressed with the intense interest which the Nanticoke in Delaware exhibited towards their Indian heritage, taught his friends a number of Indian dances and songs, and assisted them in acquiring or making ceremonial costumes of a regionally correct style." C. A. Weslager wrote that Speck did not pretend that the results were "direct survivals of their

Nanticoke forbears," but Speck wanted to assist the community's self-conscious revival and presentation of Indianness.[75] In writing for scholarly audiences, Speck differentiated between "revivals" and "survivals." Of the Rappahannock he wrote, "Some folk-dances are performed by the people, but they are hardly to be considered as direct or continuous derivations from the past. Being revivals rather than survivals, as interesting as they are, their description may be left to a more popular narrative of Virginia Indian folk-ways."[76] So Speck did not discard the notion that unbroken transmissions from pre-European-contact eras signified authentic Indian cultures. Yet he also promoted what might be called inter-tribal approaches to resources for rebuilding Indian identities in the tidewater communities he studied. For Native Americans in need of tools for asserting their Indianness in a Jim Crow world, Speck approached the straitjacket of proving continuous tradition by talking about revivals and restoration, even as he still looked for unbroken links to an aboriginal past.

Speck's confidence in his own knowledge of deep-past Algonquian traditions was based on his fieldwork among Native groups from Labrador to Oklahoma. The anthropologist William N. Fenton wrote that when he and Speck were visiting Iroquoian groups in 1945, Speck bought a pair of raccoons at a local market. Speck brought the animals back to be cooked by the "Mohawk ladies" where he and Fenton were staying and asked them to save the animals' paws. Speck wanted to find out whether his Iroquoian hosts knew of a "game and method of divination practiced among Northern Algonquian hunters" that involved raccoon paws. At least one of the local Iroquois people knew of the practice, but to Fenton, as they played, "It was soon apparent that Speck was the one who knew the rules of the game."[77] Fenton suggested that this investigation led nowhere, but it indicates Speck's confidence in his role as a scholar and as a cultural teacher or broker.

Thus, given his widespread fieldwork among varied Indian groups, Speck seems to have seen himself as a legitimate agent of the diffusion of cultural information that responded to community needs. Speck apparently thought anthropologists could help informants retrieve and revive customs and memories that seemed on the verge of extinction. He also recognized that sometimes the contexts of those memories and that knowledge had radically changed. Speck's approach to material culture among the Powhatan groups embraced the search for evidence of precontact aboriginal traditions but was broader than that. He looked for a wide range of material culture and other information about hunting, fishing, farming, and cooking that were locally distinctive. Speck thought that some traditions and objects connected with hunting and fishing showed connections with precontact practices, but he also sought information about systems, practices, and material culture that could be regarded as distinctively Indian even if not derived from precontact tradition. And despite his interests in cultural distinctiveness, Speck did not always detail whether the customs and knowledge he was documenting were shared by neighboring non-Indian rural people.[78]

In writing about Native material culture in the Chesapeake region, Speck was particularly intrigued by hunting and fishing paraphernalia. This reflected Speck's long-term interest in hunting and its relationships to social structures and land use.[79] Speck's discussion of the material cultural of hunting placed it in broad contexts, geographical and temporal, as shown in his last published text on hunting and fishing among Virginia's Powhatan groups. The Rappahannock group's "rabbit hunt with throwing clubs" had captured Speck's attention when he brought graduate students to tidewater Virginia between 1940 and 1943. Speck wrote about the organization and conduct of communal hunts for rabbits among the Rappahannock people as described to him by an informant whose memories dated from the 1890s, and he linked the rabbit hunt to other Native groups of the Southeast. Some hunters carried guns, but Speck was particularly interested in those who hunted with the "Rappahannock throwing club," presumably because he thought it gave the hunt a more "Indian" aura.[80]

Based on field work between 1938 and 1943, Speck and his collaborator, Claude Schaeffer, wrote of the Pamunkey "communal" deer drive that the "persistence of the deer drive into modern times has made possible the recovery of many details of its organization and procedure." Acknowledging that the hunt changed over time, Speck and Schaeffer framed the Pamunkey deer drive as rooted in early reservation times but also reflecting "presumably . . . aboriginal customs persisting relatively unchanged in their essential features into modern times." Speck and Schaeffer tied the communal Pamunkey deer hunt to a historical narrative of tribute to Virginia's governor stretching back to 1677, calling it, "one of the outstanding events in the social cycle of the Pamunkey Reservation."[81]

To underscore the Pamunkey deer hunt's community-building aspects and its Indian qualities, Speck wrote, "The communal deer drive takes precedence over individual forms of hunting among the Pamunkey." (Sometimes he did not dwell on whether hunting practices of Virginia's Powhatan people were shared by their Black or white neighbors, but here he probably meant to emphasize contrasts with non-Native groups' hunting traditions.) He stressed aspects of the drive that showed Pamunkey concerns about sharing the fruits of this "cooperative endeavor" within the community. He added, perhaps to connect his story with contemporary anthropological interests in hunting and his own interest in change over time: "The theoretical conflict between individual and communal prerogatives represents, most likely, a late historic condition. It dates back, presumably, only to the 17th century when the Pamunkey abandoned their communal hunting grounds in the Piedmont in favor of lands within the present reservation boundary."[82]

Speck reported that Paul Miles, a former Pamunkey chief, painted a set of panels depicting the communal deer drive, panels that by 1950 were at the Denver Art Museum. Speck said this work had "no known connection with any continuous tradition of pictography within the group," calling Miles's work "fanciful." He compared it to designs on present-day Pamunkey pottery "made for the tourist trade" and adorned with "pictographic designs," some of which were "derived from printed sources." Yet Speck also called the Miles panels a "product of ethnic intuition of the individual who made it" and "one of the unformulated traits functioning in the recent culture of the reservation." What was the source of Miles's creativity in these paintings? Did Miles accept Speck's description of his "hunting score" as a "'sub-cultural' phenomenon"? Speck asked whether Miles's creation might have sprung from "some obliterated memory or whether it constituted a response more appealing to his tradition as an Indian than to record it in faulty English"? (Given that Miles surely spoke English from birth, the word "faulty" begs for context—perhaps it was a comment on the limits of educational opportunities then available to tidewater Natives. The 1930 census noted that Miles was literate; Miles wrote letters to Speck.) Speck linked these panels to Pamunkey work to promote their Powhatan identity. Rather than accepting them as works of art, though, Speck called the panels "a historically-mysterious and etiologically-unexplained functioning attribute of the topic we present."[83]

In contrast to Miles's innovative "pictographic tablet," Speck noted in passing that a pottery school began on the Pamunkey Reservation in 1932, while Miles was chief. Speck described its purposes not as strictly revivalistic or novel but rather as an effort "to preserve and develop tribal crafts." According to Speck, "pottery has never ceased as a craft in the industrial history of the Pamunkey."[84]

Theodore Stern, one of Speck's students, carried on Speck's interest in Pamunkey pottery. Like Speck, Stern took seriously questions about what he considered aboriginal. Also, like Speck, in a 1951 article on Pamunkey pottery-making, Stern framed his subject as a traditional practice but one that was not purely aboriginal and not static. Stern asserted that pottery was among the Pamunkey's areas of cultural continuity, "fundamentally unaffected by outside methods." But, at the same time, the pottery was "illustrative of some of the acculturational forces now at work." Stern made clear that he would look at change over time and at influences from historic contacts with the Catawba and European Americans. His study emphasized a distinction the Pamunkey made between "the 'old-type' or traditional, and the 'new' method, which is taught in the State-sponsored pottery school." Stern saw these two methods as linked, not as completely separate techniques (at least when the school-based program started in 1932), noting that he was "following the native classification." He made deprecatory comments about some developments in contemporary tourism-oriented wares, some of which used generically pan-Indian motifs. Still, he understood this art and craft as historic and traditional, not timeless: "The 'old-type' technique, which is the subject of the first part of this paper, is by no means purely aboriginal. It is rather the method followed as far back as the traditional memory of informants will go. Roughly, it may be considered as having been stable in practice from about the end of the eighteenth century to recent times."[85] So Stern acknowledged Speck's conception of the continuity of pottery-making among the Pamunkey while emphasizing that it had changed over time. Competition with mass-produced goods had led to a perceived decline after the Civil War, but by 1928 there was a revival with some Pamunkey production primarily for the tourist trade. If Frank Speck's interest, and then the hard times of the Great Depression, had helped spur that revival, it was "started by the Indians themselves."[86]

Stern noted white and Catawba influences on Pamunkey pottery forms but downplayed the possibility that the Pamunkey borrowed from African American pottery-making, writing, "The putative influence of the Negro upon the crafts of their Indian neighbors is difficult to assess today. . . . It seems implausible that the free Negro might have been a source of Africanisms in pottery making. . . . Finally, the Indian, traditionally at least, has chosen to remain aloof from Negro contact." Only in a later monograph on the Chickahominy did Stern acknowledge the long history of "intermarriages" of African Americans and Native people.[87]

Stern placed Pamunkey pottery-making among other distinctively Indian facets of Pamunkey community life, noting that the Pamunkey had a centuries-old reservation and "their own laws." He put the reservation clay deposits used for pottery in the context of tribal ownership of reservation lands. One informant told Stern that the site of the clay deposits used by the whole tribe at that time was communally owned, "as a natural resource it is public."[88] This might have reassured white readers that the Pamunkey were *really* Indians, connecting them to whites' assumptions about commonality and community among traditional Native cultures.

To further emphasize traditional roots, Stern also referred to archeological evidence in the form of older potsherds on Pamunkey lands and noted that Paul Miles had "gained much from the inspection of the surface sherds which occur over the reservation." Stern felt, "after close observation of informants, that [archeological] sherds have acted as a powerful stimulus, primarily with respect to remembered modes of decoration." This affirmed the roots of pottery-making on the reservation and also the legitimacy of revivals of such practices. Writing about one aspect of the processes of preparing the clay and its temper, Stern described Paul Miles in ways that echo Speck's comments about Miles as both a traditionalist and "an innovator within the limits of his conservatism." Though Stern, like Speck, did not completely shed the straitjacket of looking for the aboriginal, he observed and acknowledged change over time in both a historic "traditional" and the "aboriginal." [89]

Frank Speck himself took an interest in aspects of Pamunkey material culture besides pottery and hunting, sometimes tapping into stereotypes of Indianness. About Pamunkey uses of animal parts in clothing and personal ornament, he conjectured that the "dignified adaptation" of fur, feathers, and such within "full dress costume" was a "reflection, as we see it, of an older concept of rapport between the people and animals."[90] Speck ruminated about animals and natural cycles and the Pamunkey sense of time and rounds of daily and seasonal activity on the reservation: "Observations determined by the movements and habits of animals seem to be a marking point for time; inevitable in a people whose food habits are so dependent upon the successive runs of shad, of alewives, of catfish of perch." But even as he noted that nineteen clocks on the Pamunkey Reservation showed the "wrong" time, Speck also recognized that modern schools and labor off the reservation were present-day realities for the Pamunkey.[91]

Speck's emphasis on material culture extended to obtaining objects for museum collections, and he paid attention to available archeological evidence. He saw archeology as helpful for investigating cultural boundaries and the diffusion of cultural traits. His notes showed him speculating about cultural transmissions around the hemisphere—and using material culture, such as the use of gourds, as evidence.[92] Speck also thought about public displays and helped develop material to support a Pamunkey "Historical Museum Project."[93]

Speck's sense that some Algonquian groups were losing aspects of their culture spurred his work at collecting objects, in order to "salvage," to document what was "vanishing," to capture "the real thing." Speck used words like "deculturation," "revival" and "survival" in talking about tidewater Indian communities' cultural lives and responses to outside pressures, sometimes obscuring his understanding that Native presents and futures would be as dynamic, fluid, and adaptive as those of their non-Native neighbors. The line between a cultural revival and a survival could be fine; at least once Speck encouraged informants to produce replicas of objects that they no longer made for their own use. Speck was excited to find a Mattaponi woman who recalled, from her mother's time, techniques for weaving feathers into textiles. She and at least one other local woman made some featherwork objects. Although he called the results "poor but tangible evidences of the old art's provenience and partial character," Speck enthusiastically linked these objects to traditional uses of feathers among Native American groups not only in North America but also in Central and South America.[94]

Speck's interest in Virginia Indians led him to look beyond academic ethnographic concerns and material-culture traditions to address the politics of race in Virginia. He felt that he could help tidewater Natives in their ongoing organizational and political work. His monographs credited Powhatan groups with strategic initiative and adaptability in staging organizational "revivals." As he wrote, "The community groups have within the last decade awakened to a self-consciousness that is stimulated by the realization of prosperity acquired through labor and thrift.... Contact with other Indian bands, and education both at home and outside the state, have created the revival movement."[95] This may be read as an effort to reassure readers that tidewater Indian communities shared conventional middle-class values, while it also affirms the Indianness of their efforts. Speck sometimes seemed overly set upon his own authority, as when he presumed to name one of the organizing Powhatan groups. He said about that non-reservation group: "For this reason, I have chosen, after consultation with Mooney and Chief Cook, to refer to them henceforth as the Upper Mattaponi band."[96] But at other times, Speck sounded respect for political initiatives of the various Powhatan groups.

Speck sometimes depicted his role as helping to facilitate movement in organizational directions that Native groups had already chosen to pursue—even as he saw himself as authoritatively speaking about what was "authentically" Algonquian and playing the "conjuror." Anthony F. C. Wallace, one of Speck's students, visited the Nanticoke with Speck in the late 1940s. Wallace wrote that the Nanticoke already had a community organization that

> was exerting political pressure, with some success, to improve things educationally, and Speck gave direct aid and comfort in this effort. The field work itself also contributed indirectly to the goal of re-creating an Indian ethnic identity, by recapturing information about aboriginal culture from the

observation of contemporary practice, much of it more recognizably Indian to Speck than to the Nanticoke themselves. With his encyclopedic knowledge of eastern Algonquian cultures, Speck could ask questions about beliefs and behavior that were suggested by his familiarity with Abenaki, Delaware, Penobscot, Pamunkey, and Montagnais-Naskapi hunting, trapping, and fishing practices.[97]

Wallace's comments raise the question of the validity of assuming, as an anthropological or historical technique, that contemporary practices were also characteristic of the past ("upstreaming"). But they also suggest Speck's regard for the political and cultural aspirations of the Nanticoke. Speck played a role in an effort by the Nanticoke of Delaware to reincorporate in the 1920s. As one scholar saw it, that effort began when a Nanticoke leader talked with Speck about how "to preserve the racial integrity of the community." For a time Speck acted as "spokesman and counselor; after representatives from the community agreed to the formation of an independent organization Speck turned the matter over to the newly elected officials."[98] Paul Miles, the Pamunkey leader, thought Speck could help develop a consensus among the non-reservation Upper Mattaponi (Adamstown) group for some form of formal organization, and it is clear that Miles was at work on this, too.[99] Speck encouraged the Rappahannock and Upper Mattaponi, and those communities ultimately built their own organizations.[100] The earlier work of Mooney and Gatschet, after all, shows that some non-reservation tidewater Powhatan groups had already made themselves publicly identifiable, and the Chickahominy had built a tribal organization before Speck arrived in the tidewater.

Given the political situation of the tidewater groups, Speck did not limit himself to publishing monographs and encouraging Native people's organizing efforts. He also directly addressed non-Indian individuals and audiences who were not likely to read his scholarly work. In 1940, when much of his fieldwork in Virginia was behind him—he was about fifty-nine years old—Speck was on the program for the annual meeting of the Virginia Conference of Social Work, to talk about "The Ethnology of Virginia Indians" in a session on "Race and Culture." The program listed that session adjacent to one led by John Powell, an advocate of Virginia's 1924 Act to Preserve Racial Integrity and adversary of indigenous Virginians. Speck's connections with tidewater Native communities were apparent when he sent a copy of the meeting program to Chief J. H. Johnson. Johnson wrote back "it gave me over joy to know John Powell who fought us so hard in VA. heard you speak for us."[101] E. P. Bradby, a Chickahominy leader, knew that Speck would be interested in hearing not only about older hunting practices, but also about legislative activity in Richmond related to the legal recognition of Virginia's Indians in the 1940s.[102]

Speck corresponded with white educators and lawyers to support tidewater Natives as they asserted their cultural identities and articulated their political needs to Virginia officials. In 1939, for example, he exchanged letters with Virginia's state supervisor of Trade and Industrial Education about the idea that an "Indian" should be involved in efforts on the Pamunkey reservation to teach "Indian arts and crafts."[103] When some members of Virginia's tidewater Native groups resisted being categorized as African Americans for draft purposes during World War II, Speck wrote to John Collier, head of the Bureau of Indian Affairs, and others on behalf of Native draftees. He sought advice from a Virginia lawyer in support of one such man, Oliver Fortune, who had been imprisoned because of this issue.[104] Speck also reached out to the Bureau of American Ethnology at this time. Presumably referring to the selective service question, in 1943 Speck sent a letter to Matthew W. Stirling, head of the BAE, through J. Oliver Adkins, the Chickahominy chief. Emphasizing his personal commitment, Speck included an informal cover note: "Here is an official statement from me. You will understand the situation. I am only too glad to stand by the Inds. of Virginia in their time of need. It is now or never in the long history of political persecution. Some one has to defend their name and status."[105] In a formal letter to Stirling, Speck wrote that he would not go into "details of an argument over the matter with those who are arbitrarily trying to deprive the Indians of Virginia of their rights to classification as such" but he wanted to re-state his position:

> It is to the effect that the people, some thousand or fifteen hundred in number, of Indian blood in Virginia are in my estimation sufficiently justified historically, ethnologically and "racially" to be classed as Indians and to enjoy the privileges and distinction they deserve as a separate element in the population of the state.
>
> I base my assertion upon almost twenty-five years contact with the various ethnic groups in the intimate relation of a field ethnologist with the people who are the subject of research. My statement applies to all the 'tribes' or bands of the Tidewater Districts of Virginia. The publications which I have brought out establish the grounds upon which I found my statement. Were the same bands to reside in any of the northern, central or western states there would be little to distinguish them from tribal groups in those states. The questions of their historical identity, the ethnic

tradition and the social separateness are satisfactorily answered in the mind of anyone who knows these sources.

In short, I regard the effort being made at this time, perhaps more drastically than heretofore, to demote [sp?] them to the status of 'colored' people—whence ergo negroes, to be unjust, unnecessary, and deplorable. It is more than that in my judgement; it is vicious, smacking of 'racial agitation' and suppression of the liberties of self-determination of Americans; little short of Hitleresque!

I believe that there are enough friends at large in sympathy with Indian ideals and aspirations to make the fanatical prejudices of Dr. W. A. Plecker of Richmond and his supporters look not only ridiculous but socially nefarious, if they were made aware of the means resorted to in the course of the policy pursued to suppress and persecute the Indians of Virginia. And I have reason to know that there are a number of such friends of the Indian in Virginia itself.[106]

This letter showed Speck responding to, and advocating for, pressing political needs among Powhatan groups. It also manifested his conception of his own authority as a white anthropologist with "intimate" knowledge of Virginia Indians. As he vouched for the Indianness of groups he had studied, in effect Speck presumed to speak for those people; likely he saw that in this setting he had more credibility than those communities themselves. Like James Mooney before him, Speck compared tidewater Virginia Native groups with more widely recognized Indian groups in the American west, north, and midwest, but here Speck's comparison could hint at a general criticism of Jim Crow segregation as a violation of "self-determination."

Still, Speck invoked "social separateness" as one of the measures of the Indianness of the tidewater Powhatan groups. He did not write that by "separateness" he meant that those communities were abiding by racialized segregation as practiced in Virginia at that time. Perhaps he meant instead to refer to the kind of group cohesion that made it possible for any small group in the United States to survive as a distinctively indigenous community. His handwriting is not entirely clear, but he seems to have used the verb "demote" in this letter. The disadvantages of "colored" or "negro" status in Jim Crow Virginia were clear—but even given the segregation, disfranchisement and extralegal violence aimed at African Americans, an anthropologist in correspondence with an ethnographer colleague in 1943 could have been more subtle in using words such as "demote" to acknowledge Virginia's racialized hierarchy. Perhaps Speck simply meant that for non-Indians to impose on an indigenous individual *any* other status or identity was unjust. In referring to the "privileges and distinction" of a separate status, maybe Speck meant to frame this as a matter of self-determination, rather than emphasizing Virginia Indians' acceptance of Jim Crow strictures. Speck's reference to Hitler suggests awareness that opposition to Nazism was influencing American thinking about race and racism by that time. He put the word "racially" in quotation marks. At this moment, did he mean to critique the very idea of race as conceived by Virginia's white segregationists, or was his attack here limited to segregation only as it was practiced against Native people? Back in 1924, Speck had written, "Some of these bands are organized with incorporated charters, others are still tribal Indians on state reservations; the Pamunkey and Mattaponi. The Rappahannock, Chickahominy, Nansamund, Nanticoke, and Upper Mattaponi succeeded in reorganizing the 'Powhatan Confederacy' in 1923, in an attempt to hold together the various bands in the region as a body. The idea of racial segregation and reconstruction is growing among them and will probably develop into an advantageous local social movement."[107] Speck likely did not intend to endorse Jim Crow practices in 1924, but he could embrace certain forms of racial segregation as advantageous to Indians.

Speck's willingness to vouch for the Indianness of Powhatan people was politically useful for Virginia Indians, although there were moments when he aroused mistrust in some individuals within those groups.[108] While it seems tidewater Virginia Natives largely welcomed his advocacy, Speck's ethnographic work illustrated some problems in the use of pre-European-contact cultural links as a tool for evaluating and affirming *real* Indianness. Speck saw "survivals" of material culture, hunting and foodways as fragmentary: "Survivals, however, are not to be found collectively intact in any one tribal community. They have come down as separate parts, some here in one band, others there in another, according to irregular factors of persistence. In these traits appear combined the characters of sedentary Iroquois culture and those of the more nomadic Algonkian."[109] In this way, Speck positioned the anthropologist/ethnographer as the authority to describe and define a "whole" to which scattered extant "survivals" from varied groups had once belonged. To Speck, such survivals were among the grounds for claims of *real* Native American identities, even if they lay broken in fragments. Potentially, this emphasis on reassembly of separated parts could weaken Speck's argument that specific groups he studied be accepted as real Indians, if each group owned only shattered pieces of a larger puzzle. Perhaps that is why Speck also embraced ideas about cultural invention and reinvention, creativity and loss, diffusion, and retention—processes that entail selective borrowing, accommodations, rejections, and appropriations from other cultures. For marginalized or liminal groups, acceptance of what James Clifford has called "creolized 'interculture'" helps address problems inherent in rigid concepts of monolithic "continuous tradition and the unified self."[110]

Speck's student Theodore Stern continued Speck's work, as he studied the western Chickahominy group in the 1940s, initially at Speck's behest. Like Speck, he grappled with ideas about change over time and continuous tradition. Stern commented that Speck's initial research interests had included "the cultural divergency that had been inferred for the aboriginal Chickahominy from their resistance to the Powhatan kingdom," and also "those facets of survivals from the Indian past, the recording of traits that even today are in the process of disappearing." He suggested that Speck understood that "many features found in common among the tidewater bands and not shared with White or Negro neighbors" in the present could very well have been "modified in the course of time. Moreover, the interchange between bands during colonial times undoubtedly disseminated elements not shared aboriginally." Stern credited Speck's work as an influence on his own recognition that "the very considerable differences between the modern Chickahominy and their aboriginal ancestors could not be ignored, and as time went on this came increasingly to occupy a central position in our research.... It seemed that the studies already published on Indian elements retained by the remnant bands of Tidewater Virginia would gain from a systematic survey of the changing context in which they have appeared. Moreover, we were struck by the successful adaptation which the Western Chickahominy have made in the course of change."[111]

Stern indicated broad interest in the nature of cultural blending and synthesis among tidewater Virginia Indian communities, and awareness of the fluidity of Chickahominy "culture-history" as reflecting "a series of movements and combinations that have incorporated diverse tribal groups and outsiders, to produce a synthesis that cannot except upon the most careful inquiry be identified with the aboriginal namesake of the band." Stern also wrote that his informants, in staking out their own Indianness, cared little about the ethnographer's interest in "whether the ultimate source of this element or that is to be found in Europe or in aboriginal Virginia." He acknowledged that this made sense since "The blending of constituent features which characterizes a given way of life is far from the mechanical addition of traits. Traditional Chickahominy represented a culture that was both Indian and European commingled and transformed, and unlike either component." Stern perhaps overestimated the extent to which any given culture can be assumed to be tightly integrated and shared as a whole by all members of a community. He may also have overestimated how much his informants thought that their ancestors lived in a unitary culture. In this passage, too, he omitted mention of African Americans. Still, Stern's recognition of the importance of change over time seems to stem from his experiences face-to-face with Chickahominy individuals, and he explicitly acknowledged that Chickahominy culture of his day was at once both traditional and synthetic. He understood that previous work by ethnographers from Mooney to Speck, while focused on the traditional, was mindful that circumstances changed the context and meaning of traditional elements.[112]

Compared to Speck, Stern wrote in more detail about social structures in Chickahominy community- and family-building. He noted that a range of shared interests drew nineteenth-century Chickahominy people together, including "a consciousness of common tradition, and the bonds of kinship," and physical proximity fostered by developing Virginia road systems. Stern also wrote that among the methods of defining the Chickahominy community was the exclusion of individuals who married Black people, in acceptance of "the racial ranking of Virginian society." He acknowledged that this exclusion could result in family ties being "dropped" or "forgotten."[113] In short, Stern in some ways took a broader view of Indianness than Speck, while embracing and extending Speck's legacy.

Perhaps the most important aspect of Frank Speck's career and his influence on other ethnographers like Stern is his expectation that "tradition" can and will be constructively, creatively used (reframed, invented, reinvented, restored, and revived) by a community. Speck himself laid out the issues concisely. He acknowledged the reality of massive and sustained cultural change among Native American groups, just as other peoples around the world had experienced change "through the agency of Europeans." He argued that the resulting transformations should not be dismissed as "lacking in value and appeal." He wrote:

> Now comes an era of reconstruction since 1920. The descendants of the Powhatan groups, to avert obliteration of their names and racial tradition, have organized into corporate associations and proceeded along modern lines to carry on a social program for consolidation of their forces. It opens another phase of their history, hopeful in certain aspects, though impeded by recollections of recent social oppression, poverty, slander, and naïve ignorance of white diplomacy. Their desire to exist as smaller nationalities is behind the move. To revive the individuality of their Indian ancestry, they have resorted to grafting customs borrowed from alien Indian groups

upon their own denuded cultural framework. This accounts for the introduction of elements of costume, ceremony, and social pageantry met with in their modern tribal life and conspicuous in some of the illustrations of this paper. The critic regards it as degenerate ethnology; but it is not, except in technique: rather is it regenerate. Now at the final move they face the alternatives of losing hold completely and turning down and out in their endeavor, or, more happily, of struggling onward with revived vigor and purpose. The future student of American folk-communities of Indian descent will find here new tribes with new trait-complexes to analyze and interpret. These contributions represent some culture aspects of the humble groups now at a climax and turning point in their history.[114]

We can reject the notion of declension implied when Speck says that these groups were rebuilding from a "denuded cultural framework," and fret about what Speck meant by "racial tradition" and "slander" here. In the name of "consolidation" and to fight "oppression," Powhatan groups in Speck's time did exclude some people who did not reject their African American ancestors and family members in order to assert their indigeneity. Powhatan groups had engaged in varied processes for publicly affirming their Native identities decades before Speck arrived among them, and those processes continue to this day—so with the advantage of hindsight, Speck's language about the crises of his time as a "final move" seems melodramatic. Yet here Speck was talking about tidewater Indians' nationalistic aspirations and celebrating their persistence and creativity. He suggested that an ethnic, rather than racialized, discourse might be available to tidewater Indians when he refers to "American folk-communities." Speck was acknowledging that culture-building processes entail creation, re-creation, and cultural borrowing. As James Clifford has commented, "Twentieth century identities no longer presuppose continuous cultures or traditions. Everywhere individuals and groups improvise local performances from a (re)collected past, drawing from foreign media, symbols, and languages."[115]

Speck's usefulness to the tidewater Native communities he studied was probably greatest when he demonstrated awareness that Indian people, like other peoples, are continuously on the move culturally and socially and draw inspiration from many, varied sources. The vitality of such ongoing moves is evident today. Danielle Moretti-Langholtz has told the story of a 1990s reburial of historic tidewater Native human remains led by the Nansemond community, a repatriation held in the context of processes modeled under the federal Native American Graves Protection and Repatriation Act. Oliver Perry, a leader of the Nansemond, planned a 1997 public ceremony that included the use of eagle feathers, tobacco pouches, sage, sweet grass, a turtle shell, and references to the "sacred hoop." As Moretti-Langholtz described it, such symbols—some "borrowed, out of necessity, from other Indian cultures"—were assembled and used in ways meaningful to the event's Native American participants. This was not a ceremony geared to foster recognition of indigeneity by non-Natives using prepackaged pan-Indian signifiers.[116]

The work of James Mooney, Albert Gatschet, Frank Speck, and Speck's students among tidewater Virginia's Native American communities illuminates the political and social roles such cultural improvisations and borrowings can play, and the importance of respectful attention to what James Clifford calls "local narratives of cultural continuity and recovery."[117] Even when some of the work of early ethnographers among tidewater Native peoples reflected stereotyping, static conceptions of Indianness, tidewater organized Native groups skillfully made use of ethnographers' advocacy to serve their own political needs, while sometimes they also accepted racialized separation as a building block of their communities.

CHAPTER 5

The Aftermath of the Racial Integrity Law, 1930s to 1950s

IN 2005, ELMER DAVIS Adams of the Upper Mattaponi described the effects of Walter Plecker's campaign to enforce the racial integrity law: "You were embarrassed to be Indian because Plecker said if you're not White, you're Black."[1] Although he spoke of "embarrassment" in the past tense, his testimony indicated the lasting power of the Plecker era to shape memories among Native Virginians. Helen Rountree, an anthropologist and ethnohistorian who has long worked with Powhatan tidewater people, told of a Chickahominy woman who had requested a copy of her birth certificate, to discover that Walter Plecker's office, in line with a general practice of amending racial categories on birth records in his Bureau of Vital Statistics, had on the back of the certificate "written a statement about the racial label of her grandparents in the county marriage registers. She told me in 1976, 'You have no idea how embarrassing that is!'"[2] Rountree did not specify what her informant found "embarrassing." Likely this woman felt the injustice of knowing that Plecker's work threatened her power to define her own identity. Perhaps she also resented an official suggestion that she had African American ancestors. That notation by Plecker's office was probably a misrepresentation of historic records, but she found it painful, nonetheless.

To examine why Virginia Natives still speak with bitterness about the Plecker era is to explore how Indian Virginians for decades after the 1924–1930 legislative battles confronted Virginia's segregation regime as a threat to their communities and personal identities. Challenges to the Indianness of tidewater Native peoples came from state officials like Plecker, but also within federal programs such as the 1930 and 1940 censuses and the World War II draft, as indigenous Virginians were called to serve in a segregated military.

In response, organized tidewater Indian communities resisted in varied ways in the 1930s and through the 1950s. They continued their focus on separate Indian institutions such as churches and schools, which remained spaces for construction and protection of tidewater Native identities, intra-and intertribal connections, and alliances with some whites. As before 1930, building those community organizations sometimes entailed the exclusion of individuals whose ancestry—indigenous, Black, and white—was comparable to that of members of organized tidewater groups, but who were unwilling or not permitted to join those bodies. As before 1930, organized tidewater Indian groups did not generally, explicitly, argue against conceptions of race that whites used to justify segregation. In that era, such arguments would have had little chance of effecting change. Nonetheless, Indian positions outside the Black/white color line posed implicit threats to Jim Crow segregation.

Federal Censuses of 1930 and 1940

Walter Plecker's opposition to official recognition of Indianness in Virginia extended to the federal census. He contacted the U.S. Bureau of the Census in advance of the 1930 decennial count to press his case that no one born in Virginia could be a real Indian, and he also tried to influence the 1940 census.[3] Data on individuals in the modern federal census is protected from public scrutiny for decades after each decennial count, but the Census Bureau produced summaries of the numbers of people enumerated as Indians in each state and county, thus publicizing and recognizing Indian populations in Virginia, and thereby contradicting Plecker's stance. As a result, Plecker and tidewater Indians had interests in individuals' racial categorization in the census, even though individuals' personal census data would not be made public in that moment.

Census Bureau figures for Virginia Indians for 1930 and 1940 likely reflect Plecker's pressure, but there was not a consistent pattern of uniform reductions in the number of people federally categorized as Indians in Virginia. Census numbers for the total Indian population in the state dropped in 1930 compared to 1920, but they were still larger than in 1890, 1900, or 1910, likely because organized Native groups were becoming more experienced and assertive.[4] Also, as tables 1 and 2 show, the census count of Indians did not decrease in every tidewater county between 1920 and 1940.

The U.S. census, of course, is a federally directed effort that historically involved localized participation. Across the country, local census enumerators brought local knowledge to bear in applying census standards for blood quantum to Indians. My assumption is that generally Southern census enumerators applied official census categories for "color or race" in subjective ways, in support of local customs of Jim Crow segregation.[5]

That subjectivity was probably especially glaring to non-reservation Native people whose families reflected centuries of kinship among Blacks, whites, and

Indians. In 1850, the census recognized and documented "an extensive mulatto population . . . nationally."[6] Census officials sometimes wrote as if "mulatto" had a clear definition (as did Walter Plecker in the 1920s). Instructions to enumerators for the 1890 census defined not only "black" and "mulatto" but also "quadroon" and "octoroon" with blood-quantum fractions, but that attempt at precision seems a departure from previous and following years' instructions. It seems unlikely that, in practice, census enumerators applied the "M" or "Mu" code to individuals based upon precise, extended genealogical inquiries.[7] Many enumerators presumably shared common stereotypes about how an African American or an American Indian should look, and relied on their impressions of the appearance of the individual and family in question, and/or on their knowledge of community reputation and associations. As a result, as shown in chapter 1, some indigenous Virginians were called mulatto in federal censuses.

The census' approach to Indian identities at any given moment did not necessarily reflect tribal or BIA practices. In counting Indians, the federal census has historically used the idea of "blood quantum," and "full" or "mixed" blood, as well as "a subjective element of communal recognition; there was no 'one drop' rule for them [Indians]."[8] Those concepts also can shape individual tribes' standards for membership, but historically, census practices for designating Indianness did not always run on the same tracks as tribal processes for determining membership.

The situation in Virginia illuminates local and regional complications in these matters. In fights about Indianness and racial integrity in 1920s Virginia outlined in chapter 2, the "blood quantum" idea of Indian identity collided with a "one-drop rule" about what made someone African American. One drop of Indian blood did not necessarily make a person Native in Virginia, any more than it did in other parts of the United States. Community reputation and residence on a reservation were also among potential factors in establishing an Indian identity in Virginia, as in the rest of the nation. In Jim Crow Virginia, though, in promoting a one-drop notion of Black identity, Plecker and his allies intended to obliterate claims to Indian identity among Virginians; they only grudgingly conceded the legal Indianness of people on Virginia's two reservations.

Given this situation, one would expect racial categorization of Virginia Indians in federal decennial censuses to reflect struggles about the positions of Indians relative to Virginia's legal Black-white color line. Indeed, the published Bureau of the Census summary figures for people enumerated as Indians in Virginia between 1890 and 1930 fluctuated from census to census in some counties (see table 1).[9] Since the figures for Native people in individual counties are comparatively small, the departure of a few indigenous Virginians for other counties, cities, or states could cause a dramatic drop in the number of Indians in a given county. Still, ordinary demographic trends and geographic mobility were not the only factors that shaped decade-to-decade fluctuations in the county-by-county figures for Virginia Indians shown in tables 1 and 2. As demonstrated in chapter 1, an individual's racialized census designation could change from one census to the next, even if that individual had not moved from one county to another. Shifts over time in tallies of Indians in tables 1 and 2 reflect inconsistent application of racial census categories.

Table 1 shows that among rural Virginia counties, variations over time in the census' counts of people enumerated as Native Americans are striking in Amherst, Caroline, Charles City, King William, Lee, and New Kent Counties. (Amherst and Lee Counties are not in the tidewater and are outside the scope of this project.) In these six counties, those fluctuations reflect geographic mobility of Indian families, but the size of those shifts could result mainly from instabilities in application of the Census Bureau's categories for "color or race." Charles City, King William, and New Kent Counties were home to considerable reservation and non-reservation tidewater Indian families, and table 2 focuses on them. Both tables reflect the fact that the Census Bureau's racial codes were malleable and complicated. For the 1930 census, the Bureau dropped "mulatto" as a racial category, in effect telling enumerators that one drop of African American ancestry made someone Black ("Negro").[10] Shedding the mulatto designation may seem like jettisoning an antiquated, demeaning word, but it was also a rejection of mixed race as a general census category. However, for the 1930 count, even though "mulatto" was no longer a formal category, notions about mixed blood were still applied to Indian people.[11] The 1930 instructions to enumerators told them, "A person of mixed white and Indian blood should be returned as Indian, except where the percentage of Indian blood is very small or where he is regarded as a white person by those in the community where he lives." Then there was this wrinkle in the one-drop conception of Blackness: "A person of mixed Indian and Negro blood should be returned a Negro unless the Indian blood predominates and the status as an Indian is generally accepted in the community."[12] Thus, the 1930 instructions on individuals with both indigenous and Black ancestors tempered a one-drop notion of what made someone African American with old concepts about degrees of mixed blood applied to Native Americans. To be Indian rather than Black in the 1930 census records entailed two markers: a blood test and a community-reputation test.[13] In contrast, enumerators were told that one of those two tests, not necessarily both, determined how to categorize someone

TABLE 1. Federal Census Figures for Indians in Virginia Counties

County/city	1890	1900	1910	1920	1930
Amherst	-	-	7	304*	278*
Bedford				6	7
Bristol city	-	1	-		
Caroline	-	-	-	-	39*
Carroll	4	-	-		
Charles City	1	-	113	104*	132*
Chesterfield	-	-	1	8	-
Culpeper	1	-	-		
Dinwiddie	1	-	-		
Elizabeth City	111	108	-	3	-
Essex	1	-	-	-	11
Fredericksburg city	-	-	1		
Giles				9	7
Goochland	1	-	-		
Grayson	1	-	-		
Halifax				6	9
Hanover	3	24	-		
Henrico	3	-	-	49	3
King and Queen	4	-	-	-	19
King William	137	152	180	232*	203*
Lee	1	-	64	6	3
Mecklenberg				-	5
New Kent	10	1	112	39	11
Norfolk	43	52	37	4	7
Norfolk city				3	13
Northampton	1	-	-		
Pittsylvania	-	-	7	5	-

Portsmouth city	-	-	2	11	3
Prince George	8	8	-	1	-
Prince William	-	1	-		
Pulaski	1	-	-		
Richmond city	-	1	3	18	9
Roanoke	8	-	-	-	-
Southampton	3	-	-		
Staunton city	-	-	2		
Washington	6	6	7	1	-
Williamsburg city	-	-	2		
Wythe	-	-	1		
All Other Counties				15	20

NOTE: For 1890–1910, numbers are for Indians in counties, "for which one or more Indians were reported;" for 1920 and 1930, figures are for counties, "in which as many as many as five Indians were enumerated" (*denotes a total that "includes a number of Indians whose classification as Indians has been questioned.")

of white and Indian ancestry. This meant that, in the census, a good deal of white blood was required to make an Indian-white person white, while a good deal of Indian blood was necessary to make an Indian-Black person Native. Perhaps these instructions reflected perceptions about supposed advantages (stemming from federal treaty and trust obligations to federally recognized tribes) accruing to Native people on reservations or in Oklahoma.

Enumerators for 1930 were instructed that someone "of mixed white and Negro blood should be returned as Negro, no matter how small the percentage of Negro blood. Both black and mulatto persons are to be returned as Negroes, without distinction." The official guidance to enumerators in 1930 also provided that "any mixture of white and non-white should be reported according to the nonwhite parents. Mixtures of colored races should be reported according to the race of the father, except Negro-Indian."[14] In the case of a "Negro-Indian" person, there was an exception to the general reliance on the race of the male parent.

These 1930 instructions reflected notions about a hierarchy of races—whiteness being hardest to get in the census framework. In effect, the bureau treated whiteness as a quality to be closely guarded by a one-drop yardstick for Blackness.

Given the tone of the 1930 instructions to enumerators, one imagines that some Census Bureau officials were sympathetic to Walter Plecker's basic assumptions, when Plecker urged the Census Bureau to adopt his position that real Indians did not exist in Jim Crow Virginia.

A 1937 bureau report on the results of 1930 census manifested the resulting ambiguities. That report commented about fluctuations in the numbers in Indians in the county-by-county national tallies from censuses from 1890 to 1910: "Much of the scattered Indian population, particularly in the eastern States, is of a migratory nature and in counties with few Indians the numbers show a relatively wide fluctuation from census to census." Perhaps white census officials found explaining those fluctuations as "migratory" patterns more palatable than fully acknowledging that, "particularly in the eastern States," the census' racial designations of Native people could shift because of subjective judgments.[15] Indeed, that 1937 report described census designations of Indians and their fluctuations over the decades as a special case, because "the size of the Indian population depends entirely upon the attention paid to the enumeration of mixed bloods, and the interpretation of the term 'Indian' in the instructions to enumerators." Bureau officials seemingly considered "Indian" more ambiguous than other racialized categories. The 1937 report grappled with variations in totals of Indians for Oklahoma, South Dakota, and North Carolina between 1910 and 1930:

> In Oklahoma, it is obvious either that the enumeration of 1920 was at least 20,000 short, or that the enumerations of 1910 and 1930 included too many with only a slight trace of Indian blood in the Indian population. The enumeration in South Dakota in 1920 also appears to have counted as white at least 3,000 who were enumerated as Indians in 1910 and 1930. The rapid increase in the Indian population of North Carolina may be due in part to a more liberal acceptance of the claims of those who wish to be considered as Indians, but there is undoubtedly a true increase, as the proportion of children in this population is unusually high.[16]

The 1930 instructions to enumerators had cautioned that "in New Mexico, Arizona, and California, enumerators should take special care to differentiate between Mexican laborers and Indians. Some Mexican laborers may endeavor to pass themselves as Indians. Persons residing in the region should have no difficulty in differentiating between the two types."[17] If this constituted a sort of recognition of ambiguities in racialized designations, the bureau here promoted the notion that physical differences of racialized "types" of Indians and "Mexican laborers" would be apparent to local enumerators.

TABLE 2: Federal Census Figures for Indians in Charles City, King William, and New Kent Counties

County	1860	1870	1880	1890	1900	1910	1920	1930	1940
Charles City	0	0	0	1	0	113*	104*	132*	104
King William	0	117	4	137	152	180*	232*	203*	243
New Kent	1	15	8	10	1	112	39	11	73

NOTE: Numbers are for Indians in counties, "for which one or more Indians were reported" in the federal census for 1890–1910 and for counties, "in which as many as many as five Indians were enumerated" in the federal census for 1920 and 1930. Figures for 1860–1880 and 1940 are from the author's searches in the manuscript census.

How did such census practices shape racialized designations of Indians in Charles City, King William, and New Kent Counties? To summarize, the numerical trends in census data for those counties between 1860 and 1940, as shown in table 2, include a sudden plateau of numbers of Indians enumerated in Charles City County after 1900, with some reductions in 1920 and 1940.[18] In King William County, there was a dip in the number of individuals enumerated as Native in 1880 compared to the 1870 count; after that, those numbers rose, except in 1930. In New Kent County, there was a steep rise in 1910, losses in the 1920 and 1930 censuses compared to the 1910 figure, then an increase in 1940. Likely, these trends in general reflect the status of reservation people in King William as well as the increasing organizational experience of non-reservation people.

In Charles City County, figures for people officially categorized as Indian were minimal until the 1910 census. Between 1910 and 1940, the numbers for Indians surely reflect the 1901 formal organization of the Chickahominy, who were prominent in Charles City County. In 1910, when a significant number of Indian designations appeared in the Charles City County census for the first time, almost all were recorded on the special form for "Indian Population" with their tribal designation "Chickahominy."

To cite just one example of the malleability of racialized designations in Charles City County censuses: Carrie P. Adkins, her husband and children were enumerated in 1910 as Indians. In 1920, she was listed as Carrie P. Sweat, remarried to John J. Sweat. In that 1920 census, Carrie and the rest of the Sweat family were categorized "mulatto," including six of Carrie's children from her previous marriage—children who in 1910 had been listed as Indian.[19] The birth parents and biological inheritance of those children had not changed in 1920, but the head of their household had, and so had their racial identity in the census.[20]

The 1860 general population census for King William County, home of the Mattaponi and Pamunkey Reservation communities, listed no one as Indian, likely reflecting the Census Bureau's general lack of attention nationally to reservation Indians at that time. In the 1870 King William County census, though, some individuals who had been categorized as "mulatto" in 1860 were listed as "Indian." Enumerations of Indians in the county continued to pick up in 1890 and afterward, with a dip in 1930 that may reflect the influence of Plecker and his allies. However, the number of Indians enumerated in King William County rose again in 1940.

In New Kent County, as in Charles City County, Indian individuals received little census recognition until 1910. For 1860, what is remarkable is not the scarcity of Indian designations in the New Kent County census, but the fact that one person, William Cooper Langston, was enumerated as Indian (as noted in chapter 1.) In a departure from the typical pattern in which census enumerators gave Indian designations, if at all, to an entire family or household, the other members of Langston's household in 1860 were designated "mulatto," though their ages and shared surname suggest a nuclear family. In 1870, as shown in chapter 1, among the handful of people listed as Indians in New Kent County was the family of John Carman Wynn and Ann Eliza Wynn, Lucy Pearman Scott's daughter, who had been categorized as "mulatto" in 1860. In 1900, only one person in New Kent County was enumerated as an Indian: Lucy Pearman Scott's son, Macfarland Pearman. After a steep increase in 1910, the numbers of Indians reported in the New Kent County census dipped in 1920 and again in 1930 but rose in 1940 (whereas in Charles City County census designations of individuals as Indian stayed comparatively closer to the 1910 figures in 1920, 1930, and 1940). The only individuals listed as Indians in the 1930 census for New Kent County were eleven people in the household of Zorobabel Adkins, who in 1920 had been enumerated in Charles City County as "mulatto." Of the thirty-nine people listed as Indian in New Kent County in 1920, at least twenty-five were still living in the county in 1930 but were not coded as "Indian."[21] Their race had changed in the view of the census, though their ancestry and their county of residence remained constant. Some of those thirty-nine New Kent County Indians recognized in 1920 had simply left the county by 1930, including Ferdinand Wynn, who lived in Richmond in 1930, and Mariah and Edward Wynn. Mariah Canaday Wynn, a granddaughter of Jones Pearman (see him in chapter 1), had married Edward Wynn, a son of Ferdinand Wynn the younger and Rebecca

Stewart Wynn. By 1930, Mariah and Edward had moved to Youngstown, Ohio; there they and their children were again enumerated as Indians.

These fluctuations in enumerated Indians in those three tidewater Virginia counties reflect the Census Bureau's engagement with the color line as drawn in the South at that time. For example, the Census Bureau's 1937 report on the 1930 census complained, "In North Carolina, and also in many other areas, the proportion of Indians shown in the census of 1930 as of full blood is much too high. This is particularly true of those tribes in which there is a large Negro admixture."[22] The notion that having African American ancestors eroded Native identities was pervasive in federal as well as state programs.

In that 1937 report on the 1930 census, the Census Bureau qualified the totals for people recorded as Indians in four Virginia counties for 1910–1930 with this note: "Includes a number of persons whose classification as Indians has been questioned." The counties where the bureau thus called into question its own figures were Amherst, Caroline, Charles City, and King William.[23] This comment likely resulted from Walter Plecker's contacts with the bureau.[24]

In summarizing and reporting on the 1930 census, the bureau further eroded its recognition of Virginia Indians when it reduced the number of "stock and tribe" categories that had been used in summarizing the results of the 1910 census; "many of the smaller tribes were thrown together into groups of tribes." In its 1930 "stock and tribe" data on Virginia Indians, the bureau lumped together several groups to create a category of "Virginia-Carolina Indians," which the published 1937 report called "one of the most important" of those changes. This separated Virginia's Powhatan Indians from their former grouping with "Algonquian stock," with the note that "this group is of mixed and somewhat uncertain origin and in the 1930 classification is not included in any linguistic stock."[25] To tidewater Powhatan groups, this likely seemed an affront to their carefully cultivated representation of themselves as the heirs and true descendants of the Powhatan people whom the English famously encountered in colonizing Virginia in 1607, whose Algonquianness was unquestionable. This recategorization distanced tidewater Indians from a major, well-recognized indigenous linguistic grouping. Further, the bureau opined, "The returns showing 43.4 percent of Virginia-Carolina Indians as 'full-blood' may be ascribed either to ignorance of racial admixture or to a desire to conceal the fact of admixture from the enumerator."[26] This echoes Walter Plecker's arguments.

The bureau's 1937 report further commented on this as a national issue not confined to the Virginia-Carolina Indians, conceding that among Native peoples generally, "after generations of associations with other races, it would be exceedingly difficult to determine the degree of admixture of blood or even to determine whether or not there was any admixture of blood. Many Indians with a trace of white or Negro blood in their remote ancestry may not be aware of such admixture, or may not consider it important. Others may desire to conceal such admixture and to claim purity of blood."[27] The bureau thus in effect recognized that its standards for Indian blood were not necessarily meaningful to Native individuals, while it defended purity of blood as an important marker. The 1937 report suggested that for "the sociologist," figures on "admixture of blood" would be interesting as reflections of how Native communities constructed "full-blood Indian" identities, but implied that Indians' uses of criteria other than blood quantum were less objective and reliable than the bureau's assessments. Presumably, the bureau's position was that there was little need to acknowledge explicitly the sovereignty of federally recognized Native groups in setting their own standards of criteria of belonging, membership and Indianness in that segregated era.[28]

Instead, that 1937 report on the 1930 census, in discussing so-called purity of blood among Indians, asserted, "The admixture of white, and to a lesser extent, of the blood of Negroes and other races, is an important factor in breaking down tribal organization and characteristics." The bureau assumed that marriages across racialized lines generally had the effect of diluting Indianness: "An admixture of the blood of other races is usually accompanied by a breakdown of tribal customs, and by adoption, in whole or in part, of the habits and life of another race." This reflected assumptions among whites about Indians as vanishing peoples. At the same time, the bureau acknowledged that many freed people among the Choctaw, Creek, Cherokee, and Chickasaw continued after emancipation to live among those tribes, "speaking the Indian language and observing many tribal customs." With that, the bureau unintentionally qualified its blanket statement about the fragility of "tribal customs" in the face of "admixture."[29]

It does seem likely that in marking the Indian identities of some Virginia Natives as questionable in its 1937 published summary of 1930 census data, the Census Bureau was addressing Plecker's recommendation that the bureau deny Indian classification to any Virginians except reservation people.[30] However, though the bureau hedged in this area, not all the figures for Indians in a given county crashed in 1930 and 1940 following Plecker's appeals. As noted, in King William County the number shrank in 1930 and expanded in 1940, while remaining higher than it had been in 1910. Similarly, in New Kent County, the number fell in 1930 but rose in 1940. In Charles City and Caroline Counties, the numbers of people federally enumerated as Indians rose in 1930. The

Rappahannock group had organized in 1921, which is probably why the Census Bureau count for Caroline County included Indians in 1930 where none had been reported since at least 1890 (see table 1).

Tidewater Native people, including the Rappahannock leader Otho Nelson, exerted counter pressures against Plecker's campaign. They got some support related to the 1930 census from a few whites sympathetic to the idea of Native identities in Virginia, including an official of Virginia's Game and Inland Fisheries Commission, a Baptist churchwoman named Martha Coleman Wester Pfaus [Mrs. Fred Pfaus] and Frank Speck.[31] After the enumeration started, Otho Nelson reported to the Census Bureau "that the enumerators either classified people 'as they see fit' or they omitted the 'race' question and then wrote what they liked later on." Rappahannock Indian people visited the head of Virginia's Fifth Census District office to insist that at least some Rappahannocks be listed as Indians.[32]

Among census enumerators in rural places like King William, New Kent, Charles City, and Caroline Counties, their work surely reflected personal and community knowledge of Indian individuals and families. Undoubtedly, some enumerators shared popular notions about interracial marriages and the danger posed by mixed-race people to racial purity and so, like Plecker, were hostile to claims of Indianness. Some enumerators, though, probably brought to their work understanding—and sometimes acceptance—of their Native neighbors' efforts to maintain Indian identities over generations. Perhaps others acquiesced if Native individuals insisted strongly enough that they be recorded as Indian rather than Black or mulatto. This kind of conflict and resistance erupts on page 40A of the 1920 Charles City County census. The enumerator wrote that Robert H. Adkins, "Refused to let me enumerate the rest of his family because I could not with truth, enumerate him as an Indian." This note, however, has been scratched out, and the rest of the family are enumerated as Indians on page 47B. One enumerator for the 1930 census in Amherst County (site of angst for Plecker, as noted in chapter 2) found the whole issue of Indianness in that part of the state too much to handle and "refused to record anyone's 'race.' "[33]

Indeed, some New Kent 1930 census sheets show that someone wrote over the initial entries for "color or race" for some individuals who had been listed as Indians in the 1920 census, making those entries illegible.[34] Such blotting out and overwriting on the census form seem like a literal representation of conflict, confusion, and inconsistencies in white officialdom. When a racial designation was overwritten in that way, did enumerators, or the Census Bureau officials who received and reviewed the enumerators' data, perceive instability in their race categories? Did the enumerators themselves do this overwriting? If so, was it on the spot or after the fact? Did the changes happen after discussion with the enumerated individuals or with officials in state government or the Census Bureau? Did bureau workers who tabulated state-by-state, county-by-county totals for the "race or color" column see these individual illegible entries? People like Plecker saw their work in denying Indian identities as corrections in the service of eugenics and white supremacy. For us, though, such overwriting in a census category with ostensibly clear-cut codes, seems a marker of the Jim Crow South's tangled and incongruous stances in matters of race.

Walter Plecker continued to try to influence the Census Bureau for the 1940 decennial count. He provided the bureau access to historical records his office had been accumulating, records that he claimed were proof that Virginia's Native people were too mixed to be considered Indian—and as we have seen, in 1940 fewer people were enumerated as Indian in Charles City County than in 1930.[35]

Overall, though, the effect of Virginia's 1920s racial integrity fights on federal census counts of tidewater Indians was uneven, reflecting tensions and congruences between local racial practices and the national program. The Census Bureau perpetuated widespread assumptions about the importance of distinguishing between full-blood and mixed-blood Native Americans, as well as one-drop ideas about what made someone Black. Still, the census counts of Virginia Indians in 1930 and 1940 also reflected Native advocacy and resistance. One-drop and full-blood notions pervaded census practices nationally and locally, but tidewater Native people challenged those ideas. Their personal and community identities were at stake.

The Military Draft

As in the census, when World War II brought Selective Service registration to the fore, Powhatan Virginians found that local, state, and federal officialdom could and would ascribe a "race" category to them against their will. Local Selective Service boards, courts, state officials, and the War Department got involved when Powhatan people confronted officials about their racialized status in the context of the wartime draft. Walter Plecker engaged this discussion to promote his belief that all Virginia Indians should be considered colored. Like Southern states' Jim Crow laws, segregation in the armed forces at that time could operate as if race were a simple Black-white binary. Local Selective Service boards generally had initial responsibility for sorting registrants and inductees by race, and there were no nationwide, standardized definitions for that purpose. As with the census, community reputation (which could mean white people's opinions) was potentially relevant in cases that seemed ambiguous or arguable.[36]

Racial classification of Virginia Indians for draft purposes raised challenges to the notion of race as a binary system and opened a debate that reached courts and the Department of War, despite the small numbers of potential soldiers involved. Would the military accept Virginia Indian inductees' assertions of their own racialized identity?[37] On that point tidewater Native leaders evidently expressed their concerns to local, state, and national officials. At least one local draft board (in King William County) asked for guidance. A state education official asked the War Department for policy clarification out of concern that categorizing tidewater Native people as Black for purposes of military service could threaten the justification for the state's Indian schools on the tidewater reservations.[38]

Some tidewater Natives were inducted and served with whites; others were placed with Black troops, and some protested that assignment. Some Chickahominy men "refused to leave their barracks" and enlisted their chief's help, to get their racial classification changed so they would serve in white units. Some Rappahannock men were prosecuted for refusing to serve with or as African Americans, and three received prison sentences.[39]

Helen Rountree and Paul T. Murray have written about this episode, so suffice it here to note that aspects of this struggle over the draft resonate with patterns in other areas where tidewater Indians contested racialized categorizations. For example, Walter Plecker and his office, in interpreting race categories in nineteenth-century documentation, continued to gloss over realities about those records, such as the catch-all nature of the antebellum category "free person of color." As in other arenas of contention, Virginia Indians strategically used white allies to appeal to white officials for recognition of their status as Indians.[40] Among the few white advocates who joined tidewater Natives in their fight about the wartime draft, Frank Speck used the weight of his scholarly credentials to testify that tidewater Powhatan groups' claims to Indianness were as valid as those of widely recognized Native groups in Oklahoma, New York, and Canada, as noted in chapter 4.[41]

In the controversies surrounding the draft, organized tidewater Native groups asserted that they lived apart from African Americans. As in other contexts, they sought not so much to contest the concept of a Black-white binary color line, but rather to position themselves as not Black. When draft board records emerged as an additional locus of governmental racialized classifications, tidewater Native Virginians could point to tribal organizations and segregated churches and schools as testament to their Indian identities and their separation from their African American neighbors.

Indian Churches

Over decades after the legislative racial integrity fights of 1924–1930, separate Indian churches remained important community-building institutions for tidewater Native people. In 1928, the Dover Baptist Association included the Pamunkey, Samaria (Western Chickahominy), and Tsena Commocko (Eastern Chickahominy) churches. That year, membership in those churches was reported at 100 for Pamunkey, 144 for Samaria and, 38 for Tsena Commocko. Though those three churches did not have Indian pastors at that time, Native leadership within each congregation remained fundamental to church functions as in preceding years. Clerks who managed church organizational and financial matters, for example, came from the Native communities.[42]

The tidewater Baptist Indian churches continued to grow after 1930. By 1950, five Indian Baptist churches in tidewater had a total membership of 487. These churches usually had the full range of auxiliary organizations typical of Southern Baptist congregations, such as Sunday schools, woman's missionary unions, and Baptist training unions. Native congregants led those auxiliary organizations. The churches thus fostered social relationships within a given Indian community, serving as sites of formal worship and community centers. As before 1930, they continued to connect Native Virginians to the larger white Southern Baptist world; Native congregants continued to represent their churches at Dover annual meetings, and around 1950, at least two of these churches were holding homecomings in which ministers from white churches participated.[43] The growth and development of Indian participation in the Dover Baptist Association thus provided support for congregations asserting their Native identities, fostering recognition of these Indian institutions among non-indigenous neighbors and within Southern Baptist institutional structures. In some cases, white Baptists helped advocate for schools for tidewater Indian children, supplementing Indian parents' investment in, and sacrifices for, those schools.

The growth of these churches and the leadership of Native people in them throughout the 1930s and 1940s look especially significant given the small, rural, and not affluent nature of the Native communities from which they drew members. For example, in 1932 the Mattaponi Reservation people organized a new church, following earlier efforts by Chief George F. Custalow to provide for services on the reservation. It drew members who had attended the Pamunkey church. When the congregation of the Mattaponi church dedicated a new building in 1935, the acting pastor, Harvey N. Custalow, came from within the congregation. He probably was related to the three Custalow men, including George F. Custalow, who helped organize the church and request its inclusion in the Dover Baptist Association in 1932.[44] By 1939, Harvey N. Custalow was serving as pastor for both Mattaponi and Samaria churches.[45] Indian View Church, of and for the Upper Mattaponi, organized in 1942. The Rappahannock people developed their own church in 1964, which became part of the Dover Baptist Association in 1965.[46] Through the 1930s and 1940s, members of Indian communities remained leaders, stewards, and managers—clerks, treasurers, and Sunday school superintendents, for example—of their churches, though it appears many of their ministers were white, except Harvey Custalow.

The newer churches of the Mattaponi, Upper Mattaponi, and Rappahannock communities were founded after the formal organization of the tribal group they served.[47] Often, Indian churches were connected to tribal organizations and their leaders. For example, in 1965 the Virginia Baptist newsletter reported that in the Pamunkey church, which dated back to 1865, "The chief of the tribe often has served as Sunday School Superintendent."[48]

Over decades after the racial integrity legislation of 1924–1930, as tidewater Native people organized additional Indian churches, those churches maintained long-term alliances with the Dover Baptist Association. That Dover connection seems especially notable considering segregation practices in Southern Baptist congregations. As noted in chapter 3, before the Civil War, some Virginia Baptist churches had white and Black members. In 1838 and 1839, Dover Baptist Association minutes provided separate tallies for white and colored membership for each association church.[49] A century later, the association made no provision for racialized distinctions in charting membership figures of churches within the association.[50] By 1939, the published constitution and by-laws of the Dover Baptist Association were silent about race in discussing membership and other organizational practices.[51] This may indicate that by that time, under the Southern Baptist Convention umbrella that covered the Dover Association, the assumption was that constituent churches were homogeneously white, so that there was no need to keep statistics on the race or ethnicities of church members. (The Dover Baptist Association included a Slovak church that dated to 1913.) Likely that was among the reasons tidewater Natives participated in Dover, as an organization that was unambiguously not Black after the Civil War.

Thus, as a Southern Baptist Convention affiliate with non-white—that is, Indian—churches, the Dover Association was perhaps in an anomalous position.

As shown in chapter 3, links to white Southern Baptist organizational structures had provided tidewater Indian churches with support for recognition of their not-Black status ever since the founding of the Pamunkey church in 1865.[52] While tidewater Indian Baptist churches could have faced a move within the Southern Baptist hierarchy to classify them as "colored," it seems that did not happen. But had such a move come to pass, it seems unlikely that in this era tidewater Indian congregations would have considered joining an association of Black Baptist churches, given the ever-looming potential for attacks on their Native identities by Virginia officials.

In the late 1930s and 1940s, male Native congregants in these churches may have been less prominent in the committee work of the Dover Baptist Association than they had been in the mid-and late 1920s. They continued to represent their own congregations regularly in the association's annual meetings, but Native men were perhaps less active in business affairs and committees at the association level. Still, the churches' financial contributions to the association were dependable, and their cultivation of auxiliary groups such as the Sunday schools was steady.

Tidewater Indian church women, though, continued their participation and leadership in the Rural Dover Sunday School Convention and in the Woman's Missionary Union (WMU) societies within the Dover Association. Annual reports of the Dover WMU between 1939 and 1947 suggest that Native churchwomen's participation in the WMU reflected significant commitments of time and energy. For example, Ruth Cook of the Pamunkey church was the leader of Group 7 of Dover's WMU from 1939 to 1947. In 1939, she was appointed to the WMU nominating committee. In 1943–1945, she served on the Time and Place Committee. Martha Coleman Wester Pfaus (Mrs. Fred Pfaus), a white woman who involved herself in advocacy for Indian schools, was active in the WMU both in the Dover Association and at the statewide level, sometimes attending Dover WMU annual meetings between 1939 and 1947.[53] Perhaps her opportunities to meet Indian women in Dover WMU work made Mrs. Pfaus more aware of their concerns, exemplifying the networks that Baptist affiliation opened to tidewater Native people.

Those annual WMU reports of 1939–1947 show matter-of-fact recognition, but little explicit discussion, of the Native churches' status as Indian congregations. For example, a mention of "Indian neighbors" in 1945 referred not to tidewater Natives, but to missionary work among Native Americans in New Mexico and Arizona. In discussing the World War II years, the superintendent of the Dover WMU organization pointed to the importance of international mission work in order "that ignorant, superstitious, uncouth, unattractive natives might know Christ as their personal Savior." Presumably, Dover's WMU superintendent did not consider the Indian Baptists in Dover churches "ignorant, uncouth, unattractive natives" or candidates for missionizing. She did refer to Dover Indians directly in this way: "Two of our girls from Pamunkey Baptist Church are students in Bacone Indian College near Muskogee, Okla., where they are preparing themselves for greater work among their own people."[54] Still, one wonders what Indian participants in Dover's Woman's Missionary Union made of her reference to primitivized "natives," as she linked racialized ideas about physical appearance to class-based notions of genteel behavior. In any case, the phrase "their own people" suggests that a racial line around tidewater Indian Baptists was firmly drawn in this woman's mind.

If by the late 1930s and 1940s many male tidewater Indian church members focused more on leading within their own congregations and less on the Dover Baptist Association's organizational structures, they were not completely absent from the latter. O. T. Custalow, sometime clerk of the Mattaponi church, was on the association's standing committee on Southwide Enterprises in 1944. He and George F. Custalow were participants in discussions at the association's general meeting that year.[55] In 1945, O. T. Custalow offered the Southwide Enterprises Committee report at the association's annual meeting. Custalow submitted the committee's brief digest of Southern Baptist "Home Mission Board" opportunities and activities, directed at Southerners who were "not ministered to by local churches or through our state mission programs," including "two hundred thousand Indians in eight Southern States" as well as Spanish-speaking, French, and Italian groups.[56] Maybe Custalow hoped his white Dover colleagues marked the contrast between his fellow Indian Baptists firmly ensconced in the Dover Association and those other, unchurched Southern Indians.

Generally, though, the voices of Indian delegates at Dover Association annual meetings got little attention in the published minutes between 1939 and 1947. For example, when the 1946 Dover Association minutes indicated that the Indian View church was an applicant for Dover membership, they read as if a white pastor, rather than the church's four delegates, who were surely Indian members of the church, did the talking at that annual meeting.[57]

In sum, the Dover Association annual meeting minutes for 1939–1947 reveal little focus on members of associated Indian churches as Indians. The Native congregations were simply listed within standard summary reporting on member churches and their activities. These published minutes of 1939–1947 did, however, include references to racialized matters, such as the American Baptist

Theological Seminary jointly supported by the National and Southern Baptist Conventions for training African American ministers; "interracial" work such as "friendly contact with Jewish neighbors;" and the need for missionary activities for "the Chinese and the Negro and the Mexican and the Russian and the Pole and the Italian" at home and abroad.[58] As in 1945, association minutes for 1946 and 1947 again mentioned unspecified Southern Indians among the potential targets for "home mission" evangelization of the unchurched of the South.[59] The Indianness of contemporary Dover Native congregants, though, was generally not highlighted in association minutes and reports beyond listing and simple acknowledgment of their churches as Indian organizations.

Two exceptions are the reference to Pamunkey young women at Bacone cited above, and an occasion in 1946 when the association agreed to help fund publication of Martha Coleman Wester Pfaus's pamphlet, "Our Indian Neighbors."[60] In 1947, the minutes of the Dover annual meeting reported that Mrs. Pfaus's "pamphlet has elicited considerable interest among our people concerning work among the Indians; and it has been an inspiration to the Indians themselves. A number of the Indian youths are applying themselves diligently to their studies and are making a creditable showing in their classes."[61] Here, "our people" seems to embrace only the whites within the Dover Association, not its Indian congregants. Doubtless, Mrs. Pfaus was useful in speaking about issues of concern to Native Dover Association Baptists, and she likely heard sincere expressions of thanks from them. We need not, though, accept an inflated estimate of how much tidewater Indian people needed white allies like Mrs. Pfaus for "inspiration." Tidewater Indian congregations had been making significant investments in the Dover Baptist Association and in their own churches and schools for decades when this pamphlet appeared. They did seek white allies who were willing to publicly support their claims to Indian identities, but their own initiatives were clear and long-standing.

Perhaps in this era, infrequent emphasis on Indian identities by the association's white Baptists (outside of Mrs. Pfaus's efforts) was intended to minimize the potential that questions of race would stir conflict within the white Dover membership. If so, then a relative quiet may have suited Native participants in the association after the noisy and painful legislative racial integrity fights of 1924–1930. Maybe Dover Indian congregations themselves avoided highlighting their racialized identity after 1930, except for efforts to secure more support for Indian schools. In any case, it seems that by the 1930s and 1940s—after Baptist engagement in the fight over a 1928 bill's proposed changes in legal definitions of Virginia's racialized categories—the association had gone as far as it would go in political advocacy for its Native members.

Around 1940, the Woman's Missionary Union advocated that Virginia Baptist Indian churches call Indian pastors from the West to replace white ministers at some of the Native churches. It seems, though, that Dover's Indian congregations generally did not pursue this idea.[62] Between 1939 and 1947, Powhatan community members led their churches in many ways and offices, although Harvey N. Custalow may have been their only Native minister. Perhaps these Dover-associated Indian Baptists did not see recruiting Native ministers from outside Virginia as a pressing need. Maybe the Indian churches of the Dover Association felt their white ministers helped to link them securely to Dover. Perhaps, instead, they were reluctant to take action that might discourage members of their own communities from seeking pulpits in the communities' Baptist churches. In either case, this episode might show that tidewater Indian Baptists valued localized networks involving whites. It could also reflect a general trend among Dover Indian Baptists, between 1939 and 1947, not to call too much attention within the association to questions of race and Indian identity.

As recently as 2004, tidewater Indian churches as historically segregated institutions led by and for Indians drew attention when the Richmond *Times-Dispatch* reported that a married couple, Lori and Jasper Battle, had been denied membership in the Rappahannock church because Lori, of the Rappahannock community, had married Jasper, an African American. In two articles, the newspaper framed this story as a matter that divided the congregation. Some viewed this episode as an opportunity to move beyond racism, while others saw denial of membership to the Battles as a matter of community preservation, necessary for "the Indian identity to stay pure."[63]

It seems that even into the twenty-first century, the legacy of Jim Crow in Virginia can still engender fears among tidewater Native people that their hard-won recognition as Indians could be eroded by social proximity to African Americans. Nationally, there are comparatively high rates of marriages by Native people to non-Natives, which could make small Native communities in the South feel particularly sensitive about out-marriages. Too, as historically segregated congregations serving distinctive small communities, the tidewater Indian churches may be more vulnerable to public accusations of racism than historically segregated white congregations in comparable rural circumstances. For couples like Lori and Jasper Battle, family ties may still be challenged along the color line.

The Battles's experience exposes potential conflicts within Indian-centered institutions long after 1924 and in the wake of modern civil rights movements.

Schools

After 1930 as before, tidewater Baptist Indian churches and separate local schools for tidewater Native children could have connections as community centers. For example, the Tsena Commocko congregation of Eastern Chickahominy people, organized in 1922, met in a schoolhouse until they moved into a nearby church building in 1932. When people on the Mattaponi Reservation organized their own church in 1932, that followed four years in which services were held in the Mattaponi school building.[64] The Upper Mattaponi met for Sunday school in the Sharon Indian School before building their Indian View church building in 1942.[65]

Some white Baptists of the Dover Association, including members of the woman's missionary groups like Martha Wester Coleman Pfaus, took an interest in schools for tidewater Natives. In 1950 an article in the Virginia Baptist weekly *Religious Herald* noted, "Hard by each Indian Church there is a school." These were the Pamunkey, Mattaponi, Sharon, Tsena Commocko, and Samaria (Chickahominy) schools. This 1950 snapshot noted that among these schools, only Samaria provided high school-level coursework. "This is the only Indian school in the state with one year of high school, which prepares their students for high school work in Bacone College, where they have ten students this year (1949–1950)." (Around that time, Lula Whitehead Shango of the Chickahominy community, who had gone to Bacone College in Oklahoma, was a teacher at the Samaria school. Her husband, a Seneca man whom she had met at Bacone, was the principal. In their case, Bacone connected a tidewater Native individual with another, well recognized indigenous group.) Reporting that twenty tidewater Indian students in all had left the state to go to school in 1949, this 1950 article was critical of state and local levels of support for the five local tidewater schools, noting that, "Indian boys and girls have nothing to look forward to beyond the grades. High school and college training is denied them in their own state and they go outside of the state for this training. The State Board of Education pays one-half of their tuitions, and one-half of the transportation when they go to other states for this training. On the Pamunkey and Mattaponi Reservations the State Board of Education provides the building and teachers for their schools. This is not true of the non-Reservation Indians."

Since, for the non-reservation groups, state and local support were inadequate, "due to crowded conditions Samaria Indian Church allows the higher grades and the recently added ninth grade pupils to use their Sunday School rooms." Also evidencing a lack of resources, at the Sharon school in 1946, a hot-lunch program required volunteer aid from the Woman's Missionary Society of the Ginter Park Baptist Church in Richmond (part of the Dover Baptist Association), and donations from two "friends" helped the community's school "patrons" build a lunchroom in 1948. (Some federal aid for hot lunches had been forthcoming in 1947.)[66]

The importance of such voluntary contributions, and the deferential relationships they might entail, are apparent as that 1950 article noted, "The patrons and pupils of these schools are deeply grateful to Mrs. Fred Pfaus, George W. Blume, and the Woman's Missionary Societies of Richmond and their many friends for all they have done for them." The fact that J. B. Rounds, the head of the Southern Baptist Convention's "Indian work," visited these schools indicates that some white Baptists saw these schools as Indian places.[67] Thus, in their schools, Indian members of the Dover Association were recipients of some Baptist home mission attention, though Dover's Indian congregants also could position themselves within the association as supporters of missionary aid, not recipients. The schools' needs were urgent, though, and doubtless tidewater Natives appreciated help from white fellow Baptists.[68]

Martha Coleman Wester Pfaus [Mrs. Fred Pfaus], who was connected with the Dover Association, wrote a 1949 pamphlet closely mirrored by that 1950 *Religious Herald* article. In it she noted the deficiencies of county-level support for schools for tidewater non-reservation or "citizen Indians," contrasting their situation with that of the two reservation groups who had better facilities due to support from the State Board of Education. Non-reservation people, "except one group, have been compelled to put up their own building and, for a time they had to pay their own teachers." She emphasized that volunteer efforts helped address some of the Samaria school's fundamental needs: "Five years ago, a fund was created by friends of the Indians to help in their education." That fund provided for the purchase of some basic equipment and furnishings. The community chipped in to fund a school bus. Pfaus went further than the 1950 *Religious Herald* article in describing inequities: "Every other nationality in the state of Virginia has the privilege of higher education—only the Indians are denied this, their just right. Can any fair-minded American feel that this treatment of the descendents of the original Virginians is just, in this 'Land of the free and the home of the brave'"?[69] In referring to the "privilege" of segregated schools for Black and white Virginians, Pfaus's use of the word "nationality" instead of "race" seems a careful choice. She pointed out that for decades tidewater Indians had positioned themselves as original, integral actors in Virginia's colonial history. She wrote also that some students at Samaria were former soldiers, calling Indians "the original American" as well as "original Virginians," thus linking them to national narratives of patriotic service and citizenship.[70] (Perhaps Pfaus was aware of international criticism of American racial segregation in the cold war era).

In another example of connections between Baptist churches and tidewater Indian schools, the principal of the reservation school in the late 1950s and through the 1963–1964 school year was a white man, Daniel Slabey, whose father had been the pastor of the Slovak Baptist Church within the Dover Baptist Association.[71] Slabey had been formally presented at the association's annual sessions in 1928—the same meeting at which R. A. Bradby had spoken about the situation of Virginia Indians as the Virginia legislature debated changes to its 1924 racial integrity law.[72] Perhaps his Dover connections helped lead Slabey to the reservation school later in his life. In 1965, he wrote a piece for a Baptist newsletter about the "First Indian Baptist Church in Virginia," noting that he was "assisting the Pamunkey people in preparing for the celebration of the 100th anniversary of the founding of their church."[73]

White Virginia Baptists supported several educational institutions in the state, from the University of Richmond and Averett College, to the Fork Union and Hargrave Military Academies. Members of tidewater Indian Baptist churches saw regular mentions of those institutions in the minutes of Dover Baptist Association annual meetings. It may be that only one of those Virginia Baptist schools, Oak Hill Academy in the western part of the state, accepted students from the tidewater Native groups, and this connection may have dated only from the mid-1950s.[74] Since tidewater Indian communities struggled to find ways to provide high school education to their children, Baptist-supported schools in Virginia could have seemed an obvious solution to that problem. But perhaps, outside the Dover Baptist Association, Virginia's white Baptists were more likely to regard tidewater Natives as colored rather than Indian.

Certainly assertions of Indian identity remained under attack, as shown in an exchange between a Virginia teacher and Walter Plecker in the summer of 1945. The teacher had requested general information about "the educational program of the Virginia Indian." Walter Plecker framed his response as a discussion not about Indians, but about "the educational program for groups of mulattoes living on two reservations in King William County." Plecker claimed that not even the reservation Mattaponi and Pamunkey should be considered "real" Indians because of a long history of "intermixture with the whites and negroes." Plecker also expressed pique about one aspect of Virginia's 1930 law (which had classified anyone with "any ascertainable degree of negro blood" as a "colored person"). Specifically, he criticized that law's provision that "those living on the reservations with one-fourth or more Indian blood and less than one-sixteenth negro blood shall be deemed tribal Indians so long as they are domiciled on said reservations. When they leave the reservation, they take their proper classification as colored. The Department of Education, however, seems to treat them as deserving of special consideration and furnishes them industrial education which is not furnished to the other negro schools of the state nor to the white schools."[75] Plecker took every opportunity to make his case against Virginian Indian identities to the end of his long career at the Bureau of Vital Statistics, even claiming that Virginia Natives received programming not available to Black or white schoolchildren.

In contrast, the State Board of Education could play up the identities of the reservation people as Indians, as in 1946 newspaper coverage of the state's effort to fill the position of teacher at the Mattaponi school. The state's director of elementary education noted that the position was at a "'modern' one-room school" with a salary "above the State minimum," and added to those selling points that "the teaching experience would be stimulating from a sociological point of view and would furnish an opportunity for study of Indian culture."[76]

Consistent with this kind of acceptance by state education officials of tidewater Native groups' Indianness, the connection to the Bacone school in Oklahoma seems to have solidified by the 1947–1948 school year. Groups of mostly Chickahominy students attended Bacone (a school with Baptist roots) for high school and some college coursework. It may be that this Virginia-Oklahoma exchange for school-age Native Virginians peaked around 1947 to 1951.[77] As late as 1954, though, the need was still acute. The non-reservation Samaria school's high school-level programming had expanded by then, but a state education official wrote to Bacone, "As you know, we only offer educational opportunities through grade eight at our Indian Reservation School because of the small enrollment. Thus we must locate high schools outside of the State" for reservation students.[78] Apparently, in the eyes of state school officials, a formal policy of sending reservation Indian high school-age children to local white or Black public schools was out of the question before the United States Supreme Court's *Brown v. Board* decision in May, 1954.[79]

Some Native students expressed interest in the Haskell Institute in Kansas, as well. Haskell's superintendent informed a Virginia state education official that "all students must be of one-fourth or more degree of Indian blood."[80] It is easy to imagine tidewater Native parents wondering what evidence would adequately fulfill this standard for their children's "degree of Indian blood."

Such parents likely hoped that going to a school like Haskell or Bacone could help make their children's Indian identity unimpeachable even if that meant separation from those children, and that acceptance and a continuing presence at institutions like Bacone would bolster their communities' position as real Indians. When the Mattaponi leader O. T. Custalow visited Virginia Native students at the North Carolina Cherokee Reservation school, he asserted his Indianness dramatically during his ongoing work to "help keep my young people satisfied to stay on the Reservation." He reported that one of the Virginia students wrote to him afterward that "all the Indians next day wanted to know who that Indian Chief was, I wore my full regalia."[81] As in the late nineteenth century, wearing such Indian regalia remained a useful strategy for representing tidewater Native identities to outsiders, including other Native groups.

Regalia was also useful at home. A feature of visits to the reservation school by outsiders was a kind of pageantry reminiscent of the public dramas enacted by tidewater Native communities as early as the 1880s. In 1955, a teacher at the reservation school wrote to a state official about a busy week of programs for scheduled visits by school children. "On Tuesday we had a load from King and Queen [County]—third grade children." Then on Wednesday, "we had a nice group from Newport News. Chief Custalow came over and we put on a few dances, etc. The visitors seemed to enjoy the show."[82] Chief Custalow's energy and leadership in representing the Indianness of the Mattaponi and Pamunkey thus extended from North Carolina Cherokee students to the reservation school.

These segregated schools helped signify Native identities and also a separation from white and Black neighbors to outsiders. One state school official expressed his impression that some tidewater reservation people were imbued with the racialized etiquette of Jim Crow, as he questioned whether African Americans should be allowed to visit the reservation school. He wrote, "Last year there were some touchy incidents since the Indian children refused to have anything to do with Negro visitors." Not everyone wanted to exclude African Americans from the reservation, though. This official admitted, "On the other hand, Chief Custalow is realizing a fee of 25¢ per Negro student when they visit his museum. Someone is going to have to say no definitely to the Chief this year. Since this is a State school, it would seem to me that State laws would apply and if students and teachers refuse to talk and deal with the Negro youngsters, they should not be encouraged to visit that school."[83] Perhaps this official was disparaging Custalow to support others in the community who shared his vision of segregation. Possibly, the students and teachers in question told him that they wanted no contact with African Americans, to emphasize their separation from Blacks (and therefore their Indianness). Maybe, instead, they simply sought to please or placate a white official who wanted to "say no" to racially integrated public gatherings.

Given the circumstances, state funding for Virginia Native high school-age students who attended schools outside the state remained inadequate. Tidewater indigenous parents in the late 1940s and into the 1950s pressed for expansion of programs at their local Indian schools. The parents wanted additional grades of high school coursework for their children locally to reduce the need to send children to faraway schools in distant states.

Some students found leaving home difficult, as seen in 1952 correspondence between a state education official, the Reverend Harvey Custalow, and Webster Custalow of the Mattaponi community. Two young Mattaponi women had fled the Cherokee Reservation school in North Carolina because of a "poor relationship with their house mother." Apparently, the two had expressed a preference for going to Bacone. The state official wrote to say that the students should return to the Cherokee school if their parents approved, but that he would not support sending them to Bacone.[84] Stresses felt by teenagers sent away from home and family were here compounded by the rigidity and condescension of a state official.

As the reservation communities worked toward high school-level classes for their children locally, they faced financial and racialized obstacles.[85] White officials who challenged the reservation schools' existence often cited small enrollment figures. Compared to North Carolina's Lumbee people, who had a system of schools in Robeson County, each tidewater Virginia Native group was indeed rather small.[86] In the eyes of white officials, this made them less viable candidates for local, publicly funded, separate schools (probably especially given national trends toward consolidation of small rural schools).

Enrollment issues also arose in connection with a non-reservation school for Indians in the Boulevard area of New Kent County that was part of the county school system at least in 1947. The county's population was waning at that time, and segregation kept enrollments at individual county schools artificially low. The county faced potential loss of state accreditation due to those small enrollments. Compounding those issues, a 1947 report on the county's school system noted that:

> In addition to the white and negro races, there is a small number of indians for whom separate school facilities must be provided, since these people will not attend the schools for negro children, and they are not allowed to

attend the schools for white children.... The presence of this additional racial group complicates the problem of adequate school facilities, though the county has not attempted to provide complete high school instruction for them. Those who want a high school education are given eighth-grade work, so that they may be able to enter high schools in other states, in which case approximately one-half of their expenses are paid by the State of Virginia.

The precarious situation of the New Kent Indian school was clear; only fourteen students were enrolled there. The county's investment in the Indian school was so small that "the school facilities for the indians in the county consist of a one-room building which the county rents for $50 a year. This building is heated by a coal stove and is in better general condition than any of the schools for negroes, though the inside walls are in such bad condition that it cannot be kept as warm as it should be in winter weather."[87] This echoes Lucy Pearman Scott's lament, a century earlier, about how hard it would be for her daughters in New Kent County to educate their children.

Virginia's local and state educational bureaucracies probably would have been stingy in their support for the Indian schools even had there been larger enrollments in those schools, given the chronic underfunding of schools for Virginia's African Americans and the hostility of some white Virginians toward tidewater Native groups. Thus, there was a need for advocacy by non-Indian allies, including Virginia Baptists like Martha Coleman Wester Pfaus. White people like Frank Speck and James Coates (more on him below) recommended greater support from federal officials for educational opportunities for tidewater Indians, with Speck again vouching that they were actually indigenous people.[88] By the early 1950s, the Society of Friends joined efforts to help fund Indian school programming.[89]

The struggle for high school classwork in-community went on for years. In 1950, probably in recognition that the state's stinginess would continue, the reservation Mattaponi and Pamunkey agreed, with some mistrust, to merge their two schools into one, urged on by the State Department of Education. Some additional state and private investment was forthcoming for the joint program, which was extended to the eighth grade.[90] Still, for a time the secondary school-level coursework at the Samaria school was more extensive than that at the reservation school, so some reservation students attended Samaria. In at least one case, the state assisted with a reservation student's room and board there, since the reservations lie far enough from Samaria to make a daily commute arduous.⁹¹ Handwritten notes from around 1956 indicate that the State Board of Education was considering further consolidation. Samaria school enrollment was larger, and at that time it offered a program through the tenth grade, so state officials entertained the notion of sending eighth and ninth graders from the reservation school to Samaria.⁹² The State Board of Education accepted that tidewater Indian parents did not want to send their children to schools for African Americans, while it continued to question the viability of separate Indian schools. In response, reservation communities kept pushing for an expanded program.

By 1956, the 1954 *Brown v. Board* decision was reshaping the terms of this debate, but desegregation did not come immediately to the reservation schools. In 1957, the Executive Committee of the Mattaponi-Pamunkey Indian Reservation told state officials that for the present school term they would accept a program that extended only to the tenth grade, but that they wanted the addition of eleventh-grade classwork soon and were "much concerned about the accreditation of the school."⁹³ The joint reservation school added twelfth-grade classes by the 1958–1959 term. Around that time the state likely ceased defraying expenses for reservation children to attend out-of-state high school programs.⁹⁴

Despite Indian parents' persistent advocacy, in 1960 State Board of Education officials were still questioning the viability of the reservation school, citing a trend of declining enrollments. One of those officials opined that, since few of the school's graduates went to college, and given the "desires, interests, capacities, attitudes and characteristics of the Indian students," the fact that the high school curriculum was "limited almost entirely to the traditional academic subject matter fields" raised questions about the "suitability of the present curriculum." He wrote that some parents had asked about including secretarial and vocational subjects in the high school program, but he noted that one man, Dr. Slabey, was doing all the high school level teaching. Presumably, Slabey would have been hard pressed to add new classes to the curriculum. This official remarked, "Some few parents have high hopes for their children, others do not care in the least about the school or what happens to their sons or daughters." It is not hard to imagine that reservation parents' desires for their children might not fit his assumptions—and that some reservation parents would resist the suggestion that the curriculum for their children should look more like a vocational-technical approach associated with education for Black students. In fact, reservation community leaders consistently stressed expansion and accreditation of their school(s). This official proposed keeping the elementary school program at the reservation school while, "the high school students should be provided for elsewhere." As justification, he cited funding constraints and reservation students' needs for "outside contacts as well as broader educational opportunities than we are able to provide under the circumstances." He did not specify where "elsewhere" might have been, but by 1960, the likely alternative was probably local county schools, rather than boarding schools such as Bacone.[95]

While these Indian schools operated, they fostered Native identities as major community institutions, but perhaps not by prioritizing curricula that consistently stressed Native histories or cultures. Around 1939–1940, white teachers taught some "Indian crafts" in the Mattaponi school.[96] In the early 1950s, proposals for teaching craft production arose, probably partly because of interest in adult-education programs to support creation and marketing of salable items to augment the sales of pottery produced at the Pamunkey Reservation. State education officials discussed "a proposed project in basketry, leatherwork, and metal work," and the need for "industrial arts" equipment and teachers.[97] In response to a proposal by a white Quaker and some state education officials, one state official familiar with the adult Pamunkey pottery school offered that "pottery making ought to be retained on the reservations since this art apparently goes back to pre-colonial days. I believe the Indians should keep alive their skill at pottery making for many reasons but certainly for the reason that it represents an activity from which they can realize a profit. I ... believe that making baskets and weaving ought to be encouraged. But not at the expense of pottery."[98] Perhaps the notion of expanding the school's training in crafts was dearer to certain whites than to the reservation communities. Take for example the tepid response by the Pamunkey leader T. D. Cook to a state official's query. Chief Cook politely indicated that "a few of our people, mostly those engaged in the making of pottery, are apparently interested in the crafts which you mentioned in your letter.... I too, feel that it would be well to plan a meeting in the near future where the members of both reservations might be able to express themselves."[99] For the most part, the reservation school program for children, if limited in facilities, staff, and funding, adhered to a basic framework of courses along standard lines for Virginia schools.[100]

If there was relatively little emphasis on generically Indian crafts, students in the schools articulated their Native identity. For an essay on the occasion of her 1960 graduation from the reservation school, Dorothy Page wrote about "Indian Women Then and Now." She noted that many aspects of the life, work, and foodways of a contemporary Indian woman resembled those of "her white sister." Still, Page was clear that those similarities did not amount to a loss of the cultural distinctiveness of the reservation communities. She cited distinctive pottery and beaded jewelry work made on the reservation and sold to tourists and the fact that reservation women served in the reservation's own church and its Missionary Society.[101]

Page's classmate Joyce Bradby chose Pocahontas as her graduation essay's subject. Like generations of tidewater Natives before her, Bradby used the image of Pocahontas to link her reservation community to the Jamestown nation-founding story. She cited Pocahontas's kindness to the English at Jamestown, and wrote that the English betrayed Pocahontas when they "returned their gratitude by capturing her in hopes that Powhatan would release some prisoners of the colony." Bradby's confidence in her community's Indian identity shone when, in emphasizing distinctive aspects of her reservation's lifeways, she attacked a popular stereotype of Indianness that did not apply to her community: "The Eastern Indians did not live in tepees."[102]

In 1966, Catherine Howell Hook of the Fredericksburg area, then on the State Board of Education, delivered a commencement address that expressed her awareness of the reservation communities' "genuine pride in your ancestors, your traditions, your way of life, your independence and the perpetuation of your ideals and aspirations for your people." Acknowledging the colonial past, Hook also embraced her memories of talking with community members at a Fredericksburg market or festival "when you displayed your lovely pottery, weaving, other crafts and tribal dances."[103]

Whites' consciousness could range from condescension to overt stereotyping, as exemplified in a commencement address by a state education official in 1962. He expressed gratitude for the "privilege" of working with community leaders and jocularly added, "We didn't always agree but I managed to come away with my scalp intact although at times I had grave doubts about doing so."[104]

Disagreements continued. A state official corresponding with Catherine Hook in 1966 alerted her "incidentally" that the Department of Education was considering "discontinuing the Indian Reservations School at the end of the current school year. All students could be transferred to the nearby King William County Schools. A final decision has not been reached. Of course, the Indian people are not in complete agreement with this action."[105] By this time, the state's interest in the economies of dismantling a hard-won community-building institution had been bolstered by national trends. The question of where Indian students would go if the reservation school closed had a potential new answer in this era of school desegregation. As the *Brown v. Board* decision slowly played out, Virginia's public schools could no longer, technically and legally, be racially segregated institutions. The reservation school closed in 1966 and the

Chickahominy lost their formal tribal connection to the Samaria school in 1967. As Helen Rountree reported, "Then, in 1971, the federal judge in Richmond readjusted the proportions of school children in the county: Samaria School became predominantly black, as is Charles City County's population. The tribe considered setting up its own academy and applying for funds under federal legislation for Indian education in order to get another school, but nothing was done in the end."[106]

Thus, segregated Indian schools survived decades of grudging state and county support, only to close in the context of the modern civil rights movement. After the *Brown v. Board* decision, organized tidewater Native peoples did not set up private segregated academies, a tactic used by white Virginians. While there was a desperate need to strike down the inequities of separate-but-inherently-unequal segregated school systems, for tidewater Indians there were costs entailed in the loss of these community institutions—just as for some African American communities there was pain when, for example, Black teachers lost jobs in the processes of consolidation and desegregating schools.

Whites' Responses

In the aftermath of the racial integrity legislative battles of 1924–1930 and into the 1950s, tidewater Natives contended with white officialdom in the Census Bureau, the wartime Selective Service and the state education system. As they battled overtly hostile officials, often even their white allies did not stray far from the racialized orthodoxies of their avowed opponents. White Dover Association Baptists for example, did not question the concept of racialized segregation, even if they accepted a special position for tidewater Natives relative to the color line. Still, as before 1930, tidewater organized indigenous groups made use of white people who helped argue for their status as Native people and for the purity of their Indian blood.

For example, a man named James R. Coates, who worked at the Norfolk Shipbuilding and Drydock Corporation, wanted to help Virginia Indians distinguish themselves from African Americans—though he did not fundamentally quarrel with Jim Crow segregation. In the aftermath of the fight about the World War II draft, Coates encouraged the development of tribal rolls and collection of documents evidencing past official recognition of tidewater Native individuals as Indians. He solicited information from Native groups and gathered testimonials from white neighbors about the Indianness of those groups. Coates intended this material to bolster a campaign for tidewater Natives' "official recognition and proper classification as native Virginia Indians," a campaign he wanted to aim at "the State or Federal Government." Coates urged leaders of tidewater indigenous groups not to include anyone on a list of tribal members whose identity might blur a line between indigeneity and African Americanness. In effect, Coates suggested that it was demeaning to tidewater Indians to call them colored people. He sent a form letter to "each chief" around early 1947, recommending that a tribal committee constituted for this purpose develop a comprehensive listing "of all persons who are members of your tribe in good standing. Do not include any one who is not entitled to the strict classification of Indian. . . . I urge you to prepare this list without undue delay and with the greatest of care to see that no one rightfully entitled to the distinction of being on the list is omitted, and to be sure that no one, under any circumstances, be permitted to appear on the list whose good standing and blood relation is other than pure Indian or Indian and white."[107] Coates wrote, "You people know who in your tribe is entitled to the distinction of being members in good standing." While asking community leaders to do classification work for this effort, he emphasized applying a familiar if unrealistic standard. People of Indian-white ancestry could be in "good standing;" individuals with African American ancestors could not.

Compared to Coates, Roy Catesby Flannagan, a white Virginia journalist, took a more sardonic yet melodramatic view of the long history of race-mixing in Virginia in his novel *Amber Satyr*, set during the 1920s legislative racial integrity fights and published in 1932. Flannagan, in the novel, poked fun at Virginia legislators' debates of 1924–1930 about bills to define Blackness and Indianness. In the end, though, Flannagan left open the notion that tidewater Native people were mulattoes trying to escape Jim Crow. Walter Plecker would have agreed about that, but had Plecker read the novel, he probably would have found it intolerable because it did not take Plecker's eugenic, segregationist vision more seriously.

Flannagan's protagonist, Luther Harris, is part of a group that Flannagan imagines as not white, yet different from African Americans in Harris's home county whose ancestors had been enslaved. To fight the proposed legislation that could hamper their efforts to claim status as Indians, Luther begins working with relatives and a white lawyer. This fictional narrative seems to refer to Chickahominy activism, but it is only barely grounded in that history.

In this novel, Flannagan satirizes those who would deny the realities of interracial sex over centuries of Virginia history. Comic scenes lampoon the deliberations in the Virginia legislature about bills to revise Virginia's legal definitions of Blackness in the wake of the 1924 racial integrity law. The actual (rather than generalized or imagined) interracial sex that occurs in the novel is not violently coerced, but it derives from a massively unbalanced power dynamic. It reflects the vulnerability of the young woman involved—Luther's daughter. The man involved is among Flannagan's most stereotypically "poor white" characters. Flannagan here frames interracial sex and sexual exploitation as a fully human, perhaps normal, occurrence, but he confines it to the non-elite characters of his novel.

Flannagan may want the reader to be outraged when in the end the decent, honorable Luther is slaughtered, but the novel depicts Southern segregation and violence as unlikely to change because they are grounded in such powerful and normal human urges and in long-established political structures. In one passage, a white man—a deputy sheriff, emblematic of official sanction of racialized violence—moves from virulent stereotypes about African American sexuality to a meditation on political power: "If the white man didn't stand for his rights, they'd [African Americans] be running the county and all the white folks would have to leave."[108] This man later murders Luther. Events that move the plot to its conclusion foreground aspects of sexuality that, though warped by Jim Crow power structures and poverty, seem, in Flannagan's vision, as powerful and intractable as the political and economic forces behind segregation. Luther's young daughter gets pregnant, dashing his hopes for her education. In the end, his murder, largely precipitated by sexual jealousies, may be read as the novelist's statement that the future did not belong to a mulatto like Luther Harris or his daughter or her child, despite the novel's satirical approach to the eugenic arguments presented in the scenes set in the state legislature.

When *Time* magazine reviewed the novel in 1932, it opined that in "dealing with the fairly thoroughly canvassed tragic situation, or lack of situation, of half-breed Negroes in the South, the book tells its story with a ruthless, rare good humor." In keeping with the novel's sardonic tone, this review labeled as a "burlesque claim" the attempt to secure legal recognition of Indianness that Luther Harris' group pressed in the state legislature.[109] *Time* so pitched the novel less as an indictment of Southern racism and more as a satirical look at a "tragic situation" well understood by mainstream audiences; Luther was a "half-breed Negro," a "tragic mulatto," not indigenous.

The eminent African American poet and literary critic Sterling A. Brown reviewed *Amber Satyr* in the pages of the Urban League's *Opportunity* magazine. He described Luther Harris as a "bronze mulatto, part Indian," taking seriously Luther's claim to an Indian identity. Brown wrote that our protagonist was "industrious, ambitious for his daughter, and nursing illusions of being considered better than a Negro because of his Indian blood."[110] In the novel, Luther Harris vacillates between hoping for a way out of Jim Crow for his daughter and saying in a time of stress "we ain't got no business down here [in the state capitol] makin' out like we's Indians. We ought to be home minding our own business."[111] Perhaps Flannagan, like Brown, saw him as "nursing illusions." Still, instead of saying, as *Time* did, that the lobbying effort of Luther's group was a "burlesque claim," Brown read the passages set in the state legislature as "good journalistic reporting of the farrago of the attempted 'race purity' bill." Brown even called Flannagan "one of the newer Southern realists," and wrote that, given its depictions of "squalor and shiftlessness" among poor whites and the "defenselessness of the poor catspaw Negroes," the novel had some critical bite. "That a Southern white man has the courage to show this miserable state of affairs unflinchingly is one of the few things keeping this bitterness from going over into despair. It was not always so; perhaps the fact that intelligent realists are now recording these wrongs is a sign that they cannot go forever unrighted."[112]

Amber Satyr's plot, though, uses racialized sexual tensions in ways that make them seem natural, widespread, and intractable, grounded in class as well as race. The novel seems implicitly to accept the notion that one drop of Black blood makes you colored, if not fully Black, when Flannagan suggests that Luther's group's Indianness is a recently invented strategy fanned by an opportunistic white lawyer. Contrary to Flannagan's fiction, Chickahominy people's assertions of their Indianness had deep roots in families and community. By the time of this novel's publication, the Chickahominy and their first church had been organized for decades. Chickahominy histories and identities were and are historically grounded in ways Flannagan did not acknowledge, although he did produce a satirically tinged commentary on the excesses of twentieth-century racist rhetoric in Virginia in this popular entertainment.

Flannagan's novel shows how easily some whites dismissed the indigeneity of Native Virginians. In his own, more virulent way, Walter Plecker continued his work to purge and head off official recognition of Indian identities in Virginia until he retired in 1946. That official dismissiveness influenced census enumerations in 1930 and arose in World War II draft episodes that exemplified federal and state policies based in assumptions about race as a white-Black binary. Even as the census modernized, federal officials articulated practices for differential treatment of Indians with African American blood and for vigilance against those who might try to "pass" as Indian rather than Black.

In the wake of the racial integrity laws of 1924 and 1930, tidewater Native groups battled those census and draft policies. They continued to develop and maintain their churches and schools as segregated Indian institutions that supported their claims to be racially and socially separate from their African American neighbors. Baptist Indian churches forged connections to other churches within the Dover Baptist Association, and through it to the white Southern Baptist Convention organizational structure. Perhaps in the late 1930s and into the 1940s the tidewater Indian churches became somewhat more inward-looking, but their Baptist connections served them in the search for support for their schools. Those schools linked Native groups to county school boards and the state educational bureaucracy in Richmond.

Today, churches continue as major community institutions. While the Indian schools eventually lost their segregated status in the wake of the *Brown v. Board* decision, former school buildings have provided havens for community activities. For example, within a few years of the consolidation of the reservation schools, the Pamunkey reached an agreement with the state that they would use a vacant school building "for purposes of displaying and selling ceramic and other types of handicraft work made by adults living on the Reservation."[113]

Expressive gestures and occasions for cultural displays of Indianness, like the selling of pottery and the annual tribute to Virginia's governor (see chapter 3), also remained important in the years after 1930. Drawing from pageantry of the late nineteenth century and 1907 Jamestown exposition, dances continued on the reservations. The establishment of a formal Pamunkey pottery school in the 1930s with state support augmented expressive public presentations of Indianness that brought in cash in those Great Depression years and following decades.[114] Building on earlier efforts to sell pottery, it was a community project to draw tourists to reservation land.

In the 1950s, O. T. Custalow established a museum at the Mattaponi Reservation, marking expanded efforts to take advantage of increasing tourism after World War II. Similarly, the emergence of the annual Western Chickahominy Fall Festival and Powwow in 1951 fostered presentation of Chickahominy Indianness on Native ground to non-Natives and to other Native groups. This event, which continues today, taps into the popularity of the powwow as a pan-Indian phenomenon, accessible to general audiences and productive of intertribal connections.[115] Given the growth of tourism in the postwar years, such cultural presentations and representations could more readily be staged in or near Indian communities. Such efforts probably helped establish footings for new kinds of activism that emerged among tidewater Indian groups in the wake of the modern civil rights movement—even as the "all-deliberate-speed" desegregation of public schools, decreed by the Supreme Court, ultimately did away with Indian schools that had been a pillar of tidewater Native identity.

In 1954, the year of the *Brown v. Board* decision, the Virginia State legislature again changed the legal definition of Indianness, broadening it to embrace more non-reservation people. The new law, though, continued the practice of defining legal Indianness using blood-quantum fractions, and provided that more than a certain fraction of Negro blood would be disqualifying.[116] In that way, it was not a radical departure from previous efforts to define Indian identities and communities. Later, though, in the context of other post-World War II civil right movements, new forms of political activism in the 1960s and 1970s created additional horizons for Virginia Natives' public assertions of their Indianness.

EPILOGUE

LONG-TERM WORK BY TIDEWATER Virginia Indians to maintain, assert, reclaim, create, and recreate their identities as Native people from the 1850s to the 1950s shows how conceptually and socially corrupt, and yet also politically powerful, was the apparatus of Jim Crow. Their life experiences demonstrated they could carve out spaces outside a racialized Black-and-white duality within a Southern segregation regime, but also showed how precarious those spaces could be. Their stories reveal their stamina and persistence in the face of pervasive state-sponsored repression that was designed not to assimilate Virginia Indians to whiteness but to cement their position on the Black side of Virginia's Jim Crow color line.

Over decades after the 1950s, the rise of multiple civil rights movements and currents of political and social change created new, additional openings for Virginia Natives to reassert their Indianness in the public sphere. Across the United States, federally recognized tribes reaffirmed their sovereignties as they "emerged from the wreckage" of aggressive 1950s federal efforts to terminate trust responsibilities to some recognized groups and to encourage Native individuals to relocate into cities. And, as Brian Klopotek pointed out, in the 1960s and later decades Native groups who were not recognized by the federal government talked together about their shared concerns, including conversations within the United Southeastern Tribes and the Coalition of Eastern Native Americans.[1]

In that context, Virginia's legislature authorized the Commission on Indians in 1983, which became the Virginia Council on Indians in 1985, to advise the governor and lawmakers about the situations of Native peoples in the commonwealth. Following that action, the state formally recognized nine Native groups in addition to the reservation-based Pamunkey and Mattaponi. The Chickahominy of Charles City County, Eastern Chickahominy of New Kent County, Rappahannock of King and Queen County, and Upper Mattaponi of King William County were recognized in 1983; the Nansemond, south of the James River in Suffolk and Chesapeake in 1985; the Monacan Indian Nation of Amherst County in 1989; and the Cheroenhaka (Nottoway) and Nottoway of Virginia, both in Southampton County, and the Patawomeck of Stafford County in 2010.

In this, Virginia participated in a trend among southeastern states to set up Indian affairs commissions intended to facilitate the work of Native groups seeking to connect with agencies and programs whose resources those groups had not yet tapped. In 1971, North Carolina established the first such commission in the region; many southeastern states followed suit through 1995, when Georgia organized its commission.[2] These Southeastern Indian affairs commissions provided spaces for Native groups to work toward state recognition; sometimes that was seen as a potential step toward federal recognition.[3] Indeed, the Virginia Council on Indians explicitly modeled its criteria for state recognition on BIA standards.[4]

Following federal recognition of the Pamunkey through the BIA petition process in 2015–2016, congressional legislation in 2018 recognized six additional Virginia Native peoples: the Chickahominy, Eastern Chickahominy, Rappahannock, Upper Mattaponi, Monacan, and Nansemond. The trajectory of these groups is exemplified by the Chickahominy people who formed a legal organization in 1901, then sought state recognition, and later received federal recognition, a sequence typical of some Southeastern Native groups in other states. The 2018 federal legislation prohibited those six Virginia groups from conducting gaming enterprises, echoing opposition from gambling interests to the Pamunkey petition a few years earlier. This legal restriction on gaming points to some of the pitfalls of federal recognition. It suggests, instead of full tribal authority and autonomy, a semi-sovereignty in which indigenous people engage in ongoing contests to try to develop appropriate government-to-government relations at the federal level.[5] While federal recognition is no panacea, this new federal status has recently facilitated access to federal funds for coronavirus-pandemic relief, which the Upper Mattaponi, for example, used to overhaul a community healthcare facility. Like other indigenous peoples throughout the Southeast, the Upper Mattaponi expect and hope to use such federal resources to foster services and jobs so that more people can remain in the community to strengthen and "keep the tribe going," as Reggie Tupponce of the Upper Mattaponi told *The Washington Post*.[6] Despite the limitations and complex bureaucratic work entailed in gaining and living with federal recognition, federal programs can potentially open narrow pathways of aid for indigenous groups who are building more stable, economically viable communities for themselves.

In the Southeast, there has been predictable backlash by people who believe that some Native groups want federal recognition only to make land claims, or to tap some of the limited federal funding available for tribal programs, or to establish gaming operations. It seems likely that some of that backlash draws on assumptions that petitioning communities are not really indigenous, but are instead white, Latinx, or Black.[7] I hope I have shown how dubious such assumptions can be, as shown in the long history of tidewater Native peoples asserting their Indianness in public and maintaining family traditions of indigeneity throughout Jim Crow times when white officialdom could treat such assertions with harsh denials.

In fact, the notion that a one-drop rule defining Blackness can diminish an individual's Nativeness continues to complicate state and federal recognition of Indian groups to this day.[8] In 2006, that was among the matters that arose when the Nottoway Indian Tribe of Virginia submitted a petition for state recognition for review by the Virginia Council on Indians, in keeping with the council's role advising state government in that area. In initially placing the petition formally before the council, the tribal chair Lynette Paige Lewis Allston wrote, "In 2006, it is tragically ironic that some Virginia Indians and Anglo-Virginians still have little reticence in accepting light-skinned descendents of Indian tribes, who readily admit and celebrate their European duality, as recognized Indians; yet anguish over the darker-skinned duality of Indian-African ancestry as somehow being of less legitimate descendancy."[9]

Clearly, in the aftermath of Virginia's segregation era, indigenous-Black relationships can still roil conversations about Native identities. This also appears, for example, in events reported by Danielle Moretti-Langholtz. In 1997, a group split from the United Rappahanock tribe because of language in the tribe's articles of incorporation that the departing group considered were designed to exclude people with African American ancestors.[10] This 1997 controversy unfolded in the context of long-term trends toward broadening recognition of multiple, plural ethnic identities, even as race continues to operate as shorthand for a Black-white divide. Joane Nagel has pointed out that in the 1980 census more Americans reported Indian ancestors than identified themselves as racially Indian. However, for some people, the one-drop notion (a standard not generally applied to questions about Native ancestry) persists today when it comes to defining someone's Black identity.[11]

In 1979, Walter Williams wrote that "*the* major problem for all southern Indians of the last century and a third has been to define their ethnic status as a third group within a biracial society."[12] (The United States has been a biracial society only in the sense that white people have poured tremendous effort into that idea.) Also, more recently, scholars including Brian Klopotek and Denise Bates have pointed out that questions of sovereignty distinguish the situations of indigenous peoples from those of other racial/ethnic groups in the United States. For years, Virginia's government denied both those distinctions—a non-Black ethnicity and First Nations status—to non-reservation indigenous Virginians. Perhaps, in the future, federal recognition will contribute to ongoing Native efforts to rectify the legacies of those long-standing denials.

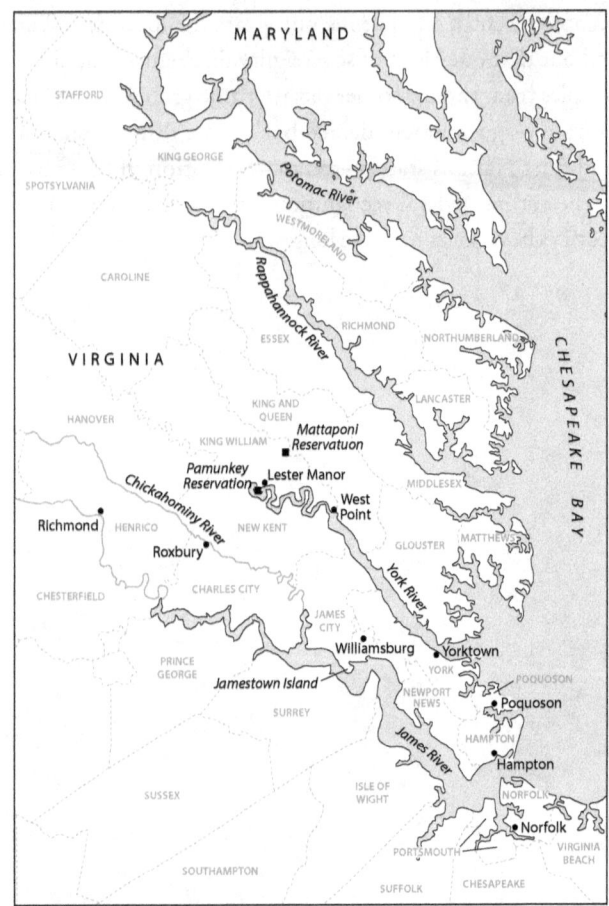

Tidewater, Virginia, Home Counties of Powhatan and Chickahominy People. Cartography by Bill Nelson.

ACKNOWLEDGMENTS

ABUNDANT THANKS AND GRATITUDE go to those on my dissertation committee at The George Washington University for expert guidance that was probing and humbling. Adele Logan Alexander, James Oliver Horton, Frederick Hoxie, Teresa Murphy, and John Michael Vlach gracefully handled the challenges of working with an old student. I hope that this book in some ways rewards their labors. Of course, while their instruction and commentary were invaluable, no flaws, errors, or omissions in this work can be laid at their scholarly doorsteps.

Another great pleasure of this project was working in a variety of archives with rich collections and skilled staff. I felt privileged to meet the stewards of records in those repositories. Constance Potter, retired from the National Archives, is a cherished friend and an expert guide to the complexities of U.S. census records. Brent Tarter, Sandy Treadway, Gregg Kimball, Patricia Ferguson Watkinson, and Virginia Dunn help make the Library of Virginia as welcoming as its facilities are well appointed. Brent is famously, fabulously generous in sharing his wisdom and encyclopedic knowledge of Virginia history. Gratitude and thanks also go to Regina Rush and others at the Albert and Shirley Small Special Collections Library at the University of Virginia, to Matthew Turi and Laura Clark Brown of the Wilson Library of the University of North Carolina at Chapel Hill, to Robert S. Cox, Earle Spamer, and Charles Greifenstein of the American Philosophical Society, to Alex Pezzati of the University of Pennsylvania Museum Archives, to Darlene Slater Herod of the Virginia Baptist Historical Society, to Leanda Gahegan of the National Anthropological Archives, to David Kilmon at the Richmond Public Library, and to the staff of the manuscript department at the William R. Perkins Library of Duke University, for their commitment to preserving the remarkable collections in their care and for making research in those collections such fun.

To Marie Tyler-McGraw go my heartfelt praise and thanks for her unfailing good humor, expert criticism, and willingness to take long walks and coffee breaks in the midst of her own packed life. Marie introduced me to Lucy Jarvis Pearman Scott and William Scott, and I am forever in her debt for that alone. For years, she patiently prodded me to get on with this project, gave me wise counsel, and read draft material that was not "ready for prime time." Dwight T. Pitcaithley has always seen the best in his fellow historians, and his generosity of spirit is always inspiring. I am deeply grateful for his friendship and his encouragement. Barbara Little's friendship and wisdom, likewise, have been sustaining. Her advice is always perceptive and well grounded. Brent Tarter read the entire manuscript at a time when I sorely needed the benefit of his catholic expertise in all aspects of Virginia history, and his collegial, magnanimous commitment to encouraging others' efforts in the field. Jane Scott's expert, gracious reading of my introduction showed me ways to improve the flow and organization of the whole text.

I am also immensely indebted to many scholars whom I know only through their work. To name just a few among them, Karen Blu, Malinda Maynor Lowery, Tiya Miles, Katherine M. B. Osburn, Claudio Saunt, Gerald Sider, and Gary Zellar provide inspiring and challenging models for anyone seeking to explore the complexities of race and Indianness in the American South. Anyone looking at the histories of Virginia's Powhatan Indians must thank Helen Rountree for her long-term, committed, indefatigable, and indispensable research and her many published works. My project's scope is much smaller than hers, and I owe much to her scholarship. Thanks go to Arica Coleman for her incisive exposition of centuries of the cultural and political history of the intersections of African American and Native American identities in Virginia. I hope she might find that my orientation toward social history complements her work.

The two scholars who read my manuscript for the University of Oklahoma Press modeled how peer review should be done; they were critical and constructive, thorough, expert in the literature of this field, and enormously generous in sharing their expertise and their time. Much gratitude also goes to Alessandra Jacobi-Tamulevich, senior acquisition editor at the University of Oklahoma Press, and the rest of the team at the press, for their expert shepherding of this project through the review and publication process.

I am beholden to my late uncle and aunt, Walter A. Feller and Judith Miller Feller, for their generosity and their interest in this project. My brother David always listened to me talk about this work as if I were making sense, even when I talked in circles, and for that gift of love I joyfully thank him here. As anyone who has done graduate school while married knows, your spouse shares his or her life with a project not of his or her choosing. John Fleckner was and is endlessly patient, wise, and critical yet warm to this project. He slogged with me through my bouts of self-doubt and, like Marie, read some very rough drafts with humor and grace. I'll be thanking him for the rest of our lives together.

NOTES

Introduction

1. Quoted in Joe Heim, "Foes of Virginia Tribes Federal Status Strike," *The Washington Post*, April 2, 2015, B1.

2. See Katherine M. B. Osburn, *Choctaw Resurgence in Mississippi: Race, Class, and Nation Building in the Jim Crow South*, on how Mississippi Choctaw status in the federal Treaty of Dancing Rabbit Creek and related Mississippi law created a context different from that faced by Virginia's tidewater indigenous people. For example, Mississippi Choctaw people received some support from segregationist politicians in early twentieth-century Mississippi in asserting that they should have access to federal programs for Indians, as Indians, in an era when much of official white Virginia denied that Virginia's indigenous people were actually Indian (see pp. 43–54, 123–25, 128–30, and 151–53, for more on Mississippi Choctaw relationships to the federal government).

3. Heim, "Foes of Virginia Tribes," B1–B2.

4. Ibid., B2

5. See Brian Klopotek, *Recognition Odysseys: Indigeneity, Race, and Federal Tribal Recognition Policy in Three Louisiana Indian Communities*, 210–11, on how this could also play out in the census in other parts of the South.

6. Heim, "Foes of Virginia Tribes," B2.

7. The anthropologist and ethnohistorian Helen C. Rountree suggested that into the 1860s, Powhatan groups may have taken an approach to group boundaries, and Indianness, that relied on "kinship and social congeniality," as well as "descent from the aborigines." She added that social "congeniality" might lead to status "as at least fringe members" of a tidewater Indian community—and while not denying the Indianness of the "fringe," she also wrote that "most such people were probably other Indians." See her *Pocahontas's People*, 189. Arica Coleman emphasizes the historic presence and participation of African Americans in Virginia Native groups, in *That the Blood Stay Pure: African Americans, Native Americans, and the Predicament of Race and Identity in Virginia*.

8. Christina Snyder, among others, discusses this in her *Slavery in Indian Country: The Changing Face of Captivity in Early America*, 5–6, 55, 153–55.

9. See Maximilian Forte's "Introduction: 'Who Is an Indian?' The Cultural Politics of a Bad Question," in his edited volume *Who Is an Indian? Race, Place, and the Politics of Indigeneity in the Americas*. See also Christina Snyder's *Slavery in Indian Country*.

10. Snyder, *Slavery in Indian Country*, 12, 156, 159–62, 194–95, 205–8, 210–12.

11. Joel Williamson, in *New People: Miscegenation and Mulattoes in the United States*, p. 125, among other scholars, has noted Herskovits's work.

12. Such laws are now commonly described as prohibiting miscegenation. Despite its aura of Greek-Latin technicality and antiquity, the word "miscegenation" was coined in the 1860s, to exploit whites' anxieties about sex across racial lines in the heat of Civil War-era debates about the rights and citizenship of African Americans. Two New York journalists, David Goodman Croly and George Wakeman, invented the word "miscegenation" for a pamphlet they published in anticipation of the campaign for the 1864 presidential election. They sought to convince voters that Republican party opposition to slavery meant that Republicans favored interracial sex, which had been described by words like "amalgamation." See Peter Wallenstein, *Tell the Court I Love My Wife: Race, Marriage, and Law: An American History*, 51–52, where he calls their pamphlet a "hoax."

13. Virginia's "Act to Preserve Racial Integrity," quoted in Walter Ashby Plecker, *Eugenics in Relation to the New Family and the Law on Racial Integrity*, 31.

14. Wallenstein, *Tell the Court I Love My Wife*, 2–3, 54, 80, 144–46, 194–98, figures 6–10, and Peter Wallenstein, *Race, Sex, and the Freedom to Marry: Loving v. Virginia*, 29–30. See also Hrishi Karthikeyan and Gabriel J. Chin, "Preserving Racial Identity: Population Patterns and the Application of Anti-Miscegenation Statutes to Asian Americans, 1910–1950," *Asian American Law Journal* 9 (2002): 1–40. As noted, the word "miscegenation" was coined by a pair of journalists during the election campaign of 1864.

15. Osburn, *Choctaw Resurgence in Mississippi*, 7, 10–11, 28.

16. Virginia Dominguez, *White By Definition: Social Classification in Creole Louisiana*, 26, 28, 34, 204; Brian Klopotek, *Recognition Odysseys*, 218, 318, 339

17. Wallenstein, *Tell the Court I Love My Wife*, 142–43; Wallenstein, *Race, Sex, and the Freedom to Marry*, 53–55.

18. Sarah Deutsch, "Being American in Boley, Oklahoma," in *Beyond Black and White: Race, Ethnicity, and Gender in the U.S. South and Southwest*, eds. Stephanie Cole and Alison M. Parker, 105.

19. Snyder, *Slavery in Indian Country*, 77–78.

20. Wallenstein, *Tell the Court I Love My Wife*, 28–35.

21. Elazar Barkan, *The Retreat of Scientific Racism: Changing Concepts of Race in Britain and the United States Between the World Wars*, 111.

22. Richard B. Sherman, in "'The Last Stand:' The Fight for Racial Integrity in Virginia in the 1920s," *Journal of Southern History* 54 (1988) provides an overview of both laws; see especially pps. 77–79; see also Rountree, *Pocahontas's People*, 220–22.

23. Matthew Frye Jacobson, *Whiteness of a Different Color: European Immigrants and the Alchemy of Race*, 3, 68.

24. Dan Kevles, *In the Name of Eugenics: Genetics and the Uses of Human Heredity*, xi.

25. Barkan, *Retreat of Scientific Racism*, 271.

26. On Indian citizenship, see, for example, Duane Champagne's "Tribal Institution Building in the Twentieth Century," in *Native Diasporas: Indigenous Identities and Settler Colonialism in the Americas*, eds. Gregory D. Smithers and Brooke N. Newman.

For a perspective on citizenship and enfranchisement of Indian peoples in Canada, see Robert Nichols's "Contract and Usurpation: Enfranchisement and Racial Governance in Settler-Colonial Contexts," in *Theorizing Native Studies*, eds. Audra Simpson and Andrea Smith.

27. See Grace Elizabeth Hale, *Making Whiteness: The Culture of Segregation in the South, 1890–1940*.

28. Osburn, *Choctaw Resurgence*, 7, 38, 43, 45–47, 52, 54–56, 117.

29. See Laura L. Lovett's "'African and Cherokee by Choice:' Race and Resistance under Legalized Segregation," *American Indian Quarterly* 22 (1998): 203, 217–19, on twentieth-century debates about African American and Native American ancestries.

30. Michael Omi and Howard Winant, *Racial Formation in the United States From the 1960s to the 1990s*, 5, 14–15.

31. Ann McMullen, "Blood and Culture: Negotiating Race in Twentieth Century New England," in *Confounding the Color Line: The Indian-Black Experience in North America*, ed. James F. Brooks, 266–67, on Native identity formation in New England.

32. Forte, "Introduction: 'Who Is an Indian: The Cultural Politics of a Bad Question," in *Who Is an Indian?*, 31, 34–39. See also Klopotek, *Recognition Odysseys*, 110–13, 122–23, 168, 206, 210. Klopotek notes that not all Jena Choctaw people think Choctaw identity should be based "strictly" in blood quantum. Since their acknowledgment by the federal government, the Jena Choctaw have lowered the blood quantum fraction required for membership, though some fear that too much outmarriage could weaken the argument for Jena Choctaw cohesion and identity in the future.

33. Karen Blu, *The Lumbee Problem: The Making of an American Indian People*, xii–xiii.

34. Omi and Winant, *Racial Formation*, 72. See Forte on pro-indigenous essentialism and pro-indigenous anti-essentialism in the conclusion to his edited volume, *Who Is an Indian?*, 236–38.

35. See, for example, not only the work of Katherine Osburn, Christina Snyder, and Brian Klopotek, but also Theda Perdue, *"Mixed Blood" Indians: Racial Construction in the Early South*; Tiya Miles, *Ties that Bind: The Story of an Afro-Cherokee Family in Slavery and Freedom*; Claudio Saunt, *Black, White, and Indian: Race and the Unmaking of an American Family*; Laura L. Lovett, "African and Cherokee by Choice: Race and Resistance under Legalized Segregation;" James H. Merrell, "The Racial Education of the Catawba Indians," *Journal of Southern History* 50, no. 3 (1984), and *The Indians' New World: Catawbas and Their Neighbors from European Contact through the Era of Removal*; Dominguez, *White By Definition*; Gerald Sider, *Living Indian Histories: Lumbee and Tuscarora People in North Carolina*; Blu, *The Lumbee Problem*; and Circe Sturm, *Blood Politics: Race, Culture, and Identity in the Cherokee of Oklahoma*. Julia M. Coates, in "'This Sovereignty Thing': Nationality, Blood and the Cherokee Resurgence" counters Sturm, emphasizing that tribal membership practices and rules function to protect tribal sovereignty, in Forte, ed., *Who Is an Indian?*.

36. See Lacy K. Ford, Jr., "Making the 'White Man's Country' White: Race, Slavery, and State Building in the Jacksonian South," in Michael A. Morrison and James Brewer

Stewart, eds., *Race and the Early Republic: Racial Consciousness and Nation-Building in the Early Republic,* 147–49.

37. See, for example, Snyder's *Slavery in Indian Country,* 6,172.

38. I am especially grateful for the work of Tiya Miles on the Cherokee, Malinda Maynor Lowery on the Lumbee, and Helen Rountree, Mikaëla Adams and Arica Coleman on Virginia Indian peoples. Ariela Gross and Eva Marie Garroute also shaped my thinking about this matter.

39. Jacobson, *Whiteness of a Different Color,* 275.

Chapter 1

1. William C. Scott and Lucy P. Scott to "My dear Children," 29 October 1854, Scott-Pearman Family Letters in Norvell Winsboro Wilson Papers. (The collection's finding aid describes the family as "possibly mulatto or part Indian.")

2. Ibid.

3. In these patterns of marriage and residence, the experiences of non-reservation tidewater indigenous people parallel and also contrast with those of Choctaw who remained in Mississippi after the removal era. In 1830, Mississippi's legislature declared that Choctaw residents in the state were citizens of Mississippi subject to state laws. This did not protect those who remained in Mississippi from Jim Crow segregation over the years. As non-whites, Mississippi Choctaw recognized the risks of associating with African Americans. Some lived in "closed endogamous communities that allowed them to support a social identity as a third racial group." See Katherine M. B. Osburn, *Choctaw Resurgence in Mississippi,* 20–21, 184–85. Lacking that kind of limited recognition of the Mississippi Choctaw based in the Treaty of Dancing Rabbit Creek, Virginia tidewater natives had even more difficulty establishing a racial identity not Black or white.

4. Certification by York County officials of Lucy Pearman Scott's status as a free person of color, dated 19 June 1848, no. 492, testifies to the requirement to carry "freedom papers" endured by free non-whites.

5. Helen C. Rountree and E. Randolph Turner, III, *Before and After Jamestown: Virginia's Powhatans and their Predecessors,* 196–99.

6. I argue that the most meaningful ways of "belonging" to an ethnic group entail participating in the life of that community, knowing its ways, and developing and performing reciprocal relationships with other members of the group. Kinship can rest on such allegiances, rather than on legalistic "blood quantum" measures of ancestry. There is a wealth of literature about this, including Eva Marie Garroute's *Real Indians: Identity and the Survival of Native America*; Lauren L. Basson's *White Enough to Be American? Race Mixing, Indigenous People, and the Boundaries of State and Nation*; essays in *Who Is an Indian? Race, Place, and the Politics of Indigeneity in the Americas,* edited by Maximilien Forte; and *Native Diasporas: Indigenous Identities and Settler Colonialism in the Americas,* edited by Gregory D. Smithers and Brooke N. Newman.

7. Helen C. Rountree, *Pocahontas's People: The Powhatan Indians of Virginia Through Four Centuries*, 190–91.

8. Ibid., 270–73.

9. Kathleen M. Brown, *Good Wives, Nasty Wenches, and Anxious Patriarchs: Gender, Race, and Power in Colonial Virginia*, 188.

10. Winthrop D. Jordan, *White Over Black: American Attitudes Toward the Negro, 1550–1812*, 20–22.

11. David D. Smits, "'Abominable Mixture:' Toward the Repudiation of Anglo-Indian Intermarriage in Seventeenth Century Virginia," *Virginia Magazine of History and Biography* 95 (1987): 161–62. Robert Tilton, *Pocahontas: The Evolution of an American Narrative*, 12–13.

12. Frederic W. Gleach, *Powhatan's World and Colonial Virginia: A Conflict of Cultures*, 127, 131, 163–69, 192–93. Rountree, *Pocahontas's People*, 87.

13. Gleach, *Powhatan's World and Colonial Virginia*, 169.

14. Not all British colonies outlawed Anglo-Indian marriage. See Michelle LeMaster, *Brothers Born of One Mother: British-Native American Relations in the Colonial Southeast*, 152–53.

15. Brown, *Good Wives, Nasty Wenches, and Anxious Patriarchs*, 197–98.

16. Warren M. Billings, "The Law of Servants and Slaves in Seventeenth Century Virginia," *Virginia Magazine of History and Biography* 99 (January 1991):61.

17. Brown, *Good Wives, Nasty Wenches, and Anxious Patriarchs*, 182, 215–16. See also Peter Wallenstein, "Race, Marriage, and the Law of Freedom: Alabama and Virginia, 1860s–1960s," *Chicago-Kent Law Review* 70 (1994): 371–437.

18. Brown, *Good Wives, Nasty Wenches, and Anxious Patriarchs*, 213.

19. Helen C. Rountree, "Ethnicity Among the 'Citizen' Indians of Tidewater Virginia," in *Strategies for Survival: American Indians in the Eastern United States*, edited by Frank W. Porter, III, 177.

20. Ibid., 182.

21. Brown, *Good Wives, Nasty Wenches, and Anxious Patriarchs*, 120–23, 216, 218–19.

22. Ibid., 242–44. See also Peter Wallenstein, *Tell the Court I Love My Wife: Race, Marriage and the Law—An American History*, 27–37.

23. Tilton, *Pocahontas*, 12–25. See Robert Beverley's *The History and Present State of Virginia.*, ed. Louis B. Wright, 38–39. Arica L. Coleman, in *That the Blood Stay Pure: African Americans, Native Americans, and the Predicament of Race and Identity in Virginia*, pages 60–61, argues that Jefferson's vision of white-Indian unions likely did not extend to Virginia Indians of his own day, because he "believed the Virginia aborigines' intermixture with Blacks placed them outside the possibility of intermixing with Whites."

24. Helen C. Rountree and Thomas E. Davidson, *Eastern Shore Indians of Virginia and Maryland*, 173–76, 186–99.

25. On the Nottoway lands, see Arica L. Coleman, *That the Blood Stay Pure*, especially pages 84–85 and 228–29.

26. Transcription of "A Petition from Citizens of King William County, Virginia" (MS petitions, King William County, B 1207), 20 January 1843, file 3695, National Anthropological Archives, Washington, DC.

27. Karen Blu, *The Lumbee Problem: The Making of an American Indian People*, 65, 73, 81. See also Lacy K. Ford, Jr., "Making the 'White Man's Country' White: Race, Slavery, and State Building in the Jacksonian South," in Michael A. Morrison and James Brewer Stewart, eds. *Race and the Early Republic: Racial Consciousness and Nation-Building in the Early Republic*, 147–49.

28. Gerald Sider, *Living Indian Histories: Lumbee and Tuscarora People in North Carolina*, 243.

29. Laura L. Lovett, "African and Cherokee by Choice: Race and Resistance under Legalized Segregation," 222.

30. Sider, *Living Indian Histories*, 86–90.

31. Blu, *The Lumbee Problem*, 124.

32. Rountree, *Pocahontas's People*, 190, 193, 343.

33. Jack D. Forbes, *Africans and Native Americans: The Language of Race and the Evolution of Red-Black Peoples*, 257–58, 262–64.

34. Rountree, *Pocahontas's People*, 188–89.

35. A summary is at Brendan Wolf's entry in *Encyclopedia Virginia*, "Racial Integrity Laws, 1924-1930," https://www.encyclopediavirginia.org/racial_integrity_laws_of_the_1920s. Accessed 26 May 2016.

36. Deposition of William H. Brisby, 19 July 1877; Southern Claims Commission, file no. 21949, no. 51446, William C. Langston; Records of the U.S. Southern Claims Commission; National Archives Building, Washington, DC. Accessed at https://www.fold3.com/image/34/222372377, 18 May 2016. Brisby's mother was of Pamunkey descent. In 1901, as a widower, he married Victoria Pearman Holmes, child of Jones Pearman and his wife Lizzie, who was William Cooper Langston's daughter Rebecca Elizabeth. See Brisby's Southern Claims Commission file, no. 19204, no. 48617, and John T. Kneebone's "William H. Brisby," in the *Encyclopedia Virginia*, https://www.encyclopediavirginia.org/Brisby_William_H_1836-1916. Accessed 12 June 2016. Brisby's cousin Martha Holt, when she was enumerated in his household in the New Kent County censuses of 1910, 1900, and 1880, was listed as "mulatto" or Black, like others in that household. In the King William County census in 1870, and in 1920 New Kent County, Holt appeared as Indian.

37. Testimony of John H. Langston, 18 March 1874; Southern Claims Commission file no. 21949, no. 51446, William C. Langston; Records of the U.S. Southern Claims Commission, National Archives Building, Washington, DC. Accessed at https://www.fold3.com/image/34/222372377, 18 May 2016.

38. Rountree, *Pocahontas's People*, 187.

39. In contrast, the Mississippi Choctaw of the post-removal and Jim Crow eras routinely displayed multiple cultural markers clearly differentiating them from white and Black Mississippians in dress, language, and practices such as stickball games; Katherine M. B. Osburn, *Choctaw Resurgence in Mississippi*, 20–21. See also Brian Klopotek, *Recognition Odysseys: Indigeneity, Race, and Federal Tribal Recognition Policy in Three*

Louisiana Indian Communities on language persistence (or lack thereof) among Louisiana indigenous groups, 94–95, 103–4, 130–31, 174–75.

40. William Scott and Lusey *(sic)* Scott, to "Dear Children," 26 August 1849; and E. Porter to "Dear Sister," 21 February 1842, both letters in Scott-Pearman Family Letters in Norvell Winsboro Wilson Papers.

41. Typically, but not always in 1940, individual census pages have more than one page number. One set of numbers orders the sheets in an individual census district; the other series represents consecutive numbering of all sheets for the entire county that included that district. Where it was available, for brevity, I have cited the page number in the county-wide numbering system. For the 1940 census, I cite page numbers for the census district.

42. I base this speculation on several sources. One is the microfilmed Register of Free Negroes and Mulattoes in Henrico County for 6 July 1840 at Library of Virginia, which lists William Scott and Richard P. Scott as sons of William and Frances Scott. Others are the entries for William P. Scott and Richard Scott in the 1850 Henrico County census just mentioned, the New Kent County Chancery Court case 1918-004 (cited later in this chapter), family letters cited later, and listings of the three Scott families in the 1861 census for Brantford, Canada, also cited later. While William's sons listed in the 1840 register may not have been the same William and Richard Scott who married Lucy's daughters, I will not ignore that possibility.

43. Gregg Kimball, "Place and Perception: Richmond in Late Ante-bellum America" (Ph.D. diss., University of Virginia, 1997), 190–1.

44. Rountree, *Pocahontas's People*, 200.

45. Gregg Kimball, *American City, Southern Place: A Cultural History of Antebellum Richmond*, 126–27. On Baptist deacons, I am also indebted to Marie Tyler-McGraw. See also Brian Klopotek's *Recognition Odysseys* for commentary on the leadership of Baptist deacons in Indian communities in more recent times, 199.

46. Kimball, *American City*, 127–29, 289.

47. Ibid., 128,136.

48. See David Brion Davis, *The Problem of Slavery in the Age of Emancipation*, 207–9, and 198–99.

49. Bill filed 15 January 1827, and Report of Commissioners dated January 1827. York County (Va.) Chancery Causes, 1768–1891. Fanny Jarvis, et al., vs. Executor of William Jarvis, box 7, folder 1832-004, Accession BC 1134480. Local Government Records Collection, York County Court Records. Library of Virginia, Richmond.

50. The one exception may be William Newman, on page 435 in the 1830 York County census.

51. It is possible that Lucy's father was the William Jarvis listed in York County's register of "free Negroes" in 1810 (entry no. 59), who had been emancipated years earlier in the will of one Thomas Jarvis. See microfilmed Free Negro registers for York County, 1798–1824. York County Records, reel 42. Library of Virginia, Richmond.

52. Peter Wallenstein, *Cradle of America: Four Centuries of Virginia History*, 88–90. See also Eva Sheppard Wolf, *Almost Free: A Story about Family and Race in Antebellum Virginia*.

53. William F. Pearman to "My Dear Brother," 25 August 1854, Scott-Pearman Family Letters in Norvell Winsboro Wilson Papers.

54. Lucy P. Scott to "My Dear Children," 5 September 1854, Scott-Pearman Family Letters in Norvell Winsboro Wilson Papers.

55. Thanks to Marie Tyler-McGraw for suggesting that Lucy here was meditating on sympathetic whites' reactions to deteriorations in the legal status for free people of color and a resulting decline in daily opportunities for peer-to-peer interactions between her family and white neighbors.

56. Wallenstein, *Cradle of America: Four Centuries of Virginia History*, 157. Kimball, *American City, Southern Place: A Cultural History of Antebellum Richmond*, 68–69. Rountree, *Pocahontas's People*, 182–83.

57. William F. Pearman to "Capt. Wm. Scott," 27 October 1852, Scott-Pearman Family Letters in Norvell Winsboro Wilson Papers.

58. William C. Scott and Lucy P. Scott, to "My dear Children," 29 October 1854, Scott-Pearman Family Letters in Norvell Winsboro Wilson Papers.

59. See the record of the second marriage of George Fleming Pearman (son of George Anderson Pearman and Letitia Scott Pearman) in Ontario *Registrations of Marriages, 1869–1928*, Series: MS 932. Archives of Ontario, Ontario, Canada. Accessed on Ancestry.com 3 July 2013. See also the entry for Letitia Scott in microfilmed Register of Free Negroes and Mulattoes in Henrico County for 1840. Library of Virginia, Richmond. Possibly Letitia was a daughter of William Scott.

60. William C. Scott to "My dear Children," 25 April 1859, Scott-Pearman Family Letters in Norvell Winsboro Wilson Papers.

61. Robin W. Winks, *The Blacks in Canada: A History*, 144, 149, 365–68.

62. William C. Scott and Lucy P. Scott, to "My dear Children," 29 October 1854, Scott-Pearman Family Letters in Norvell Winsboro Wilson Papers.

63. Lucy P. Scott to "My dear Children," undated, Scott-Pearman Family Letters in Norvell Winsboro Wilson Papers.

64. William C. Scott to "My dear Children," 25 April 1859, Scott-Pearman Family Letters in Norvell Winsboro Wilson Papers.

65. Ibid.

66. William C. Scott and Lucy P. Scott to "My dear Children, 27 October 1869, Scott-Pearman Family Letters in Norvell Winsboro Wilson Papers. For Ellen Charity, see microfilmed Register of Free Negroes and Mulattoes in Henrico County for 6 July 1840. Library of Virginia, Richmond.

67. Lucy P. Scott to "my dear children," 30 January 1862, Scott-Pearman Family Letters in Norvell Winsboro Wilson Papers.

68. William C. Scott to "My dear Children," 25 April 1859, and William C. Scott and Lucy P. Scott to "my dear children," 27 October 1869, both in Scott-Pearman Family Letters in Norvell Winsboro Wilson Papers.

69. These two sisters may have been the only ones among Lucy's Pearman children who stayed in Virginia; court records of the settlement of Macfarland Pearman's estate recount that only Ann Eliza Pearman Wynn, and Susan Pearman Howell, remained in the state. See an undated copy of a bill of complaint to Hon. D. G. Tyler, judge of the

Circuit Court for New Kent County. New Kent County (Va.) Chancery Causes, 1848–1956. Heirs of M. F. Pearman vs. Heirs of M. F. Pearman, 1918-004. Local Government Records Collection, New Kent County Court Records. Library of Virginia, Richmond.

70. Rountree, *Pocahontas's People*, 190, 342.

71. As Jim Crow regimes tightened, it seems unlikely that many enumerators in the postbellum South would have accepted an individual's articulation of his or her racial identity if that identity differed from the enumerator's perceptions. Probably many enumerators relied on whether the appearance of an individual, and of his or her family members, fit racialized stereotypes. Enumerators were also influenced by community reputation and associations, when and if an enumerator was familiar with the families, individuals, and communities in his or her district.

72. Deposition of Ferdinand Wynn, 6 February 1873, Southern Claims Commission file no. 19374, Ferdinand Wynn; Records of the U.S. Southern Claims Commission, National Archives Building, Washington, DC. Accessed at https://www.fold3.com/image/697249, 29 December 2016.

73. The U.S. census slave schedules for 1860 Charles City County do not indicate that Ferdinand Wynn owned slaves.

74. See chapter 2 on the Indian connections of the Stewart-Bullifant family in which Rebecca was born and the Indian identity of Rebecca Stewart's mother.

75. Census instructions prescribed "Ot" for "other," for individuals "not falling within" one of the other standard "classes."

76. Ferdinand the younger and his brother Winslow each had a son named Ferdinand; see the 1870 Charles City County census, p. 570B; 1880 Charles City County census, p. 193D; 1900 New Kent County census p. 10B, Black Creek Magisterial District. When Winslow married Joanna Holmes in 1880, the New Kent County Marriage Register (volume 1, 1865–1911) called the couple Indian.

77. Theodore Stern, "Chickahominy: The Changing Culture of a Virginia Indian Community," *Proceedings of the American Philosophical Society* 96 (1952): 204.

78. Brian Klopotek pointed out that in the long term, "All tribes are intertribal to some extent, incorporating new members through marriage, adoption, trade lines, and enslavement," and also that at some points in an indigenous group's history, practices of endogamy—including cousin marriage—could be a signifier of a group's conception and construction of its distinctive Native identity, and a way of keeping individuals within the community. In-group and cousin-marriage might have been common among their non-Native neighbors but it had specific and distinctive resonance among small Native groups in the Jim Crow South. See Klopotek, *Recognition Odysseys*, 205, 222–23, 224, 255.

79. New Kent County federal census for 1850, page 336B. See also a copy of the will of Thomas Pearman, witnessed in 1884. New Kent County (Va.) Chancery Causes, 1848–1956. Albert Williams, et al., v. J. P. Miles, Curator, etc., 1893-001. Local Government Records Collection, New Kent County Court Records. Library of Virginia, Richmond.

80. Through 1860, identifications of Indians in federal decennial censuses were uncommon, so the small numbers of Indians enumerated in mid-nineteenth-century Virginia reflect nationwide census trends as well as Virginia's racial politics. The 1870

instructions to census enumerators reminded them that, in keeping with the Constitution, "Indians not taxed" were not to be enumerated on the primary federal form (schedule 1) for tallying population, since Indians "not taxed" did not count for purposes of apportioning congressional representation to states. However, "Indians out of their tribal relations, and exercising the rights of citizens under State or Territorial laws, will be included" in schedule 1. Given the situation in Virginia, the classification of these Pearman families in 1870 (and the household of William and Lucy Pearman Scott in 1850) as mulatto seems predictable, even though in 1870 the printed census schedule 1 form added Indian to white, mulatto and Black as an option for the column noting someone's "color." See National Archives and Records Administration, "American Indians in the Federal Decennial Censuses, 1790–1930" information sheet, November 2004, and U.S. Department of Commerce, Bureau of the Census, *Twenty Censuses: Population and Housing Questions, 1790–1980*, 14–19.

81. James Mooney, "Circulars and Other Material Concerning Indians and Traces of Indians in Virginia, Maryland, Delaware, and North Carolina, 1889–1912," file no. 2190, National Anthropological Archives, Washington, DC.

82. Rountree, *Pocahontas's People*, 191, 342.

83. See William Walter Pearman's Certificate of Death, Commonwealth of Virginia, Charles City County, no. 9419, 27 March 1934. Accessed on Ancestry.com 25 January 2017.

84. Report by special agent George Tucker, 17 April 1876; Southern Claims Commission file no. 21949, no. 51446, William C. Langston; Records of the U. S. Southern Claims Commission, National Archives Building, Washington, DC. Accessed at https://www.fold3.com/image/34/222372377, 18 May 2016. For more on Native Americans in the context of the Southern Claims Commission, see Susanna Michele Lee's *Claiming the Union: Citizenship in the Post–Civil War South*, 125–32.

85. Deposition of William C. Langston, 19 July 1877; Southern Claims Commission file no. 21949, no. 51446, William C. Langston; Records of the U. S. Southern Claims Commission; National Archives Building, Washington, DC. Accessed at https://www.fold3.com/image/34/222372377, 18 May 2016. In the will of the elder Thomas Pearman as entered into court records in February 1865, he left lands, livestock, and "my carpenter and Shoe making tools," to his children, showing that like others in the extended Pearman-Howell-Wynn families, he was a person of some property and skills; see the will at pages 17 and 18 of volume 1, 1864–1887, of the will book of the Clerk of the New Kent County Circuit Court.

86. Marriage license of John C. Howell and Grace L. Stewart, 15 March 1910. New Kent County (Va.) Chancery Causes, 1848–1956. John C. Howell vs. Grace Stewart Howell, 1913–001. Local Government Records Collection, New Kent County Court Records. Library of Virginia, Richmond.

87. Microfilmed New Kent County Marriage Register, vol. 2, 1909–1950, p. 8. Library of Virginia, Richmond. See also certificate of marriage for her brother Ferdinand D. Wynn, 8 April 1955, no. 7910 in Richmond City.

88. His death certificate also calls him white. Certificate of Death, Commonwealth of Virginia, State file no. 3061, February 1947. Accessed on Ancestry.com, 26 January 2017.

89. Deposition of John Howell, 21 October 1913. New Kent County (Va.) Chancery Causes, 1848–1956. John C. Howell v. Grace Stewart Howell, 1913-001. Local Government Records Collection, New Kent County Court Records. Library of Virginia, Richmond.

90. Bill of exceptions, testimony of John C. Howell. New Kent County (Va.) Chancery Causes, 1848–1956. John C. Howell v. Charles H. Langston, 1921-004. Local Government Records Collection, New Kent County Court Records. Library of Virginia, Richmond. See also deposition of Olivia (Olive) Langston, 18 February 1920, in that same case, and John Clayton Howell's World War II-era draft registration card, serial no. 1567. Accessed on Ancestry.com, 2 April 2015.

91. See, for example, the undated copy of a bill of complaint to D. G. Tyler. New Kent County (Va.) Chancery Causes, 1848–1956. Heirs of M. F. Pearman v. Heirs of M. F. Pearman, 1918-004. Local Government Records Collection, New Kent County Court Records. Library of Virginia, Richmond. Rountree, in *Pocahontas's People*, 191, 207, and 347, mentions these surnames.

92. Microfilmed New Kent County Marriage Register, vol. 1, 1865–1911, p. 40. Library of Virginia, Richmond. A twenty-four-year-old man named Archer Collins appeared in the New Kent County household of John and Susan Howell in the 1850 census, working, like John Howell, as a wheelwright. Perhaps his presence indicates a generations-long connection to the family of Pinkey's husband, Simeon.

93. Microfilmed New Kent County Marriage Register, vol. 2, 1909–1950, p. 1. Library of Virginia, Richmond.

94. Microfilmed King William County Marriage Register, 1884–1943 (entry for 20 January 1909). Library of Virginia, Richmond.

95. In another example of how intertwined the affairs of these families were, James P. Miles was executor of the estate of Thomas Pearman, the younger, after Thomas's death around 1887. See New Kent County (Va.) Chancery Causes, 1848–1956. Albert Williams, et al., v. J. P. Miles, Curator, etc., 1893-001. Local Government Records Collection, New Kent County Court Records. Library of Virginia, Richmond.

96. Microfilmed New Kent Register of Marriages, vol. 1, 1865–1911, p. 32. Library of Virginia, Richmond. (The Richard Stewart household on 107A in 1920 New Kent County is not the same family.)

97. So were Martha Canaday (a daughter of Jones Pearman) and her children, listed on the same page as the family of Olivia Stewart Howell Langston (John Clayton Howell's mother) and Charles Langston (John Clayton Howell's stepfather) in 1910 New Kent (p. 225B), apparently living near Stewart and Wynn families.

98. Microfilmed New Kent County Register of Marriages, vol. 1, 1865–1911, p. 100. Library of Virginia, Richmond. See also Llewellyn Stewart's World War II-era draft

registration card, state file no. 85-009711, serial no. U1890. Accessed on Ancestry.com, 5 September 2017.

99. Microfilmed New Kent County Register of Marriages, vol. 1, 1865–1911, p. 53. Library of Virginia, Richmond, Virginia

100. Microfilmed King William County Marriage Register, 1884–1943. Library of Virginia, Richmond, has a record of Walter Miles's marriage to Hattie Stewart in 1913, which identified them as Indian.

101. Bill to D. G. Tyler, 30 October 1919, and deed dated 5 November 1889. New Kent County (Va.) Chancery Causes, 1848–1956. John C. Howell v. Charles H. Langston, 1921-004. Local Government Records Collection, New Kent County Court Records. Library of Virginia, Richmond.

102. Bill to Frank Armistead, 29 June 1942. New Kent County (Va.) Chancery Causes, 1848–1956. John C. Howell v. Ferdinand Wynn, et als., 1942-003. Local Government Records Collection, New Kent County Court Records. Library of Virginia, Richmond. (See also Hanover County Chancery Cause 1878-037.)

103. Copy of 1853 property tax record for "Camm Wynne." New Kent County (Va.) Chancery Causes, 1848–1956. John Camm Wynne v. Administrator of James Stamper, 1882-018. Local Government Records Collection, New Kent County Court Records. Library of Virginia, Richmond. See also "Wynn, John C. (Indian)" notation in an entry (no page number) in a New Kent County Land Tax, Personal Property and Sheriff's Receipt Book, 1851–1852. Local Government Records Collection, New Kent County Court Records. Library of Virginia, Richmond.

104. See Chancery Cause 1895-004, in New Kent County (Va.) Chancery Causes, 1848–1956. Richmond T. Lacy, Administrator of Henley B. Sherman, Creditors of Thomas B. Sherman v. Sherman, Creditors of Henley B. Sherman, Heirs of Thomas B. Sherman, 1895-004. Local Government Records Collection, New Kent County Court Records. Library of Virginia, Richmond.

105. Undated copy of a bill of complaint to D. G. Tyler. New Kent County (Va.) Chancery Causes, 1848–1956. Heirs of M. F. Pearman v. Heirs of M. F. Pearman, 1918-004. Local Government Records Collection, New Kent County Court Records. Library of Virginia, Richmond. Listing of the 1884 marriage of J. S. Wynn and Lena L. Howell is microfilmed in the New Kent County Marriage Register, vol. 1, 1865–1911, p. 46. Library of Virginia, Richmond.

106. "Exceptions of Virginia Wynn and Hiram Wynn to Commissioners Report," 26 April 1888. Hanover County (Va.) Chancery Causes, 1831–1913. John Solomon Wynn v. H. Wynn, et als., 1903-027. Local Government Records Collection, Hanover County Court Records. Library of Virginia, Richmond. (See also Lucile Wynn v. Virginia White, et als., 1904-022, in those Hanover County (Va.) Chancery Court Cases, 1831–1913.)

107. Undated copy of a bill of complaint to D. G. Tyler. New Kent County (Va.) Chancery Causes, 1848–1956. Heirs of M. F. Pearman vs. Heirs of M. F. Pearman, 1918-004. Local Government Records Collection, New Kent County Court Records. Library of Virginia, Richmond.

108. William C. Scott to "My dear Children," 25 April 1859, and William C. Scott and Lucy P. Scott to "my dear children," 27 October 1869, in Scott-Pearman Family Letters in Norvell Winsboro Wilson Papers.

109. Bill to D. Gardner Tyler, accepted by the court 14 July 1904. New Kent County (Va.) Chancery Causes, 1848–1956. M. F. Pierman v. Albert Williams, et als., 1905-005. Local Government Records Collection, New Kent County Court Records. Library of Virginia, Richmond.

110. U.S. Department of Commerce, Bureau of the Census, *Twenty Censuses,* 22.

111. Ibid., 39.

112. Undated copy of a bill of complaint to D. G. Tyler. New Kent County (Va.) Chancery Causes, 1848–1956. Heirs of M. F. Pearman vs. Heirs of M. F. Pearman, 1918-004. Local Government Records Collection, New Kent County Court Records. Library of Virginia, Richmond.

113. As noted, two daughters of the elder Thomas Pearman, Mary Ann and Martha, lived in the Park Bailey family. I have not been able to connect Alice and Ballard Bailey to Park Bailey's family, but it seems possible that the family of Ballard and Alice Bailey had multiple extended-family ties to Macfarland Pearman.

114. Microfilmed King William County Marriage Register, 1884–1943. Library of Virginia, Richmond.

115. Undated copy of a bill of complaint to D. G. Tyler. New Kent County (Va.) Chancery Causes, 1848–1956. Heirs of M. F. Pearman vs. Heirs of M. F. Pearman, 1918-004. Local Government Records Collection, New Kent County Court Records. Library of Virginia, Richmond.

116. Brown, *Good Wives, Nasty Wenches, and Anxious Patriarchs,* 110.

117. Teresia Teaiwa, "The Ancestors We Get to Choose: White Influences I Won't Deny," in *Theorizing Native Studies,* eds. Audra Simpson and Andrea Smith, 44.

118. Barbara Krauthamer, *Black Slaves, Indian Masters: Slavery, Emancipation and Citizenship in the Native American South,* 30.

Chapter 2

1. Quoted in Walter Ashby Plecker, *Eugenics in Relation to the New Family and the Law on Racial Integrity,* 31.

2. "At an Interview Between William Archer Thaddeus Jones and Hon. Albert O. Boschen Held in the Office of the Bureau of Vital Statistics, the Following Questions Were Asked and Answered, January 31st, 1925," box 41, Papers of John Powell, Albert and Shirley Small Special Collections Library, University of Virginia. Jones's sister, whose children attended the Indian School at Roxbury, was Mattie B. O. Jones, the first wife of Curtis Wynn who was a son of Ferdinand and Rebecca Wynn.

3. Peter Wallenstein, on pages 42–44 in *Race, Sex, and the Freedom to Marry: Loving v. Virginia* pointed out that in some states, Jim Crow legal definitions of racial identity

could differ from one context to another, in different areas of segregation, from schools, sex, and marriage, to public transportation.

4. Brian William Thomson remarked on this, in his dissertation "Racism and Racial Classification: A Case Study of the Virginia Racial Integrity Legislation," 182–83, 301–03.

5. See Lee D. Baker's *Anthropology and the Racial Politics of Culture*, 200, on Cox's efforts to find financial support for his publication.

6. Richard B. Sherman, "'The Last Stand:' The Fight for Racial Integrity in Virginia in the 1920s," *Journal of Southern History* 54 (February 1988): 71–73.

7. See, for example, Peter Wallenstein's *Tell the Court I Love My Wife: Race, Marriage, and Law: An American History*, 33. For other cases in which Virginia courts looked at race "socially speaking" and at physical appearance, and a case in which Indian "blood" was an issue before the court in the postbellum era (1877's *McPherson v. Commonwealth*), see Samuel N. Pincus, *The Virginia Supreme Court, Blacks, and the Law, 1870–1902*, 52–53, 55–57.

8. Sherman, " 'The Last Stand,' " 70. See also Brendan Wolf's entry in *Encyclopedia Virginia*, "Racial Integrity Laws, 1924–1930." https://www.encyclopediavirginiaorg/racial_integrity_laws_of_the_1920s. Virginia Foundation for the Humanities, 4 November 2015. Accessed 26 May 2016.

9. Peter Wallenstein has remarked on this, in *Blue Laws and Black Codes: Conflicts, Courts, and Change in Twentieth-Century Virginia*, 147–48, and *Tell the Court I Love My Wife*, 140.

10. A. Leon Higginbotham Jr., *In the Matter of Color: Race and the American Legal Process: The Colonial Period*, 43–44.

11. Ibid., 44.

12. Dan Kevles pointed out that in England, by the 1880s, some "reformers were forging [social] Darwinism into a weapon against laissez-faire." See *In the Name of Eugenics: Genetics and the Uses of Human Heredity*, 21–23.

13. Edward J. Larson, *Sex, Race, and Science: Eugenics in the Deep South*, 30.

14. Virginia Governor (1922–1926: Trinkle) Executive Papers, 1922–26, boxes 19, 20, 29. Accession 21567b, State Government Records Collection, Library of Virginia, Richmond.

15. Betsy L. Nies, *Eugenic Fantasies: Racial Ideology in the Literature and Popular Culture of the 1920s*, 65–66.

16. Robert. F. Berkhofer Jr., *The White Man's Indian: Images of the American Indian from Columbus to the Present*, 177–78. The Indian Citizenship Act of 1924 can be seen as an assimilative measure. Berkhofer points out that it also had to do with political efforts to rein in the power of the Department of the Interior and suggests parallels with the idea that immigrants had to be "Americanized," even as the flow of new immigrants was being slowed in the 1920s.

17. Thomson, "Racism and Racial Classification," 87, 201.

18. Paul A. Lombardo, "Miscegenation, Eugenics, and Racism: Historical Footnotes to *Loving v. Virginia*," *University of California-Davis Law Review* 21(1998): 427–28.

19. Thomson, "Racism and Racial Classification," 201–5.

20. Walter Plecker to Rev. Wendell White, 10 May 1924; Walter Plecker to Dr. C.W. Garrison, 5 January 1925, both in box 41, Powell Papers.

21. Earnest Sevier Cox to unnamed correspondent, 1907, box 1, Earnest Sevier Cox Papers, William R. Perkins Library, Duke University.

22. Earnest Sevier Cox to Alliance of Colored American Citizens of the United States of America, 7 July 1924, box 2, Earnest Sevier Cox Papers.

23. Earnest Sevier Cox to Mr. and Mrs. E. D. Pines, 29 September 1906, box 1, Earnest Sevier Cox Papers.

24. Earnest Sevier Cox to Henry L. West, draft, n. d., box 1, Earnest Sevier Cox Papers; and Henry L. West to Earnest Sevier Cox, 13 December 1923, box 2, Earnest Sevier Cox Papers.

25. Earnest Sevier Cox to Mrs. E. D. Pines, 30 January 1918, box 1, Earnest Sevier Cox Papers.

26. Earnest Sevier Cox to G. P. Putnam's Sons ("Mr. Putnam, the younger") 20 November 1919; and undated draft of that letter, both in box 1, Earnest Sevier Cox Papers

27. On Cox's relationship to Grant, see pages 245–48 of Jonathan Peter Spiro's *Defending the Master Race: Conservation, Eugenics, and the Legacy of Madison Grant*.

28. Earnest Sevier Cox to Madison Grant, 6 December 1920, box 1, Cox Papers. Indicating his need to flatter Grant, Cox wrote that in discussing his ideas with Richmond College faculty, they were impressed that Grant had agreed to read Cox's manuscript. At that moment, those faculty members knew of Grant as the author of an introduction to Lothrop Stoddard's *The Rising Tide of Color Against White World-Supremacy* and likely also as author of *The Passing of the Great Race*. Stoddard wrote supportive letters, including one congratulating Cox on the passage of Virginia's 1924 Act to Preserve Racial Integrity, but seems not to have exerted himself to become more widely and publicly associated with Cox, Powell, and Plecker. See Lothrop Stoddard to Earnest Sevier Cox, 25 March 1924, box 2, Cox Papers.

29. Earnest Sevier Cox to Madison Grant, 6 December 1920, box 1, Cox Papers

30. Madison Grant to Earnest Sevier Cox, 12 January 1921, box 2, Cox Papers. Apparently, at least one Klan leader admired Grant's efforts to spread such "information;" see Spiro, *Defending the Master Race*, 171.

31. W. Clyde Maddox to John Powell, 3 May 1931, box 40, Powell Papers.

32. J. Douglas Smith, *Managing White Supremacy: Race, Politics, and Citizenship in Jim Crow Virginia*, 78–80. See also John T. Kneebone's entry on the "Ku Klux Klan in Virginia," in Encyclopedia Virginia. https://www.encyclopediavirginia.org/Ku_Klux_Klan_in_Virginia. Virginia Foundation for the Humanities, 4 November 2016. Accessed 11 May 2018.

33. Katherine Osburn notes that the Mississippi Choctaw "drew support from both advocates and opponents of the Klan." Given the Mississippi Choctaw's historical legal position under federal treaty and state law, and their separatism, some white supremacists saw them as not exactly colored, if not white. This did not mean that the Mississippi Choctaw escaped Jim Crow segregation. See Osburn's *Choctaw Resurgence in Mississippi*, 89–91, 95–97.

34. Earnest Sevier Cox to Will Buford, 19 January 1923, box 2, Cox Papers.

35. Madison Grant to Earnest Sevier Cox, 18 March 1924, box 2, Cox Papers.

36. See, for example, Earnest Sevier Cox to Marcus Garvey, 8 June 1925; and Marcus Garvey to Earnest S. Cox, 10 June 1925, both in box 2, Cox Papers.

37. See Sherman, "The Last Stand," 74–77, on the Anglo-Saxon Clubs and their activities.

38. Powell Papers, box 38. The Anglo-Saxon Clubs constitution cited here was printed in a pamphlet included in Powell's papers.

39. Madison Grant to John Powell, 1 February 1924, box 39, Powell Papers.

40. Powell Papers, box 38. Like the Anglo-Saxon Club constitution, the 5 June 1923, newspaper piece cited here was reprinted in a pamphlet included in Powell's papers.

41. Ibid. Also see Sherman, "The Last Stand," 70–71, for a discussion of fears among white Virginians about whether the mixed population in Virginia was increasing, and whether more African Americans were successfully "passing" as white.

42. Ibid.

43. Powell Papers, box 38. Along with the Anglo-Saxon Club constitution and newspaper piece of 5 June 1923, the 22 July 1923 piece cited here was reprinted in a pamphlet included in Powell's papers. His mention of history and ethnology evokes Peggy Pascoe's observation that for nineteenth-century racialists, race was not determined by biology alone. Rather, it was "understood as an indivisible essence that included not only biology but also culture, morality, and intelligence." Peggy Pascoe, "Miscegenation, Law, Court Cases, and Ideologies of 'Race' in Twentieth-Century America," *Journal of American History* 83 (1996): 48.

44. See the above-cited pamphlet that reprinted the newspaper piece of 22 July 1923, in the Powell Papers, box 38.

45. Ibid.

46. Pascoe, "Miscegenation Law," 48.

47. See the above-cited pamphlet that reprinted the other newspaper pieces of 5 June and 22 July 1923, in the Powell Papers, box 38.

48. Ibid.

49. Ibid.

50. Ibid.

51. Ibid.

52. Sherman, "The Last Stand," 77–78.

53. Lombardo, "Miscegenation, Eugenics, and Racism," 438; Thomson, "Racism and Racial Classification," 269.

54. Larson, *Sex, Race and Science* (2, 83–84, 93, 153–55), argued that in the era when Plecker began his campaign against interracial marriage, white Southern eugenicists generally focused their efforts to control reproduction by people they considered mentally unfit (through gender segregation or sterilization, for example) on whites rather

than on African Americans, because their concern was preventing "deterioration of the Caucasian race," not the African American "race."

55. Brian William Thomson focused on these aspects of the racial integrity campaign in his "Racism and Racial Classification."

56. Thomson, "Racism and Racial Classification," 235–37.

57. "Killed," *Religious Herald*, 18 March 1926, 11.

58. "Chief Cook's Lament," *The Richmond Planet*, 11 February 1928 and reprinted 18 February 1928. See also Thomson, "Racism and Racial Classification," 239–42.

59. Louise Burleigh (Powell) to John Powell, n.d., box 40, Powell Papers.

60. Typescript "Racial Integrity Legislation," apparently prepared by Louise Burleigh for a use as an editorial for a Farmville newspaper, and mailed to Powell on 28 February 1928, box 38, Powell Papers.

61. Walter Plecker to J. Griswold Webb, 3 March 1926, box 41, Powell Papers.

62. Walter Plecker to editor, Richmond *Times-Dispatch*, 28 April 1925, box 41, Powell Papers.

63. Walter Plecker to E. Lee Trinkle, 5 October 1925, box 43, Trinkle Papers. School segregation concerned Plecker, as he worked to extend his reach under the 1924 law beyond questions of marriage; see, for example, *Virginia Health Bulletin*, vol. xvi, extra no. 2, March 1924, "The New Virginia Law to Preserve Racial Integrity," box 43, Trinkle Papers.

64. Walter Plecker to E. Lee Trinkle, 5 October 1925, box 43, Trinkle Papers.

65. E. Lee Trinkle to Chief E. P. "Bradley" (Bradby), 1 December 1925, box 43, Trinkle Papers.

66. E. Lee Trinkle to Walter Plecker, 1 December 1925, box 43, Trinkle Papers.

67. E. Lee Trinkle to Walter Plecker, 4 December 1925, box 43, Trinkle Papers.

68. Virginia Acts of Assembly, 1929–1930, quoted in Helen C. Rountree, *Pocahontas's People*, 221.

69. *Notes on the History of Defining a "Colored Person,"* a typescript in box 38, Powell Papers, provide more detailed discussion of why promoters of this bill thought a new law was needed (including the suggestion that an old standard defining "colored" status at one-fourth or more of "negro blood" resulted from "ignorance of the law of heredity"); of school segregation; and of how class factored into their vision of the history of legal definitions of race and interracial marriage in Virginia.

70. Virginius Dabney, "Virginia Takes Up Racial Integrity," *New York Times*, 16 February 1930.

71. Typescript "Racial Integrity Legislation," apparently prepared by Louise Burleigh for a use as an editorial for a Farmville newspaper, and mailed to Powell on 28 February 1928, box 38, Powell Papers.

72. Walter A. Plecker to [name not apparent on this copy], 12 February 1924, box 41, Powell Papers.

73. See Smith, *Managing White Supremacy*, 83–84.

74. *Virginia Health Bulletin*, vol. xvi, extra no. 1, March 1924, "Instructions to Local Registrars and Other Agents in Administration of the Law to Preserve Racial Integrity," box 38, Powell Papers.

75. Ibid.

76. Ibid.

77. Local registrar [name redacted in this copy] to Dr. W. A. Plecker, SR, 28 July 1923, box 41, Powell Papers.

78. Walter Plecker to M. B. Booker, 15 February 1924, box 41, Powell Papers.

79. *Virginia Health Bulletin*, vol. xvi, extra no. 1, March 1924, "Instructions to Local Registrars and Other agents in Administration of the Law to Preserve Racial Integrity," box 38, Powell Papers.

80. Walter A. Plecker to Mrs. A. P. Bohannon, 3 May 1938, box 41, Powell Papers; Walter A. Plecker to E. C. Lacy, 3 February 1943, box 42, Powell Papers.

81. Walter Plecker to Samuel L. Adams, 11 December 1924, box 41, Powell Papers.

82. Walter Plecker to the Clerks of Rockbridge, Amherst, and Augusta Counties, 29 April 1924, box 41, Powell Papers.

83. Walter Plecker to W. H. Clark, 29 July 1924, box 41, Powell Papers. See also a letter to the editor that Walter Plecker wanted the editor of the Lexington *County News* to publish, 17 September 1924, box 2, Cox Papers.

84. Walter Plecker to John Powell, 30 July 1924, box 41, Powell Papers.

85. Walter Plecker to Earnest Sevier Cox, 9 August 1924, box 41, Powell Papers.

86. Walter Plecker to the American Medical Association, 19 September 1924, box 2, Cox Papers.

87. Sherman, "The Last Stand," 80–81.

88. See, for example, Plecker's letter to a local clerk about the Johns case for an example of his assertions of the value of his evidence in this case: Walter Plecker to W. E. Sandidge, 4 October 1924, box 41, Powell Papers.

89. Lombardo, "Miscegenation, Eugenics, and Racism," 440–42.

90. Thomson, "Racism and Racial Classification," 233–35.

91. Leon M. Bazile to John Powell, 26 November 1924, box 39, Powell Papers.

92. Walter Plecker to William R. Kennedy, 16 September 1924, box 2, Cox Papers. See also Walter Plecker to Matthew W. Paxton, 17 September 1924, forwarding to him as editor, *County News*, a letter to the editor also dated 17 September 1924 that he wanted Paxton to publish, box 2, Cox Papers.

93. See Bruce Dain, *A Hideous Monster of the Mind: American Race Theory in the Early Republic*, vii–ix, 203; and Elazar Barkan, *The Retreat of Scientific Racism*, 15.

94. Walter Plecker to Mrs. Robert H. Cheatham, 30 April 1924, copy with text of undated letter to Mary Gilden, box 41, Powell Papers.

95. See, for example, Walter Plecker to Harry E. Davis, 4 October 1924, box 41, Powell Papers.

96. Walter Plecker to Augusta Fothergill, 21 January 1928, box 41, Powell Papers.

97. Walter Plecker to Samuel L. Adams, 11 December 1924, box 41, Powell Papers.

98. "Stenographic Report of an Interview Regarding the So-Called 'Indians' of Charles City County between Mr. E. H. Marston of Charles City County and Dr. W. A. Plecker, State Registrar, Held in the Bureau of Vital Statistics, February 1925," box 41, Powell Papers.

99. Walter Plecker to L. M. Nance, 19 December 1924, box 41, Powell Papers.

100. "Stenographic Report of an Interview Regarding the So-Called 'Indians' of Charles City County between Mr. E. H. Marston of Charles City County and Dr. W. A. Plecker, State Registrar, Held in the Bureau of Vital Statistics, February 1925," box 41, Powell Papers.

101. Clarence Jennings to Albert O. Boschen, 27 January 1925, box 41, Powell Papers.

102. "At an Interview between William Archer Thaddeus Jones and Hon. Albert O. Boschen," 31 January 1925," box 41, Powell Papers.

103. Walter Plecker to D. E. Harrower, 27 April 1925, box 41, Powell Papers.

104. Ibid.

105. Walter Plecker to John Powell, 27 April 1925, box 41, Powell Papers.

106. Frank G. Speck to Walter Plecker, 6 September 1924, box 2, Cox Papers.

107. Walter Plecker to W. M. Steuart, 14 January 1925, box 29, Trinkle Papers.

108. Walter Plecker, "Shall America Remain White?," typescript copy, box 38, Powell Papers; Walter Plecker to A. W. Thompson, 12 December 1924, Cox Papers.

109. Walter Plecker, "Virginia's Attempt to Adjust the Color Problem," typescript copy (a reprint summary appeared in *The Literary Digest,* 7 March 1925), box 38, Powell Papers. There was also a reprint of this article in Walter Ashby Plecker, Bureau of Vital Statistics, Public Health Bureau, "Eugenics in Relation to the New Family and the Law on Racial Integrity," second edition (Richmond, Virginia: Superintendent of Public Printing, 1924).

110. Plecker, "Eugenics in Relation to the New Family and the Law on Racial Integrity," 1–11.

111. See, for example, a 1924 letter from Walter Plecker to Warner Ames; and Walter Plecker to Earnest Sevier Cox, 10 September 1924, both in box 2, Cox Papers; and Thomas Dabney to Earnest Sevier Cox, 31 March 1924, box 2, Cox Papers.

112. Walter Plecker to Alliance of Colored American Citizens, 1 April 1924; Walter Plecker to Earnest Sevier Cox, 18 June 1924; and Earnest Sevier Cox to Alliance of Colored American Citizens of the United States of America, 7 July 1924, all in box 2, Cox Papers.

113. Broadside of the Alliance of Colored American Citizens of the United States of America, n.d., box 2, Cox Papers.

114. Copy in box 38, Powell Papers.

115. Marcus Garvey to Earnest Sevier Cox, 10 June 1925, box 2, Cox Papers.

116. See Walter Plecker to the President of the United States, 19 March 1927, box 41, Powell Papers.

117. John J. Fenner Jr., to Earnest Sevier Cox, 17 June 1925, box 2, Cox Papers.

118. See Sherman, "The Last Stand," 86–88, on these articles and responses to them in the white and Black press.

119. Scrapbook with text of "The Last Stand: The Necessity of Racial Integrity Legislation in Virginia as Shown by an Ethnological Survey of the State by Congressional Districts," n.d., box 38, Powell Papers.

120. Walter Plecker to E. Lee Trinkle, 19 April 1924; E. Lee Trinkle to Walter Plecker, 23 April 1924, both in box 43, Trinkle Papers. See also E. H. Anderson, to E. Lee Trinkle, 17 April 1924, box 43, Trinkle papers. The latter letter thanks the governor, on behalf of the Virginia Post, no. 1, of the Anglo-Saxon Clubs of America, for sending a message through "Anglo-Saxon Powell" praising the 1924 law, for "the promptness of the registration of yourself and family," and for his intention to send copies of the law to other governors urging that other states pass similar legislation.

121. See, for example, Walter Plecker to Rev. Wendell White, 10 May 1924, box 41, Powell Papers.

122. Walter Plecker to L. E. Stephens, 12 December 1924, box 2, Cox Papers.

123. Walter Plecker to J. Griswold Webb, 3 March 1926, box 41, Powell Papers.

124. Walter Plecker to Harry E. Davis, 4 October 1924, box 41, Powell Papers.

125. Walter Plecker to John K. Gailey, 21 May 1925, box 41, Powell Papers.

126. Walter Plecker to Earnest Sevier Cox, 9 August 1924, box 41, Powell Papers.

127. See, for example, Walter Plecker to F. M. Register, 9 August 1924, box 41, Powell Papers.

128. Walter Plecker to C. W. Garrison, 5 January 1925, box 41, Powell Papers.

129. Walter Plecker to Morris Sheppard, 12 March 1925, box 41, Powell Papers.

130. Sherman, "The Last Stand," 69.

131. Undated petition, Richmond City, School Board Minutes, barcode 1051019, Minutes/Notes of 23 October 1925 and 27 November 1925, Concerning Children of Ray Wynn, Library of Virginia, Richmond. This text appears to be a draft, not final, version.

132. "Bar Six Indians From City School," *Richmond Times-Dispatch*, 23 October 1925; "Begin Battle to Admit Six to Classroom," *Richmond Times-Dispatch*, 24 October 1925; "Standing of Six Indian Students to Be Considered," *Richmond News Leader*, 23 October 1925; "Will Resume School Hearing November 3," *Richmond Times-Dispatch*, 25 October 1925; "Protest Ban on Indian Children," *Richmond News Leader*, 24 October 1925; "Negro Blood Here Causes Trouble," *The Richmond Planet*, 31 October 1925.

133. Ibid.

134. Superintendent of the Richmond Public Schools, *Fifty-Ninth Annual Report of the Superintendent of the Public Schools of the City of Richmond, Virginia, for the Scholastic Year Ending June 30, 1928* (Richmond: Curtiss-Neal, Incorporated,1928) 9, 13, 32, 75, 112–13, 116–17, 134.

135. Superintendent of the Richmond Public Schools, *Sixtieth Annual Report of the Superintendent of the Public Schools of the City of Richmond, Virginia, for the Scholastic Year Ending June 30, 1929*, 9. See also page 9 in the *Sixty-First Annual Report of the Superintendent of the Public Schools of the City of Richmond, Virginia for the Scholastic*

Year Ending June 30, 1930 and the *Sixty-Second Annual Report of the Superintendent of the Public Schools of the City of Richmond, Virginia, for the Scholastic Year Ending June 30, 1931.*

136. Isola Myrtle was the daughter of John Clayton Howell's mother Olivia Stewart Howell and Olivia's second husband Charles Langston.

137. Microfilmed New Kent County Marriage Register, vol. 2, 1909–1950, 2, Library of Virginia. See also Myrtle Wynn's death certificate, which described her as white. Commonwealth of Virginia Certificate of Death, State File no. 10952, April 1920. Accessed on Ancestry.com, 21 January 2017.

138. 1920 Richmond City census, p. 236 (1A). John Jones was the one petitioner who was not in Richmond at the time of his family's census enumeration in 1920; in 1920 they lived in Charles City County (p. 32A, Charles City County census)

139. See her Certificate of Death, Commonwealth of Virginia file no. 22841, of October 1940.

140. Keziah and her children were enumerated in 1870 and 1880 Petersburg's census as Indians (pp. 195B and 277D); but in 1900 Keziah was back in King William County, along with two of her sons, including twenty-three-year-old Tom (called Thomas S. Dennis Jr., in the 1880 census); the 1900 census listed all three on the Indian Population form as Powhatan people (p. 140B). When Keziah Dennis died in King William County in 1917, her Virginia state death certificate (file no. 20170; accessed on Ancestry.com, 11 July 2017) noted that she was Indian and the daughter of James Langston and Nancy Wynn.

141. Draft registration card for John T. Jones, serial no. 327, order number 243, 12 September 1918. Accessed on Ancestry.com, 26 April 2016. See also microfilmed New Kent County Marriage Register, vol. 2, 1909–1950, p. 11 (in which the couple are noted to be Indian). Library of Virginia, Richmond.

142. See Isola Myrtle's 30 April 1920, Certificate of Death, Commonwealth of Virginia file no.10952.

143. George E. Haw and Morton L. Wallerstein to Albert H. Hill, 5 November 1925, Richmond City, School Board Minutes, barcode 1051019, Minutes/Notes of 23 October 1925 and 27 November 1925, Concerning Children of Ray Wynn, Library of Virginia, Richmond.

144. Notarized affidavit of testimony of Sarah J. Bradby, 10 December 1925, Richmond City, Hustings Court, Ended Causes, December 1925, barcode 1011709; *The Commonwealth of Virginia vs. Ray Winn*, 11 December 1925, Library of Virginia, Richmond. The 1860 census for Charles City County lists F. J. Bullifant and Margaret A. Stuart in a household with seven children eleven years of age and younger (page 124), including Rebecca, James, and Marion Stuart.

145. Deposition of H. T. Douglas, 21 November 1925, Richmond City, Hustings Court, Ended Causes, December 1925, barcode 1011709, *The Commonwealth of Virginia vs. Ray Winn*, 11 December 1925, Library of Virginia, Richmond.

146. Deposition of J. J. Cardine, 21 November 1925, Richmond City, Hustings Court, Ended Causes, December 1925, barcode 1011709, *The Commonwealth of Virginia vs. Ray Winn*, 11 December 1925, Library of Virginia, Richmond.

147. Bill of indictment, 2 November 1925, Richmond City, Hustings Court, Ended Causes, December 1925, barcode 1011709, *The Commonwealth of Virginia vs. Ray Winn*, 11 December 1925, Library of Virginia, Richmond.

148. See Thomson, "Racism and Racial Classification," 233–35.

149. Court Instructions, n.d., Richmond City Hustings Court, Ended Causes, December 1925, barcode 1011709, *The Commonwealth of Virginia vs. Ray Winn*, 11 December 1925, Library of Virginia, Richmond. In the papers of John Powell there are copies of the court's instructions: box 38, Papers of John Powell, Albert and Shirley Small Special Collections Library, University of Virginia.

150. Ray Wynn died in 1958 in his seventies because of injuries he suffered in an accident at the Richmond Abbatoir. His death certificate (Commonwealth of Virginia no. 9961) lists his "color or race" as white.

Chapter 3

1. Hazel W. Hertzberg, *The Search for an American Indian Identity*, 26.

2. Moble Hopson interview, in *Weevils in the Wheat: Interviews with Virginia Ex-Slaves,* edited by Charles L. Perdue Jr., Thomas E. Barden, and Robert K. Phillips, 143, 146. The uses of dialect in these Federal Writers Project narratives raise important questions. I have quoted the text as it was printed by the Writers Project.

3. See chapter 1 for a brief, selective overview of seventeenth-and eighteenth-century whites' views of Blacks and Indians.

4. Rountree, *Pocahontas's People,* 189–92, 204–5. See also pp. 174–75 on out-marriage among the Pamunkey.

5. John Garland Pollard, "The Pamunkey Indians of Virginia," Bureau of American Ethnology Bulletin 17, 16. Similar formal exclusions were not unusual, but not uniform, in the indigenous South. For example, the Tunica-Biloxi of Louisiana did not include people with African American forebears on their tribal rolls as late as the 1970s, and have barred people who married a Black individual from the reservation. Klopotek, *Recognition Odysseys,* 79, 221–22.

6. James Mooney, draft of "The Powhatan Confederacy, Past and Present," *American Anthropologist* 9, no. 1 (1907): 31, in MS. 2199, National Anthropological Archives, Washington, DC.

7. Rountree, *Pocahontas's People,* 189, 210–11.

8. Copy of certificate, dated 8 November 1904, MS. 112, National Anthropological Archives, Smithsonian Institution, Washington, DC. See also Rountree, *Pocahontas's People,* 212–13.

9. Rountree, "Ethnicity Among the 'Citizen' Indians of Tidewater Virginia," 190–91.

10. Minutes of the Dover Baptist Association 223rd meeting 22 October 2006, copy in file folder on Samaria Baptist Church at Virginia Baptist Historical Society, Richmond.

11. Virginia Historical Records Survey Project, Division of Professional and Service Projects, Works Projects Administration, *Inventory of the Church Archives of Virginia: Dover Baptist Association*, 8.

12. Daniel Slabey, "First Indian Baptist Church in Virginia," *Religious Herald*, 2 September 1965, 6.

13. Colosse/Dover Minute Book, 1814–1834, microfilm at Virginia Baptist Historical Society.

14. Ibid.

15. Slabey, "First Indian Baptist Church in Virginia," 6.

16. Fred Anderson, "Pathways in Baptist History," *Religious Herald*, 15 May 2003.

17. Virginia Historical Records Survey Project, Division of Professional and Service Projects, Works Projects Administration, *Inventory of the Church Archives of Virginia: Dover Baptist Association*, xxiii.

18. In contrast, as African Americans established their own churches in Mississippi after the Civil War, some of those Black congregations held separate services for Mississippi Choctaw people. As more churches for and among Choctaw people developed later in the century, those provided additional support for Choctaw ethnicity, schools, and community-building, like Baptist Indian churches in tidewater Virginia. It seems that some Mississippi Choctaw found the relatively autonomous organizational structure for Baptist congregations appealing, as did Virginia's Indian Baptists, and there was even a Choctaw Baptist Association. See Katherine M. B. Osburn, *Choctaw Resurgence in Mississippi*, 28–30, and Clara Sue Kidwell, *Choctaws and Missionaries, 1818–1918*, 178–80, 182–83, 190.

19. Slabey, "First Indian Baptist Church in Virginia," 6.

20. The proposed change had to do with "admitting messengers from the Pamunkey Indian Church to seats in the Association." See photocopy of page 12 from 1868 Minutes of the Dover Baptist Association; photocopy of page 13 from 1869 Minutes of the Dover Baptist Association; and copy of typescript page with handwritten header, "Pamunkey (Indian) Baptist Church," all in Virginia Baptist Historical Society folder on the "Pamunkey Indian" Church, Virginia Baptist Historical Society, Richmond.

21. Slabey, "First Indian Baptist Church in Virginia," 6–7

22. Ibid., 6

23. Ibid., 6–7

24. Ibid., 7.

25. "Indian Churches and Schools in Virginia," *Religious Herald*, 9 March 1950, 12.

26. Virginia Historical Records Survey Project, Division of Professional and Service Projects, Works Projects Administration, *Inventory of the Church Archives of Virginia: Dover Baptist Association*, 34.

27. Rountree, *Pocahontas's People*, 202.

28. P. E. Throckmorton, notarized statement, 4 February 1920, MS. 112, National Anthropological Archives, Washington, D.C.

29. Rountree, *Pocahontas's People*, 218.

30. "History of Tsena Commocko Baptist Church," single page in Virginia Baptist Historical Society folder on "Tsena Commocko" Church, Virginia Baptist Historical Society, Richmond.

31. "Indian Churches and Schools in Virginia," *Religious Herald*, 9 March 1950, 12; Rountree, *Pocahontas's People*, 189.

32. Virginia Historical Records Survey Project, Division of Professional and Service Projects, Works Projects Administration, *Inventory of the Church Archives of Virginia: Dover Baptist Association*, 42. Despite this reference to missionary activity, the nineteenth-and twentieth-century experiences of indigenous Virginia tidewater peoples in the Baptist church contrasted sharply with those of the Mississippi Choctaw, who had formal missions from the Catholic Church and the American Board of Commissioners for Foreign Missions; see Kidwell, *Choctaws and Missionaries in Mississippi, 1818–1918*, 176–78.

33. J. B. Hill, "Dedication of Mattaponi Indian Baptist Church," *Religious Herald*, 6 June 1935, 8.

34. "History of Indian View Baptist Church," printed page in Virginia Baptist Historical Society folder on "Indian View Indian" Church, Virginia Baptist Historical Society, Richmond. Rountree; *Pocahontas's People*, 160.

35. "Indian Churches and Schools in Virginia," *Religious Herald*, 9 March 1950, 13.

36. Minutes of the One Hundred and Thirty-Eight Annual Session of the Dover Baptist Association/Held with Hebron Baptist Church, King William County, Va., 19, 20, 21 July 1921 (Richmond, Virginia: Clyde W. Saunders, 1921), 3–4, 25, 33, 40.

37. On missionaries among the Mississippi Choctaw, see Osburn, *Choctaw Resurgence in Mississippi*, 28–29; and Kidwell, *Choctaws and Missionaries in Mississippi, 1818–1918*.

38. Minutes of the One Hundred and Forth-Fifth Annual Session of the Dover Baptist Association Held with Hopeful Baptist Church, Hanover County, Virginia, 17–18 July 1928 (Richmond, Virginia: Interstate Printing Corporation, 1928), 4–7, 10.

39. Ibid., 21.

40. William L. Lumpkin, in *A Chronicle of Christian Heritage: Dover Baptist Association of Virginia, 1783–1983*, 173–74, echoed this, saying the 1928 bill would have altered "the traditional civic and social standing of Virginia Indians. Several Indian churches were affiliated with the Dover."

41. "The Dover on the Present Situation," *Religious Herald*, 2 August 1928.

42. "Tribe of Pamunkey: Conclusion of Their Most Interesting History," Richmond, Virginia, *Daily Times*, 2 November 1890, copy in MS. 2197, National Anthropological Archives, Washington, DC.

43. Some Mississippi counties continued to fund Indian schools after 1900. The federal Office of Indian Affairs stepped in to establish day schools for Mississippi Choctaw students after a Mississippi Choctaw agency was established in 1918. See Osburn, *Choctaw Resurgence in Mississippi*, 32–34, 61, 63–68; and Kidwell, *Choctaws and Missionaries in Mississippi, 1818–1918*, xiv, 28, 32–35, 49, 182–83, 188, 193–94, 201.

44. Hertzberg, *Search for an Indian Identity*, 14–15.

45. Rountree, *Pocahontas's People*, 355, note 113. See also Klopotek, *Recognition Odysseys*, 134, 143, 212–14, 216–19, 318. He argues that Louisiana's Jena Choctaw bolstered their case for not being considered colored by refusing to attend Louisiana schools for Black students, and also that in Louisiana in some instances the word "white" could be used to connote the status of not being Black, rather than being a denial of Native ancestry— a sort of variation on Virginia's "Pocahontas exception."

46. Indigenous groups in Mississippi and Louisiana who were unrecognized by the federal government also faced this situation of being excluded from public schools for whites and unwilling to attend those for Black students for at least some part of the era of segregation. See Osburn, *Choctaw Resurgence in Mississippi*, Kidwell, *Choctaws and Missionaries in Mississippi, 1818–1918*, and Klopotek, *Recognition Odysseys*, 53, 61–62 131–46, 148–49, 216–18, 323. Klopotek points out that school segregation could exemplify the "ambiguous status in the racial caste system" of indigenous groups in the United States; for example, the Coushatta people of Louisiana attended a high school for whites by 1931, and after World War II, Jena Choctaw students enrolled in schools for white, rather than Black, children. As Arica Coleman pointed out, clearly if a Native group did not historically set up separate schools, that in no way indicates that that group was not "Indian enough"; see *That the Blood Stay Pure*, 228–29.

47. "Information Sheet" for participants in a 21 May 1954, "Exhibit Day" at Mattaponi Reservation, Virginia Department of Education Indian School Files, 1936–1967. Accession 29632, R. G. 27, series 1, box 1, folder 11. State Government Records Collection, Library of Virginia, Richmond.

48. Albert S. Gatschet, "Virginia Letter: The Pamunky Indians and Their Little Reservation," Washington *Chronicle*, 14 December 1890, clipping in National Anthropological Archives, MS. 55, Washington, DC.

49. Rountree, *Pocahontas's People*, 201.

50. Ibid., 201, 215.

51. J. B. Hill, "Dedication of Mattaponi Indian Baptist Church," *Religious Herald*, 6 June 1935, 8.

52. Rountree, *Pocahontas's People*, 202.

53. Ibid., 217–18. 5 November 1982, Testimony before the Joint Subcommitee Studying the Relationship between the State and Indian Tribes, "Submitted by Chickahominy Indian Tribe," box 4, folder 63, Records of the Virginia Council on Indians, 1988–2012. Accession 50420, state government records collection, Library of Virginia, Richmond.

54. "Indian Churches and Schools," *Religious Herald*, 9 March 1950, 13.

55. Julie H. Ernstein, Buck H. Woodard, Danielle Moretti-Langholtz, and Angela L. David, National Register of Historic Places Registration form, "Sharon Indian School," accepted for National Register listing 2007, section 7, page 2; section 8, pages 6–9; page 22, note 22.

56. File of Virginia's Office of the Second Auditor; Second Auditor in account with city and county treasurers, 1916–1928. Second Auditor Inventory, entry no. 9. Record Group 50, SAI 9, State Government records collection, Library of Virginia, Richmond.

(The Halifax County entries relate to the group in that county who also attracted Walter Plecker's attention, near the North Carolina border. These funds were linked to North Carolina's program for Indian schools, which seems to have been far more extensive than Virginia's efforts, particularly among the Lumbee of Robeson County.)

57. "Indian Churches and Schools," *Religious Herald*, 9 March 1950, 13.

58. Rountree, *Pocahontas's People*, 213.

59. Donal F. Lindsey, *Indians at Hampton Institute, 1877–1923*, 203–5, 208.

60. "Powhatan's Men Yet Live," Washington *Evening Star*, 25 April 1894, MS. 2197, National Anthropological Archives, Washington, DC.

61. Ernstein, Woodard, Moretti-Langholtz, and David, National Register of Historic Places Registration form, "Sharon Indian School" section 8, page 11, quoting an oral history interview of 1987.

62. Christian F. Feest, *The Powhatan Tribes*, 34, 89–90.

63. Rountree, *Pocahontas's People*, 147, 175, 187.

64. James Mooney, Pamunkey Notes, Pamunkey Reservation, Prince [sic] William County, Va., post 1899, MS. 2218, National Anthropological Archives, Washington, DC.

65. Broadside "Notice" of performance by "Powhatan's Indian Braves," 1898, file 4969, National Anthropological Archives, Washington, DC.

66. Feest, *Powhatan Tribes*, 80, 90.

67. Steven Conn, *History's Shadow: Native Americans and Historical Consciousness in the Nineteenth Century*, 213.

68. Rountree, *Pocahontas's People*, 225.

69. Feest, *Powhatan Tribes*, 80.

70. George Pierre Castile, "On the Tarascanness of the Tarascans and the Indianness of the Indians," in George Pierre Castile and Gilbert Kushner, eds., *Persistent Peoples: Cultural Enclaves in Perspective*, 178. This argument arose in the context of Castile's discussion of how a group may survive as a recognizable cultural group when surrounded as an enclave by a larger society, even in the absence of obvious unifying factors such as "racial" homogeneity, a shared homeland or language, or a relatively static distinctive complex of shared "culture." Given that, he argued that most important for such groups is "a continuity of common identity" that is based upon a shared understanding about "the meaning of a set of symbols." Those symbols develop out of historical experiences shared within the group, but they are not unchanging and are not necessarily historically "accurate" in a conventional sense. See also Castile's "Issues in the Analysis of Enduring Cultural Systems," in Castile and Kushner, eds., *Persistent Peoples*, xvii–xviii.

71. Hertzberg, *The Search for an American Indian Identity*, 57.

72. Ibid., 198.

73. Ibid., viii.

74. Ibid., 194–97.

75. Philip Deloria's *Playing Indian* analyzes the history of whites pretending to be Indians, from the Boston Tea Party to the counterculture of the 1960s.

76. Ibid., 76–85, 94.

77. Ibid., 123–24.

78. Feest, *Powhatan Tribes*, 80.

79. "Tribe of Pamunkey: Conclusion of Their Most Interesting History," Richmond, Virginia, *Daily Times*, 2 November 1890, copy in MS. 2197, National Anthropological Archives, Washington, DC.

80. Feest, *Powhatan Tribes*, 90–92.

81. Photographs 74-4903 and 74-4896: Photographs: Smithsonian, Pamunkey. Cook Family Collection, Photographic Lot 87-6 (loaned to the National Anthropological Archives by a Cook or Bradby family member and copied for the NAA collections in 1974), National Anthropological Archives, Washington, DC.

82. Photographs: Smithsonian, Pamunkey. Cook Family Collection, Photographic Lot 87-6, including photo number 74-4911, National Anthropological Archives, Washington, DC.

83. Rountree, *Pocahontas's People*, 260.

84. Photographs 74-4903, 74-4896, 74-4894, 74-4908, 74-4911, 74-4857, 74-4910, 74-4892, 74-4861, 74-4863, 74-4891, 74-4906: Smithsonian, Pamunkey. Cook Family Collection, Photographic Lot 87-6, National Anthropological Archives, Washington, DC.

85. Photographs 74-4858, 74-4864, 74-4867, 74-4868, 74-4869, 74-4870, 74-4872, 74-4873, 74-4876, 74-4877, 74-4878, 74-4879, 74-4882; 74-4883; 74-4885, 74-4888, 74-4897, 74-4900: Smithsonian, Pamunkey. Cook Family Collection, Photographic Lot 87-6, National Anthropological Archives, Washington, DC.

86. Ibid., Photographs 74-4860, 74-4862, 74-4871, 74-4884, 74-4893, 74-4856, 74-4887, 74-4895.

87. Ibid., Photographs 74-4854, 74-4855, 74-4859, 74-4865, 74-4866, 74-4874, 74-4875, 74-4880, 74-4881, 74-4886, 74-4889, 74-4890, 74-4899, 74-4902, 74-4904, 74-4905.

88. Rountree, *Pocahontas's People*, 202.

89. Mooney himself worked to present the fruits of his labor among the Kiowa to exposition audiences.

90. Gatschet's handwritten notes, MS. 2197, National Anthropological Archives, Washington, D.C.

91. Rountree, *Pocahontas's People*, 208–10, and Pamunkey notes, Pamunkey Reservation, Prince [sic] William County, Va., post 1899, of James Mooney, from informant Terrill Bradby, MS. 2218, National Anthropological Archives, Washington, DC.

92. Pamunkey notes, Pamunkey Reservation, Prince [sic] William County, Va., post 1899, of James Mooney, from Informant Terrill Bradby, MS. 2218, National Anthropological Archives, Washington, DC.

93. Untitled newspaper clipping from *Indian Journal* of Muskogee, Eufaula, Indian Territory, 3 August 1893, MS. 2197, National Anthropological Archives, Washington, DC. See also Feest, *The Powhatan Tribes*, 79–80.

94. Pamunkey notes, Pamunkey Reservation, Prince *[sic]* William County, Va., post 1899, of James Mooney, from Informant Terrill Bradby, MS. 2218, National Anthropological Archives, Washington, DC.

95. "Pamunkeys Want a Sea Trip," *Times* of Washington, DC., 6 July 1899, MS. 2197, National Anthropological Archives, Washington, DC.

96. Pamunkey notes, Pamunkey Reservation, Prince *[sic]* William County, Va., post 1899, of James Mooney, from Informant Terrill Bradby, MS. 2218, National Anthropological Archives, Washington, DC.

97. Photograph 74-4898 noted as "Jamestown Exposition," in Smithsonian, Pamunkey. Cook Family Collection, Photographic Lot 87-6, National Anthropological Archives, Washington, DC.

98. As noted in chapter one, Journey Miles was listed as white in the federal census of 1880, and Black in 1900. In the census for 1920 and 1930, he and his family were classified as Indians (page 50A, 1920 King William County; page 245B, 1930 King William County). In 1920 the enumerator specified that they were living on the Pamunkey Reservation.

99. Frederick E. Hoxie, *A Final Promise: The Campaign to Assimilate the Indians, 1880–1920*, x–xii, 28.

100. Ibid., 87–89.

101. Ibid., 90–92, 94.

102. Frederic W. Gleach, "Pocahontas at the Fair: Crafting Identities at the 1907 Jamestown Exposition," *Ethnohistory* 50 (2003): 419–21.

103. Jamestown Exposition Company, *The Jamestown Exposition: Special Events, Military and Naval Features. . .*, 6.

104. Ibid., 43 and ff.

105. "Notes: Jamestown Exposition," *Smithsonian Miscellaneous Collections* 50 (1907): 285–86.

106. Smithsonian Institution, *The Exhibits of the Smithsonian Institution and United States National Museum at the Jamestown Tercentennial Exposition, Norfolk, Virginia, 1907*, 15.

107. *The Official Blue Book of the Jamestown Ter-centennial Exposition, A.D. 1907*, 410–11.

108. Lucy Red Wise, "Romantic Sewell's Point, *Jamestown Magazine* 1 (1906), no. 5: 24– 25; Gleach, "Pocahontas at the Fair," 419; Jamestown Official Publication Co. *Jamestown Tercentennial Exposition Official Daily Program* for July 13, 1907.

109. Jamestown Exposition Company, *The Jamestown Exposition: Special Events, Military and Naval Features. . .*, 40, 43; *The Official Blue Book of the Jamestown Ter-centennial Exposition, A.D. 1907*, 177–78.

110. William H. Lee, *Glimpses of the Jamestown Exposition and Picturesque Virginia*, not paginated.

111. Gleach, "Pocahontas at the Fair," 436–39.

112. A. S. Kelton, "Tuscarora Indians to Have Exhibit at the Jamestown Exposition," *Jamestown Magazine* 1 (1907), no. 10: 36–39.

113. Jeffrey Kosiorek, "Masquerading Indians and Unsightly Blacks: Racial Policy, the American Past, and National Identity at Colonial National Monument," *Virginia Magazine of History and Biography* 120 (2012): 34, 40–41, 49–51.

114. Rountree, *Pocahontas's People*, 212–13.

115. Ibid., 218, 350 n. 224.

Chapter 4

1. Frank G. Speck, *Chapters on the Ethnology of the Powhatan Tribes of Virginia*, Indian Notes and Monographs, vol. 1, no. 5, 232.

2. George W. Stocking, Jr., ed. *Colonial Situations: Essays on the Contextualization of Ethnographic Knowledge. History of Anthropology*, vol. 7, 4.

3. National Anthropological Archives, Smithsonian Institution, Washington, DC. Papers of James Mooney and Albert Gatschet related to Indians of Virginia. MSS. 1449, 2014, 2190, 2197, 2199, 2215, 2218, 2497, 3579, 3695, 4969.

4. Steven Conn, *History's Shadow: Native Americans and Historical Consciousness in the Nineteenth Century*, 182–92.

5. Ibid., 192–95.

6. Ibid., 195–96.

7. As argued in chapter 3, tidewater Indians tapped into ubiquitous pan-Indian imagery representing supposedly timeless Indianness, but also rooted their Indianness in a well-known narrative of national origins at Jamestown, constructing a historical continuity from Virginia's colonial past and positioning themselves in a broad stream of United States history.

8. John C. Ewers, introduction to the 1979 edition, *Calendar History of the Kiowa Indians,* by James Mooney (1898; reprint Washington, DC: Smithsonian Institution Press, 1979), viii.

9. In addition to the work of Mooney and Gatschet, the bureau also published a report on the Pamunkey by John Garland Pollard, a prominent Virginia politician.

10. Conn, *History's Shadow*, 106–7, 179–80.

11. Curtis M. Hinsley, Jr., *Savages and Scientists: The Smithsonian Institution and the Development of American Anthropology, 1846–1910*, 150–51.

12. Albert Gatschet, Annual Report to the Director for 1893, MS. 4734, National Anthropological Archives, Washington, DC.

13. Rountree, *Pocahontas's People*, 202.

14. Mason quoted in Theodore Stern, "Pamunkey Pottery Making," *Southern Indian Studies* 3 (1951): 6, 45.

15. John Wesley Powell, *Tenth Annual Report of the Bureau of Ethnology to the Secretary of the Smithsonian Institution 1888–'89*, 20.

16. James Mooney, *The Powhatan Confederacy, Past and Present* draft typescript (with original notes), 29, MS. 2199, National Anthropological Archives, Washington, DC (published in *American Anthropologist* 9, no. 1 of 1907).

17. Here, Mooney's interest in antiquities reminds us of early nineteenth-century debates about the Mississippian mound-builders, and whether ancestors of present-day North American Indians had been capable of the kinds of technologies and political centralization that whites saw as markers of a march toward "civilization."

18. James Mooney, "Circulars and other materials concerning Indians and traces of Indians in Virginia, Maryland, Delaware, and North Carolina, 1889–1912...," MS. 2190, National Anthropological Archives, Washington, DC.

19. Mooney, draft of *The Powhatan Confederacy, Past and Present*, 28–29.

20. Hinsley, *Savages and Scientists*, 34–35, 47–48, 221–23.

21. Response of Garthon (sp?) Archer, in James Mooney, "Circulars and other material concerning Indians and traces of Indians in Virginia, Maryland, Delaware, and North Carolina, 1889–1912...," MS. 2190, National Anthropological Archives, Washington, DC.

22. Response probably of B. C. Harrison, in ibid.

23. Response of E. C. Wynne, in ibid.

24. Response of Cynthia B. T. Coleman, in ibid.

25. Response of Robert Hales, M.D., in ibid.

26. Response of L. B. Anderson, M.D., in ibid.

27. Response of Joseph W. Southall, M.D. in ibid.

28. Response of Isabella H. Harrison, in ibid.

29. Response probably of Dr. H. N. Hewitt, in ibid.

30. Response of H. W. Mimas, in ibid.

31. Response of William B. Shands, including a letter dated 30 June 1889 from Shands to Mooney, in ibid.

32. Response of I. T. Edwards, M.D., in ibid.

33. Response of Thomas Satane, in ibid.

34. Response of S. F. Harwood, in ibid.

35. Response of W. A. Bradby, in ibid.

36. James Mooney, Pamunkey Notes, post 1899, MS. 2218, National Anthropological Archives, Washington, D.C.

37. Mooney, draft of *The Powhatan Confederacy, Past and Present*, 29–30, MS. 2199.

38. James Mooney to Prof W. J. McGee, 22 October 1899, Records of the Bureau of American Ethnology, series 1, Correspondence, Letters Received 1888–1906, box 109, National Anthropological Archives, Washington, DC.

39. Rountree, *Pocahontas's People*, 207.

40. A. A. Bass to James Mooney, 5 December 1899, in James Mooney, "Circulars and other material concerning Indians and traces of Indians in Virginia, Maryland, Delaware, and North Carolina, 1889–1912. . .," MS. 2190, National Anthropological Archives, Washington, DC.

41. Mooney, draft of *The Powhatan Confederacy, Past and Present*, 29–31.

42. Ibid., 45.

43. Rountree, *Pocahontas's People*, 190–91, noted that some of those New Kent people "married both Chickahominies and Pamunkeys."

44. Albert S. Gatschet, Pamunkey notebook, post 1893, MS. 2197, National Anthropological Archives, Washington, DC.

45. Ibid.

46. "Virginia Letter. The Pamunky Indians and Their Little Reservation," Washington *Chronicle*, 14 December 1890, clipping in MS. 55 and in Gatschet's Pamunkey notebook, MS. 2197, National Anthropological Archives, Washington, DC.

47. James Mooney to Prof. W. J. McGee, 22 October 1899, Records of the Bureau of American Ethnology, series 1, Correspondence, Letters Received 1888–1906, box 109, National Anthropological Archives, Washington, DC.

48. Mooney, draft of *The Powhatan Confederacy, Past and Present*, 31.

49. James Mooney to Albert S. Gatschet, 20 September 1887, Albert S. Gatschet. Letters Received, 1880–1891, MS. 4047, National Anthropological Archives, Washington, DC.

50. Albert S. Gatschet, Pamunkey notebook, post 1893, MS. 2197, National Anthropological Archives, Washington, DC.

51. Albert S. Gatschet, Annual Report for 1892, MS. 4734, Annual Reports to the Director, National Anthropological Archives, Washington, DC.

52. Raphael Semmes to John Swanton, 12 March 1940, and Frank Speck to John Swanton, 21 April 1940, MS. 4069, National Anthropological Archives, Washington, DC.

53. O. Oliver Adkins to Bureau of American Ethnology, 6 April 1943 and 10 April 1943, in "Documents in support of the Indian racial status of the Chickahominy tribe... 1904–1942," MS. 112, National Anthropological Archives, Washington, DC. In 1974, a group of Pamunkey family photos were copied for the National Anthropological Archives as noted in chapter 3. See "Smithsonian, Pamunkey. Cook Family Collection," Photographic Lot 87-6 (loaned to the National Anthropological Archives by a Cook or Bradby family member and copied for the NAA collections in 1974), National Anthropological Archives, Washington, DC.

54. Rountree, *Pocahontas's People*, 207–8.

55. Frederic W. Gleach, "Anthropological Professionalization and the Virginian Indians at the Turn of the Century," *American Anthropologist* 104 (2002): 500.

56. Danielle Moretti-Langholtz used "administrative genocide" to describe that denial, in "Other Names I Have Been Called: Political Resurgence Among Virginia Indians in the Twentieth Century" (Ph.D. diss., University of Oklahoma, 1998), 109.

57. John Witthoft, "Frank Gouldsmith Speck, 1881–1950; Ethnologist and Teacher," *Southern Indian Studies* 2, no. 1 (1950): 2, 39–40.

58. For an example of Speck's use of language that suggests a hierarchy of cultures or cultural traits from "simple to complex," see *Chapters on the Ethnology of the Powhatan Tribes*, 229, 451.

59. Witthoft, "Frank Gouldsmith Speck, 1881–1950," 2, 41–43. Like Albert Gatschet before him, Speck also did work among the Catawba that involved efforts to preserve linguistic information among them.

60. See for example J. Walter Fewkes to Frank Speck, 14 February 1921, Records of the Bureau of American Ethnology, series 1, Correspondence, Letters Received, 1909–1949, box 223, National Anthropological Archives, Washington, DC.

61. Speck, *Chapters on the Ethnology of the Powhatan Tribes,* 227–30; and Speck, "The Ethnic Position of the Southeastern Algonkian," *American Anthropologist* 26 (1924): 193–98.

62. Speck, *Chapters on the Ethnology of the Powhatan Tribes,* 231.

63. Thomas J. Blumer, "Wild Indians and the Devil: The Contemporary Catawba Spirit World," *American Indian Quarterly* 9 (1985): 150. Frank G. Speck, *Catawba Texts,* Columbia University *Contributions to Anthropology* 24, 1934.

64. See Klopotek, *Recognition Odysseys,* for a comment on Speck's value as an advocate for Louisiana Native groups, 58.

65. Speck, *Chapters on the Ethnology of the Powhatan Tribes,* 236

66. Ibid., 237.

67. As Henry Bascom Collins of the BAE studied Mississippian mounds in 1925, he also measured and wrote about bodily characteristics—including skin color and hair texture—of a group of Mississippi Choctaw people "to evaluate their degrees of Indian blood." Relatively speaking, Speck's attitude about how to gauge someone's Indianness seems comparatively less wedded to such physical markers. But Collins's study suggests how normal were phenotypically based ideas about "full blood" among anthropologists and archeologists at that time. It also seems to show that the Mississippi Choctaw, like tidewater Virginia indigenous people, were willing to work with white scholars to promote their identities as "pure blood" Indians, despite Collins's use of methods that appear to us today based in "scientific" racism; see Osburn, *Choctaw Resurgence in Mississippi,* 90–92. See also Klopotek, *Recognition Odysseys,* 20–21, about other comparable efforts by physical anthropologists.

68. Peggy Pascoe, "Miscegenation Law, Court Cases, and the Ideologies of Race," *Journal of American History* 83 (1996): 54–55.

69. Frank G. Speck, *The Nanticoke Community of Delaware,* 2–3.

70. Frank G. Speck, *The Rappahannock Indians of Virginia,* Indian Notes and Monographs 5, no. 3, vii–viii.

71. Speck, "The Ethnic Position of the Southeastern Algonkian," 194.

72. See the transcription of "A Petition from Citizens of King William County, Virginia" in James Mooney's papers (ms petitions, King William County, B 1207), 20 January 1843, file 3695, National Anthropological Archives, Washington, DC.

73. George L. Hicks, "Cultural Persistence Versus Local Adaptation: Frank G. Speck's Catawba Indians," *Ethnohistory* 12 (1965): 351.

74. Rappahannock Field Notes of Robert R. Sollenberger, 1940, Frank G. Speck Papers, Freeman Guide no. 3027 [170 (20:4F3b)], American Philosophical Society, Philadelphia, Pennsylvania.

75. Frank W. Porter, III, "Anthropologists at Work: A Case Study of the Nanticoke Indian Community," *American Indian Quarterly* 4 (1978): 6–7.

76. Speck, *Rappahannock Indians of Virginia*, 81.

77. William N. Fenton, "Frank G. Speck's Anthropology (1881–1950): Mentor, Colleague, Friend" in *The Life and Times of Frank G. Speck*, University of Pennsylvania Publications in Anthropology, no. 4, edited by Roy Blankenship, 12–13.

78. Some exceptions are in his monograph on *The Nanticoke Community of Delaware*, 38, and *The Rappahanock Indians of Virginia*, 69.

79. Witthoft, "Frank Gouldsmith Speck, 1881–1950," 41. See Harvey A. Feit, "The Construction of Algonquian Hunting Territories: Private Property as Moral Lesson, Policy Advocacy, and Ethnographic Error," in George W. Stocking Jr., ed. *Colonial Situations*, 109–11; and Janet Chute, "Frank G. Speck's Contributions to the Understanding of Mi'kmaq Land Use, Leadership, and Land Management," *Ethnohistory* 46 (1999): 481–540.

80. Frank G. Speck and Claude E. Schaeffer, "The Deer and the Rabbit Hunting Drive in Virginia and the Southeast," *Southern Indian Studies* 2, no. 1 (1950): 3, 14–17.

81. Ibid., 19–20, 3–5, 7–9, 10–11, 14.

82. Ibid., 9–10.

83. Ibid., 10–14.

84. Ibid., 11.

85. Stern, "Pamunkey Pottery Making," vii, 17, 31, 50–51, 61–63, 67.

86. Ibid., 48–49, 56–59, 67–69.

87. Ibid., 48–49. Stern, "Chickahominy: The Changing Culture of a Virginia Indian Community," *Proceedings of the American Philosophical Society* 96 (1952), 191.

88. Stern, "Pamunkey Pottery Making," xiii, 2.

89. Ibid., 5, 16, 31, 32, 38.

90. "Costume Ornaments with Talismanic Significance," notes in Frank G. Speck Papers, Freeman Guide no. 3045 [170 (21:4F2b)], Pamunkey Hunting and Fishing [1938–1939, 1945], American Philosophical Society, Philadelphia, Pennsylvania.

91. "Measurement" notes, Frank G. Speck Papers, Freeman Guide no. 3047 [170 (21:4F2k)], Pamunkey Mensuration, American Philosophical Society, Philadelphia, Pennsylvania.

92. George Heye to Frank G. Speck, 18 April 1940, and note cards, in Frank G. Speck Papers, Freeman Guide no. 3036 [170 (20:4F1d)], Miscellaneous notes: Virginia Indians [1939–1947], American Philosophical Society, Philadelphia, Pennsylvania.

93. W. S. Bradby to Speck, 19 November 1940, Frank G. Speck Papers, Freeman Guide no. 3050 [170 (20:4F2r], American Philosophical Society, Philadelphia, Pennsylvania.

94. Speck, *Chapters on the Ethnography of the Powhatan Tribes of Virginia*, 433, 435, 444–50.
95. Speck, *Rappahannock Indians of Virginia*, viii–ix.
96. Speck, *Chapters on the Ethnology of the Powhatan Tribes of Virginia*, 265.
97. Anthony F. C. Wallace, "A Field Trip to Indian River with Frank G. Speck," in *The Life and Times of Frank G. Speck*, University of Pennsylvania Publications in Anthropology, no. 4, edited by Roy Blankenship, 86.
98. Porter, "Anthropologists at Work," 6–7.
99. Paul Miles to Speck, 27 November 192; and Paul Miles to Speck, 10 December 1921, both in Frank G. Speck Papers, Freeman Guide no. 3040 [170 (21:4F2s], American Philosophical Society, Philadelphia, Pennsylvania.
100. Rountree, *Pocahontas's People*, 216–17.
101. Materials in Miscellaneous notes: Virginia Indians [1939–1947] including a letter from "Chief J. H. Johnson" to Speck of 1 May 1940, Frank G. Speck Papers, Freeman Guide no. 3036 [170 (20:4F1d)], American Philosophical Society, Philadelphia, Pennsylvania.
102. E. P. Bradby to Speck, 2 June 1945, Frank G. Speck Papers, Freeman Guide no. 3045 [170 (21:4F2b], American Philosophical Society, Philadelphia, Pennsylvania.
103 B. H. Van Oot to Speck, 14 December 1939, Frank G. Speck Papers, Freeman Guide no. 3040 [170 (21:4F2s], American Philosophical Society, Philadelphia, Pennsylvania.
104. Paul T. Murray, "Who Is an Indian? Who Is a Negro?: Virginia Indians in the World War II Draft," *The Virginia Magazine of History and Biography* 95(1987): 225–26; Charles Edgar Gilliam to Speck, 24 July 1943 and 17 August 1943, Frank G. Speck Papers, Freeman Guide no. 3021 [170 (20:4F1i)], American Philosophical Society, Philadelphia, Pennsylvania.
105. Frank Speck to Matthew W. Stirling, 3 February 1943, and H. W. Dorse to Frank Speck, 15 February 1943, Records of the Bureau of American Ethnology, series 1, Correspondence, Letters Received, 1909–1949, box 223, National Anthropological Archives, Washington, DC.
106. Frank Speck to Dr. M. W. Stirling, 4 March 1943, Records of the Bureau of American Ethnology, series 1, Correspondence, Letters Received, 1909–1949, box 223, National Anthropological Archives, Washington, DC.
107. Speck, "The Ethnic Position of the Southeastern Algonkian," 188.
108. Otho S. Nelson to Speck 23 August 1940, Frank G. Speck Papers, Freeman Guide no. 3053 [170 (20:4F3c], American Philosophical Society, Philadelphia, Pennsylvania.
109. Speck, *Rappahannock Indians of Virginia*, ix.
110. Clifford, *Predicament of Culture*, 10, 14–15.
111. Stern, "Chickahominy," 157.
112. Ibid., 157–58, 193, 199–200.
113. Ibid., 204, 206.
114. Speck, *Chapters on the Ethnology of the Powhatan Tribes of Virginia*, 452–53.
115. Clifford, *Predicament of Culture*, 14.

116. Danielle Moretti-Langholtz, "Other Names I Have Been Called," 268–81.
117. Clifford, *Predicament of Culture*, 15.

Chapter 5

1. Julie H. Ernstein, Buck H. Woodard, Danielle Moretti-Langholtz, and Angela L. Daniel, National Register of Historic Places Registration form, "Sharon Indian School," accepted for National Register listing 2007, 9, 22, note 21.

2. Helen C. Rountree, *Pocahontas's People*, 232.

3. Over time, before his retirement in 1946, Plecker came to regret that earlier, in his dealings with some specific Indian communities (as noted in chapter 2), he had sometimes compromised his stance that no Virginia Natives should be recognized as Indians because of their (in his view) mixed and so tainted blood.

4. U.S. Department of Commerce, Bureau of the Census, *Fifteenth Census of the United States 1930: The Indian Population of the United States and Alaska*, 3.

5. In 1900 and after, federal guidelines led to more consistent counting of Native people living on reservations, not just citizen Indians without tribal connections and off reservation lands. See James P. Collins, "Native Americans in the Census, 1860–1890," *Prologue* 38 (2006): 56, and National Archives and Records Administration, "American Indians in the Federal Decennial Censuses, 1790–1930," information sheet, November 2004.

6. Joel Perlmann and Mary C. Waters, eds., *The New Race Question: How the Census Counts Multiracial Individuals,* introduction by the editors, 4.

7. U.S. Department of Commerce, Bureau of the Census, *Twenty Censuses: Population and Housing Questions, 1790–1980* prepared by Frederick G. Bohme (Washington, DC: U.S. Government Printing Office, 1979), 28. See also Margo J. Anderson, "Counting by Race: The Antebellum Legacy" in Perlmann and Waters, eds., *The New Race Question*, 280–81.

8. Perlmann and Waters, eds., *The New Race Question*, introduction by the editors, 5; and C. Matthew Snipp, "American Indians: Clues to the Future of Other Racial Groups," in Perlmann and Waters, eds., *The New Race Question*, 194–99.

9. Data for 1890–1930 in tables 1 and 2 are from U.S. Department of Commerce, Bureau of the Census, *Fifteenth Census of the United States 1930: The Indian Population of the United States and Alaska*, 20. These figures should be interpreted with care. For example, variations in Elizabeth City County could reflect changes in the presence or ways of counting Native students at Hampton Institute.

10. See U.S. Department of Commerce, Bureau of the Census, *Twenty Censuses: Population and Housing Questions, 1790–1980*, 52.

11. Enumerators that year were using the general population schedule to enumerate Indians, not a special form for Indian populations. They were to note on the general schedule whether an Indian was "full or mixed blood" and his or her tribe in the spaces on the

general schedule form otherwise devoted to the birthplaces of an individuals' parents. However, they also used a "Supplemental Schedule for Indian Population" on which individuals were cross-referenced to their entries on the general population schedule.

12. U.S. Department of Commerce, Bureau of the Census, *Fifteenth Census of the United States 1930: The Indian Population of the United States and Alaska*, 1. Enumerators' instructions are quoted in National Archives and Records Administration, *1930 Federal Population Census: Catalog of National Archives Microfilm*, xiii.

13. In the application of a community-reputation test, of course, an important question was whose opinion mattered to the enumerator.

14. National Archives and Records Administration, *1930 Federal Population Census: Catalog of National Archives Microfilm*, xiii.

15. U.S. Department of Commerce, Bureau of the Census, *Fifteenth Census of the United States 1930: The Indian Population of the United States and Alaska*, 7. The 1930 tabulation for Virginia shows urban Indians at 4.5 percent of the state's Native population. This small percentage raises questions about whether Virginia Indians who moved, like Virginian African Americans at some times, were more likely to leave the state than whites who relocated. Before and after the 1924 racial integrity law, some tidewater Native people did leave the state. See Rountree, *Pocahontas's People*, 225.

16. U.S. Department of Commerce, Bureau of the Census, *Fifteenth Census of the United States 1930: The Indian Population of the United States and Alaska*, 2, 4.

17. Quoted in George B. L. Arner's introduction, U.S. Department of Commerce, Bureau of the Census, *Fifteenth Census of the United States 1930: The Indian Population of the United States and Alaska*, 1.

18. Post-1890 figures are from U.S. Department of Commerce, Bureau of the Census, *Indian Population in the United States and Alaska, 1910*, 30; and the U.S. Department of Commerce, Bureau of the Census, *Fifteenth Census of the United States 1930: The Indian Population of the United States and Alaska*, 20.

19. See page 46B in 1910, and page 20B in 1920, in the Charles City County census, Harrison District.

20. Had Carrie Adkins Sweat been listed as a "mulatto" and head of her household (in the absence of a husband), one would expect that her children would receive the same classification as their mother, but with John Sweat present, it seems possible that assumptions about male roles shaped the enumerator's designations of the mother's and children's race.

21. It does not appear that any of those twenty-five Indians were called white in the 1930 census. For example, the family of Robert A. and Mary E. Bradby, Indian in 1920, was listed as "neg" in 1930. For the family of Robert W. and Susie F. Atkins, in 1930 the coding in the column for "color or race" is so overwritten that it is illegible; they too had been enumerated as Indians in 1920.

22. Introduction by George B. L. Arner, U.S. Department of Commerce, Bureau of the Census, *Fifteenth Census of the United States 1930: The Indian Population of the United States and Alaska*, 1.

23. U.S. Department of Commerce, Bureau of the Census, *Fifteenth Census of the United States 1930: The Indian Population of the United States and Alaska*, 20.

24. Rountree, *Pocahontas's People*, 228, 353.

25. U.S. Department of Commerce, Bureau of the Census, *Fifteenth Census of the United States 1930: The Indian Population of the United States and Alaska*, 33, 34, 36.

26. Ibid., 39.

27. Ibid., 70.

28. Ibid., 2, 70.

29. Ibid., 70, 71.

30. Rountree, *Pocahontas's People*, 226–28.

31. I thank Brent Tarter for pointing out Mrs. Pfaus's 1955 obituary in the *Richmond Times-Dispatch*.

32. Rountree, *Pocahontas's People*, 227–28.

33. Ibid., 228.

34. For example, see the listing of Robert W. Atkins's family for 1930, on page 253B (sheet 8B for the Cumberland Magisterial District), and the family's 1920 listing on pages 102A and B (sheets 4A and B for the Cumberland Magisterial District).

35. Rountree, *Pocahontas's People*, 230.

36. Paul T. Murray, "Who Is an Indian? Who Is a Negro?: Virginia Indians in the World War II Draft," *Virginia Magazine of History and Biography* 95 (1987): 218–20, 222–23, 226–27, 229–30.

37. Ibid., 229.

38. Rountree, *Pocahontas's People*, 230; Murray, "Who Is an Indian? Who Is a Negro?," 220–21, 225–26.

39. Rountree, *Pocahontas's People*, 233.

40. See Murray, "Who Is an Indian? Who Is a Negro?," 215–31.

41. See Frank G. Speck's "Testimonial for Indians of Virginia Approving Their Claim for Indian Classification," 8 December 1944, in James R. Coates Collection, Records Concerning the Ancestry of Indians in Virginia, 1833–1947. Accession 31577, Library of Virginia, Richmond.

42. Dover Baptist Association, Minutes of the One Hundred and Forty-Fifth Annual Session of the Dover Baptist Association Held with Hopeful Baptist Church, Hanover County, Virginia, 17–18 July, 1928 (Richmond, Virginia: Dover Baptist Association by Interstate Printing Corporation, 1928), 4–7, 44–51.

43. "Indian Churches and Schools in Virginia," *Religious Herald*, 9 March 1950, 12–13.

44. Virginia Historical Records Survey Project, Division of Professional and Service Projects, Works Projects Administration, *Inventory of the Church Archives of Virginia: Dover Baptist Association*, 42, and J. B. Hill, "Dedication of Mattaponi Indian Baptist Church," *Religious Herald*, 6 June 1935, 8.

45. Minutes of the One Hundred and Fifty-Seventh Annual Session of the Dover Baptist Association, Virginia, Held with the Glen Allen Baptist Church, Henrico County, Virginia, 11–12 April 1939 and Annual of Dover Woman's Missionary Union (Richmond, Virginia: Richmond Press, 1939), 65.

46. William L. Lumpkin, *A Chronicle of Christian Heritage: Dover Baptist Association of Virginia, 1783–1983*, 197.

47. Rountree, *Pocahontas's People*, 216, dates the modern formal organization of the Upper Mattaponi to 1923 and that of the Rappahannock to 1921.

48. Daniel Slabey, "First Indian Baptist Church in Virginia," *Religious Herald*, 2 September 1965, 7.

49. Minutes of the Dover Baptist Association: Convened at Beulah Church, King William County, Virginia, 13–15 October 1838 (Richmond, Virginia: Wm. Sands, at the *Herald* Office, 1838), 3–4; and Minutes of the Dover Baptist Association: Convened at Bethel M. H., Elizabeth City County, Virginia, 12–14 October 1839 (Richmond, Virginia: Wm. Sands, at the Office of the *Religious Herald*, 1839), 3–4.

50. See, for example, Minutes of the One Hundred and Fifty-Seventh Annual Session of the Dover Baptist Association, Virginia, Held with the Glen Allen Baptist Church, Henrico County, Virginia, 11, 12 April 1939 and Annual of Dover Woman's Missionary Union (Richmond, Virginia: Richmond Press, 1939), 72–73. Minutes of Dover Baptist Association annual meetings between 1939 and 1947 are available at the Library of Congress.

51. Ibid., 7–10

52. In the 1860s, several African American congregations had transferred from the Dover Association to the Shiloh Baptist Association of Black churches. See Virginia Historical Records Survey Project, Division of Professional and Service Projects, Works Projects Administration, *Inventory of the Church Archives of Virginia: Dover Baptist Association*, xxiii.

53. See, for example, Minutes of the One Hundred and Fifty-Seventh Annual Session of the Dover Baptist Association, Virginia, 11–12 April 1939, 49, 54; Minutes of the One Hundred and Fifty-Ninth Annual Session of the Dover Baptist Association, Virginia, Held with Ginter Park Baptist Church, Richmond, Virginia, 15–16 April 1941, and Annual of Dover Woman's Missionary Union (Richmond, Virginia: Richmond Press, 1941), 69–71, 73; Minutes of the One Hundred and Sixty-First Annual Session of the Dover Baptist Association, Virginia, Held with First Baptist Church, Richmond, Virginia, 5–6 May 1943, Minutes of Dover Rural Sunday School Convention, and Annual of Dover Woman's Missionary Union (Richmond, Virginia: Richmond Press, 1943), 76–77, 79, 81; Minutes of the One Hundred and Sixty-Second Annual Session of the Dover Baptist Association, Virginia, Held with Biltmore Baptist Church, Henrico County, Virginia, 11–12 April 1944 and Minutes of Dover Rural Sunday School Convention, and Annual of Dover Woman's Missionary Union (Richmond, Virginia: Richmond Press, 1944), 76–77, 79, 80.

54. Minutes of the One Hundred and Sixty-Third Annual Session of the Dover Baptist Association, Virginia, Held with Barton Heights Baptist Church, Richmond, Virginia, 17–18 April 1945, Minutes of Dover Rural Sunday School Convention, and Annual of Dover Woman's Missionary Union (Richmond, Virginia: Richmond Press, 1945), 27, 29.

55. Minutes of the One Hundred and Sixty-Second Annual Session of the Dover Baptist Association, Virginia, 11–12 April 1944, 3, 17, 36, 47.

56. Minutes of the One Hundred and Sixty-Third Annual Session of the Dover Baptist Association, Virginia, 17–18 April 1945, 30.

57. Minutes of the One Hundred and Sixty-Fourth Annual Session of the Dover Baptist Association, Virginia, Held with New Bridge Baptist Church, Henrico County, Virginia, 16–17 April 1946 and Annual of Dover Woman's Missionary Union (Richmond, Virginia: Richmond Press, 1946), 14–15.

58. See, for example, Minutes of the One Hundred and Sixty-Second Annual Session of the Dover Baptist Association, Virginia, 11–12 April, 1944, 27, 29, 31, 82.

59. See, for example, Minutes of the One Hundred and Sixty-Fifth Annual Session of the Dover Baptist Association, Virginia, Held with Park View Baptist Church, Richmond, Virginia, 15–16 April 1947, and Annual of Dover Woman's Missionary Union (Richmond, Virginia: Richmond Press, 1947), 35.

60. Minutes of the One Hundred and Sixty-Fourth Annual Session of the Dover Baptist Association, Virginia, 16–17 April 1946, 34.

61. Minutes of the One Hundred and Sixty-Fifth Annual Session of the Dover Baptist Association, Virginia, 15–16 April, 1947, 42.

62. Rountree, *Pocahontas's People,* 230.

63. Arica L. Coleman, "Notes on the State of Virginia: Africans, Indians and the Paradox of Racial Integrity," 106–9.

64. Virginia Historical Records Survey Project, Division of Professional and Service Projects, Works Projects Administration, *Inventory of the Church Archives of Virginia: Dover Baptist Association,* 40, 42.

65. "Indian Churches and Schools in Virginia," *Religious Herald,* 9 March 1950, 13. It was not unusual for Baptist congregations to use available community buildings such as schools. For Native tidewater organized groups, though, such borrowings and links were perhaps especially important because of the Indian churches' small pool of potential members.

66. Ibid., 13, 21; Mrs. Fred Pfaus [Martha Coleman Wester Pfaus], "The Indians of the Old Dominion (Our Debt to Virginia Indians)" (no information on publisher, 1949), 2, 16.

67. "Indian Churches and Schools in Virginia," *Religious Herald,* 9 March 1950, 21; Mrs. Fred Pfaus, "The Indians of the Old Dominion (Our Debt to Virginia Indians)," 17.

68. Of course, African American parents throughout the South also faced scanty public funding for education and school facilities, and many, like the parents of students in the tidewater Indian schools, volunteered their labor and made financial sacrifices to supplement meager public support for their children's separate, segregated schools.

69. Mrs. Fred Pfaus, "The Indians of the Old Dominion (Our Debt to Virginia Indians)," 6–8, 12–13.

70. Ibid., 7, 12–13. See Brian Klopotek, *Recognition Odysseys,* 147–49, for comparable arguments about school attendance by the Jena Choctaw in Mississippi in the postwar era.

71. Annual High School Reports for Mattaponi-Pamunkey Indian Reservation School, 1957–58 through 1963–64, series 1, box 1, folder 2, Virginia Department of Education, Indian School Files, 1936–1967. Accession 29632. State Government Records

Collection, Library of Virginia, Richmond; Virginia Historical Records Survey Project, Division of Professional and Service Projects, Works Projects Administration, *Inventory of the Church Archives of Virginia: Dover Baptist Association*, 36.

72. Rev. W. Thorburn Clark, "The Dover," *Religious Herald*, 9 August 1928, 3.

73. Daniel Slabey, "First Indian Baptist Church in Virginia," *Religious Herald*, 2 September 1965, and Daniel Slabey to Henry M. Hambrecht Jr., 12 May 1965, series 1, box 1, folder 14, Virginia Department of Education, Indian School Files, 1936–1967. Accession 29632. State Government Records Collection, Library of Virginia, Richmond.

74. See G. F. Poteet to Thomas Custalow, 30 January 1956; G. F. Poteet to L. D. Ussery, 11 October 1955, and G. M. Turner to G. F. Poteet 19 March 1955, all in series 1, box 2, folder 6, Virginia Department of Education, Indian School Files, 1936–1967. Accession 29632. State Government Records Collection, Library of Virginia, Richmond.

75. W. A. Plecker to State Board of Education 23 July 1945 (quoting Annie Belle Crowder's post card); and W. A. Plecker to Annie Belle Crowder, 23 July 1945, series 1, box 1, folder 13, Virginia Department of Education, Indian School Files, 1936–1967. Accession 29632. State Government Records Collection, Library of Virginia, Richmond.

76. "Lack of Teacher Is Keeping 22 Indians Out of School," Richmond *Times-Dispatch*, 12 November 1946.

77. See copies of Annual Catalogue of Bacone College for 1948–1949, 1949–1950, and 1951–1952, with registers of students for the 1947–1948, 1948–1949, and 1950–1951 school years, respectively, in series 1, box 1, folder 4, Virginia Department of Education, Indian School Files, 1936–1967. Accession 29632. State Government Records Collection, Library of Virginia, Richmond.

78. G. F. Poteet to Roger William Getz, 10 February 1954, series 1, box 1, folder 5, Virginia Department of Education, Indian School Files, 1936–1967. Accession 29632. State Government Records Collection, Library of Virginia, Richmond.

79. Klopotek, *Recognition Odysseys*, 12–13, 61, 132–34, 142, 146–49, 217–18, shows that in some cases indigenous Louisianans attended schools for white students before the *Brown v. Board* decision—though this could be contentious. Clifton-Choctaw children in Louisiana were excluded from Rapides Parish high schools for white students until 1971. In Alabama, Calvin McGhee's activism led the Escambia County School Board to agree both to upgrade the existing grammar school for the Poarch Creek Band community and also to bus Creek students to local high schools for whites. See Denise E. Bates, *The Other Movement: Indian Rights and Civil Rights in the Deep South*, 22–24.

80. Solon G. Ayers to Gerald Bosch, 16 June 1953, series 1, box 1, folder 16, Virginia Department of Education, Indian School Files, 1936–1967. Accession 29632. State Government Records Collection, Library of Virginia, Richmond; and G. F. Poteet to Solon G. Ayers, 10 February 1954, series 1, box 1, folder 16, Virginia Department of Education, Indian School Files, 1936–1967. Accession 29632. State Government Records Collection, Library of Virginia, Richmond.

81. Chief O. T. Custalow to Gerald Bosch, 9 February 1953, series 1, box 1, folder 15, Virginia Department of Education, Indian School Files, 1936–1967. Accession 29632. State Government Records Collection, Library of Virginia, Richmond.

82. Maggie F. Dickinson to Mr. Poteet, 13 May 1955, series 1, box 2, folder 21, Virginia Department of Education, Indian School Files, 1936–1967. Accession 29632. State Government Records Collection, Library of Virginia, Richmond.

83. Gerald Bosch to Davis Y. Paschall, 18 August 1953, series 1, box 1, folder 7, Virginia Department of Education, Indian School Files, 1936–1967. Accession 29632. State Government Records Collection, Library of Virginia, Richmond.

84. Davis Y. Paschall to Rev. Harvey Custalow and Webster Custalow, 30 October 1952, series 1, box 1, folder 8, Virginia Department of Education, Indian School Files, 1936–1967. Accession 29632. State Government Records Collection, Library of Virginia, Richmond.

85. Similarly, before the 1920s, few communities had public high schools for Blacks in the Jim Crow South. Even in the mid-1930s, when about half of Southern whites between the ages of fourteen and seventeen attended high school, the average for Southern African Americans in that age group was "less than 20 percent." See Jennifer Ritterhouse, *Growing Up Jim Crow: How Black and White Southern Children Learned Race*, 183.

86. In the late 1940s, the Pamunkey school had five pupils, the Mattaponi school served twenty-two students, and Tsena Commocko seventeen. See Mrs. Fred Pfaus, "The Indians of the Old Dominion (Our Debt to Virginia Indians)," 10, 12, 14.

87. Wilson K. Doyle, "Report and Recommendations on the Public School System of New Kent County" (Charlottesville, Virginia: Division of Publications of the Bureau of Public Administration, University of Virginia, July 1947) i, 2, 16, 24. In New Kent County (Va.) School Records, 1872–1922; 1947 (barcode 1045071), Local Government Records Collection, New Kent County. Library of Virginia, Richmond.

88. Rountree, *Pocahontas's People*, 236.

89. "Report of Indian Education Fund 1951–1952," series 1, box 1, folder 7, Virginia Department of Education, Indian School Files, 1936–1967. Accession 29632. State Government Records Collection, Library of Virginia, Richmond.

90. Library of Virginia, "A Guide to Department of Education R. G. 27 Indian School Files, 1936–1967;" and text of speech delivered at 12 June 1959 graduation ceremony at Mattaponi-Pamunkey Reservation School, series 1, box 1, folder 14. Accession 29632. State Government Records Collection, Library of Virginia, Richmond.

91. G. F. Poteet to Mrs. Anita Emery, 20 October 1955, series 1, box 2, folder 9, Virginia Department of Education, Indian School Files, 1936–1967. Accession 29632. State Government Records Collection, Library of Virginia, Richmond; and G. F. Poteet to Glenn Brands, 11 October 1955, series 1, box 2, folder 9, Virginia Department of Education, Indian School Files, 1936–1967. Accession 29632. State Government Records Collection, Library of Virginia, Richmond.

92. "Data on the Samaria School," series 1, box 2, folder 9, Virginia Department of Education, Indian School Files, 1936–1967. Accession 29632. State Government Records Collection, Library of Virginia, Richmond.

93. G. F. Poteet to Alfred S. Curtis, 12 August 1957, series 1, box 2, folder 10, Virginia Department of Education, Indian School Files, 1936–1967. Accession 29632. State Government Records Collection, Library of Virginia, Richmond.

94. "Final Annual High School Report" for Mattaponi-Pamunkey School, 1957–1958, series 1, box 1, folder 2, Virginia Department of Education, Indian School Files, 1936–1967. Accession 29632. State Government Records Collection, Library of Virginia, Richmond; "Indian Education Fund Budget" for 1956–1958 biennium and "Indian Education Fund, 1958–1959," both in series 1, box 1, folder 7, Virginia Department of Education, Indian School Files, 1936–1967. Accession 29632. State Government Records Collection, Library of Virginia, Richmond.

95. G. L. Quirk to Dr. Davis Y. Paschall, 2 June 1960, series 1, box 2, folder 19, Virginia Department of Education, Indian School Files, 1936–1967. Accession 29632. State Government Records Collection, Library of Virginia, Richmond.

96. Rountree, *Pocahontas's People, 230*.

97. Gerald Bosch to Davis Y. Paschall, 18 August 1953, series 1, box 1, folder 7, Virginia Department of Education, Indian School Files, 1936–1967. Accession 29632. State Government Records Collection, Library of Virginia, Richmond; and Mr. Paschall to Dr. Bosch, 21 October 1952, series 1, box 1, folder 15, Virginia Department of Education, Indian School Files, 1936–1967. Accession 29632. State Government Records Collection, Library of Virginia, Richmond; and Davis Y. Paschall to Gerald Bosch and Luther McRae, 3 November 1952, series 1, box 1, folder 15, Virginia Department of Education, Indian School Files, 1936–1967. Accession 29632. State Government Records Collection, Library of Virginia, Richmond.

98. Gerald Bosch to Mr. Paschall, 14 October 1952, series 1, box 1, folder 15, Virginia Department of Education, Indian School Files, 1936–1967. Accession 29632. State Government Records Collection, Library of Virginia, Richmond; and Dr. Bosch to Davis Y. Paschall, 23 December 1952, series 1, box 1, folder 15, Virginia Department of Education, Indian School Files, 1936–1967. Accession 29632. State Government Records Collection, Library of Virginia, Richmond.

99. T. D. Cook to Gerald Bosch, 19 January 1953, series 1, box 1, folder 15, Virginia Department of Education, Indian School Files, 1936–1967. Accession 29632. State Government Records Collection, Library of Virginia, Richmond; and Gerald Bosch to Chief T. D. Cook, 29 December 1952, series 1, box 1, folder 15, Virginia Department of Education, Indian School Files, 1936–1967. Accession 29632. State Government Records Collection, Library of Virginia, Richmond.

100. See, for example. "Schedule of Classes/Mattaponi-Pamunkey Indian Reservations Schools" for 1956–1959, series 1, box 2, folder 10, Virginia Department of Education, Indian School Files, 1936–1967. Accession 29632. State Government Records Collection, Library of Virginia, Richmond.

101. Dorothy Page, "Indian Women Then and Now," series 1, box 1, folder 14, Virginia Department of Education, Indian School Files, 1936–1967. Accession 29632. State Government Records Collection, Library of Virginia, Richmond.

102. Joyce Bradby, "Pocahontas," series 1, box 1, folder 14, Virginia Department of Education, Indian School Files, 1936–1967. Accession 29632. State Government Records Collection, Library of Virginia, Richmond.

103. Catherine Howell Hook, Commencement Address for 31 May 1966," series 1, box 1, folder 14, Virginia Department of Education, Indian School Files, 1936–1967. Accession 29632. State Government Records Collection, Library of Virginia, Richmond.

104. G. L. Quirk, Commencement Address for 8 June 1962, series 1, box 1, folder 14, Virginia Department of Education, Indian School Files, 1936–1967. Accession 29632. State Government Records Collection, Library of Virginia, Richmond.

105. Henry M. Hambrecht, Jr., to Mrs. Catherine Hook, 20 May 1966, series 1, box 1, folder 14, Virginia Department of Education, Indian School Files, 1936–1967. Accession 29632. State Government Records Collection, Library of Virginia, Richmond.

106. Rountree, *Pocahontas's People*, 241–42.

107. Copy of form letter attached to handwritten "Inter Office Information" note, from "Jim" to "Ken," 14 January 1947, James R. Coates Collection, Records Concerning the Ancestry of Indians in Virginia, 1833–1947. Accession 31577, Library of Virginia, Richmond.

108. Roy Flannagan, *Amber Satyr* (Garden City, New York: Doubleday, Doran, and Company, 1932), 290.

109. "Hehonee Hero," *Time*, 16 May 1932 [accessed at www.time.com, 3 June 2008].

110. Sterling A. Brown, "Amber Satyr," *Opportunity: Journal of Negro Life* 10 (number 11, November 1932): 352.

111. Flannagan, *Amber Satyr*, 171.

112. Brown, "Amber Satyr," 352.

113. G. L. Quirk to Chief T. D. Cook, 8 October 1958, series 1, box 1, folder 1, Virginia Department of Education, Indian School Files, 1936–1967. Accession 29632. State Government Records Collection, Library of Virginia, Richmond.

114. Theodore Stern, "Pamunkey Pottery Making," *Southern Indian Studies*, 3 (1950): 59–60.

115. Rountree, *Pocahontas's People*, 239–40.

116. Ibid., 239.

Epilogue

1. Klopotek, *Recognition Odysseys*, 23, 64.

2. Bates, *The Other Movement*, x, 33–34.

3. Klopotek, *Recognition Odysseys*, 69, 149–55, 199–202; Rountree, *Pocahontas's People*, 212, 217–18; and Bates, *The Other Movement*, 34–36.

4. See, for example, a copy of "Recognition Criteria" described as "based on the criteria established by the U.S. Department of the Interior, Bureau of Indian Affairs" and "Approved by Virginia Council on Indians 9-18-89" at box 4, folder 37; and Recognition Committee Report to the VCI, Nottoway Tribe of Virginia Petition for State Recognition, Presented 27 January 2009, page 18, box 4, folder 25—both in Records of the

Virginia Council on Indians, 1988–2012, Accession 50420, State Government Records Collection, Library of Virginia, Richmond.

5. Klopotek, *Recognition Odysseys*, 22–23, 49, 156–57, 197, 200–1.

6. Jenna Portnoy, "The Beginning of a Future," *The Washington Post,* 4 June 2021, B1-B2; Klopotek, *Recognition Odysseys*, 4, 97–98, 163–64, 184.

7. Klopotek, *Recognition Odysseys*, 4, 163–64, 203–4.

8. Ibid., 215–16, 337.

9. Lynette Paige Lewis Allston to Karenne Wood, 17 October 2006, box 4, folder 25, Records of the Virginia Council on Indians, 1988–2012, Accession 50420, State Government Records Collection, Library of Virginia, Richmond. See Coleman on the Nottoway petition, in *That the Blood Stay Pure*.

10. Moretti-Langholtz, "Other Names I Have Been Called," 177, 197–98, 234–43.

11. Joane Nagel, *American Indian Ethnic Renewal: Red Power and the Resurgence of Identity and Culture*, 91. See also comments by Native leaders in Alabama and Louisiana in the wake of that 1980 census, in Bates, *The Other Movement*, 146–47.

12. Walter L. Williams, in his preface to *Southeastern Indians Since the Removal Era*, edited by Walter L. Williams, xv.

BIBLIOGRAPHY

Unpublished/Manuscript Sources

Records of the Bureau of American Ethnology, Series 1, Correspondence, Letters Received 1888–1906. National Anthropological Archives, Smithsonian Institution, Washington, DC.

Records of the Bureau of American Ethnology, Series 1, Correspondence, Letters Received, 1909–1949. National Anthropological Archives, Smithsonian Institution, Washington, DC.

Coates, James R. Collection, Records Concerning the Ancestry of Indians in Virginia, 1833–1947. Accession 31577. Library of Virginia, Richmond.

Colosse Baptist Church Minute Book, 1814–1834. Virginia Baptist Historical Society, Richmond.

Cox, Earnest Sevier Papers. William R. Perkins Library, Duke University, Durham, NC.

National Anthropological Archives Mss. 55, 112, 1449, 2014, 2190, 2197, 2199, 2214, 2215, 2218, 2497, 3579, 3619, 3695, 4047, 4069, 4734, 4969, and photographic lot 87-6. National Anthropological Archives, Smithsonian Institution, Washington, DC.

Powell, John Papers. Small Special Collections Library, University of Virginia, Charlottesville.

Scott-Pearman Family Letters in the Norvell Winsboro Wilson Papers. #2957, Southern Historical Collection, University of North Carolina Library, Chapel Hill, North Carolina.

Speck, Frank G. Papers. American Philosophical Society. Philadelphia, Pennsylvania.

Speck, Frank G. Papers. University of Pennsylvania Museum Archives, Philadelphia.

United States Department of Commerce, Bureau of the Census, General Population Schedules for Charles City, King William, and New Kent Counties, 1860–1930.

Records of the Virginia Council on Indians, 1988–2012. Accession 50420. State Government Records Collection, Library of Virginia, Richmond.

Virginia Secretary of the Commonwealth, Executive Papers of Andrew Jackson Montague (Governor 1902–1906). R. G. 3. State Government Records Collection, Library of Virginia, Richmond.

Virginia Secretary of the Commonwealth, Executive Papers of E. Lee Trinkle (Governor 1922–1926). R. G. 3, Accession 21567b. State Government Records Collection, Library of Virginia, Richmond.

Virginia State Department of Education Indian School Files, 1936–1967. R. G. 27. Accession 29632. State Government Records Collection, Library of Virginia, Richmond.

Virginia State Office of the Second Auditor; Second Auditor in account with city and county treasurers, 1916–1928. R. G. 50, SAI 9. State Government Records Collection, Library of Virginia, Richmond.

Published Works and Dissertations

Adams, Byron S. *See! See! See! Guide to Jamestown Exposition, Historic Virginia and Washington.* Washington, DC: Byron S. Adams, 1907.

Adams, Mikaëla M. *Who Belongs?: Race, Resources and Tribal Citizenship in the Native South.* New York: Oxford University Press, 2016.

Adkins, Elaine, and Ray Adkins. *Chickahominy Indians-Eastern Division: A Brief Ethnohistory.* No place of publication noted: Elaine Adkins and Ray Adkins, 2007.

Ahern, Willbert A. "Assimiliationist Racism: The Case of the 'Friends of the Indian.'" *The Journal of Ethnic Studies* 4: 23–32.

Archer, Armstrong. *A Compendium of Slavery as It Exists in the Present Day in the United States of America.* London: Armstrong Archer, 1844.

Axtell, James. *The Indians' New South: Cultural Change in the Colonial Southeast.* Baton Rouge: Louisiana State University Press, 1997.

Baker, Lee D. *Anthropology and the Racial Politics of Culture.* Durham, NC and London: Duke University Press, 2010.

Barkan, Elazar. *The Retreat of Scientific Racism: Changing Concepts of Race in Britain and the United States Between the World Wars.* Cambridge and New York: Cambridge University Press, 1992.

Basson, Lauren L. *White Enough to Be American? Race Mixing, Indigenous People, and the Boundaries of State and Nation.* Chapel Hill: University of North Carolina Press, 2008.

Bateman, Rebecca B., "Africans and Indians: A Comparative Study of the Black Carib and Black Seminole." *Ethnohistory* 37, no. 1 (1990): 1–24.

———. "Naming Patterns in Black Seminole Ethnogenesis." *Ethnohistory* 49 (2002): 227–57.

Bates, Denise E. *The Other Movement: Indian Rights and Civil Rights in the Deep South.* Tuscaloosa: University of Alabama Press, 2012.

Bayart, Jean-François. *The Illusion of Cultural Identity.* 1996. Rev. ed. Translated by Steven Rendall, Janet Roitman, Cynthia Schoch, and Jonathan Derrick. Chicago: University of Chicago Press, 2005.

Beale, Calvin L. "An Overview of the Phenomenon of Mixed Racial Isolates in the United States." *American Anthropologist* 74 (1972): 704–10.

Berkhofer, Robert. F., Jr. *The White Man's Indian: Images of the American Indian from Columbus to the Present*. New York: Knopf, 1978.

Berry, Brewton. *Almost White*. New York: Macmillan, 1963.

Berlin, Ira. *Slaves Without Masters: The Free Negro in the Antebellum South*. New York: Pantheon Books, Random House, 1974.

Bernstein, Alison R. *American Indians and World War II: Toward a New Era in Indian Affairs*. Norman and London: University of Oklahoma Press, 1999.

Beverley, Robert. *The History and Present State of Virginia.*, ed. Louis B. Wright (London, 1705; reprint, Chapel Hill: University of North Carolina Press, 1947).

Billings, Warren M. "The Law of Servants and Slaves in Seventeenth Century Virginia." *Virginia Magazine of History and Biography* 99 (January 1991): 45–62.

Blaeser, Kimberley M. *Gerald Vizenor: Writing in the Oral Tradition*. Norman and London: University of Oklahoma Press, 1996.

Blankenship, Roy, ed. *The Life and Times of Frank Speck*. University of Pennsylvania Publications in Anthropology, no. 4. Philadelphia: University of Pennsylvania, 1991.

Blu, Karen I. *The Lumbee Problem: The Making of an American Indian People*. Cambridge, London, and New York: Cambridge University Press, 1980.

Blumer, Thomas J. "Wild Indians and the Devil: The Contemporary Catawba Indian Spirit World." *American Indian Quarterly* 9 (1985): 149–68.

Bonney, Rachel A., and J. Anthony Paredes, eds. *Anthropologists and Indians in the New South*. Tuscaloosa and London: University of Alabama Press, 2001.

Briggs, Charles, and Amy Shuman, eds. *Theorizing Folklore: Toward New Perspectives on the Politics of Culture*. Special issue of *Western Folklore* 52 (1993).

Bright, W. H. *Official Guide of the Jamestown Ter-Centennial Exposition*. Norfolk, Virginia: Albert Hess, 1907.

Brooks, James F., ed. *Confounding the Color Line: The Indian-Black Experience in North America*. Lincoln and London: University of Nebraska Press, 2002.

Brown, Kathleen M. *Good Wives, Nasty Wenches, and Anxious Patriarchs: Gender, Race and Power in Colonial Virginia*. Chapel Hill: University of North Carolina Press for the Institute of Early American History and Culture, 1996.

Brown, Sterling A. "Amber Satyr." *Opportunity: Journal of Negro Life* 10 (no. 11, November 1932): 352.

Brundage, W. Fitzhugh. *Lynching in the New South: Georgia and Virginia, 1880–1930*. Urbana and Chicago: University of Illinois Press, 1993.

———, ed. *Where These Memories Grow: History, Memory, and Southern Identity*. Chapel Hill and London: University of North Carolina Press, 2000.

Buchanan, Shonda. *Black Indian: A Memoir*. Detroit: Wayne State University Press, 2019.

Bynum, Victoria E. " 'White Negroes' in Segregated Mississippi: Miscegenation, Racial Identity, and the Law." *The Journal of Southern History* 64 (1998): 247–76.

Calloway, Colin G., and Neal Salisbury, eds. *Reinterpreting New England Indians and the Colonial Experience*. Boston: Colonial Society of Massachusetts, 2003.

Cantwell, Robert. *Ethnomimesis: Folklife and the Representation of Culture*. Chapel Hill and London: University of North Carolina Press, 1993.

Castile, George Pierre, and Gilbert Kushner, eds. *Persistent Peoples: Cultural Enclaves in Perspective*. Tucson: University of Arizona Press, 1981.

Chute, Janet. "Frank G. Speck's Contributions to the Understanding of Mi'kmaq Land Use, Leadership, and Land Management." *Ethnohistory* 46 (1999): 481–540.

Clifford, James. *The Predicament of Culture: Twentieth Century Ethnography, Literature, and Art*. Cambridge, MA: Harvard University Press, 1988.

Cohen, William. *At Freedom's Edge: Black Mobility and the Southern White Quest for Racial Control, 1861–1915*. Baton Rouge and London: Louisiana State University Press, 1991.

Cole, Stephanie and Alison M. Parker, eds. *Beyond Black and White: Race, Ethnicity and Gender in the United States South and Southwest*. College Station: University of Texas at Arlington by Texas A&M University Press, 2004.

Coleman, Arica L. "Notes on the State of Virginia: Africans, Indians and the Paradox of Racial Integrity." Ph.D. dissertation, Union Institute and University, Cincinnati, Ohio, 2005.

———. *That the Blood Stay Pure: African Americans, Native Americans, and the Predicament of Race and Identity in Virginia*. Bloomington and Indianapolis: Indiana University Press, 2013.

Collins, James P. "Native Americans in the Census, 1860–1890." *Prologue* 38 (2006): 54–59.

Coltelli, Laura. *Winged Words: American Indian Writers Speak*. Lincoln: University of Nebraska Press, 1990.

Conn, Steven. *History's Shadow: Native Americans and Historical Consciousness in the Nineteenth Century*. Chicago and London: University of Chicago Press, 2004.

Cowger, Thomas W. *The National Congress of American Indians: The Founding Years*. Lincoln and London: University of Nebraska Press, 1999.

Crenshaw, Kimberlé, Neil Gotanda, Gary Peller, and Kendall Thomas, eds. *Critical Race Theory: The Key Writings that Formed the Movement*. New York: New Press; distributed by W. W. Norton, 1995.

Dailey, Jane. *Before Jim Crow: The Politics of Race in Postemancipation Virginia*. Chapel Hill and London: University of North Carolina Press, 2000.

Dain, Bruce. *A Hideous Monster of the Mind: American Race Theory and the Early Republic*. Cambridge, MA and London: Harvard University Press, 2002.

Dane, J. K., and B. Eugene Griessman. "The Collective Identity of Marginal Peoples: The North Carolina Experience." *American Anthropologist* 74 (1972): 694–704.

Darrell, Regna. "The Emergence of Academic Anthropology at the University of Pennsylvania." *Journal of the History of the Behavioral Sciences* 6 (1970): 80–92.

Davis, Darnella. *Untangling a Red, White, and Black Heritage: A Personal History of the Allotment Era.* Albuquerque: University of New Mexico Press, 2018.

David Brion Davis, *The Problem of Slavery in the Age of Emancipation.* New York: Vintage Books, 2015.

Deal, J. Douglas. *Race and Class in Colonial Virginia: Indians, Englishmen, and African on the Eastern Shore during the Seventeenth Century.* New York: Garland, 1993.

Degler, Carl. *Neither Black Nor White: Slavery and Race Relations in Brazil and the United States.* New York: Macmillan, 1971. Reprint Madison: University of Wisconsin Press, 1986.

Deloria, Philip J. *Playing Indian.* New Haven and London: Yale University Press, 1998.

Deloria, Vine, Jr., ed. *American Indian Policy in the Twentieth Century.* Norman and London: University of Oklahoma Press, 1985.

DeMarce, Virginia Easley. "Looking at Legends—Lumbee and Melungeon: Applied Genealogy and the Origins of Tri-Racial Isolate Settlements." *National Genealogical Society Quarterly* 81 (March 1993): 24–45.

———. "'Verry Slitley Mixt': Tri-Racial Isolate Families of the Upper South: A Genealogical Study." *National Genealogical Society Quarterly* 80 (March 1992): 5–35.

Den Ouden, Amy E. *Beyond Conquest: Native Peoples and the Struggle for History in New England.* Lincoln and London: University of Nebraska Press, 2005.

Dominguez, Virginia. *White By Definition: Social Classification in Creole Louisiana.* New Brunswick, NJ: Rutgers University Press, 1986.

Dorr, Gregory Michael. "Assuring America's Place in the Sun: Ivey Foreman Lewis and the Teaching of Eugenics at the University of Virginia, 1915–1953." *The Journal of Southern History* 66 (2000): 257–96.

———. "Principled Expediency: Eugenics, *Naim v. Naim,* and the Supreme Court." *American Journal of Legal History* 42, no. 2 (1998): 119–59.

Dorr, Lisa Lindquist. "Arm in Arm: Gender, Eugenics, and Virginia's Racial Integrity Acts of the 1920s." *Journal of Women's History* 11 (1999): 143–66.

———. *White Women, Rape, and the Power of Race in Virginia, 1900–1960.* Chapel Hill and London: University of North Carolina Press, 2004.

Dover Baptist Association. Minutes of the Annual Sessions of the Dover Baptist Association for 1838, 1839, 1921, 1928, 1939–1947.

Dowd, Gregory Evans. *A Spirited Resistance: The North American Indian Struggle for Unity, 1745–1815.* Baltimore and London: Johns Hopkins University Press, 1992.

Edwards, William A. "Racial Purity in Black and White: The Case of Marcus Garvey and Earnest Cox." *The Journal of Ethnic Studies* 15 (1987): 117–42.

English, Daylanne K. *Unnatural Selections: Eugenics in American Modernism and the Harlem Renaissance.* Chapel Hill and London: University of North Carolina Press, 2004.

Ernstein, Julie H., Buck H. Woodard, Danielle Moretti-Langholtz, and Angela L. David. National Register of Historic Places Registration form, "Sharon Indian School" prepared by authors at the American Indian Resource Center, Department of Anthropology, College of William and Mary, 2006, and accepted for National Register listing 2007.

Fear-Segal, Jacqueline. "Nineteenth-Century Indian Education: Universalism Versus Evolutionism." *Journal of American Studies* 33 (1999): 323–41.

Feest, Christian F. *The Powhatan Tribes*. New York: Chelsea House Publishers, 1990.

Fields, Barbara J. "Ideology and Race in American History." In *Region, Race, and Reconstruction: Essays in Honor of C. Vann Woodward*. Edited by J. Morgan Kousser and James M. McPherson. New York: Oxford University Press, 1982.

Fixico, Donald L. *Termination and Relocation: Federal Indian Policy, 1945–1960*. Albuquerque: University of New Mexico Press, 1986.

Flannagan, Roy. *Amber Satyr*. Garden City, New York: Doubleday, Doran, 1932.

Forbes, Jack D. *Africans and Native Americans: The Language of Race and the Evolution of Red-Black Peoples*, 2nd ed. Urbana and Chicago: University of Illinois Press, 1993.

Forte, Maximilian C., ed. *Who Is an Indian? Race, Place, and the Politics of Indigeneity in the Americas*. Toronto; Buffalo, NY; and London: University of Toronto Press, 2013.

Foster, Morris F. *Being Comanche: A Social History of an American Indian Community*. Tucson: University of Arizona Press, 1991.

Frederickson, George M. *The Comparative Imagination: On the History of Racism, Nationalism, and Social Movements*. Berkeley and Los Angeles: University of California Press, 1997.

———. *White Supremacy: A Comparative Study in American and South African History*. New York and Oxford: Oxford University Press, 1981.

Gallay, Alan. *The Indian Slave Trade: The Rise of the English Empire in the American South, 1670–1717*. New Haven and London: Yale University Press, 2002.

Garroute, Eva Marie. *Real Indians: Identity and the Survival of Native America*. Berkeley, Los Angeles, and London: University of California Press, 2003.

Gilbert, William H., Jr. *Synoptic Survey of Data on the Survival of Indian and Part-Indian Blood in the Eastern United States*. Washington, DC: Library of Congress, Legislative Reference Service, General Research Section, 1947.

Gleach, Frederic W. "Anthropological Professionalization and the Virginia Indians at the Turn of the Century." *American Anthropologist* 104 (2002): 499–507.

———. "Pocahontas at the Fair: Crafting Identities at the 1907 Jamestown Exposition." *Ethnohistory* 50 (2003): 419–45.

———. *Powhatan's World and Colonial Virginia: A Conflict of Cultures*. Lincoln and London: University of Nebraska Press, 1997.

Goldberg, David Theo. "The Social Formation of Racist Discourse." In *Anatomy of Racism*. Edited by David Theo Goldberg. Minneapolis: University of Minnesota Press, 1990.

Green, Michael K., ed. *Issues in Native American Cultural Identity*. New York: P. Lang, 1995.

Green, Rayna. "The Pocahontas Perplex: The Image of Indian Women in American Culture." *Massachusetts Review* 16 (1975): 698–714.
Gross, Ariela J. *What Blood Won't Tell: A History of Race on Trial in America.* Cambridge, MA and London: Harvard University Press, 2008.
Grounds, Richard A., George E. Tinker, and David E. Wilkins, eds. *Native Voices: American Indian Identity and Resistance.* Lawrence: University Press of Kansas, 2003.
Guinn, Jeff. *Our Land Before We Die: The Proud Story of the Seminole Negro.* New York: Jeremy P. Tarcher/Putnam, 2002.
Guterl, Matthew Pratt. *The Color of Race in America, 1900–1940.* Cambridge, MA and London: Harvard University Press, 2001.
Hale, Grace Elizabeth. *Making Whiteness: The Culture of Segregation in the South, 1890–1940.* New York: Random House, Pantheon Books, 1998.
Haney López, Ian. *White by Law: The Legal Construction of Race.* New York and London: New York University Press, 1996.
Harmon, Alexandra. "Tribal Enrollment Councils: Lessons on Law and Indian Identity." *Western Historical Quarterly* 32 (2001): 175–200.
Harring, Sidney L. *Crow Dog's Case: American Indian Sovereignty, Tribal Law, and United States Law in the Nineteenth Century.* Cambridge: Cambridge University Press, 1994.
Hassian, Marouf Arif, Jr. *The Rhetoric of Eugenics in Anglo-American Thought.* Athens and London: University of Georgia Press, 1996.
"Hehonee Hero." *Time,* 16 May 1932.
Hendry, Joy. *Reclaiming Culture: Indigenous People and Self-Representation.* New York: Palgrave Macmillan, 2005.
Hertzberg, Hazel W. *The Search for an American Indian Identity: Modern Pan Indian Movements.* Syracuse, NY: Syracuse University Press, 1971.
Hicks, George L. "Cultural Persistence Versus Local Adaptations: Frank G. Speck's Catawba Indians." *Ethnohistory* 12 (1965): 343–54.
Higginbotham, A. Leon, Jr., *In the Matter of Color: Race and the American Legal Process: The Colonial Period.* Oxford and New York: Oxford University Press, 1978.
Higginbotham, A. Leon, Jr., and Kopytoff, Barbara K. "Racial Purity and Interracial Sex in the Law of Colonial and Antebellum Virginia." *Georgetown Law Journal* 77 no. 6 (1989): 1967–2029.
Hinsley, Curtis M., Jr., *Savages and Scientists: The Smithsonian Institution and the Development of American Anthropology, 1846–1910.* Washington, DC: Smithsonian Institution Press, 1981.
Holloway, Pippa. *Sexuality, Politics, and Social Control in Virginia, 1920–1945.* Chapel Hill: University of North Carolina Press, 2006.
Holt, Thomas C. "Marking: Race, Race-Making, and the Writing of History." *American Historical Review* 100 (1995): 1–20.

Horn, James. *Adapting to a New World: English Society in the Seventeenth Century Chesapeake.* Chapel Hill and London: University of North Carolina Press for the Institute of Early American History and Culture, 1994.

Horse, Perry G., "Reflections on American Indian Identity." In *New Perspectives on Racial Identity Development: A Theoretical and Practical Anthology.* Edited by Charmaine L. Wijeyesinghe and Bailey Anderson, III. New York and London: New York University Press, 2001.

Hoxie, Frederick E. *A Final Promise: The Campaign to Assimilate the Indians, 1880–1920.* Lincoln and London: University of Nebraska Press, 1984.

Hoxie, Frederick E., Ronald Hoffman, and Peter J. Albert, eds. *Native Americans and the Early Republic.* Charlottesville and London: United States Capitol Historical Society by the University Press of Virginia, Charlottesville, 1999.

Hudson, Angela Pulley. *Creek Paths and Federal Roads: Indians, Settlers, and Slaves and the Making of the American South.* Chapel Hill: University of North Carolina Press, 2010.

Hultkrantz, Åke. "North American Indian Religion in the History of Research: A General Survey. Part I and Part II." *History of Religions* 6 (1966): 91–107, 183–207.

Jacobson, Matthew Frye. *Whiteness of a Different Color: European Immigrants and the Alchemy of Race.* Cambridge, MA: Harvard University Press, 1998.

———. *Barbarian Virtues: The United States Encounters Foreign Peoples at Home and Abroad, 1876–1917.* New York: Hill and Wang, 2000.

Jamestown Exposition Company. *Jamestown Exposition on Hampton Roads, 1907... Official Classification of Exhibit Departments.* Norfolk, Virginia: Jamestown Exposition Company, 1907.

Jamestown Exposition Company. *The Jamestown Exposition: Special Events, Military and Naval Features....* Norfolk, Virginia: Department of Congresses and Special Events, Jamestown Exposition Company, 1907.

Jamestown Official Photograph Corporation. *Scenes at the Jamestown Exposition with Historic Sites in Old Virginia.* New York: Jamestown Official Photograph Corporation by Isaac H. Blanchard, 1907.

Jamestown Official Publication Co. *Jamestown Tercentennial Exposition Official Daily Program* for July 13, 1907. Norfolk, Virginia: Jamestown Official Publication, 1907.

Jamestown Tercentennial Commission. *Final Report of the Jamestown Ter-centennial Commission.* Washington, DC: Government Printing Office, 1909.

Johnston, James Hugo. *Race Relations in Virginia and Miscegenation in the South, 1776–1860.* Amherst: University of Massachusetts Press, 1970.

Jones, Martha S. *Birthright Citizens: A History of Race and Rights in Antebellum America.* Cambridge: Cambridge University Press, 2018.

Jordan, Winthrop D. *White Over Black: American Attitudes Toward the Negro, 1550–1812.* Baltimore: Penguin Books edition, 1969.

Karthikeyan, Hrishi, and Gabriel J. Chin. "Preserving Racial Identity: Population Patterns and the Application of Anti-Miscegenation Statutes to Asian Americans, 1910–1950," *Asian American Law Journal* 9 (2002): 1–40.

Kelton, A. S. "Tuscarora Indians to Have Exhibit at the Jamestown Exposition," *Jamestown Magazine* 1 (1907), no. 10.

Kerr-Ritchie, Jeffrey. *Freedpeople in the Tobacco South: Virginia, 1860–1900*. Chapel Hill and London: University of North Carolina Press, 1999.

Kevles, Daniel J. *In the Name of Eugenics: Genetics and the Uses of Human Heredity*. Cambridge, MA and London: Harvard University Press, 1995; originally published in 1985 by Knopf.

Kidwell, Clara Sue. *Choctaws and Missionaries in Mississippi, 1818–1918*. Norman and London: University of Oklahoma Press, 1995.

Kimball, Gregg D. *American City, Southern Place: A Cultural History of Antebellum Richmond*. Athens: University of Georgia Press, 2000.

———. "Place and Perception: Richmond in Late Ante-bellum America." Ph.D. dissertation, University of Virginia, Charlottesville, 1997.

Kirshenblatt-Gimblett, Barbara. *Destination Culture: Tourism, Museums, and Heritage*. Berkeley, Los Angeles, and London: University of California Press, 1998.

Kline, Wendy. *Building a Better Race: Gender, Sexuality, and Eugenics from the Turn of the Century to the Baby Boom*. Berkeley, Los Angeles, and London: University of California Press, 2001.

Klopotek, Brian. *Recognition Odysseys: Indigeneity, Race, and Federal Tribal Recognition Policy in Three Louisiana Indian Communities*. Durham, NC and London: Duke University Press, 2011.

Konkle, Maureen. *Writing Indian Nations: Native Intellectuals and the Politics of Historiography, 1827–1863*. Chapel Hill and London: University of North Carolina Press, 2004.

Kosiorek, Jeffrey. "Masquerading Indians and Unsightly Blacks: Racial Policy, the American Past, and National Identity at Colonial National Monument." *Virginia Magazine of History and Biography* 120 (2012): 33–61.

Krauthamer, Barbara. *Black Slaves, Indian Masters: Slavery, Emancipation and Citizenship in the Native American South*. Chapel Hill: University of North Carolina Press, 2013.

LaCapra, Dominick, ed. *The Bounds of Race: Perspectives on Hegemony and Resistance*. Ithaca, NY and London: Cornell University Press, 1991.

Larson, Edward J. *Sex, Race, and Science: Eugenics in the Deep South*. Baltimore: Johns Hopkins University Press, 1995.

———. "Belated Progress: The Enactment of Eugenic Legislation in Georgia." *Journal of the History of Medicine and the Allied Sciences* 46 (1991): 44–64.

Lee, Susanna Michele. *Claiming the Union: Citizenship in the Post–Civil War South*. New York: Cambridge University Press, 2014.

Lee, William H. *Glimpses of the Jamestown Exposition and Picturesque Virginia*. Chicago: Laird and Lee, 1907.

LeMaster, Michelle. *Brothers Born of One Mother: British-Native American Relations in the Colonial Southeast*. Charlottesville and London: University of Virginia Press, 2012.

Lemire, Elise. *"Miscegenation:" Making Race in America*. Philadelphia: University of Pennsylvania Press, 2002.

Lindsey, Donal F. *Indians at Hampton Institute, 1877–1923*. Urbana and Chicago: University of Illinois Press, 1995.

Litwack, Leon. *Trouble in Mind: Black Southerners in the Age of Jim Crow*. New York: Random House, 1998.

Lombardo, Paul A. "Miscegenation, Eugenics, and Racism: Historical Footnotes to *Loving v. Virginia*." *University of California, Davis, Law Review* 21 (1988): 421–52.

Lowery, Malinda Maynor. *Lumbee Indians in the Jim Crow South: Race, Identity, and the Making of a Nation*. Chapel Hill: University of North Carolina Press, 2010.

Lovett, Laura L. "'African and Cherokee by Choice:' Race and Resistance under Legalized Segregation." *American Indian Quarterly* 22 (1998): 203–29.

Lumpkin, William L. *A Chronicle of Christian Heritage: Dover Baptist Association of Virginia, 1783–1983*. Richmond, Virginia: Skipworth, 1983.

Maddox, Lucy. *Citizen Indians: Native American Intellectuals, Race, and Reform*. Ithaca, New York, and London: Cornell University Press, 2005.

Mandell, Daniel. *Behind the Frontier: Indians in Eighteenth Century Massachusetts*. Lincoln and London: University of Nebraska Press, 1996.

———. *Tribe, Race, History: Native Americans in Southern New England, 1780–1880*. Baltimore: Johns Hopkins University Press, 2008.

Martin, Joel W. *Sacred Revolt: The Muskogee's Struggle for a New World*. Boston: Beacon, 1991.

McClintock, Anne. *Imperial Leather: Race, Gender, and Sexuality in the Colonial Conquest*. New York and London: Routledge, 1995.

Melish, Joanne Pope. *Disowning Slavery: Gradual Emancipation and "Race" in New England, 1780–1860*. Ithaca, NY: Cornell University Press, 1998.

Merrell, James H. *The Indians' New World: Catawbas and Their Neighbors from European Contact through the Era of Removal*. Chapel Hill: University of North Carolina Press for the Institute of Early American History and Culture, 1989. Reprint, New York and London: W.W. Norton, 1991.

———. "The Racial Education of the Catawba Indians." *Journal of Southern History* 50 (1984): 363–84.

———. "Reading 'An Almost Erased Page:' A Reassessment of Frank G. Speck's Catawba Studies." *Proceedings of the American Philosophical Society* 127 (1983): 248–62.

Merritt, Jane T. *At the Crossroads: Indians and Empires on a Mid-Atlantic Frontier, 1700–1763*. Chapel Hill and London: University of North Carolina Press for the Omohundro Institute of Early American History and Culture, 2003.

Meyer, Carter Jones, and Diana Royer, eds. *Selling the Indian: Commercializing and Appropriating American Indian Cultures*. Tucson: University of Arizona Press, 2001.

Miles, Tiya. *Ties That Bind: The Story of an Afro-Cherokee Family in Slavery and Freedom*. Berkeley: University of California Press, 2005.

Mitchell, Michele. *Righteous Propagation: African Americans and the Politics of Racial Destiny after Reconstruction.* Chapel Hill and London: University of North Carolina Press, 2004.

Mooney, James. "The Powhatan Confederacy, Past and Present." *American Anthropologist* (1907): 9:129–52.

Moretti-Langholtz, Danielle. "Other Names I Have Been Called: Political Resurgence Among Virginia Indians in the Twentieth Century." Ph.D. dissertation, University of Oklahoma, Norman, 1998.

Morgan, Philip D. *Slave Counterpoint: Black Culture in the Eighteenth Century Chesapeake and Low Country.* Chapel Hill and London: University of North Carolina Press for the Omohundro Institute of Early American Culture, 1998.

Morrison, Michael A., and James Brewer Stewart, eds. *Race and the Early Republic: Racial Consciousness and Nation-Building in the Early Republic.* Lanham, MD: Rowman and Littlefield, 2002.

Mulroy, Kevin. *The Seminole Freedmen: A History.* Norman: University of Oklahoma Press, 2007.

Murray, Paul T. "Who Is an Indian? Who Is a Negro?: Virginia Indians in the World War II Draft." *Virginia Magazine of History and Biography* 95 (1987): 215–31.

Nagel, Joane. *American Indian Ethnic Renewal: Red Power and the Resurgence of Culture and Identity.* New York: Oxford University Press, 1996.

National Archives and Records Administration. *1930 Federal Population Census: Catalog of National Archives Microfilm.* Washington, DC: National Archives Trust Fund Board, 2002.

Naylor, Celia E. *African Cherokees in Indian Territory: from Chattel to Citizens.* Chapel Hill: University of North Carolina Press, 2008.

Nesper, Larry. "The Meshingomesia Indian Village Schoolhouse in Memory and History." In *Social Memory and History: Anthropological Perspectives.* Edited by Jacob J. Climo and Maria G. Catell. Walnut Creek, CA: Altamira, 2002.

Ngai, Mae M. "The Architecture of Race in American Immigration Law: A Reexamination of the Immigration Act of 1924." *Journal of American History* 86 (1999): 67–92.

Nicholls, Michael L. "Passing Through this Troublesome World: Free Blacks in the Early Southside." *Virginia Magazine of History and Biography* 92 (1984): 50–70.

Nies, Betsy L. *Eugenic Fantasies: Racial Ideology in the Literature and Popular Culture of the 1920s.* New York and London: Routledge, 2002.

Oakley, Christopher Arris. *Keeping the Circle: American Indian Identity in Eastern North Carolina, 1885–2004.* Lincoln and London: University of Nebraska Press, 2005.

Oberg, Michael Leroy. *Dominion and Civility: English Imperialism and Native America, 1585–1685.* Ithaca, NY and London: Cornell University Press, 1999.

O'Brien, Jean M. *Firsting and Lasting: Writing Indians Out of Existence in New England.* Minneapolis and London: University of Minnesota Press, 2010.

The Official Blue Book of the Jamestown Ter-centennial Exposition, A.D. 1907. Norfolk, Virginia: Colonial Publishing, 1909.

Omi, Michael and Howard Winant. *Racial Formation in the United States From the 1940s to the 1960s*, 2nd ed. New York and London: Routledge, 1994.

Osburn, Katherine M. B. *Choctaw Resurgence in Mississippi: Race, Class and Nation Building in the Jim Crow South, 1830–1977.* Lincoln and London: University of Nebraska Press, 2014.

Pagden, Anthony. *The Fall of Natural Man: The American Indian and the Origins of Comparative Ethnography.* Cambridge and New York: Cambridge University Press, 1982.

Paredes, J. Anthony, ed. *Indians of the Southeastern United States in the Late 20th Century.* Tuscaloosa and London: University of Alabama Press, 1992.

Pascoe, Peggy. "Miscegenation Law, Court Cases, and the Ideologies of Race." *Journal of American History* 83 (1996): 44–69.

Perdue, Charles L., Jr., Thomas E. Barden, and Robert K. Phillips, eds. *Weevils in the Wheat: Interviews with Virginia Ex-Slaves.* Charlottesville: University Press of Virginia, 1976, 4th printing 1999.

Perdue, Theda. *"Mixed Blood" Indians: Racial Construction in the Early South.* Athens and London: University of Georgia Press, 2003.

———. *Slavery and the Evolution of Cherokee Society, 1540–1866.* Knoxville: University of Tennessee Press, 1979.

Perlman, Joel, and Waters, Mary C., eds. *The New Race Question: How the Census Counts Multiracial Individuals.* New York: Russell Sage Foundation and Levy Economics Institute of Bard College, 2002.

Perman, Michael. *Struggle for Mastery: Disfranchisement in the South, 1888–1908.* Chapel Hill and London: University of North Carolina Press, 2001.

Pfaus, Mrs. Fred [Martha Coleman Wester Pfaus]. "The Indians of the Old Dominion." In "Our Debt to Virginia Indians." No information on publisher, 1949.

Pincus, Samuel N. *The Virginia Supreme Court, Blacks, and the Law, 1870–1902.* New York and London: Garland, 1990.

Plecker, Walter Ashby. *Eugenics in Relation to the New Family and the Law on Racial Integrity.* Richmond, Virginia: Bureau of Vital Statistics, State Board of Health and D. Bottom, Superintendent of Public Printing, 1924, 1925.

———. "Racial Improvement." Paper read at the 56th Annual Meeting of the Medical Society of Virginia, 3 October 1925, at Richmond, Virginia, and reprinted from the *Virginia Medical Monthly* of November 1925.

Pollard, John Garland. *The Pamunkey Indians of Virginia.* Bureau of American Ethnology Bulletin 17. Washington, DC: U.S. Government Printing Office, 1894.

Porter, Frank W., III. "Anthropologists at Work: A Case Study of the Nanticoke Indian Community." *American Indian Quarterly* 4 (1978): 1–18.

———, ed. *Strategies for Survival: American Indians in the Eastern United States.* Westport, CT: Greenwood, 1986.

Porter, Kenneth W. *The Black Seminoles: History of a Freedom-Seeking People*. Edited by Alcione M. Amos and Thomas P. Senter. Gainesville: University Press of Florida, 1996.

Powell, John Wesley. *Tenth Annual Report of the Bureau of Ethnology to the Secretary of the Smithsonian Institution 1888–'89*. Washington: Government Printing Office, 1893.

Reséndez, Andrés. *The Other Slavery: The Uncovered Story of Indian Enslavement in America*. Boston and New York: Houghton Mifflin Harcourt, 2016.

Reyhner, Jon and Jeanne Elder. *American Indian Education: A History*. Norman: University of Oklahoma Press, 2004.

Richter, Daniel K. *Facing East from Indian Country: A Native History of Early America*. Cambridge, MA and London: Harvard University Press, 2001.

Ritterhouse, Jennifer. *Growing Up Jim Crow: How Black and White Southern Children Learned Race*. Chapel Hill: University of North Carolina Press, 2006.

Roediger, David R. *The Wages of Whiteness: Race and the Making of the American Working Class*. London and New York: Verso, 1991.

Rogers, Edward S., ed. *A Northern Algonquian Source Book: The Papers of Frank G. Speck*. New York: Garland, 1985.

Rothman, Joshua D. *Notorious in the Neighborhood: Sex and Families across the Color Line in Virginia, 1787–1861*. Chapel Hill and London: University of North Carolina Press, 2003.

———. "'To Be Freed From Thate Curse and Let at Liberty:' Interracial Adultery and Divorce in Antebellum Virginia." *Virginia Magazine of History and Biography* 106 (1998): 443–81.

Rountree, Helen C. "Ethnicity Among the 'Citizen' Indians of Tidewater Virginia." In Frank W. Porter, III, ed., *Strategies for Survival: American Indians in the Eastern United States*. Westport, CT: Greenwood, 1986.

———. *Pocahontas's People: The Powhatan Indians of Virginia Through Four Centuries*. Norman and London: University of Oklahoma Press, 1990.

———. *The Powhatan Indians of Virginia: Their Traditional Culture*. Norman: University of Oklahoma Press, 1989.

———. "Powhatan Priests and English Rectors: World Views and Congregations in Conflict." *American Indian Quarterly* 16 (Autumn, 1992): 485–500

———, ed. *Powhatan Foreign Relations, 1500–1722*. Charlottesville and London: University Press of Virginia, 1993.

Rountree, Helen C., and E. Randolph Turner, III. *Before and After Jamestown: Virginia's Powhatans and their Predecessors*. Gainesville: University Press or Florida, 2002.

Rountree, Helen C., and Thomas E. Davidson. *Eastern Shore Indians of Virginia and Maryland*. Charlottesville and London: University Press of Virginia, 1997.

Russell, John H. *The Free Negro in Virginia, 1619–1865*. Baltimore: Johns Hopkins University Press, 1913. Reprint, New York: Dover Publications, 1969.

Saunt, Claudio. *Black, White, and Indian: Race and the Unmaking of an American Family.* Oxford and New York: Oxford University Press, 2005.

Saxton, Alexander. *The Rise and Fall of the White Republic.* London and New York: Verso, 1990.

Scheckel, Susan. *The Insistence of the Indian: Race and Nationalism in Nineteenth Century America.* Princeton: Princeton University Press, 1998.

Schwarz, Philip J. *Twice Condemned: Slaves and the Criminal Laws of Virginia, 1705–1865.* Baton Rouge: Louisiana State University Press, 1988.

———. *Slave Laws in Virginia.* Athens and London: University of Georgia Press, 1996.

———. *Migrants Against Slavery: Virginians and the Nation.* Charlottesville and London: University Press of Virginia, 2001.

Sheehan, Bernard W. *Savagism and Civility: Indians and Englishmen in Colonial Virginia.* Cambridge and New York: Cambridge University Press, 1980.

Sherman, Richard B. " 'The Last Stand:' The Fight for Racial Integrity in Virginia in the 1920s." *Journal of Southern History* 54 (February 1988): 69–92.

———. "The 'Teachings at Hampton Institute:' Social Equality, Racial Integrity, and the Virginia Public Assemblage Act of 1926." *Virginia Magazine of History and Biography* 95 (1987): 275–300.

Sider, Gerald. *Living Indian Histories: Lumbee and Tuscarora People in North Carolina.* Cambridge: Cambridge University Press, 1993. Reprint, with a new preface by the author. Chapel Hill and London: University of North Carolina Press, 2003.

Silver, Timothy. *A New Face on the Countryside: Indians, Colonists, and Slaves in South Atlantic Forests, 1500–1800.* Cambridge and New York: Cambridge University Press, 1990.

Simpson, Audra, and Andrea Smith, eds. *Theorizing Native Studies.* Durham, NC and London: Duke University Press, 2014.

Smith, J. Douglas. "The Campaign for Racial Purity and the Erosion of Paternalism in Virginia, 1922–1930: 'Nominally White, Biologically Mixed, and Legally Negro.'" *The Journal of Southern History* 68 (2002): 65–106.

———. *Managing White Supremacy: Race, Politics, and Citizenship in Jim Crow Virginia.* Chapel Hill and London: University of North Carolina Press, 2002.

Smith, Mark M. *How Race Is Made: Slavery, Segregation, and the Senses.* Chapel Hill: University of North Carolina Press, 2006.

Smithers, Gregory D., and Brooke N. Newman, eds. *Native Diasporas: Indigenous Identities and Settler Colonialism in the Americas.* Lincoln and London: University of Nebraska Press, 2014.

Smithsonian Institution. *The Exhibits of the Smithsonian Institution and United States National Museum at the Jamestown Tercentennial Exposition, Norfolk, Virginia, 1907.* Washington, DC: Smithsonian Institution by Judd and Detweiler, 1907.

Smithsonian Institution. "Notes: Jamestown Exposition." *Smithsonian Miscellaneous Collections* 50 (1907): 285–86.

Smits, David D. "'Abominable Mixture:' Toward the Repudiation of Anglo-Indian Intermarriage in Seventeenth-Century Virginia." *Virginia Magazine of History and Biography* 95 (1987): 157–92.
Smoak, Gregory E. *Ghost Dances and Identity: Prophetic Religion and American Indian Ethnogenesis in the Nineteenth Century.* Berkeley, Los Angeles, and London: University of California Press, 2006.
Snyder, Christina. *Slavery in Indian Country: The Changing Face of Captivity in Early America.* Cambridge, MA: Harvard University Press, 2010.
Sollors, Werner. *Beyond Ethnicity: Consent and Descent in American Culture.* New York: Oxford University Press, 1986.
———. *Interracialism: Black-White Intermarriage in American History, Literature, and Law.* Oxford and New York: Oxford University Press, 2000.
———. *Neither Black nor White Yet Both: Thematic Explorations of Interracial Literature.* Cambridge, MA and London: Harvard University Press, 1997.
Speck, Frank Gouldsmith. *Catawba Texts.* Columbia University *Contributions to Anthropology* 24, 1934. Reprint. New York: AMS Press, 1969.
———. *Chapters on the Ethnology of the Powhatan Tribes of Virginia.* Indian Notes and Monographs, vol. 1, no. 5. New York: Museum of the American Indian, Heye Foundation, 1928.
———. "The Ethnic Position of the Southeastern Algonkian." *American Anthropologist* 26 (1924): 184–200.
———. *Indians of the Eastern Shore.* Baltimore: Springfield State Hospital Press, 1922.
———. *The Nanticoke Community of Delaware.* 1915. Reprint. New York: AMS Press, 1981.
———. *The Nanticoke and Conoy Indians with a Review of Linguistic Material from Manuscript and Living Sources: On a Historical Study.* Wilmington: Historical Society of Delaware, 1927.
———. *The Rappahannock Indians of Virginia.* Indian Notes and Monographs, vol. 5, no. 3. New York: Museum of the American Indian, Heye Foundation, 1925.
Speck, Frank G., Royall B. Hassrick, and Edmund S. Carpenter. *Rappahannock Taking Devices; Traps, Hunting and Fishing.* Philadelphia: University Museum, 1946.
Speck, Frank G., and Claude E. Schaeffer, "The Deer and the Rabbit Hunting Drive in Virginia and the Southeast." *Southern Indian Studies,* 2, no. 1 (1950): 3–20.
Spiro, Jonathan Peter. *Defending the Master Race: Conservation, Eugenics, and the Legacy of Madison Grant.* Burlington: University of Vermont Press, 2009.
Steinzor, Nadia. *The Web of Self Determination: A Focus on Native Americans.* Göteborg: Peace and Development Research Institute, University of Göteborg, 1992.
Stern, Theodore. "Chickahominy: The Changing Culture of a Virginia Indian Community." *Proceedings of the American Philosophical Society* 96 (1952): 157–225.
———. "Pamunkey Pottery Making." *Southern Indian Studies,* 3 (1951): vii–78.

Stewart, Polly. "Regional Consciousness as a Shaper of Local History." In *Sense of Place: American Regional Cultures*. Edited by Barbara Allen and Thomas J. Schlereth. Lexington: University Press of Kentucky. 1990.

Stocking, George W., Jr., ed. *Colonial Situations: Essays on the Contextualization of Ethnographic Knowledge. History of Anthropology*, vol. 7. Madison: University of Wisconsin Press, 1991.

Stremlau, Rose. *Sustaining the Cherokee Family: Kinship and the Allotment of an Indigenous Nation*. Chapel Hill: University of North Carolina Press, 2011.

Strong, Pauline Turner, and Barrik Van Winkle. "'Indian Blood': Reflections on the Reckoning and Refiguring of Native North American Identity." *Cultural Anthropology* 11(1996): 547–76.

Sturm, Circe. *Blood Politics: Race, Culture, and Identity in the Cherokee Nation of Oklahoma*. Berkeley, Los Angeles, and London: University of California Press, 2002.

Thomson, Brian William. "Racism and Racial Classification: A Case Study of the Virginia Racial Integrity Legislation." Ph.D. dissertation, University of California, Riverside, 1978.

Tilton, Robert. *Pocahontas: The Evolution of an American Narrative*. Cambridge: Cambridge University Press, 1994.

Townsend, Kenneth W. *World War II and the American Indian*. Albuquerque: University of New Mexico Press, 2000.

Trigger, Bruce G., ed. *Handbook of North American Indians: Volume 15, Northeast*. Washington, DC: Smithsonian Institution, 1978.

United States Department of the Interior, Bureau of Indian Affairs. *U. S. Indian Population (1962) and Land (1963)*. Washington, DC: U.S. Department of the Interior, Bureau of Indian Affairs, 1963.

United States Department of Commerce, Bureau of the Census. *Indian Population in the United States and Alaska, Department of Commerce, Bureau of the Census, 1910*. Washington, DC: Government Printing Office, 1915. Reprint, Millwood, NY: Kraus Reprint, 1973.

United States Department of Commerce, Bureau of the Census. *Fifteenth Census of the United States 1930: The Indian Population of the United States and Alaska*. Washington, DC: Government Printing Office, 1937; reprint, Millwood, NY: Kraus Reprint, 1973.

United States Department of Commerce, Bureau of the Census. *Twenty Censuses: Population and Housing Questions, 1790–1980*. Prepared by Frederick G. Bohme. Washington, DC: U.S. Government Printing Office, 1979.

Virginia Commission on Indians. Report of the Commission on Indians to the Governor and General Assembly of Virginia, December 1983.

Virginia Historical Records Survey Project, Division of Professional and Service Projects, Works Projects Administration. *Inventory of the Church Archives of Virginia: Dover Baptist Association*. Richmond: Virginia Historical Records Survey Project, 1939.

Virginia State Department of Health, Bureau of Vital Statistics. *Annual Report of the Bureau of Vital Statistics* for 1935, 1936, and 1937. Richmond: Virginia State Department of Health.

Vizenor, Gerald. *Earthdivers: Tribal Narratives on Mixed Descent.* Minneapolis: University of Minnesota Press, 1981.

Wadlington, Walter. "The *Loving* Case: Virginia's Anti-Miscegenation Statue in Historical Perspective. *Virginia Law Review* 52 (1966): 1189–1223.

Wallenstein, Peter. *Blue Laws and Black Codes: Conflicts, Courts, and Change in Twentieth-Century Virginia.* Charlottesville and London: University of Virginia Press, 2004.

———. *Cradle of America: Four Centuries of Virginia History.* Lawrence: University Press of Kansas, 2007.

———. "Race, Marriage, and the Law of Freedom: Alabama and Virginia, 1860s–1960s." *Chicago-Kent Law Review* 70 no. 2 (1994): 371–437.

———. *Race, Sex, and the Freedom to Marry: Loving v. Virginia.* Lawrence: University Press of Kansas, 2014.

———. *Tell the Court I Love My Wife: Race, Marriage, and Law: An American History.* New York: Palgrave Macmillan, 2002.

Waselkov, Gregory A., Peter H. Wood, and Tom Hatley. *Powhatan's Mantle: Indians in the Colonial Southeast.* Rev. ed. Lincoln and London: University of Nebraska Press, 2006.

Wickman, Patricia Riles. *The Tree That Bends: Discourse, Power, and the Survival of the Maskókî People.* Tuscaloosa and London: University of Alabama Press, 1999.

Wilkinson, Charles. *Blood Struggle: The Rise of Modern Indian Nations.* New York and London: W.W. Norton, 2005.

Williams, Walter L., ed. *Southeastern Indians Since the Removal Era.* Athens: University of Georgia Press, 1979.

Williamson, Joel. *The Crucible of Race: Black-White Relations in the American South since Emancipation.* New York: Oxford University Press, 1984.

———. *New People: Miscegenation and Mulattoes in the United States.* New York: Free Press, Macmillan, 1980.

Winks, Robin W. *The Blacks in Canada: A History.* New Haven and London: Yale University Press, 1971.

Witthoft, John "Frank Gouldsmith Speck, 1881–1950; Ethnologist and Teacher." *Southern Indian Studies* 2 (1950): 2, 39–44.

Wolf, Eva Sheppard, *Almost Free: A Story about Family and Race in Antebellum Virginia.* Athens and London: University of Georgia Press, 2012.

Wright, J. Leitch, Jr. *Creeks and Seminoles: The Destruction and Regeneration of the Muscogulge People.* Lincoln and London: University of Nebraska Press, 1986.

———. *The Only Land They Knew: American Indians in the Old South.* New York: Free Press, Macmillan, 1981. Reprint, Lincoln and London: University of Nebraska Press, Bison Books, 1999.

Writers' Program of the Works Project Administration in the State of Virginia. *The Negro in Virginia*. New York: Hastings House, 1940. Reprint, with foreword by Charles L. Perdue, Jr., Winston-Salem, NC: John F. Blair, 1994.

Wynes, Charles E. "The Evolution of Jim Crow Laws in Twentieth Century Virginia." *Phylon: The Atlanta University Review of Race and Culture* 28 (1967): 416–25.

Young, Robert J. C. *Colonial Desire: Hybridity in Theory, Culture, and Race*. London, New York: Routledge, 1995.

Zellar, Gary. *African Creeks: Estelvste and the Creek Nation*. Norman: University of Oklahoma Press, 2007.

INDEX

References to illustrations appear in italic type.

acculturation. *See* assimilation/ acculturation

Act to Preserve Racial Integrity (1924): impact and legacy of, 83–89; implementation of, 65–70; origins and evolution of, 4–9; overviews, 49–50, 51–52; passage of, 64; repeal of, 9; surveillance and enforcement, 70–79. *See also* Plecker, Powell, and Cox and racial integrity act

Adams, Elmer Davis, 158

Adkins, O. Oliver, and family, 93, 138, 151, 165, 166, 169

admixture of races. *See* "amalgamation" concepts; racial purity ideology

African Americans: churches, 25–26, 94–96, 97, 224n18; repatriation movement, 26, 57–58, 59, 61; schools, 100, 101, 103–4. *See also* Blacks, Native disassociation from; Black-white binary paradigm

Alliance of Colored American Citizens, 80–81

Allston, Lynette Paige Lewis, 196

"amalgamation" concepts, 21, 53, 63, 80. *See also* "mongrelization"

Amber Satyr (Flannagan), 189–91

American Colonization Society, 26, 58

American Journal of Public Health, 80

anglicization of Natives, 25, 105, 112, 113, 136. *See also* assimilation/acculturation

"Anglo-Saxon Clubs," 59–61, *60*

anthropological viewpoints, 18, 105, 107, 108–9, 128. *See also* Mooney, James; Speck, Frank

appearance and race. *See* physical traits as racial markers

Asian immigrants, 5, 59, 61

assimilation/acculturation, 8, 79, 108, 117, 120, 136, 149. *See also* anglicization of Natives

"authenticity," cultural, 12, 13, 126, 127–28, 144, 149. *See also* primitivism; "vanishing race" narrative

Bacone College (Muskogee, Okla.), 101, 104, 175, 178, 181, 182

Bailey family, 38–40, 47–48

Banaba people, 50

Baptist Churches. *See* churches, Baptist

Barkan, Elazar, 6, 8

Bass, Augustus, 134–35

Bates, Denise, 197

Battle, Jasper and Lori, 177–78

Bazile, Leon M., 74–75

Berkhofer, Robert, 56

biological determinism, 5, 6. *See also* eugenics movement

birth records, 56–57

Blacks, Native disassociation from: contemporary outlook, 196–97; and culture of segregation, 8–9; Pearman-Scott family, 31–32, 40, 86; by reservation Indians, 22, 92; in response to Black-white racial divide, 2–3, 4, 66–67, 92–93, 158–59, 196–97; and rise in endogamy, 36–37, 115–16, 142; and separate schools/churches, 97, 101, 103–4, 172–78, 182–83. *See also* Black-white binary paradigm; tribal recognition (state/federal)

Black-white binary paradigm: Plecker, Powell, and Cox argument for, 53–54, 84; and racial integrity act, 7; and racialization of Natives, 2, 8–11, 16; white construction of, overviews, 16–17, 37, 51, 90–93. *See also* blood quantum concept

blood quantum concept: effects on Native cultural identity, 2, 8–11, 16; mixture definitions and legal standards, 4–5, 5, 7, 54, 160, 181, 193; under racial integrity act, 51. *See also* mixed-ancestry argument, overviews and concepts; non-reservation Indians; "one-drop rule"

Blu, Karen, 10, 22, 23

boarding schools (BIA), 100–101

Boas, Franz, 6, 128, 139–40, 142

Bradby family: E. P., 68, 150–51; John, 112–13; Joyce, 187; R. A., 99, 180; Sarah J., 99; W. A., 133–34; William Terrill, 105, 115, 116, 117, 121. *See also* Cook/Cook-Bradby families

Brisby, William H., 24, 39

British influences, 1, 10, 12, 19, 55, 105. *See also* Pocahontas narrative

Brown, Kathleen, 19, 20, 48

Brown, Kevin, 1

Brown, Sterling A., 190–91

Brown v. Board of Education of Topeka decision, impact of, 101, 181, 185, 188, 192–93

Buck v. Bell, 7

Bullifant family, 87, 88–89

Bureau of American Ethnology (BAE) (Smithsonian), 13, 114, 126, 129–38, 151–52

Bureau of Indian Affairs (BIA), 101, 119, 120, 151

Bureau of Vital Statistics, Virginia: creation of, 56; Plecker as head of, 52, 53, 57, 63, 71, 85, 158, 181

Burleigh, Louise, 66–67, 69–70

Canada, Pearman-Scott migrations to, 11, 15–16, 25, 26, 28–34, 45

Cardine, James J., 88–89

Castile, George Pierre, 107

Catawba people, 140

Catawba Texts (Speck), 140

census information, ambiguities of (and examples): 1980 census, 196; Bailey and Pearman families, 38–39; Canadian, 32; changes over time, 160–80; Dennis family, 87; enumerators' instructions and biases, 47, 48–50, 161, 164, 210n71, 211n80, 236n11; Howell family, 37–38, 39, 41–42, 87; overviews, 2; Pearman-Scott family, 16, 45–47; Plecker's influence on, 79, 158, 159–60, 164–70, 170; Stewart family, 87; Wynn family, 35–36, 37–38, 43–44

Cherokee Reservation (North Carolina), 101, 104, 129, 182–83

Cherokee "type" and whiteness concept, 62–63

Chicago Exposition (1893), 117

Chickahominy people: churches, 93, 97; donations to Smithsonian, 137–38; east-west split of, 97; endogamy within, 36; Plecker's focus on, 68–69, 76–79; and "Powhatan Confederacy," 153; schools, 102; tribal organization/recognition efforts, 93, 121–22, 194, 195

Choctaw people, Mississippi: churches for, 224n18, 225n32; cultural markers of, 207–8n39, 233n67; legal/racial status of, 5, 202n2, 205n3, 217n33; racial mixing in, 8–9; schools for, 100
churches, Baptist: historical overview, 93–99; racial integration in antebellum churches, 22, 25–26, 94, 173. *See also* churches, Black; churches, Native American
churches, Black, 25–26, 94–96, 97, 224n18
churches, Native American, 93–99, 172–78, 182–83, 192, 224n18, 225n32
citizenship issues: Indian Citizenship Act, 46–47, 56; nineteenth century standards, 33; and racial integrity act, 7–8; and racialized stereotypes, 4, 5; reservation *v.* non-reservation Indians, 46–47
civil rights and race, 2, 20, 178, 188, 193, 194
Clifford, James, 128, 154, 156, 157
clothing and regalia, pan-Indian. *See* pan-Indian material culture and public performance
Coates, James T., 188–89
Collins, Henry Bascom, 233n67
Collins family (Native family), 41–42, 87
"colored," definitions of, 54, 65, 68–69. *See also* "free persons of color" concept/label
Colosse Baptist Church, 94–95
Commission on Indians (Virginia), 194
"common identity" concept, 227n70. *See also* cultural and social customs as racial marker
community/reputation factors in racial designation: and instructions to census enumerators, 160, 161–62; in Plecker's fight for racial purity, 54, 64, 67, 78, 88–89, 102; in selective service draft, 170–71. *See also* cultural and social customs as racial marker
Cook/Cook-Bradby families, 111–14; Capitola, 112; George M., 66, 96, 98; Ruth, 174; Tecumseh Deerfoot, 111, 113, 114, 186
coronavirus-pandemic relief, 195
County News (Lexington), 75
Cox, Earnest Sevier, 53, 57–59, 62–63, 80–81. *See also* Plecker, Powell, and Cox and racial integrity act
"creolized interculture," 154
"Croatan Indians," 92
cultural and social customs as racial marker, 9–11, 92, 134–35, 139–45, 141, 152, 172, 205–6n6, 227n70. *See also* community/reputation factors in racial designation
cultural exchange/borrowing, 139–45, 154–57
Cushing, Frank Hamilton, 109
Custalow family, 172–73, 175, 177, 182–83, 183, 192
customs and community traditions. *See* cultural and social customs as racial marker

Dabney, Virginius, 69
Daily Times (Richmond), 99–100, 101–2, 109–10
Dalrymple, Edwin A., 130, 133, 137
"deculturation," 149. *See also* assimilation/acculturation
deer drives, 145–46
Deloria, Philip, 109
Dennis family, 85, 87, 113, 114
desegregation. *See* integration/desegregation
Deutsch, Sarah, 6

dilution of race concept. *See*
    "amalgamation" concepts
disassociation from Blacks. *See* Blacks,
    Native disassociation from
dispossession, land, 6, 9, 21–22
Douglas, H. T., 88
Dover Baptist Association, 93, 96, 97,
    98–99, 172, 173–74, 175–77

Eastman, Charles, 109
economic opportunities, racial
    limitations on, 17, 26, 29, 91–92
education and literacy: and impact of
    desegregation, 101; in Indian traditions
    and handicrafts, 186; Natives emphasis
    on, 17; Pearman-Scott family pursuit
    of, 26, 29, 30–31, 32–33, 86; secondary
    education for non-whites, 103–4, 178,
    178–80, 181–85, 183; vocational, 185,
    186. *See also* schools
employment concerns, 17, 59, 188
endogamy, 36–37, 115–16, 142. *See also*
    "paired sibling marriage"
English colonial influence. *See* British
    influences
Estabrook, Arthur, 73
"ethnographic present" concept, 128
eugenics movement: historical
    profile and background, 4–6; and
    immigration limitations, 8; Plecker,
    Powell, and Cox support of, 53, 56–59,
    58, 64, 79–80, 83–84; and whiteness
    standards, 6–7
Europeans (Southern and Eastern) as
    threat to racial purity, 8, 56, 58

Feest, Christian, 106, 107
Fenton, William N., 144
Flannagan, Roy Catesby, 189–91
Forbes, Jack, 23–24
"free persons of color" concept/label, 2,
    16, 18, 23–24, 48, 92, 171

"fringe" people concept, 18
Fugitive Slave Act (1850), 26, 31

gambling enterprise prohibitions, 195
Garvey, Marcus, 59, 81
Gatschet, Albert, 102, 114–15, 126, 129,
    134, 136–38. *See also* Mooney, James
Gazette (Lexington), 75
Gingaskin Reservation, 21–22
Grant, Madison, 8, 58–59

Hale, Grace Elizabeth, 8
Halifax community
    "compromise," 63, 72–73
Hampton Institute (Hampton
    University), 103–4
Haskell Institute, Kansas, 104,
    181, 181–82
Henry, Joseph, 131
Herskovits, Melville, 4
Hertzberg, Hazel, 101
Holt, Henry, 74–75
home missions (Baptist), 98, 175, 176, 179
homogamy, 142. *See also* endogamy
Hook, Catherine Howell, 187
Hopson, Moble, 4, 22, 91–92
Howell family: family connections and
    profile, 36–43, 86–87; John and Susan
    (née Pearman), 15, 18, 33, 34; John
    Clayton, 40–41, 43, 68
Hoxie, Frederick, 117, 120

identity construction, Native: and
    challenges of racial integrity laws, 8–9,
    49–50; and churches, 93–99, 172–78;
    and dispossession of land, 6, 9, 21–22;
    interracial marriage prohibitions, 92,
    104, 135, 177; and schools, 99–104; as
    threat to racial purity of whites, 56, 60,
    62, 69–70; tribal recognition efforts,
    1–3, 91–93, 103–4, 121–22, 169, 194–95.
    See also Blacks, Native disassociation

from; cultural and social customs as racial marker; "Indianness"; intertribal connections; pan-Indian material culture and public performance; "vanishing race" narrative
immigration, racial limitations on, 8, 56, 58, 59, 61, 117
Immigration Act of 1924, 56
Indian affairs commissions, 195
Indian Citizenship Act (1924), 56
"Indianness," 3–11, 54, 68–69, 202n7. *See also* Blacks, Native disassociation from; identity construction, Native; pan-Indian material culture and public performance
institutional racism, normalization of, 60
integration/desegregation: in antebellum churches, 22, 25–26, 94, 173; *Brown v. Board of Education of Topeka* decision, impact of, 101, 181, 185, 188, 192–93
interracial marriage prohibitions, historical overviews, 4–9, 19–25, 54–55. *See also* Act to Preserve Racial Integrity (1924)
interracial marriage prohibitions among Natives, 92, 104, 135, 177. *See also* endogamy
intertribal connections: marriages, 104, 115–16, 135; and pan-Indian Native identity, 93, 108, 138, 139, 192, 210n78

Jacobson, Matthew Frye, 7, 14
Jamestown Tercentennial Exposition (1907), 116, 118, *125*
Jarvis, Lucy. *See* Scott, William C. and Lucy Pearman (née Jarvis)
Jarvis, William, 27
Jefferson, John J., 93
Johns case (Dorothy), 74, 75, 80
Johnson, J. H., 150
Jones, William Archer Thaddeus, 51–52, 77–78

Kevles, Dan, 8
Kimball, Gregg, 26
kinship and racialized identities. *See* cultural and social customs as racial marker
Klopotek, Brian, 194, 197, 210n78
Krauthamer, Barbara, 50
Ku Klux Klan, 58–59, 84

land, dispossession of, 9, 21–22, 81, 112
land ownership as racial status marker, 91
Langston, William Cooper, and family, 24, 39–41, 87
language: and anglicization of Natives, 25; English in intertribal relationships, 101; as marker of community cultural identity, 11, 134; study of Algonquian tongues, 129, 136–37, 139
Lindsey, Donal, 104
linguistics. *See* language
literacy. *See* education and literacy
Literary Digest, 80
Lombardo, Paul, 64
Louisiana Club for Segregation, 82
Louisiana interracial marriage prohibitions, 5–6
Louisiana Purchase Exposition (1904), 117
Loving v. Virginia, 9, 75, 89
Lower College Baptist Church, 94
Lumbee people, 10, 22–23, 92, 100, 183

Mason, Otis, 107, 115, 116, 130
material culture, Native, 105, 144–49, 153. *See also* pan-Indian material culture and public performance; "survivals" and "revivals" (cultural)
Mattaponi people (state-recognized reservation group): census data on, 166; church/schools, 97–98, 102–3, 172–73, 175, 178, 181, 183–86; cultural organization and identity,

12, 93, 133; federal tribal recognition for, 194; and pan-Indian material culture, 111, 114, 120, 121, 182, 192; as reservation Indians, 3, 9, 12, 22. *See also* Upper Mattaponi people (non-reservation group)
McDougle, Ivan E., 73
Methodist churches, 96
Miles, Journey, 42, 116
Miles, Paul, 146, 148, 150
military draft. *See* Selective Service policy on race
miscegenation, 5–6, 203n12. *See also* interracial marriage prohibitions, historical overviews
mission/missionary work, 98, 174–76, 177, 178
Mississippi Choctaw people. *See* Choctaw people, Mississippi
Mississippi interracial marriage prohibitions, 5
"mixed," definition as racial term, 72
mixed-ancestry argument, overviews and concepts, 1–2, 8–11, 16. *See also* Black-white binary paradigm; "mongrelization"; racial purity ideology
Monacan people, 3, 63, 64, 71–72, 73, 195
"mongrelization," 65, 80, 81. *See also* "amalgamation" concepts
Mongrel Virginians (McDougle and Estabrook), 73
Mooney, James: aid to Native organizing efforts, 121–22; ethnographic work overview, 126–28; on Native disassociation from Blacks, 92; tidewater Indians research and fieldwork, 39, 115, 129–38, 150. *See also* Gatschet, Albert
Moretti-Langholtz, Danielle, 156–57, 196
Morgan, Lewis Henry, 108–9
"mulatto" label: census ambiguity examples, 2, 16, 25–26, 32, 38–39, 44, 160–61, 166; definitions, 19–25, 23–25, 55, 72, 160; and Plecker's obsession with one-drop rule, 64, 72, 75; and racial binary extremism, 19–20, 22, 121, 136, 142
museum collections and displays, 115, 117, 128, 130, 146, 148, 192

Nagel, Joane, 196
Nansemond people, 23, 81–82, 96, 134–35, 153, 156–57, 194–95
Nanticoke people, 139, 142, 143–44, 149–50, 150, 153
Native American Graves Protection and Repatriation Act, 156–57
New Orleans Exposition (1884), 115
News Leader (Richmond), 60, 62, 85
New York Times, 69
Nies, Betsy, 56
1924 act. *See* Act to Preserve Racial Integrity (1924)
non-reservation Indians: cultural identity, concentration and preservation of, 11, 12, 17–18, 36–37, 49–50, 86, 101; in ethnological research projects, 135–36, 149; lack of state/local financial support for, 178–79, 181; legalized racial bias against, 49, 67, 69–70, 160, 168; organization of and tribal recognition efforts, 10, 85, 92–93, 121, 194–95; racial identity labeling *v.* reservation groups, 6, 9, 12, 20, 20–21, 35, 193
North Carolina: census enumeration in, 164; Cherokee Reservation, 101, 104, 129, 182–83; Lumbee people, 10, 22–23, 92, 100, 183; Native affairs commission in, 195; Native disassociation from Blacks in, 23; Native schools in, 100
Nottoway people, 3, 133, 195, 196

Oak Hill Academy, 180
Obergefell v. Hodges, 89

"octoroon," 72, 160
Oklahoma: Bacone College, Muskogee, 101, 104, 175, 178, 181, 182; census enumeration in, 164; interracial marriage laws, 6
Omi, Michael, 9, 10
"one-drop rule": current status of, 196–97; overviews of ideology, 2, 11; Plecker's obsession with, 64, 67–71, 70–71, 75; and racial purity ideology, 48–50, 53–54, 61–62, 65. *See also* Black-white binary paradigm; eugenics movement
Opportunity (magazine), 190–91
Osburn, Katherine M. B., 8–9
"Our Indian Neighbors" (pamphlet), 176

Page, Dorothy, 186–87
"paired-sibling marriage," 25, 36, 43
Pamunkey Baptist Church, 95–96, 172
Pamunkey people, overviews, *123*, *124*, *125*; churches, 94–96, 180; exogamous marriage prohibitions, 92; federal tribal recognition of, 1–3, 194–95, *195*; as reservation Indians, 9, 12, 22, 67; schools, 100, 102, 178, 182, 183–86. *See also* identity construction, Native; Pamunkey Baptist Church
pan-Indian material culture and public performance, *124*, *125*; adoption of in response to racial purity legislation, 66–67; ethnological interest in, 105, 130, 144–49, 153; and homogenized/romanticized cultural markers, 106–8; misrepresentations of and primitivism, 117–21; pageantry/cultural display, 192–93; Pocahontas depictions, 105–6, 111, 114, 116, 118–19, 187; to promote/emphasize "Indianness," 12, 107, 108, 109, 111–12, 114–17, 182, 192–93; as "strategic essentialism," 10; and tourism, 109, 146–47, 192–93
Parker, Arthur C., 107, 108, 109

Pascoe, Peggy, 217n43
Passing of the Great Race, The (Grant), 58
Pearman, William F., 28
Pearman family, 38–39; Jones, 38, 38–40, 131; Macfarland and family, 16, 45–48; Michael, 15, 25, 27; Susan and Ann Eliza, 15, 18. *See also* Pearman-Scott family
Pearman-Scott family: background and departure from Virginia, 25–27; disassociation with Blacks, 31–32, 40, 86; family profiles and racial identity issues, 27–31, 33–34, 45–48; migrations to Canada, 11, 15–16, 25, 26, 28–34, 45; overview of experiences, 15–19; Wynn family connections, 34–36; Wynn/Howell family connections, 34–45. *See also* Pearman family
Perdue, Theda, 50
Perry, Oliver, 156–57
Pfaus, Martha Coleman Wester, 174, 176, 179–80
physical traits as racial markers: census enumerators' reliance on, 79, 160; in ethnological study, 134, 135, 136, 142, 233n67; limitations of, 17, 54, 142; Plecker's reliance on, 63, 64, 79; and white stereotyping of Natives, 105, 174–75
Plecker, Powell, and Cox and racial integrity act: attempts to influence other states, 82–83; campaign to pass, 52–60; continuing public advocacy, 79–82; and eugenics movement, 53, 56, 58, 79–80; impact and legacy of, 83–89; implementation of, 65–70; surveillance and enforcement, 70–79. *See also* Cox, Earnest Sevier; Plecker, Walter Ashby; Powell, John
Plecker, Walter Ashby, 7, 52, 53, 191; advocacy of eugenic racism, 79–80; attempts to influence other states, 82–83; community racial classification

observations, 63; concern for accuracy of records, 63–64; enforcement stuff, 55–56, 70–79; influence on census, 79, 158, 159–60, 164–70; obsession with white racial purity, 61–63, 67–68, 70–71, 75, 180–81; on weaknesses of registration program, 67, 73. *See also* Plecker, Powell, and Cox and racial integrity act

Pocahontas narrative, *125*; Black relations to Pocahontas, 81; depictions of and Native identity construction, 105–6, 111, 114, 116, 118–19, 187; descendants of Pocahontas, 21, 131–32; exception clause in racial integrity law, 4, 6, 7, 65, 70, 82–83, 89, 132; romanticization of, 21, 105–6

pottery making, 130, 146–48, 186, 192

Powell, John, 53, 59, 61–62, 81–82, 150. *See also* Plecker, Powell, and Cox and racial integrity act

Powell, John Wesley, 128, 129

primitivism: ethnographic stereotyping, 115, 127–28; popularity of, 107, 108–9, 117–20; and white stereotyping of Natives, 24–25, 174–75. *See also* stereotyping, racialized

public performance. *See* pan-Indian material culture and public performance

Putnam, Frederic Ward, 115, 117, 128

"quadroon," 72, 160

race mixing. *See* mixed ancestry argument, overviews and concepts

race *v.* ethnicity concepts, 9–11, 62, 141

racial binary. *See* Black-white binary paradigm

racial integrity act. *See* Act to Preserve Racial Integrity (1924)

racial integrity laws outside Virginia, 22, 82–83

racialized identities: evolution of racial identities in United States, 3–11, 217n43; historical review, 19–25; and human ancestry theories, 57–58, 59; policing/enforcement of, 55–56, 70–79. *See also* blood quantum concept; cultural and social customs as racial marker; stereotyping, racialized

racial purity ideology, 49–50, 59, 65. *See also* eugenics movement; "one-drop rule"

Rappahannock people: churches, 173, 177; Mooney's observations on, 135; Plecker's focus on, 76, 78–79; and "Powhatan Confederacy," 153; Speck's observations on, 142, 143, 144, 145; tribal organization/recognition efforts, 169, 194, 195

reburials, 156–57

regenerate ethnology, 156. *See also* "survivals" and "revivals" (cultural)

registration programs for racial identity, 57, 60, 67, 71

religion: Baptist churches historical overview, 93–99; mission/missionary work, 98, 174–76, 177, 178; Pearman-Scott family focus on, 33; views on racial integrity act, 65–66. *See also* churches, Baptist; churches, Black; churches, Native American

Religious Herald, 65, 178

repatriation movement (of African Americans), 26, 57–58, 59, 61

reputation and racial designation. *See* community/reputation factors in racial designation

"revivals," 148–49. *See also* "survivals" and "revivals" (cultural)

Richmond Planet, 85

Rolfe, Thomas, 21

Rountree, Helen C.: on Black integration in schools, 188; on cultural anglicization, 25; on early interracial marriage restrictions, 20; on "fringe" Powhatan people, 18; on Indianness, 202n7; on John Carman Wynn family, 35; on Mattaponi using pan-Indian material culture, 111; on Powhatan racial/social mixing, 24; on separation from Black churches, 97

"salvage" ethnography, 138–39
Samaria Baptist Church and school, 93, 97, 102, 172, 173, 184–85, 188
Schaeffer, Claude, 145
schools: attendance/enrollment data, 183–84, 242n85; Baptist supported, 180; Black, 100, 101, 103–4; closing of reservation schools, 187–88; deficiencies of support/funding for, 178–80, 183; government supported, 100–101, 102, 103, 178–79, 181, 182–83; Native American, 86, 96–97, 99–104, 178–88, 192; segregation in, 51–52, 68, 69, 77, 85–88, 99. *See also* education and literacy; *under* churches, Native American
"scientific" racism, 4, 6, 57, 75, 80, 83–84, 127, 233n67
Scott, Lucy Pearman (née Jarvis). *See* Scott, William C. and Lucy Pearman (née Jarvis)
Scott, William C. and Lucy Pearman (née Jarvis), 15–19, 25–27, 32–33, 45. *See also* Pearman-Scott family
Scott family. *See* Pearman-Scott family
secondary education for non-whites, 103–4, 178, 178–80, 181–85, 183
segregation: Plecker, Powell, and Cox devotion to, 53–54, 84–85; in post–Civil War South, 5–6; in schools, 51–52, 68, 69, 77, 85–88, 99. *See also* integration/desegregation
Selective Service policy on race, 151, 158–59, 170–72

self-determination, activism for, 108, 152–53
separatism, 57–58, 59, 108
Shands, William B., 133
Shango, Lula Whitehead, 178
shared experience and cultural identity. *See* cultural and social customs as racial marker
Sheppard, Morris, 83
Sherman, Richard B., 83
Sider, Gerald, 23
Slabey, Daniel, 180, 185–86
slavery/enslaved people: Baptist church membership denial, 94; creation of through forced intermixture, 135; and forced racial intermixture, 135; Fugitive Slave Act (1850), 26, 31; historical overviews, 6, 19–22; owned by Native Americans, 27, 28, 35, 37; as strategy to avoid state expulsions, 27
Smith, John. *See* Pocahontas narrative
Smithsonian Institution: Bureau of American Ethnology (BAE), 13, 114, 126, 129–38, 151–52; and promotion of Native cultural identity, 107, 115, 116, 117, 118–20, 120, 130, 137. *See also* Gatschet, Albert; Mooney, James
social and cultural traditions. *See* cultural and social customs as racial marker
Society of American Indians (SAI), 107–8, 109
Sollengerger, Robert, 143
Sorrells decision, 74–75, 82–83
Southern Baptist organization and structure, 172–74, 174, 175–76, 192. *See also* churches, Baptist
Speck, Frank: advocacy for Powhatan cultural and racial identity, 149–54, 171, 184; cultural change and exchange, 139–43; cultural markers and racial labeling, 142; overviews and legacy of, 13, 126–29, 138–39, 155–57; Plecker's efforts to suppress, 78–79,

137; Stern's continuation of work, 154–55; survival/revival of material culture and traditions, 143–49
stereotyping, racialized: ethnographic perpetuation of, 115, 126–28; evolution of, 4–5; and Pocahontas narrative, 21, 105–6; romanticization and homogenization of racial/cultural markers, 105–9, 160, 187; and white racial bias, 24–25, 174–75. *See also* physical traits as racial markers; racialized identities
sterilization laws and practices, 7, 64
Stern, Theodore, 25, 36, 146–48, 154–57
Stewart family, 42–43, 86–87, 88–89. *See also* Wynn family
Stirling, Matthew W., 151–52
"strategic essentialism," 10
"survivals" and "revivals" (cultural), 140, 141, 144, 148–49, 153–54, 155–57

taxonomic ethnological classifications, 128, 129
Teaiwa, Teresia, 50
tepees, 121, 187
terminology and racial identities, 19–25, 72, 160. *See also* "colored," definitions; "free persons of color" concept/label; "mulatto" label
Thomson, Brian William, 64
Throckmorton, Philip, 97
tidewater Natives: historical overview, 3–11; map of territories, 119, *198*
Time (magazine), 190, 191
Times-Dispatch (Richmond), 61–62, 63, 67, 69, 81, 85, 177
tourism and Native cultural identity, 109, 146–47, 192–93. *See also* pan-Indian material culture and public performance
Treaty of Dancing Rabbit Creek, 202n2, 205n3

tribal recognition (state/federal): organization efforts, 1–3, 91–93, 103–4, 121–22, 169, 194–95; Plecker, Powell, and Cox disapproval of, 85; racialized determination methods, 9–10, 11. *See also* cultural and social customs as racial marker
tribute presentation narrative, 109–13, 145. *See also* pan-Indian material culture and public performance
Trinkle, Elbert Lee, 55, 64, 68, 76–77, 82
Tsena Commocko Church and school, 97, 99, 102, 172, 178
Tupponce, Reggie, 195
Turner, Nat, 19, 22
Tuscarora people, 23, 92, 120

Universal Negro Improvement Association (UNIA), 59, 81
Upper Mattaponi people (non-reservation group): church/school, 98, 102–3, 173, 178; ethnological studies of, 135, 149–50; and "Powhatan Confederacy," 153; tribal recognition efforts, 194, 195
U.S. National Museum (Smithsonian). *See* Smithsonian Institution

"vanishing race" narrative: among ethnographers, 13, 130, 134, 139, 140, 148–49, 154; white viewpoint, 110, 132, 133, 138, 168
Virginia Conference of Social Work, 150
Virginia Council on Indians, 194–95
vital statistics records, 56–57. *See also* Bureau of Vital Statistics, Virginia

Wallace, Anthony F. C., 149–50
Wallenstein, Peter, 5
Washington Post, 195
Weslager, C. A., 143–44
White America (Cox), 53, 58, 80

whiteness: legal standards for, 7, 19–20, 51, 54, 64, 65, 68–69; Plecker, Powell, and Cox campaign for racial purity, 60, 60–61, 62, 62–63, 70, 163

whites "playing Indian," 108–9, 119, 120

white supremacy ideology, 17, 60, 70. *See also* eugenics movement

white testimony and advocacy for Native Americans, 78, 86, 102, 174, 184, 185–91. *See also under* Speck, Frank

Wild West mythos, 106–7, 119–20

Williams, Walter, 196

Winant, Howard, 9, 10

Woman's Missionary Union (WMU), 174–75, 177, 178

work and employment, 17, 59, 188

World War II, 151, 158, 170

Wynn family: Ann Eliza (nee Pearman), 15, 43–45; family connections and profiles, 34–36, 43–45, 86–88; Ferdinand (the elder), 35, 43; Ferdinand (the younger), 35, 35–36, 42, 78; John Carman, 34–36, 37, 43–45; Ray and Isola and school attendance issues, 85–86; Ray and May marriage challenge, 87–89, 223n150; Rebecca Stewart, 35–36, 37

Yorktown sesquicentennial exposition, 121